ADVANCE PRAISE FOR THE BOOK

'The complex environment of emerging markets offers unparalleled opportunities for agile players who combine strong execution, customer-oriented innovation and the drive to create new markets. The book captures these approaches through detailed insights and a number of cross-industry success stories. It is a must-read for managers who want to understand what it takes to become a successful emerging market MNC'—**Adi Godrej, chairman, Godrej Industries Ltd**

'*Riding the Tiger* showcases an intimate knowledge of the complexities and contradictions of doing business in India and the skills it takes to succeed. It displays an innate understanding of India's social fabric, economic issues, historical context and political nuances which is evident in the objective rigorous data-driven analysis. I am positive that this book will educate businesspeople across the world (and Indians too!) about the uniqueness of doing business in India, which, in the author's words, will be an "absolute necessity" going forward'—**Anand Mahindra, chairman and managing director, Mahindra Group**

'For many years, stakeholders from across the automotive value chain benefited from Wilfried's deep domain knowledge about the industry. Now, through *Riding the Tiger*, Wilfried presents a compelling business case about India.'

'He identifies success factors of firms that overcame odds in this country. He delineates how different levels of innovation have helped firms genuinely stand out. He shares best practices from around the world, and explains how these could be tailored for an Indian context. Wilfried also asks some uncomfortable questions—but he is constructive in his criticism as he lays out an agenda for India-centric businesses in an increasingly dynamic and competitive world.'

'*Riding the Tiger* provides valuable pathways for sustaining the Make in India dream. As Wilfried observes: "A national brand, like any other brand, requires constant deposits in the brand equity account."'

'Several tomes have mapped India's great economic opportunity since reforms began in 1991. Yet, Wilfried still manages to break fresh ground. To ensure longevity and earn pride of place on a bookshelf, a research-based book must be insightful, authentic, multi-faceted and readable. Wilfried's book is all of these. A must-read for India watchers, baiters and investors alike'—**Sunil Kant Munjal, chairman, Hero Corporate Service Pvt. Ltd**

'In today's volatile world, emerging markets continue to be extremely sensitive to global fluctuations. With the India business case starting to have more relevance, it has become critical to account for these changes and prepare for them in order to ride the storm. A growing share of strategic partnerships are taking place between the government and corporate sector and it becomes even more important to look at India's history from an economic, social and political perspective to actively learn from our follies and bring about positive change.

'*Riding the Tiger: How to Execute Business Strategy in India* highlights this required outlook. India's economy has weathered the test of time despite the uncertainty seen around the globe, and could continue to hold its position as one of the faster growing economies given the right funding and regulations. The case studies analysed excellently point out how companies are innovating to address previously untapped customer segments while still bringing about social impact in developing economies. This, coupled with the government's programmes to promote entrepreneurship, has resulted in making India the third largest start-up hub in the world resulting in its immense traction.

'India is poised on the edge of becoming a market where doing business is now necessary and not just an option'—**Ratan Tata, chairman emeritus, Tata Sons; ex-chairman, Tata Group**

'A fascinating read detailing nuances of what it takes for companies to succeed in India. The authors showcase a vast number of companies that have demonstrated a finer edge, despite extant challenges. Undoubtedly, *Riding the Tiger* is the catalyst to boost the Make in India agenda'—**Deepak Parekh, chairman, HDFC Ltd**

'A very smart book by Dr Aulbur. Over the years he has seen all angles and sides of India. A must-read for the young entrepreneurs, and those who wish to do business in India'—**Vivek Chaand Sehgal, chairman and co-founder, Samvardhana Motherson Group**

'As someone who has worked for long in India, and yet has true awareness of the most competitive firms in the world and what it takes to make them so, Wilfried Aulbur provides an excellent analysis of how the companies he has referenced have excelled in establishing themselves as world leaders in their respective fields'—**Farhad Forbes, co-chairman, Forbes Marshall Pvt. Ltd**

'The book provides great learning for all of us who own, lead and manage companies in India'—**Naushad Forbes, co-chairman, Forbes Marshall Pvt. Ltd; president (2016–17), Confederation of Indian Industry**

'Strategy is only as good as its execution. Through well-chosen diverse case studies of several successful Indian companies, the author explains what it takes to win in India. This is an interesting read'—**N.R. Narayana Murthy, co-founder, Infosys**

'Clear choices, strong leadership and alignment across the organization are key to driving global success for emerging market multinationals. The book highlights this recipe for success via a detailed analysis of leading companies. It is a must-read for people who want to understand how to succeed in volatile markets in India and beyond'—**Rajiv Bajaj, managing director, Bajaj Auto Ltd**

'A superb analysis of success stories, from a wide cross section of businesses, revealing the key ingredients of winning strategies. Contains invaluable lessons for all investors in the hugely attractive, but complicated, country that is India'—**R.C. Bhargava, chairman, Maruti Suzuki Ltd**

'*Riding the Tiger* by Dr Wilfried G. Aulbur is a great book which traces how a focused approach towards continuously improving and harnessing unique propositions has enabled various eminent corporates to reach the pinnacle of success. A fine outline of the key driving factors, challenges faced and what can be done to surmount them highlights the wisdom of years captured in these pages. The book is a must-read for entrepreneurs wanting to master the challenges of a volatile, diverse and dynamic environment in emerging markets like India in keeping with the global and local context which is always evolving based on different parameters'—**Nishant Arya, executive director, JBM Group**

'Riding the Indian business tiger is not easy, given the country's complex environment. Wilfried Aulbur's fascinating book documents sixteen companies, both Indian and transnational, that have succeeded in the volatile markets of India. They have done this through a combination of strategies which essentially calls for a relentless focus on excelling at what they do best, by being quick to learn from mistakes and adapting to change.

'From the individual strands of winning strategies that companies weave, this useful book presents the case for a sustaining tapestry of industrial ecosystem, essential for India if it has to realize its potential, and for companies if they are to flourish here'—**Meher Pudumjee, chairperson, and Pheroz Pudumjee, director, Thermax Group**

'The authors have impeccable credentials on the subject, with one of them having actually having successfully ridden the tiger during his tenure as head of Mercedes-Benz India. The book reflects their excellent understanding of the challenges and opportunities of doing business in India and will be very useful to managers and investors in India alike'—**Anees Noorani, managing director, Zodiac Clothing Company**

'In the fast-changing business environment of India, companies across the spectrum seek the path to successful performance. They need go no further than this highly readable book which unravels the secret sauce of India's outstanding companies. With his experience in managing a leading multinational in India and consulting for some of the best companies, Wilfried Aulbur is uniquely placed to write this book'—**Rishikesha T. Krishnan, director, IIM Indore**

'Wilfried Aulbur and Amit Kapoor's analysis is world-class. They provide examples of both success and failure in the Indian marketplace. Drawing on extensive data from dozens companies, the authors offer critical insights into the keys for commercial survival—and prosperity—in India. This is required reading for businesses looking to capitalize on India's remarkable growth potential'—**Anup Malani, Lee and Brena Freeman Professor, University of Chicago**

'This is a very impressive book on Indian business and its contribution to the wider economy. The authors combine their extensive practical experience with sound analysis to reveal the secrets to success in emerging markets. A particular highlight is the rich diversity and detail of the cases in the book. These offer deep insights into operational efficiencies, innovation, strategic choices and trade-offs as well as the alignment and leadership needed to succeed in today's volatile environment'—**Jaideep Prabhu, Jawaharlal Nehru professor of Indian business and enterprise, director, Cambridge Centre for Indian and Global Business, Judge Business School, University of Cambridge**

'The complexities of doing business in emerging markets such as India are extreme. Solid strategies, consistent execution and constant innovation allow emerging market MNCs to create value in such a volatile and uncertain environment—a fact that is captured well in the book by Wilfried and Amit. It is a must-read for people who would like to learn how to navigate emerging markets such as India successfully'—**Sanjay Kirloskar, chairman and managing director, Kirloskar Brothers Ltd**

'The possibilities and the diversity are unique in India—especially for the economy. But everyone who wants to start a business in India has to be familiar with the unique characters of the so called "Indian jungle". With this book written by two experienced and well-known India experts, you will get along successfully through this "jungle". It is a must-read for everyone who deals with the Indian economy'—**Bernhard Steinrücke, director general, Indo-German Chamber of Commerce**

'In the 1990s, the Western media portrayed India as a slumbering elephant that needs to be awakened. In the mid-2000s, they showed India as a crouching tiger ready to pounce on the world scene. In recent years, however, India has been depicted as a tiger running at full speed and overtaking the Chinese dragon. Indeed, India's time has come: with its huge consumer market and vast pool of young talent and frugal ingenuity, India is becoming the world's global economic and innovation engine. Yet, India is a highly complex market that can test the patience of even seasoned business executives. This book is a must-read "survival guide" for intrepid senior leaders who wish to explore the rich Indian business jungle and learn to "ride the tiger"'—**Navi Radjou, co-author, *Jugaad Innovation* and *Frugal Innovation***

'Complexity of doing business in India is a well-known fact. The authors have been able to use their vast personal experiences in India to distil the essence and simplify it for easy understanding, without compromising on the quality of their insights. A worthy read'—**Neeraj Kanwar, vice-chairman and managing director, Apollo Tyres Ltd**

'*Riding the Tiger* is an extremely appropriate study of the opportunities and challenges of being successful in India. Co-written by Wilfried Aulbur and Amit Kapoor, it combines the practical knowledge of managing a successful MNC in India together with the later experience of studying the Indian environment through consulting and the academic experience of leading the Indian Institute for Competitiveness and curating the Porter Prize.

'The book gives excellent practical examples of companies which have been successful in the Indian environment through combination of operational performance, innovation and leadership. This book would be very useful for those MNCs who wish to be successful in India, not necessarily by following their traditional models, as well as for Indian entrepreneurs and businesses who wish to succeed from the opportunities offered by the Make in India initiative.

'I highly recommend this book to business leaders and practising managers'—**Nirmal Bhogilal, chairman, Batliboi Ltd**

'A lot has been made of the complexity of the Indian market. *Riding the Tiger* rightly focuses on why some companies succeed where others fail. Winning is all about a relentless pursuit of category creation, specialization, innovation and faultless execution. The companies featured in the book have not just redefined the way we look at "value for money", but have created competitive, world-class brands'—**Shereen Bhan, managing editor, CNBC-TV18**

'*Riding the Tiger* is a compelling read for anyone interested in India. The book brings together multiple facets to help develop a true sense of what's needed to manage the complexities, and exploit the opportunities, presented by India'—**Vikas Sehgal, global partner, Rothschild; advisor, Government of India**

'India has comparable complexity to Europe in terms of geographic, cultural and linguistic differences. Being successful in the country requires strong execution, constant focus on customer value and clarity of purpose. *Riding the Tiger* captures the essentials of doing business and being successful in India very well. A must-read for anyone interested in doing business in India as well as emerging markets'—**Prakash Chhabria, managing director, Finolex Industries Ltd**

'It is a fascinating book to read for all who are already present in the Indian market or plan investments here. It inspires you to have a wider look at business opportunities in India and what role your Indian company can play to secure the future for your global operation. The book is based on a very rich experience in the local market and many case studies on how ideas got converted into success stories'—**Huber Reilard, managing director, EFD Induction; president, Indo-German Chamber of Commerce**

'India is seen by many as a unique country with such diversity that it is like a continent. Therefore, the best of strategies elsewhere may not meet success here. There's no silver bullet to tap the big opportunities across various sectors in this strongest pillar of the BRICS wall. However, the deep insights and elaborate case studies in *Riding the Tiger* can equip the reader with that much-needed knowledge that is critical for success. This book will be helpful for anyone who wants to understand the Indian business environment, deeply.

'Sometimes, an "outsider" discovers some really interesting aspects on a "local" subject because of his/her strong interest in and experience of it. Dr Wilfried Aulbur has managed to do that in this book'—**Sumantra B. Barooah, associate editor, AutoCar Professional**

'India is becoming increasingly central to the growth and innovation strategies of the world's multinationals. It is the world's fastest-growing large economy and, by 2025, is likely to emerge as the world's third largest, overtaking not just Germany but also Japan. Given these trends, it is incumbent upon the leaders of any global company to become more knowledgeable about India and smarter about how to develop and implement the right strategies for India. *Riding the Tiger* is one of the best books, by far, to address these needs. Wilfried Aulbur and Amit Kapoor know India inside out and have written a thoroughly well-researched and highly readable book. I recommend it as a must-read for CEOs and senior executives of every global company'—**Anil K. Gupta, Michael Dingman chair in strategy and globalization, Smith School of Business, University of Maryland; co-author,** *The Quest for Global Dominance* **and** *Getting China and India Right*

'In this important book, Aulbur and Kapoor paint a vivid portrait of what it takes to succeed in the turbulent environment that is today's India: strategic flexibility, customer-centric innovation, a focus on value for money, frugal innovation and operational excellence. It just may turn out that learning to "ride the tiger" in India will hold the key to business success around the world as digitization and rapid change, combined with corruption, environmental degradation and income inequality, become the new normal'—**Stuart L. Hart, professor, Steven Grossman endowed chair in sustainable business, University of Vermont; author,** *Capitalism at the Crossroads*

'How to think about the complex Indian domestic market has confounded many companies seeking to do business and operate there. Now, thanks to the keen intellect of Wilfried Aulbur and Amit Kapoor, this task is much easier. *Riding the Tiger* is a must-read for scholars, investors, and in-country business operations leaders'—**Roy Kamphausen, senior vice-president, Research; director, Washington DC office, National Bureau of Asian Research**

RIDING
THE TIGER

How to Execute
Business Strategy in India

Wilfried Aulbur with Amit Kapoor

RANDOM BUSINESS

RANDOM BUSINESS

USA | Canada | UK | Ireland | Australia
New Zealand | India | South Africa | China

Random Business is part of the Penguin Random House group of companies
whose addresses can be found at global.penguinrandomhouse.com

Published by Penguin Random House India Pvt. Ltd
7th Floor, Infinity Tower C, DLF Cyber City,
Gurgaon 122 002, Haryana, India

Published in Random Business by Penguin Random House India 2016

ISBN 9788184007534

Typeset in Minion Pro by Manipal Digital Systems, Manipal
Printed at Replika Press Pvt. Ltd, India

To our families

CONTENTS

List of Abbreviations   xiii

Acknowledgements   xvii

Introduction   xxi

1   India's Economy: Remarkably Resilient   1

2   Operational Excellence: The Pressure to Get
    the Basics Right   26

3   Made in India: The Long Road towards
    Building Industry-Wide Excellence   67

4   Indian Innovation: Driving Differentiation   98

5   Start-ups and Incubation in India: The Start
    of an Innovation Explosion   151

6   Choices and Trade-Offs: What You Do and
    Don't Do Matters   177

7   Alignment: Directing an Orchestra versus
    Playing One Instrument   229

8   Leadership: Having the Courage to Provide Direction   262

9   To Sum It Up: What You Need to Know to Ride the Tiger   299

Appendix   325

Notes   347

Index   405

LIST OF ABBREVIATIONS

APSEZL	Adani Ports and Special Economic Zone Ltd
ASEAN	Association of Southeast Asian Nations
ACMA	Automotive Component Manufacturers Association
BAVA	Bajaj Automotive Vendor Association
BoP	Balance of payment
BPS	Basis points
BYBY	By yourself better yourself
BSE	Bombay Stock Exchange
B2B	Business to business
B2C	Business to consumer
CAGR	Compound annual growth rate
CSR	Corporate social responsibility
CSA	Country-specific advantage
CRM	Customer relationship management
CV	Commercial vehicle
CY	Calendar year
DPSU	Defence public sector undertaking
EBITDA	Earnings before interest, tax, depreciation and amortization
EU	European Union
FMCG	Fast-moving consumer goods

FDI	Foreign direct investment
FICV	Future infantry combat vehicle
GIC	Global in-house centre
GHG	Greenhouse gas
GCPL	Godrej Consumer Products Ltd
GST	Goods and services tax
GSA	Government-specific advantage
GMV	Gross merchandise value
HUL	Hindustan Unilever Ltd
HLS	Homeland security
HDFC	Housing Development Finance Corporation
HPS	Husk Power Systems
IIM	Indian Institute of Management
IIT	Indian Institute of Technology
ISRO	Indian Space Research Organisation
IGCC	Indo-German Chamber of Commerce
ITP	Institutional trading platform
IRDA	Insurance Regulatory and Development Authority
IP	Intellectual property
ILO	International Labor Organization
IoT	Internet of things
JV	Joint venture
LIC	Life Insurance Corporation
LCC	Low-cost carrier
M&A	Merger and acquisition
MENA	Middle East and North Africa
MNC	Multinational company
NDA	National Democratic Alliance
NHB	National Housing Bank
NREGA	Mahatma Gandhi National Rural Employment Guarantee Act

NSE	National Stock Exchange
NPA	Non-performing asset
OEM	Original equipment manufacturer
OFDI	Outward foreign direct investment
OHSAS	Occupational Health and Safety Assessment Series
PV	Passenger vehicle
PE	Private equity
P&G	Procter and Gamble
PSU	Public sector undertaking
PPP	Purchasing power parity
R&D	Research and development
RO	Reverse osmosis
RTC	Road transport corporation
RBEI	Robert Bosch Engineering and Business Solutions Ltd
SEBI	Securities and Exchange Board of India
SAIL	Steel Authority of India Ltd
TPM	Total productive maintenance
ULIPs	Unit-linked products
UPA	United Progressive Alliance
USFDA	US Food and Drug Administration
UV	Ultraviolet
VC	Venture capital
VUCA	Volatility, uncertainty, complexity and ambiguity

ACKNOWLEDGEMENTS

This book has benefited immensely from the insights of many owners and managers that are actively and positively involved in driving India's economy to greater heights. Mentioning all of them would be futile; however, some deserve special mention as without them this book would have lost insights and value. Rahul Bharti and R.C. Bhargava at Maruti Suzuki have been constant companions during the past few decades, and have provided much guidance. Sudipta Bhattacharya, Captain Unmesh Abyankar and Malay Mahadevia provided us an in-depth look into globally competitive port operations in India. Hubert Reillard helped us to bring the challenges and successes of a hidden champion to life. At Godrej, Vivek Gambhir, Sunder Mahadeva, Sunil Kataria and Praveen Dalal helped us understand how frugal emerging market MNCs can out-compete established global players. Sunil Mathur from Siemens and his team explained their approach to frugal engineering. At Bosch, Vijay Rathnaparkhe and Dr Steffen Berns helped us understand the immense value that global in-house centres can bring to MNCs. Phanindra Sama from redBus highlighted the successes and potential of the Indian start-up scene. Rajiv Bajaj and his team, namely Pradeep Shrivastava, Abraham Joseph, S. Ravikumar, Eric Vas and Amruth Rath, emphasized the importance of clear choices and alignment to drive global market success. Dr Ashwin Naik explained the journey of Vaatsalya and how concern for his parents drove him and his team to invent a new business model. At HDFC Life, Amitabh Chaudhry explained the challenges of the VUCA world and an uncertain regulatory environment. This theme was reiterated by Sajjan Jindal and his team in the Indian steel industry. At IndiGo, Aditya Ghosh drove the message that every little thing matters. Rajinder Bhatia, Amit and Baba Kalyani from Bharat Forge as well as Chaand Sehgal from Motherson demonstrated that fortune favours the bold. Sanjiv Mehta and his team from Hindustan Unilever shared their insights into shared value business models. Anuj Mehra from Mahindra Rural Finance and Dharmesh Vakharia from Mahindra Housing Finance highlighted the need for innovative business models to increase quality of life as well as job opportunities in rural India. To all of them, a very big and heartfelt thank you!

Other industry stalwarts that have provided support and guidance during numerous discussions shall not go unnamed either. In no particular order, some of them are: Sanjiv Bajaj, Abhay and Prasan Firodia, Farhad and Naushad Forbes, Sanjay, Alok and Rama Kirloskar, Sailesh Mehta, Nishant Arya, Narayana Murthy, Pawan Goenka, Günter Butschek, Cyrus Mistry, Naomi Ishi, Sunil Munjal, V.R. Tanti, Ravi Pandit, Meher and Pheroz Pudumjee, John Edwin, Vinod Dasari.

We also would like to thank the team at Roland Berger for their positive support and enthusiasm despite long days of sifting through documents and analysing information. First and foremost, Nitya Vishwanathan was instrumental and tireless in driving data analysis for the book. This analysis has added depth to our discussion, and we couldn't have written the book without it. Others, such as Kriti Jain, Vandhna Babu, Rijul Bharadwaj, Shekhar Mishra, Volkmar Noeske, Himank Shanker, Vaibhav Jain and Harsh Singh were of great help as well. The rest of the team contributed by creating a positive and dedicated work environment that makes any task fun.

We would like to thank Katherine Nölling and Maximilian Mittereder for their support in marketing the book. The competence, dedication and attention to detail in the editing done by Holly Michelson and Heidi Benson, from Burton, van Iersel & Whitney, Munich, was crucial for the final version of the book and is very much appreciated.

We would like to thank the editorial team at Penguin Random House for their support and insights. Without their belief in the work and flexibility on timelines, this book would not have been possible. We are deeply indebted to both Milee Ashwarya and Lohit Jagwani.

We would like to thank our families who have borne the brunt of the work as weekend after weekend was spent thinking, reading or writing about business in emerging markets. Their support has made all the difference.

INTRODUCTION

INDIA: A VIBRANT AND VOLATILE BUSINESS OPPORTUNITY

We live in a VUCA world—a world characterized by volatility, uncertainty, complexity and ambiguity. The Internet is (finally) revolutionizing the retail and media industries. Green technologies are shaping our growth path. Biotechnology and material science are on the verge of ever more fundamental breakthroughs. Digitalization and robotization are putting industrial capabilities at risk. Germany is about to switch off nuclear power. Europe is faced with a violent geopolitical conflict on her doorsteps. Britain just decided to leave the European Union (EU). The US has proclaimed the 'Pacific Age' and faces probably the most divisive presidential election campaign in its history. Unethical behaviour by bankers has not only led to the great financial crisis of 2008 but also to a series of scandals relating to Libor[1] and exchange rate fixing. Car company executives have cheated on the emission values of their vehicles. Oil prices, exchange rates and stock markets have undergone fluctuations that have left even the hardiest investors breathless. The long list of facts that we would have at best considered as unlikely trends just a little while ago continues to grow longer at ever shorter time intervals.

Emerging markets, while often delivering higher growth rates than the so-called developed economies, tend to be more exposed to these critical uncertainties. Internal factors increase volatility and complexity beyond the levels seen in developed markets. Most emerging markets face key challenges; for instance, governance issues such as the recent corruption scandal in Brazil or the corruption scandals in India a couple of years ago. Rule of law is often either inadequate or not enforceable.[2] Political uncertainty is high in both democratic and non-democratic emerging markets, often leading to internal and external tensions as witnessed by the Ukraine crisis, the current war in Yemen and the dangerous ongoing tensions in the South China Sea. Institutional voids[3] prevent a simple application of global business models and sometimes imply that it is not the best contender but the best connected who wins. Operating in emerging markets does require a unique combination of stamina, commitment, flexibility and speed.

India is no exception. Just a couple of years ago, global coverage about India focused almost entirely on gaps in governance. Massive corruption scandals embroiled the government and the administration and led to extensive policy paralysis. At the height of the crisis, more than INR[4] 6.2 trillion of projects[5] were held up at various stages of the investment process with a corresponding negative impact on the overall economy. During the second half of the Congress-led United Progressive Alliance (UPA) government, sudden bans on iron ore and coal mining disrupted access to raw material for energy and steel producers. GDP growth slowed down to an unsatisfactory level of 4–5 per cent and growth-oriented companies were forced to focus on operational efficiency and cost savings as they struggled for survival. The sweeping win of the opposition National Democratic

Alliance (NDA) in 2014 and the focus of the new government on investment and pro-business policies has created cautious optimism within India and abroad. However, it remains to be seen how many of the election promises will be executed on the ground.

Yet, despite these challenges, India's democracy has enabled remarkable economic and political development. India managed to keep a collection of independent nations together in a single state after shaking off the yoke of foreign occupation. The current discussion in Europe around Greece, Britain and potentially other countries clearly serves as a reminder that this is no mean feat. India's GDP is 4.3 times greater compared to 1991[6] and the country has pulled about 225 million citizens out of poverty.[7] Telecommunications penetration has gone from 6 million in 1991 (1 per cent penetration) to 915 million in 2013[8] (73 per cent penetration). Between 1991 and 2013, 45,466 km of national highways were built, as compared to 13,839 km between 1951 and 1991.[9] The addition since 1991 alone is four times the length of Germany's total autobahn network.

Change and progress in India are palpable and visible everywhere. When I[10] arrived in India for the first time in 1994, I was mesmerized by India's colours and the diversity of her people. But I remember clearly the nagging thoughts and growing frustration that such a beautiful country did not seem to be able to offer exciting careers to her young people. Most of India's best and brightest were determined to secure seats at US universities in the hope of settling there. Today, things have changed dramatically for the better. In most fields, careers in India are as exciting and fulfilling as in any other part of the world—with the challenges of operating in an emerging nation, probably even more exciting.

Today, India means opportunity. There are clearly significant business opportunities here that can and should be leveraged.

Successfully riding the Indian tiger requires a sound, flexible strategy, operational excellence and a dedication to customer-centric innovation.

Typical strategy frameworks that look at a ten-year planning horizon may not be applicable to emerging markets in general and India in particular. With doubts about the predictability of the future—new competitive dynamics driven by digitalization, frugal innovations and business models, fast-changing consumer needs and aspirations, etc.—strategic approaches in India require flexibility. While firmly centred on a common purpose, strategies and organizations need to be able to adapt quickly to changing market environments.

Besides strategy, operational excellence is of key importance to survive in the hyper-competitive Indian environment. Prices in India, such as those for passenger cars, are significantly lower than in developed and other emerging markets.[11] While disposable

0 FIGURE 1

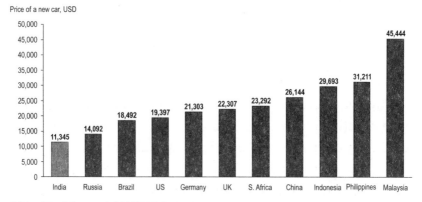

Purchasing a Car in India Is Cheaper Than in Most of the Developed as Well as Developing Nations

Price of a new car: Country comparison

Price of a new car, USD

1) Price of New Volkswagen Golf 2.0 TDI 140 CV 6 vel. (or equivalent), with no extras has been considered for comparison

Source: The Random Walk, 'Mapping the World's Prices 2015', DB Research, http://ftalphaville.ft.com/files/2015/04/DB_RandomWalk_2015-04-14_0900b8c0898020b1-1.pdf

income has increased significantly over the last few decades,[12] large sections of the population remain very price-sensitive. The key challenge in providing value at a consumer-defined price point can only be met by companies that relentlessly pursue cost reductions and process improvements across the value chain.

Indian consumers are value-for-money devotees. Satisfying their demands for performance at acceptable price points drives business model and process innovations. Price/performance equations of products need to be constantly improved via frugal engineering in order to both secure existing markets and open up whole new market segments for consumption.[13] Real technological innovation breakthroughs have been less prominent in the Indian market and are generally more relevant to furthering the global aspirations of Indian multinational companies (MNCs).

THE PROTAGONISTS: LEVERAGING THE RESURGENCE OF INDIA

Successful players in India come from all backgrounds—large and well-connected family businesses, hardy MNCs, new entrants that have built their empires over the last ten to twenty years, as well as the latest wave of e-commerce companies. Each of these companies has leveraged different strengths and overcome different challenges in order to establish itself firmly in the country.

India's early economic history has been written by large families and conglomerates. Business families and groups—such as Tata, Birla, Godrej and others—have had a major impact on the country and some have become global household names. These companies boast formidable competitive advantages such as access to capital, legal and political support, brand reputation, distribution footprint, research and development (R&D)

capability and a solid talent pipeline. Backed by the specific advantages of their firms, these Indian leaders have entered new lines of businesses, leveraged their position for joint ventures (JVs) with MNCs and, in a more recent phenomenon, driven innovation by acting as venture capital (VC) investors. Many have looked beyond India's shores to drive global expansion of their firms and brands.

Newer additions to this group, such as Reliance, Adani Ports and Special Economic Zone Ltd (APSEZL), Bharti and others, have grown at extraordinary speed, fully leveraging the opportunities that a liberalized economy has presented to them. Many have been innovation leaders in their fields, e.g., Bharti Airtel, a company that redefined the way the telecom business is run globally, and APSEZL, a company that built best-in-class port infrastructure in India and competes head-on with the best ports globally.

MNCs typically leveraged their brand, processes and technologies to penetrate the mind and the wallet of the Indian consumer. Some, such as Siemens, who built the Indo-European telegraph line from London to Calcutta in 1865–70, have been active in the country for more than a century and have become local household names. Others such as Maruti Suzuki are newer additions, but their product portfolio and approach to the Indian market has made them part and parcel of the Indian economy and cultural fabric.

A new set of companies born out of the start-up environment in Bangalore, Gurgaon, Mumbai, Pune and Chennai is also entering the scene. Here, local players either adopt global models to an Indian context or solve real-life issues for Indian customers. With nine unicorns[14] (Flipkart, Snapdeal, Ola Cabs and others) at the time of writing, the Indian start-up scene is likely to remain interesting over the next few years.

OUR PURPOSE

This book looks at successful and sometimes-not-so-successful strategies, operations and innovations within India. We have distilled lessons from our decades of practical work experience in the country. We leverage more than 200 client engagements in India and other emerging markets as well as countless research assignments on India's macro- and micro-economic environment. In addition, more than 100 case studies created in the last few years in the context of the Porter Prize provide us with detailed insights into the way business is done in India. The book clearly addresses the Indian context; however, many approaches and ideas can be applied to other emerging markets as well.

We hope that our work will offer useful insights to practitioners and professionals working in any one of the four company types described above or those trying to establish their own enterprise. We also hope that students with an interest in emerging markets and their challenges will find reading our book useful. Some twenty cases in nearly as many different industries are covered. To increase the impact of our case studies, each case is preceded by an overview of the relevant industry to establish context and relevance.

Overall, we are guided by two seminal works on strategy: Porter's *Harvard Business Review's* article, 'What Is Strategy?',[15] and Lafley and Martin's more recent book, *Playing to Win*.[16] Rather than identifying yet another framework, our book is loosely guided by the ideas in these works and focuses more on the practical implications of strategy, operations and innovation in emerging markets. As can be seen from many of the cases that we discuss, success in India is often the result of unsuccessful attempts, quick course corrections, customer-focused innovations and relentless push for cost optimization and scale. Being successful in India is not rocket science, but it does require entrepreneurs to get all the various pieces of the puzzle right and to work on a value proposition that makes sense to discerning Indian customers.

The structure of the book is as follows: Chapter 1 sets the stage by looking at India's development from an economic, social and political point of view. The main focus of the analysis is India's journey post-liberalization. We show that India's economy is remarkably resilient despite all the challenges that the macro-economic environment and her own political parties throw at her. We also point out that the country's performance versus its main rival China is reasonable once the liberalization time difference is taken into account.

Chapter 2 focuses on operations as the basic enabler to execute strategy in a price-sensitive, value-for-money-focused environment. We are looking at operational excellence efforts in the wake of liberalization and also at the journey that still needs to be covered by many Indian companies. Key case studies include Maruti Suzuki, APSEZL and EFD Induction.

Chapter 3 analyses challenges in the Indian textile and machine-tool industry which serve as a reminder of the work that still needs to be done. A review of the history of 'Made in Germany' will provide potential lessons for the current government initiative 'Make in India'. We will point out the achievements as well as the challenges that India faces in establishing herself as a major manufacturing power in the face of low-cost competition and re-industrialization trends in the West (e.g., Industry 4.0).

Clearly, operational excellence is necessary but insufficient to compete in India. Sustainable economic value is created not by competing to be the best but by competing to be unique, and hence is directly dependent on the companies' capability to innovate. Chapter 4 will analyse the importance of innovation, both for the Indian domestic market as well as for conquering developed and other emerging markets abroad. We will focus on several areas of innovation—business models, repurposing of products for a different set of applications and product innovation through frugal engineering. Case studies such as Godrej, Tata Chemicals, Hindustan Unilever Ltd (HUL), Husk Power Systems (HPS), Siemens and Bosch will shed light on the vibrant Indian innovation ecosystem. This book will discuss India's low performance on fundamental research, its leadership role in frugal innovation, as well as India's importance for R&D centres of leading global MNCs.

Chapter 5 highlights a relatively new phenomenon in India, namely the development of its incubation and start-up ecosystem. India is currently the third largest start-up hub in the world, and case studies such as redBus and Kyron provide us with interesting views of innovation activities in this exploding market segment.

Chapter 6 looks at choices and trade-offs. To create unique value, companies have to create activity systems that perfectly fit with customer needs. Optimizing one activity system prevents the company from getting into another activity system to deliver alternative products. While strategy development is often the result of trial and error, successful Indian companies end up with a clearly defined understanding about who they are and what they do. We will discuss the cases of Bajaj Auto, Vaatsalya Healthcare and HDFC Life Insurance.

Chapter 7 details the importance of company purpose to drive alignment through organizations. There needs to be a good fit between all activities to drive performance and create activity systems that cannot easily be copied by other companies. We analyse the alignment between strategy, innovation, internationalization and operations for Indigo and JSW, a leading steel company in India.

Chapter 8 talks about leadership, i.e., the courage and drive it takes to create and grow aligned global businesses. We focus, in particular, on two relevant avenues of growth, one via global expansion and M&As (mergers and acquisitions) and the other by creating entirely new businesses at the bottom of the pyramid via shared value initiatives. We look at the history of outgoing Indian foreign direct investment (FDI) and highlight its unique structure versus other emerging markets such as China. We also highlight that shared value rather than corporate social responsibility (CSR) is the only scalable answer to solve India's many challenges. The cases that we discuss are HUL, Mahindra Rural Finance, Motherson and Bharat Forge's defence business.

Chapter 9 is a short summary of our analysis and deliberations.

In contrast to many other writers, we have presented our case studies in full length rather than sprinkling insights gleaned from their examples across chapters. As the reader will immediately recognize, none of these cases exhibits only one topic, e.g., operational excellence. Rather, they reflect all of the themes that are discussed in this book—operational excellence, innovation and differentiation, choices and trade-offs, alignment and leadership. Successful companies are successful because they integrate all these approaches into one holistic whole. We felt that describing these holistic approaches in one go was more adequate and a better reflection of the achievements of the various companies that we discuss.

Writing a book about India is a truly humbling experience. The country is vast, its differences in terms of culture and business pronounced. India's development is sometimes chaotic and always fast-paced. Consistent data is often impossible to obtain. We realize that some of our observations are a reflection of India's particular state of development at the end of 2015/beginning of 2016. We believe that many of the strategic and operational approaches exhibited by our case studies will remain relevant for practitioners trying to find their way through the VUCA world of the twenty-first century.

During our discussions with executives, students, etc. around the world, we have often come across a significant amount of scepticism. Is India moving fast enough or is the country falling irrevocably behind? Is her political system the right one? Corruption is so endemic, will it ever be solved? Such questions, and many others, are fair questions to ask and important ones for India to answer. However, it is absolutely crucial to recognize how far India has come. India did not start from a level playing field but suffered the effects of colonialization and had to work hard to overcome the same. While this discussion is not part of our book, it will be helpful for some readers to consider reading Will Durant's *The Case for India*, written in 1930. Durant paints a vivid picture of the challenges faced by India's founding generation and their descendants when building a new nation out of a conglomerate of independent states and people.[17]

1

INDIA'S ECONOMY

REMARKABLY RESILIENT

INDIA'S ELEPHANT: A DIFFERENT TYPE OF DRAGON?

Over the last thirty-five years, India's economic power has steadily increased. The compound annual growth rate (CAGR)[18] of India's GDP from 1980 to 2014 was 6.3 per cent,[19] enabling the country to increase its output by about 7.9 times. India's GDP today stands at USD 2096.8 billion, and India ranks tenth in global GDP rankings (2013 rank) and third in purchasing power parity (PPP)-adjusted GDP rankings (2013 rank).[20] More importantly, pre- and post-liberalization growth has always been consistently above 5 per cent, as shown in Figure 1.1.

Despite all the vagaries of global markets, internal strife and politics, India's economy has not disappointed beyond a certain point and has proven itself to be remarkably resilient. Time periods of slower growth are linked to major events in India's history: the aftermath of the balance of payment (BoP) crisis in which the effect of reforms had not yet fully taken root (1990–95, 5.1 per cent) and the recent governance and global economic crisis (2010–14, 6.5 per cent).

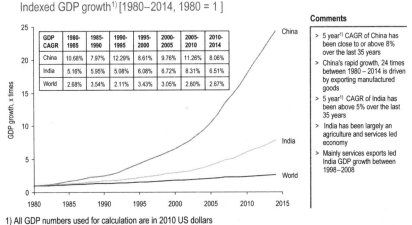

FIGURE 1

India's GDP Increased by About 7.9x since 1980, Three Times Faster Than Global Expansion but Only a Third of Chinese Achievements

Indexed GDP growth[1) [1980–2014, 1980 = 1]

GDP CAGR	1980-1985	1985-1990	1990-1995	1995-2000	2000-2005	2005-2010	2010-2014
China	10.68%	7.97%	12.29%	8.61%	9.76%	11.26%	8.06%
India	5.16%	5.95%	5.08%	6.08%	6.72%	8.31%	6.51%
World	2.68%	3.54%	2.11%	3.43%	3.05%	2.60%	2.67%

Comments

> 5 year[1) CAGR of China has been close to or above 8% over the last 35 years
> China's rapid growth, 24 times between 1980 – 2014 is driven by exporting manufactured goods
> 5 year[1) CAGR of India has been above 5% over the last 35 years
> India has been largely an agriculture and services led economy
> Mainly services exports led India GDP growth between 1998–2008

1) All GDP numbers used for calculation are in 2010 US dollars

Source: US Department of Agriculture Economic Research Service, Real GDP (2010 Dollars) Historical, http://www.ers.usda.gov/data-products/international-macroeconomic-data-set.aspx; Roland Berger analysis

While India fares well in comparison to global averages, her growth trails that of China significantly. Catching up to replicate the 'Chinese economic miracle' does not seem likely over the next twenty to thirty years. China's growth has never dipped below 8 per cent in each of the six-year intervals that we have considered. Chinese GDP increased by a factor of twenty-four since 1980, about three times larger than India's achievement. China's focus on (over) investment in infrastructure and export of manufactured goods to create well-paying jobs has lifted hundreds of millions more out of poverty than India's socialist and democratic efforts could muster.

Taking the thirteen-year difference between the beginnings of economic reforms into account (1978 in China versus 1991 in India), things do not look quite as bleak. Assuming the historic growth rate of 6.1 per cent (most analysts expect at least 7 per cent going forward), India's GDP would be about sixteen times as large as its 1980 GDP and about 56 per cent of China's 2014 GDP. To put things in perspective in a different way, India's GDP in 2014 equals 88.4 per cent of China's GDP in 2001. While both countries have been operating at different speeds, the difference may not be as large as it is generally portrayed in the public domain. Going forward, India is projected to continue to grow faster than China.[21] However, it seems likely that China's economically dominant position will remain unchallenged for some time to come. Nevertheless, India's economic weight on the global scale will be substantial over the next decades.

Contrary to China's manufacturing-led growth model, India's growth has been driven by services. Industry, manufacturing and mining have been at a relatively constant share of 43–45 per cent of GDP (see Figure A.1 in the Appendix). Services have grown at the expense of agriculture and allied services. From a mere 38.6 per cent of the overall economy, services accounts for a staggering 60 per cent of overall GDP today, a ratio that is very similar to that of developed nations such as the US. Recent announcements regarding a 'Make in India' approach target a 10 per cent market share gain of manufacturing, bringing manufacturing to a rather high 25 per cent of GDP. While these intentions are positive, whether they will be successful remains to be seen.

A Large Market + Reasonable Labour Cost = An Opportunity Too Attractive to Pass Up

While the consistent growth of the Indian economy is encouraging, the growth of some of India's largest companies has been nothing short of spectacular. Take Bharat Forge as an example. When Baba Kalyani, the current chairman and managing director of Bharat Forge, joined the company in 1972, its turnover was USD 1.3 million. In the financial year ending on 31 March 2014, the consolidated turnover of Bharat Forge had comfortably crossed the USD 1 billion mark. Overall, the CAGR of India's top fifty companies during the last decade[22] equals

21 per cent, a clear indication that once India's entrepreneurial talent was unleashed, it did find ways for value creation.

India's potential has been recognized not only by local players. FDI of MNCs took off around the mid-2000s. From a relatively modest, sub-USD 5 billion-a-year level, FDI shot up to a yearly level of about USD 25–30 billion (see Figure 1.2).[23] Hardly surprising, this strong increase in FDI coincided with a period of strong growth in India's GDP (8.3 per cent in 2005–10). Not only did foreign companies want to participate in India's growth, they contributed to creating jobs and wealth in the country, thereby increasing their customer base and supporting the creation of a virtuous cycle. Services, telecommunications, construction, and computer software and hardware sectors brought the majority of FDI into India. Mauritius, Singapore and the US are responsible for more than 50 per cent of the total FDI inflows into the country.

1 FIGURE 2

FDI as Well as FII Flows Have Grown Significantly since 1991; Cumulative Inbound FDI of USD 371 bn, FII/FPI Investment of USD 190 bn

India FDI inflow, outflow, FDI equity inflow and FPI/FII investment [1991–2016, USD bn]

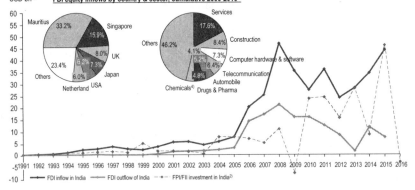

1) USD billion at current prices and current exchange rates 2) INR/USD exchange rate = 60 has been used 3) For the period Apr 2000 to Mar 2016 4) Except fertilizers

Source: UNCTAD World Investment Report 2016: Annex Tables 01 and 02, http://unctad.org/en/Pages/DIAE/World%20 Investment%20Report/Annex-Tables.aspx NSDL, FPI /FII Investment details (Financial Year), https://www.fpi.nsdl.co.in/web/ Reports/Yearwise.aspx?RptType=5; DIPP, Factsheet on FDI, April 2000 to March 2016, http://dipp.nic.in/English/Publications/ FDI_Statistics/2016/FDI_FactSheet_JanuaryFebruaryMarch2016.pdf; Roland Berger Analysis

Take German investments as an example. According to the Indo-German Chamber of Commerce (IGCC), about 1680 German companies (including branches and sales offices) are present in India, with hubs centred in Maharashtra (638), Karnataka (213), Tamil Nadu (213) and NCR[24] (145). In addition, the IGCC lists about 320 German companies that have established JVs with Indian players. The performance of German companies in the country is remarkable as indicated by the IGCC 15 Index which includes the daily stock prices of fifteen German companies[25] that are listed on the Bombay Stock Exchange (combined market cap in excess of EUR 27 billion).[26]

While FDI did retract somewhat during the economic slowdown and the challenging environment during the last years of the previous government (see below), it did not collapse. Foreign investors' trust in India's medium-to-long-term potential did not seem to waver even as political parties and the government created one of the largest economic downturns in recent Indian history. Similar observations hold for foreign institutional investments. Overall, investments of foreign institutional investors saw a significant increase around 2004, dipped shortly into negative territory in 2009 due to liquidity issues abroad, and then rebounded after the crisis.

A key motivator of foreign and Indian direct investment has always been the large and growing middle class of the country that is increasingly willing to spend hard-earned money. On a GDP per capita level, India's growth accelerated in each of the six-year intervals starting with a growth rate of 3.0 per cent in 1980–85 and ending with a growth rate of 6.75 per cent in the six-year period from 2005 to 2010 (see Figure A.2 in the Appendix). There are only two exceptions to this trend, the previously discussed periods from 1990 to 1995 and 2010 to 2014.

Again, while India fared better in terms of growth rates than global averages, the comparison with China is hardly flattering. The Chinese

GDP per capita was about 16 per cent lower than that of India in 1980 (USD 342 versus USD 409). While economic growth and restrictive population growth drove China's GDP per capita up by more than seventeen times, India achieved a four-fold increase in GDP per capita and trails China today by a factor of three (USD 6,050 versus USD 1,778 in 2014). Accounting for the thirteen-year difference and extrapolating with India's historic GDP per capita growth rate of 4.4 per cent leads to a GDP per capita of USD 3,118 or 52 per cent of China's 2014 GDP per capita number. This rather large difference reflects faster population growth and slower economic development in India versus China. Both areas need government attention going forward.

1 FIGURE 3

Net Domestic Savings and Personal Disposable Income with Strong Increase since 1990. Lending Interest Rates Are Falling

India net domestic savings [INR bn], lending rates [%], PDI per capita[1] [INR] and avg amount of debt per household [INR]

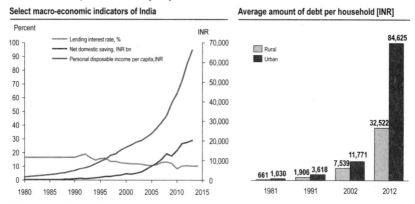

1) PDI = Personal Disposable Income
Source: World Development Indicators, World Bank , Lending interest rates (%), http://data.worldbank.org/indicator/FR.INR. LEND RBI macroeconomic aggregates, September 2014, https://www.rbi.org.in/scripts/PublicationsView.aspx?id=15790 NSS reports: Household Assets & Liabilities in India, 59th round, November 2005 release, Key Indicators of All India Debt & Investment, 70th round, December 2014 release; Roland Berger analysis

While less impressive than China, wealth creation in India over the last thirty-five years has been dramatic. Wealth is concentrated among a young population that enjoys spending money and is not afraid to take on debt. Economic growth has driven an exponential increase in disposable income per capita as shown in Figure 1.3. Combined with falling interest rates and a strong increase in net domestic savings as well as consumer credit, India's consumption story will remain strong in the foreseeable future. Significant penetration has been reached across many categories. However, as shown in Table 1.1, significant potential versus developed markets remains to be exploited.

1 TABLE 1

Indian Consumer Goods Ownership/1000 Households Varies a Lot across Categories. Overall Significant Potential vs Developed Nations

Durable consumer goods ownership per 1000 households

Category	India[1]	China[3]	Japan[2]
Motorcycle[2]	313 *(378/184)*	245	135
Washing machine	132 *(213/29)*	907	1035
Refrigerator	296 *(438/94)*	917	1168
Television	703 *(804/496)*	1220	1913[3]
Camera	86 *(136/17)*	352	1171
Air Conditioner	141[4] *(235/59)*	1074	2376
Computer	74 *(149/15)*	762	1372[5]
Cell phone	868 *(922/776)*	2166	1878[6]
Automobile	71[7] *(80/20)*	257	1101[8]

(xx/yy) - Urban/rural ownership of goods per 1000 households
1) All India numbers calculated as - Goods per 1000 households = (no. of urban+rural households reporting possession/ Total no. of households surveyed)*1000; Data as per survey of 2011-12
2) Data for year 2014 3) Data as per survey of 2015
4) Includes scooters 5) Excludes Barun tube TV sets 6) Includes air coolers 7) Motor car and Jeep 8) Only cars considered
Source: Household Consumption of Various Goods and Services in India 2011-12, NSS 68th Round, Statistical Yearbook of China 2015, Japan 2014 National survey of Family Income and Expenditure; Roland Berger analysis

While India's consumers are getting wealthier, they are far from homogeneous. Strong regional differences exist, e.g., in the purchase of luxury goods. A large (3200 households) quantitative study across luxury car customers, for example, identified six distinct consumer groups among the target group: young car enthusiasts, mature car enthusiasts, heavy users, fun-seeking affluents, cost-conscious consumers and traditionalists (see Figures A.3 and A.4 in the Appendix). All of these groups have different purchasing patterns, socio-economic backgrounds, etc.

Even more importantly, the distribution of these groups is not homogeneous across the country, necessitating different go-to-market approaches in the various regions. This phenomenon is not limited to luxury goods but can also be found in the purchase of industrial goods as well as consumer goods and services.

As purchasing power spreads across the country, reaching the Indian consumer is an important and challenging task. With low urbanization projected to continue into the future (32.7 per cent in 2015, 50 per cent in 2050[27]), most B2C (business to consumer) businesses must find innovative and cost-effective ways to penetrate India's cities as well as her rural population. HUL found an innovative solution to this challenge. Leveraging 'Shakti Ammas' and 'Shaktimaans', women and men whose families belong to the lowest income bracket in their village, for last-mile distribution, the company is able to reach 1,65,000 villages in India. This provides HUL with a low-cost distribution channel that (including income generated from selling non-competing products for other companies) is nearly as profitable as its ordinary sales channels, according to company interviews.[28]

India's attractiveness is not only driven by her consumers but also by massive investments in infrastructure. A staggering EUR 830 billion will be invested in the Indian economy over the FY13–FY17 period (see Figure A.5 in the Appendix). The focus of key investments is electricity, roads and bridges, telecommunications, railways and metro, irrigation, airports, ports and other key infrastructure areas. This investment will not only create jobs and opportunities by itself, it will also have a significant impact on the overall competitiveness of India's economy. In accordance with the planning commission, expenditure targets for the tenth and eleventh plan were largely met. Hence we can be fairly confident that comparable results will be achieved for the twelfth plan. Past performance and the current commitment of the new government to push infrastructure investments will give a significant economic push to the country and provide grounds for optimism.

Last but not least, on average, India's public, corporate and household debt as a percentage of GDP is relatively low by international standards. All combined account for 121 per cent of GDP, a number lower than that of Brazil (138 per cent) and China (225 per cent) as well as of most developed nations. Clearly, there are remaining reserves left for both consumption and investment (see Figure 1.4).

1 FIGURE 4

Overall Debt Levels (Households, Corporates, Public) Are Low Compared to Global Averages and Allow for Future Investments

Household debt [1980–2014, % GDP], Corporate debt [1980–2014, % GDP], Public debt [1980–2014, % GDP]

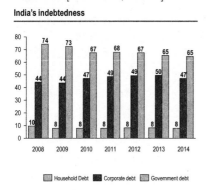

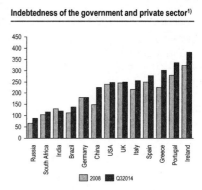

1) Data include indebtedness of households, non-profit Institutions serving households, non-financial corporations and the government as a per cent of GDP. Government indebtedness data are actuals/estimates for 2014.

Source: Reserve Bank of India, Financial stability report, Issue 11, June 2015; Roland Berger analysis

Crossing the Sea: India's Increased Integration in Global Business

Not to be outdone, India's outward direct investments showed strong performance. Outward direct investments grew from USD 6 million in 1990 to USD 1.9 billion in 2003[29] and then reached a respectable level of USD 15–20 billion between 2005 and 2011. India's corporate heroes across diverse sectors such as automotive, pharma, renewable energy, information technology (IT) and engineering services increasingly look outside to establish a strong global foothold. Reasons for foreign investments and acquisitions are many. In some cases, assets in developed economies are being bought for technology and customer access. Technology acquisition, brand extension and diversification of business risks were, for example, the outcomes of the successful takeover of Jaguar Land Rover by Tata Motors. In other cases, companies in emerging markets such as Africa or Southeast Asia drive an opportunity for market access and cross-leverage of products. Godrej, for example, very successfully bought brands in both these geographies that extend its core line-up of consumer products in India.[30]

1 FIGURE 5

India's Import and Export Intensity Has Consistently Grown over the Last 35 Years, Comparable with China During the Last 5 Years

Import/Export Share [1980–2014, % GDP]

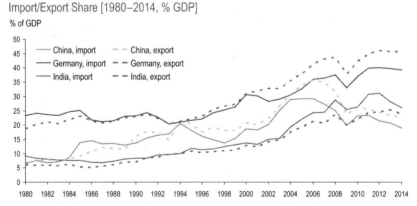

Source: World Development Indicators, World Bank , 'Imports of goods and services (% of GDP)' and 'Exports of goods and services (% of GDP)', http://data.worldbank.org/indicator/NE.IMP.GNFS.ZS and http://data.worldbank.org/indicator/NE.EXP.GNFS.ZS; Roland Berger analysis

India's engagement with international business and markets has only increased as a function of time. The years of splendid self-sufficiency are definitively over. Since 1991, the import and export share in India's GDP has gone up about three times. Imports in 2014 amounted to 26 per cent of GDP, exports to 24 per cent. In 2014, India's export and import intensity compares favourably with China, as shown in Figure 1.5.[31]

While India's integration with the rest of the world is increasing, her share of world merchandise exports, for example, is still small at 1.7 per cent in 2013.[32] Compared to other players (China 11.7 per cent, US 8.4 per cent, Germany 7.7 per cent, Japan 3.8 per cent, France 3.1 per cent, South Korea 3.0 per cent, Brazil 1.3 per cent), India outperforms Brazil but clearly bats below her medium-to-long-term potential. Particularly striking is the difference in export composition. India's manufacturing export as a percentage of total exports stands at 50 per cent, which is higher than Brazil's 33 per cent but lower than other relevant countries (China 93 per cent, Japan 88 per cent, South Korea 85 per cent, Germany 83 per cent, US 64 per cent).[33] This fact highlights untapped opportunities that the current government is trying to address via the 'Make in India' campaign.

While 'Make in India' may be a new slogan, companies have recognized for some time that India can potentially play an important role in their global engineering and manufacturing footprint. Currently, a window of opportunity seems to be opening as China tries to move further up the value chain. With costs rising in China, the Chinese government is pushing a policy of 'innovate' rather than 'make' in China. Lower-cost, labour-intensive parts of the manufacturing value chain may be available for the taking. India's manufacturing manpower costs about a third as much as comparable labour in China as shown in Figure 1.6. With a large working population and a fair amount of English-speaking people, India can potentially establish herself as a serious competitor for low-cost manufacturing versus alternatives such as Vietnam, Indonesia and the Philippines.

Nevertheless, India has to take these and similar competitors seriously. All of them offer attractive wages as well as additional advantages. Indonesia, for example, boasts a large internal market and a high penetration of English; the Philippines offers state support for 'Make in Philippines' and a predominantly English-speaking workforce. As a consequence, consistent policy action and government reform will be crucial to realize India's ambitions.

1 FIGURE 6

China's Rising Wage Rates Create an Opportunity for Other Asian Economies to Replace It as the Go-To Manufacturing Destination

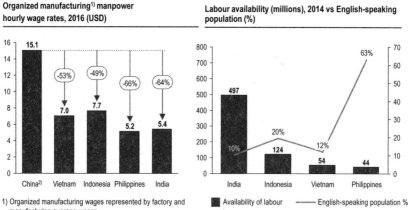

Organized manufacturing[1] manpower hourly wage rates, 2016 (USD)

Labour availability (millions), 2014 vs English-speaking population (%)

1) Organized manufacturing wages represented by factory and manufacturing average wages
2) Mainland China Wages

Availability of labour — English-speaking population %

Source: Salaryexplorer, 'Hourly Wage Rates', http://www. salaryexplorer.com/hourly-wage.php; Payscale, http://www. payscale.com/research/IN/Industry=Manufacturing/Hourly_ Rate#by_Years_Experience; Roland Berger analysis

Source: World Development Indicators, World Bank, 'Labor Force, total', http://data.worldbank.org/indicator/SL.TLF. TOTL.IN; Wikipedia, https://en.wikipedia.org/wiki/List_of_ countries_by_English-speaking_population; Secondary research, Roland Berger estimates

Critics are fast to point out that cost advantages add up to nothing unless they come with adequate productivity and consistent productivity gains. Positive news on this front comes from the statistics of the International Labor Organization (ILO). According to the ILO's Global Wage Report 2012/2013, India's productivity gains over the period 1999–2007 and 2008–2011 have clearly outpaced increases in salaries (see Figure 1.7).[34]

Initial results from this development can be seen in the fact that several capital goods companies have moved their export basis for key products from China to India over the last three to four years.

1 FIGURE 7

India Has Shown Similar Increase in Labour Productivity as China, but Average Wages in India Have Not Grown at the Same Rate

Growth in wages and labour productivity in Asia, 1997–2007 and 2008–11 (%)

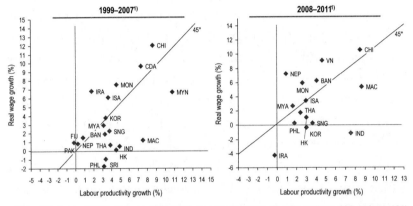

1) China CHI, Cambodia CDA, Indonesia ISA, Islamic Republic of Iran IRA, Republic of Korea KOR, Malaysia MYA, Singapore SNG, Bangladesh BAN, Thailand THA, India IND, Macau (China) MAC, Hong Kong (China) HK, Sri Lanka SRI, Philippines PHL, Myanmar MYN, Mongolia MON, Nepal NEP, Pakistan PAK, Fiji FIJ

Source: Global Wage Report 2012/13, International Labor Organization

All Is Not Well: India's Business Environment Challenges

While the overall scenario points to positive fundamentals, challenges for growth exist. One of the key obstacles to investment in the country is the notoriously low ease of doing business index (see Figure A.6 in the Appendix). Based on the World Bank 2016 report, India ranked 130 out of 189 nations, far behind many relevant emerging market competitors. The new Indian government is taking aggressive measures to ensure India's ranking improves significantly. Improvement in the regulatory environment, reduction in documentation procedures for exports and imports and the 'Make in India' campaign are some of the initiatives taken so far. Execution of consistent policies will be key to achieving real improvement on the ground as well as in rankings.

In addition, doing business varies from one region to another and one size definitely does not fit all. For example, India's business environment holds significantly more challenges for the construction industry in the south and east due to lower 'ease of doing business' rankings and a lower penetration of the organized sector (see Figure A.7 in the Appendix). Again, these findings are valid across industries, albeit to different degrees. Foreign visitors to India are tempted to compare it to the cultural, economic and regional differences in their home country (e.g., within Germany—Hamburg versus Stuttgart). However, a comparison with the EU is much more adequate. Differences in India are in many respects far more similar to the differences that one finds, for example, between Germany and Greece or Romania.

A significant part of India's 'ease of doing business' challenge is the country's legal system. India's legal system is de facto useless, driving more and more companies to sign contracts with offshore arbitration in locations such as Singapore. The case load in front of the country's Supreme Court is so high that clearing all cases would require 466 years, as we mentioned earlier.[35] Lower courts are plagued by corruption, which is one of the reasons why it typically takes ten to fifteen years to get legal disputes settled. Since justice delayed is justice denied, the only practical solution is to avoid involvement with the Indian judicial system to the maximum extent possible.

Lastly, due to weak growth in the years 2010–14, India's banking system is stressed and suffers from high non-performing assets (NPAs) and corporate restructuring burden. NPA levels and restructured advances in Indian banks hover around 15 per cent on average for public sector banks, limiting their capability to lend. Due to better risk procedures and less political influence, the situation of the private banks in India is significantly better, as shown in Figure 1.8.

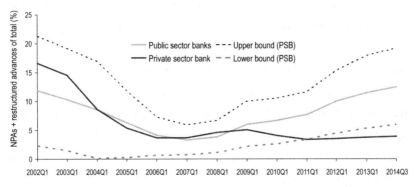

1) NPAs = Non-Performing Assets

Source: Economic Survey of India 2014-15, Ministry of Finance, Government of India

INDIA'S POLITICAL SYSTEM: CHANGE IS THE ONLY CONSTANT

As a typical emerging country, India faces numerous challenges. IPR security, red tape, distribution, corruption, etc., are just some of the challenges that make life in India interesting. Unfortunately, India's political system often seems to be part of the problem rather than the solution. It would be worthwhile to trace the key political events during the last twenty-five years. A summary of relevant trends is given in Table A.2 in the Appendix.

1991 to 1998: A New Economy Is Born

Economically, the period up to 1991 was a closed and relatively isolated period for India thanks to the Licence Raj or Permit Raj regime. Licence Raj refers to the elaborate licences, regulations and accompanying red tape that were required to set up and run businesses in India between 1947 and 1990.[36] The driving force behind the Licence Raj was the social and economic model of a state-controlled economy born out of the socialist leanings of India's founding fathers. As in many other countries, government control sapped growth and competitiveness and stifled innovation by disallowing a free-market reign. Licences were given to a select few who had to meet the requirements of sometimes up to eighty government agencies. The inefficiencies created by the government led to a situation where even essential goods and services such as phone lines, gas connections, airline tickets and automobiles were scarce. Waiting times for a car could be as long as twenty-five years, forcing parents to order a vehicle as soon as their son or daughter was born. Product quality was mostly shoddy and choice extremely limited, as signified by the duopoly of Ambassador and Fiat Padmini cars that dominated the roads during those years.

1991 was a seminal year in world history, not only for India. The collapse of the Soviet Union signified the end of the Cold War and meant that India lost one of her most important trade partners. India had traditionally been friendly with the USSR and more suspicious of the US. A lot of her trade with the USSR had been on barter basis—essential goods, machines, oil and gas were exchanged against India's products. This mechanism of trade collapsed and the problem was exacerbated by the Kuwait crisis. The war in Kuwait drove oil prices up, which very quickly depleted India's currency reserves. In a short time, India had to fly her gold reserves to London and Zurich as a security for her foreign debts.

The national embarrassment of these events led to a change in government. Pushed against the wall, the new Indian ruling team around Narasimha Rao, who served as prime minister between 1991 and 1996, and former Prime Minister Manmohan

Singh, who served as finance minister in the Rao government, drove radical economic reforms. With foreign exchange reserves that could hardly finance three weeks' worth of imports, Rao and his team acted on three main problem areas. Government schemes and subventions were massively reduced for a short-term improvement of state finances. Several areas of the economy were opened up for private investments and the Licence Raj was abolished. In addition, the economy was opened up to the world. A 20 per cent devaluation of the Indian Rupee supported Indian exports, and the door to FDI was opened up when majority ownership or even 100 per cent subsidiaries of foreign companies were allowed to operate in India. In contrast to east European nations, however, privatization of state-owned companies was not given priority.

The Foreign Investment Promotion Board was set up to streamline FDI procedures. The limit on foreign equity holdings was raised from 40 per cent to 51 per cent under the automatic route in thirty-five industries (expanded to 111 industries in 1996). The outcome saw approved FDI going from INR 500 crore in 1992 to over INR 55,000 crore in 1997, as per the 2001–02 economic survey of India. In 1997, 100 per cent FDI in cash and carry wholesale trading was permitted.

The market regulator Securities and Exchange Board of India (SEBI), which was established in 1988, was given statutory powers in 1992 through the SEBI Act (1992). India's leading stock exchange, the National Stock Exchange (NSE) was established in 1992. IT companies that had started in the 1980s became internationalized thanks to the economy opening up. US companies started outsourcing work to low-cost and skilled talent pools in India. Automotive companies such as South Korea's Hyundai Motors entered the country. Other sectors such as airlines and telecom also gained momentum.

However, despite sweeping changes, the Indian consumer remained cautious. Consumerism was subdued in the early days of liberalization because of the baggage from the Licence Raj. Consumer choices were very few. Businesses on their part were not yet exposed to global competition, and quality was often not up to the mark. Disposable income was limited. With no adequate social systems in place, the immediate focus of many consumers remained the education of their children, ideally in the US, the possession of an apartment or a house and an adequate nest egg for retirement. All of these required sufficient savings. In 1995, India's gross domestic savings rate as a percentage of GDP was 24.4 per cent as compared, for instance, to the US (16.9 per cent), the UK (17 per cent) and Germany (22.7 per cent).[37]

While the Congress had led India out of the Licence Raj, it found it difficult to leverage this success and harness the fruit of its labour. As mentioned earlier, significant policy changes do not immediately translate into larger growth but do take their own time to percolate through the system. The Congress, despite being able to stay in power for a full five-year term, found governing increasingly difficult as the impending doom of the BoP crisis started to wane. On the one hand, The Congress did not have a clear mandate but depended on unpredictable left parties. On the other, minority regional parties started growing in strength as they were more adept at reflecting India's large ethnic and cultural diversity.

The number of prime ministers that India went through during the 1991–98 period is a reflection of this political uncertainty. The BJP's Atal Bihari Vajpayee held the post for thirteen days before Rao, but had to resign because the party failed to muster enough support to obtain a majority. Chandra Shekhar Singh of The Janata Dal was prime minister for about seven months during 1990–91, but had to resign when the Congress withdrew support and he could not bring out a full-fledged budget. H.D. Deve Gowda was prime minister from 1996 to 1997, heading the United Front (a conglomeration of non-Congress and non-BJP regional parties), and was succeeded by Inder Kumar Gujral, who stayed in office for about a year.

1998 to 2003: Governments Change but Economic Policies Remain the Same

A factious thirteenth Lok Sabha election in 1998 brought the BJP to power. With the support of regional parties in the NDA alliance, the BJP served a full term in office that was interspersed with events that posed a significant challenge to the government. The BJP-led government declared India as a full-fledged nuclear power after conducting nuclear tests at the Indian Army's Pokhran Test Range. This brought on some global alienation against India in the form of a variety of sanctions by countries such as the US and Japan. The Kargil war, which took place between India and Pakistan between May and July 1999, started because of an infiltration of Pakistani soldiers and Kashmiri militants into Indian territory. The spectre of the infiltration leading to a full-fledged war between two nuclear nations created significant concern among India's trade partners and the world at large. Communal riots in Gujarat, which led to the killing of approximately 3000 people, brought widespread international condemnation in 2002.

On the economic front, the BJP continued the Congress' liberalization work and in many ways drove it further along. The government introduced institutional reforms in areas such as infrastructure that continue to benefit India's economy today. For instance, the National Highways Authority of India's Golden Quadrilateral project was launched in 2001 by the BJP, and stands to date as the largest highway project in India, connecting Delhi, Mumbai, Kolkata, Chennai and other metropolitan cities. In 2001, FDI also opened up in the defence and insurance sectors. These initiatives countered some of the adverse impact created by the Kargil conflict and the sanctions brought on by the nuclear tests. Also in the same year, the NDA instituted the department of disinvestment; which was tasked with further dismantling the Licence Raj and divesting non-performing public sector companies to private enterprises. In addition, the telecommunications sector enjoyed exponential growth during this period and the IT sector finally appeared on the global radar as India was increasingly seen as a reliable offshoring destination.

2003 to 2008: 'India Shining' Does Not Ensure Political Success

Riding a positive economy and a wave of election wins in states such as Madhya Pradesh, Rajasthan and Chhattisgarh, the Vajpayee-led BJP government called for early Lok Sabha elections in 2004. While almost all newspapers, opinion polls and psephologists[38] predicted a resounding win for the NDA, the Congress-led UPA came to power instead. Critics felt the BJP's 'India Shining' campaign was removed from the reality of vast parts of India, especially rural India. *India Today*, a leading political magazine, pointed to the lopsided focus of the campaign on the urban growth story that neglected the distress and backwardness of the rural landscape.[39]

The new UPA government continued down the path of economic reform and did not change the BJP policies initially. Overall, the first five years of the Congress government, the so-called UPA I, have been credited with faster growth (also on the back of a rapidly expanding global economy), higher savings and investments, growing foreign trade and capital inflows, and investments in infrastructure under public–private partnership models.

Besides a focus on urban areas, the Congress was aware that the 60 per cent of the population that depended either directly or indirectly on agriculture held the voting power. During its first five years in power, the Congress initiated various populist schemes, such as the National Rural Employment Guarantee Act (NREGA),[40] Bharat Nirman[41] and the National Food Security Act.[42] At the same time, it also introduced strong legislation in the form of the Right to Information Act[43] and the Forest Rights Act.[44] While leakages and graft limit the effectiveness of government schemes,[45] NREGA increased rural income in India and thereby increased demand coming from rural India. Attractive to the majority of the electorate, these schemes gathered speed during UPA II, the second five-year term of the Congress-led government, and drove up deficits in public finances.

As in its previous tenure, the Congress did rely on the support of the Communist Party as its key ally, and again the left proved to be unreliable. The important nuclear deal with the US was signed during the first term of the UPA government but not supported by the left. Hence, the Congress was forced to take support from the ideologically distinct Samajwadi Party to get the deal ratified and to end India's nuclear apartheid.

2008 to 2014: Policy Paralysis Reigns in Economic Growth

The political and economic scenario deteriorated during the second term of the UPA. The 2008 global financial crisis had an impact on the overall Indian economy and GDP growth contracted, albeit only for a short time. Internal problems exacerbated external pressures. While key legislation such as the Lokpal,[46] Land Acquisition Act[47] and Right to Education Act[48] were passed, the government got caught in a string of high-profile corruption cases. Scams related to the 2010 Commonwealth Games in Delhi, the 2G telecom spectrum auctions and the Coalgate bribery cases marred the government's reputation in India and had a negative impact on the global view of India as a place to do business. The last two cases, respectively, led to the imprisonment of the telecom minister and a judicial probe order on the now former prime minister by the Central Bureau of Investigation in relation to coalfield allocations.

In an environment of intense public scrutiny, the administration became extra cautious and deferred making project decisions for investment proposals across the board. Hence, while economic growth slowed down linearly to a low of 4.5 per cent on a quarterly basis, the average value of quarterly stalled projects grew by a staggering CAGR of 27.5 per cent between FY09 and FY14. The total value of stalled projects in FY14 amounted to about INR 6.2 trillion.[49] Overall, some 521 projects were stalled, about 40 per cent of them due to land acquisition issues. The largest hit was in the manufacturing sector, with total stalled projects worth INR 3.2 trillion. The steel and metal sectors particularly suffered from the slow rate of project execution. Forty-five projects worth INR 565 billion were impacted during FY14 due to de-allocation of coal blocks and environmental clearance issues. The railway sector suffered from INR 277 billion in stalled projects, which were intended to build railway infrastructure. Private sector interest in the road and highway sector sank to a low with INR 270 billion worth of projects not receiving any bids. With consumer confidence increasingly shaken, key consumer markets were feeling the heat. Car sales, credit growth and sales reported by consumer goods firms all floundered and fell during the 2011–13 period. Sales for passenger cars (in units) for instance dropped from 2.78 million units in 2012 to 2.55 million in 2013.

2014 Onwards: The Good Days Are Here

With widespread dissatisfaction regarding the UPA's performance and strong anti-incumbency feelings, the sixteenth Lok Sabha elections turned into a landslide election for the BJP. For the first time since 1984, a single party won 282 seats and hence obtained a clear, single-party majority. Together with its coalition partners, the BJP's NDA got a comfortable majority of 336 seats in the lower house of Parliament. The Congress party's performance was the clear opposite, with just a dismal forty-four seats. This was the party's lowest tally in the Lok Sabha ever and a clear reflection of India's impatience and lack of acceptance of political parties that do not drive the growth agenda aggressively and consistently.

The new Modi government is driving a number of relevant reforms. An important example is greater fiscal federalism. The fourteenth finance commission has recommended the increase of central assistance to states to 42 per cent from the earlier 32 per cent. This move will provide an opportunity for enlightened state governments to drive change and progress in their more homogeneous constituencies. FDI limits in key sectors such as defence, insurance and railways have been further opened up. Coupled, for example, with lucrative defence contracts and the need to generate 30 per cent offset,[50] these initiatives are beginning to drive investment interest in the country.

The Pradhan Mantri Jan Dhan Yojana plans to roll out bank accounts for every household. The ultimate goal is to enable direct transfer of subsidy disbursement and to limit graft and corruption. An ambitious '100 Smart City' programme has been announced as well as challenging targets for green energy (solar and wind) generation across the country. Many projects that stalled under the previous government have since been cleared and some are currently under implementation. The 'Make in India' campaign intends to bring high-volume, low-value-add manufacturing jobs to India to ensure that India's demographic dividend does not become a demographic nightmare. The government has passed a goods and services tax (GST) which will turn India into one seamless market and bring 30–40 per cent cost savings in logistics. This is one of the most substantial changes in India's indirect tax system, with far-reaching consequences in terms of improving the ease of doing business.

Additionally, the Modi government has reached out to a large number of foreign players to improve India's global standing and to reinforce or build new alliances. China, Japan and the US have all committed multi-billion-dollar investments to the country, which should give growth and investment a significant boost.

Factors are currently positive. Economic growth has bottomed out and picked up of late. Inflation is low, in particular driven by low oil prices. The key challenge going forward will be to ensure that policy reforms are consistent and will be diligently implemented. Time is of essence both for the country and the BJP, as the anti-incumbency votes in 2004 and 2014 have shown.

IN SUMMARY

India's economy has grown consistently over the last thirty-five years to create a market that is too large to miss. Various corporate players—Indian, MNCs, family-owned, public-listed, start-ups, etc.—have found ways to deal with the volatility of India's environment. They create value for discerning customers and by extension for themselves. Successful players ride the Indian tiger by building organizations aligned around a clear common purpose. Their strategies are flexible and centred around the cornerstones of operational excellence and customer-centric innovations. The aspirations of Indian players are not limited to India herself but are regional and global, leveraging an ever-increasing integration of India with global markets.

Challenges in India are many and include a turbulent political landscape. However, all parties in India today feel the acute need to generate economic growth and to improve transparency. As a consequence, economic policy has been fairly constant during changes of political leadership.

The overall, the best is yet to come. India is currently the fastest growing major economy in the world and is likely to carry that title for several years. Finding the right approach to doing business in India is therefore not an option but an absolute necessity.

2

OPERATIONAL EXCELLENCE

THE PRESSURE TO GET THE BASICS RIGHT

Indian consumers pose a very difficult challenge for foreign and local companies alike. In India, being successful means serving your customers at China's prices and providing Japan's quality. It implies marrying German engineering, US innovation and Italian design with Korean efficiency. Clearly, like other emerging markets, companies in India have to identify holistic, sustainable, customer-driven solutions to survive and potentially thrive in such a challenging environment.

Operational excellence hence becomes the entry ticket to doing business in India. Value for money is defined by the size of the Indian customer's wallet and his/her willingness to spend a certain amount for your product. Your price must match this amount or sales will be restricted to relatively small sections of the overall Indian economy. Cost reduction through strategies such as Kaizen, continuous improvement, product value management or 5S are, therefore, not an option but a *conditio sine qua non*, a necessary condition without which no strategy will be successful.

This chapter looks at the positive impact of liberalization on the operational performance of Indian companies. We will understand the remaining challenges that need to be overcome to create a level playing field for companies operating in India. Success stories from Maruti Suzuki, APSEZL and EFD Induction provide insights on how to beat the odds. Challenges in building a 'Made in India' national brand will be discussed in the following chapter. There we will analyse the textile and machine tool industry to highlight the need for broad-based performance improvements beyond select companies. We will look at national branding and outline some lessons learned from the genesis of 'Made in Germany'. We will also emphasize the importance and timeliness of the current 'Make in India' campaign.

FACING THE WORLD: THE IMPACT OF INDIA'S LIBERALIZATION

India's liberalization in 1991 spawned the country's foray into productivity enhancement and modern management techniques. Key drivers for the same were the reduction of tariffs on inputs and final goods, increased FDI, delicensing and reforms in supporting service sectors such as banking, telecommunications, transportation and insurance. Productivity growth in India was mostly dominated by 'within-plant' productivity improvements.[51] Existing plants and companies became more competitive in the face of increased competition as well as improved access to input materials and technologies. Reallocations—that is, the exit of non-productive companies that succumbed to competitive pressures—also happened, but overall seemed to have played a lesser role.[52]

Productivity increases in India as a result of liberalization have been analysed in detail. Take high import tariffs or import restrictions on raw materials and foreign goods as an example. Typically, they drive up the cost of raw materials and production for firms and industries. As a consequence, both internal consumption and exports are affected due to high prices. Demand for imported goods goes down and gives rise to monopolistic or oligopolistic competition in the home market, which leads to low quality at a high price and negatively impacts consumers. Smuggling and black markets are typically the result of import barriers as well.

Reducing tariffs for import of products has a positive influence on plant productivity due to the increased accessibility of capital goods and technology that can be used to modernize plants and equipment.[53] Two-thirds of all imports after liberalization resulted from products that were not imported before liberalization. Access to raw materials and technologies increased dramatically.[54] This in turn led to the local production of different products, such that during the 1990s, around a quarter of overall production was driven by new products. Import tariff reduction also exposed the Indian industry to international competition and forced rapid upgrading of management practices.[55]

FDI has had a positive impact on productivity gains. However, its relevance for Indian companies is less pronounced than that of import and final product tariff reductions.[56] Analysis in other emerging markets[57] has shown that foreign ownership typically leads to significant productivity improvements in the acquired plants. Typical improvements of foreign-owned plants include restructuring, increased investments, enhanced integration of acquired plants into global supply networks via exports, etc. However, compared with import-duty reduction, FDI tends to affect in-country productivity with a certain time lag. Foreign companies need to set up or restructure businesses, which takes time. Employees need to be trained in the latest management techniques and the diffusion of this knowledge via attrition is also not immediate.

Removing industrial licensing requirements had a positive effect on the investments in a given state, for instance, the number of factories.[58] Until the 1980s, India required every firm with more than fifty employees (100 employees without power) and a certain amount of assets to obtain an operating licence. The licence specified how much and what type of output the firm could produce, its location, etc. By 1991, most of the restrictions of the 'Licence Raj' were lifted, spurring on manufacturing investments and making it easier for companies to set up plants. Not surprisingly, this effect was more pronounced in states with less labour-restrictive policies.

Reforms in services such as banking, telecommunications, insurance and transportation all resulted in substantial productivity improvements for Indian manufacturing firms.[59] According to Arnold et al., productivity increases amounted to 11.7 per cent for domestic firms and 13.2 per cent for foreign enterprises during 1991–2004.[60] Clearly, the impact of further professionalization of banking, telecommunications and transportation on India's global manufacturing competitiveness is substantial. As India's services reform is not complete (see, for example, the recent introduction of a uniform goods and services tax), significant opportunity for productivity enhancements exists and is only waiting to be tapped by a conscious bureaucracy.

Indian companies that adapted quickly to the changed environment and adopted modern management techniques early were able to reap significant benefits. Productivity and quality tools such as ISO certifications, Kaizen, value stream mapping and total productive maintenance (TPM) are widely used in larger Indian companies.[61] Benefits achieved via these techniques include enhanced operational performance, improved customer satisfaction, improved global competitiveness, improved image and or brand perception and solutions for chronic problems. Examples of these benefits can be seen in the spectacular success of the companies described in the case studies below.

In particular, global quality certifications proved to be an important tool in overcoming negative country-of-origin perceptions. India's Automotive Component Manufacturers Association (ACMA) represents more than 700 member companies from the organized sector and about 85 per cent of the industry by turnover. ACMA reports[62] a large number of member companies with coveted certifications. Clearly, these certifications are impressive and go a long way in convincing global and domestic clients about the capabilities of Indian suppliers. They are a significant driving force behind the USD 38.5 billion turnover of the industry (FY15) as well as the USD 11.2 billion of exports. However, work remains to be done. For one, quality and productivity tools need to percolate down to Tier-2 and Tier-3 suppliers. Also, according to original equipment manufacturer (OEM[63]) feedback, certification and actual supplier performance are not always aligned, pointing to the need for consistent implementation of processes versus a mere focus on meeting certification criteria. Similarly, as shown in Figure 2.1, the Indian pharmaceutical industry boasts the second highest number of US Food and Drug Administration (USFDA) approved facilities outside of the US itself.[64] The strength of certifications is combined with a reasonable performance on patents, part of the innovation ecosystem in India that we will talk about in Chapters 4 and 5.

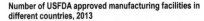 FIGURE 1

Operational Excellence and Innovation Count among the Strengths of the Indian Pharmaceutical Industry

Number of USFDA approved manufacturing facilities in different countries, 2013

Major patent applicants from Indian pharmaceutical industry, 2009-10

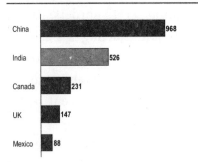

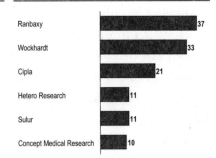

Source: Centre for Monitoring Indian Economy Pvt. Ltd, 'Indian drug makers draw more FDA scrutiny in 2013', 26 September 2013, http://www.cmie.com/kommon/bin/ sr.php?kall=wclrdhtm&nvdt=20130926161313473&nvpc =099000000000&nvtype=INSIGHTS&ver=pf; Roland Berger analysis

Source: Indian Federal Office of the Controller General of Patents, Designs and Trade Marks, Annual Report 2009–10, p. 18; Roland Berger analysis

REMAINING BARRIERS: RUN JUST TO STAND STILL

However, in today's highly competitive environment, companies have to run just to stand still. To survive, they need to live by the Olympic motto *citius, altius, fortius*— faster, higher, stronger. Even today, this is more important for companies operating out of India as they have several additional challenges to overcome compared to rivals from developed and other emerging countries. Some of the factors include the lack of infrastructure, the availability of electricity, the cost of and access to capital, the implicit cost of institutional voids, the challenge of a country-of-origin disadvantage and the lack of an adequately trained workforce.

India's logistics performance has declined over the last seven to eight years due to capacity constraints at major ports and their low mechanization levels, slow inland freight movement and lack of last mile connectivity. India's logistics performance index rank is now 54, down from 39 in 2007.[65] According to a World Bank study, the return on sales[66] of heavily logistics-dependent companies is 200 bps[67] lower in India than in best-in-class countries. In terms of ease of doing business, India faces clear challenges in enforcing contracts, trading across borders, paying taxes, dealing with building permits and starting a business. Labour law complexities continue to encourage companies to hire temporary rather than permanent labour. In many manufacturing companies, temporary labour makes up 30–70 per cent of the total workforce.

Inverted duty structures—which means that finished goods are taxed at lower rates than raw materials or intermediate products—discourage domestic value addition.[68] Mostly as a result of regional and bilateral free-trade agreements with countries such as Japan, South Korea and ASEAN (Association of Southeast Asian Nations), manufacturers of aluminium products, capital goods, cement, chemicals, electronics, paper, steel, textiles and tyres are subject to duty inversion.[69] While some inverted duties have been addressed in the recent 2014–15 budget, more needs to be done.

It does not come as a surprise then, that 'access to imported inputs at competitive prices' and 'high cost or delays caused by domestic transportation' top the list of grievances for companies exporting out of India.[70] 'Technical requirements and standards abroad' and 'difficulties in meeting quality/quantity requirements of buyers' take the third and fourth place, respectively, as areas of concern, pointing to a remaining skill and performance gap for Indian companies versus global requirements. We will focus on this aspect in the following chapter.

From an import perspective, 'burdensome import procedures', 'tariffs', 'corruption at the border' and 'high cost or delays caused by domestic transportation' lead the list of concerns. Clearly, these can be tackled by determined government policies and need to be addressed to turn 'Make in India' into a reality.

Corruption—both external corruption to influence government authorities and internal corruption in companies in areas such as purchasing, marketing, logistics, HR or dealer networks—exacts a high price of doing business from Indian and foreign companies. Beyond the financial impact of losing orders, inflated input prices and operating costs, the organizational impact on firms operating in India is noticeable.[71]

Social capital characterized by regional trust and the rule of law can improve company performance. Increased trust of an owner or a CEO in his or her management team and teams down the line allows for decentralized decision-making and hence company growth. Increased rule of law and timely decisions from the courts provide the necessary safety net in case employees betray the trust placed in them. Today, many organizations in India are still run with very high management control and Indian employees regularly succumb to delegating responsibility upwards. Both approaches do not lend themselves to facing the challenges that the VUCA world throws at corporations. In this new environment, all other factors being equal, it is conceivable that low-trust nations with a comparative disadvantage in decentralization may face lower productivity growth than nations with high social capital. Figure 2.2 shows the decentralization of companies across a number of countries. Nordic and Anglo-Saxon countries tend to be quite decentralized in comparison to Southern European and emerging markets. Not surprisingly, Greece is the country with the highest degree of centralization, which reflects a social context that is marred by tax evasion, corruption and chronic underperformance.

FIGURE 2

Indian Companies Have Relatively Centralized Operations, whereas Major European Companies Are More Decentralized

Average decentralization by country: Survey findings

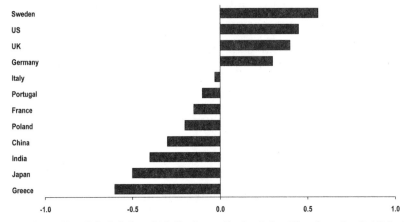

Source: Nicholas Bloom, Raffaella Sadun and John Van Reenen, 'The Organization of Firms Across Countries' (National Bureau of Economic Research, NBER Working Paper 15129, July 2009), http://www.nber.org/papers/w15129.

Misallocations of production factors such as capital and labour can have severe negative impacts on total factor productivity.[72] As we have seen in Chapter 1, NPAs[73] of Indian state-owned banks and their exposure to restructured advances under the corporate debt restructuring mechanism are very high. Firms with political connections seem to have benefited from access to (subsidized) credit, even if their circumstances would have cut off funding otherwise. Since political influence rather than company performance can drive access to credit, this is a clear example of misallocation of resources with resulting negative consequences for India's overall total productivity factor. In addition, state-owned banks may have to be recapitalized by the government in an effort to bring liquidity back into key industries. As a consequence, taxpayers would finance the failures of poorly managed but well-connected companies rather than investments in infrastructure, health or education, which would benefit India's citizens and her performing companies.[74] Other distortions relate to laws restricting easy entry and exit of companies. In the case of state-owned companies in particular, closure is dragged out even in cases where losses have accumulated over decades. Hsieh and Klenow[75] have quantified the effects of labour and capital misallocation in India and China and identified potential manufacturing total factor productivity gains to the tune of 30–50 per cent in China and 40–60 per cent in India.

BEATING THE ODDS: INDIA'S HEROES

While the challenges may seem daunting, all is not lost. A number of companies have developed operating models that enable profitable growth in India. Many of these (see Table A.1 in the Appendix) have done exceedingly well. Let's look at three outstanding examples of successful companies from different industries.

Maruti Suzuki: Driving India since 1983

With a current market share of around 50 per cent, which is close to its historic highs, Maruti Suzuki has defined mobility for Indians since the 1980s. Its relentless pursuit of a 'volume up, cost down' strategy has created a virtuous cycle that continues to create sustainable competitive advantage. The automotive manufacturer is poised to profit from the growth of the Indian passenger vehicle (PV) market like no other company in India.

India's Passenger Vehicle Market: On Its Way to a Global Top 3 Position

India's PV market has grown at a healthy clip, with a CAGR of 14 per cent between 2005 and 2012. While the overall market stagnated at around 2.6 million vehicles between 2012 and 2014, growth seems to have resumed in 2015 due to a change in government and improved customer sentiment. Going forward, growth of the PV market to about 4.6 million units in 2020 is expected.[76] This volume would put India firmly in a top spot by volume behind China and the US. Clearly, India is too large a market for any OEM to ignore.

India, in many ways, proves herself to be different than other markets. We highlighted the value focus of Indian customers in the Introduction (see Figure 0.1). India's PV consumers make very complex value evaluations before making the purchase decision. New vehicle concepts may gain volume quickly but then lose volume equally quickly if they do not hit the sweet spot in terms of exterior styling, interior finesse, engine performance, space, fuel efficiency and of course price. Since the road conditions are tough and consumers tend to take 'safe' decisions for a 'safer tomorrow', the availability, proximity and affordability of after-sales service plays a major role in the purchase decision. Lifecycles tend to be much more sharply defined than in developed economies, necessitating constant product and marketing interventions to keep vehicles fresh and interesting. Price differences matter to the extent that a difference as low as INR 10,000 could change a choice for a vehicle costing INR 4,00,000.[77]

Additionally, NREGA, Bharat Nirman, guaranteed minimum-support prices for agricultural products and other schemes have driven rural incomes up, as discussed earlier. As a consequence, rural India has become a force to reckon with for car companies. Prosperity has spread to smaller towns, and their transporters, traders and shopkeepers, village bankers and teachers are looking for reliable and affordable mobility. Maruti Suzuki's sales in smaller towns and rural areas, for example, amounted to 3.5 per cent of total unit sales in FY08. In FY15, a third of the company's sales came from such areas.[78] Maruti Suzuki's approach to rural marketing is extensive. 7,800 local villagers are nominated as resident dealer sales executives, the first point of contact between the rural population and Maruti Suzuki. Complementary marketing channels, such as ITC's e-choupal[79] are leveraged for further penetration. Factory visits for villagers are part of the outreach programme, as are support for rural sporting events and rural fairs. Detailed profiles of villagers in terms of their choices, lifestyles and consumption patterns are developed to fine-tune Maruti's value proposition to their needs. Maruti's success has not gone unnoticed. Toyota, Hyundai and other major players have announced plans and are in the process of establishing rural networks of their own.

2 FIGURE 3

During the Last Few Years, Compact and UV Segment Sales Increased; Number of Market Offerings in These Segments Also Increased

Emergence of compact and UV segment

PV sales – FY11 vs FY16 [% of total PV sales]

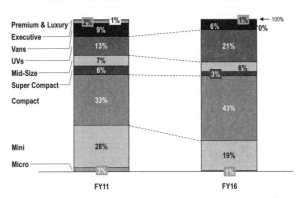

Source: Society of Indian Automobile Manufacturers (SIAM), monthly flash reports, http://www.siamindia.com/, Roland Berger analysis

The Indian PV market is also structurally different from many other markets. As shown in Figure 2.3, the Indian PV market is mainly dominated by two segments—utility and compact vehicles.

Together, mini[80] and compact[81] vehicles make up more than 60 per cent of total car sales in India. With about 1.7 million vehicles, small cars are the vehicle of choice for Indian consumers and are likely to remain the vehicle of choice in the future. Total sales of 2.7 million small cars are anticipated in FY20. The high demand for small cars is a reflection of a number of factors, including the limited spending power of India's middle class, the congestion in India's cities, the struggle to find adequate parking space and the excise duty support for cars within certain engine and length restrictions. Demand and government support create volumes substantial enough for India to become a global lead market in small cars, which should continue to open up opportunities in terms of value addition on both the production and R&D side.

The Indian PV market is potentially the most demanding in terms of price levels and customer expectations. The additional stagnation of PV sales during FY12 and FY15 had created a market environment that was extremely challenging for most players. Overall, industry capacity utilization was in the range of 55–60 per cent in FY15. While the market leaders Maruti Suzuki and Hyundai had a comfortable capacity utilization of more than 90 per cent, players such as Tata Motors, Mahindra, Renault–Nissan, Toyota Kirloskar, General Motors, Skoda and Fiat struggled with utilization levels around or significantly below 50 per cent. Honda, Ford and Volkswagen managed capacity utilization rates around 80 per cent, either on the back of new launches or via focused exports. Hardly surprising, many OEMs posted negative EBITDA[82] margins in the timeframe between FY13 and FY15.

Since the Indian market is different, every MNC hoping to garner a relevant market share in India has had to develop market-adequate vehicles. Price pressure mandates deep[83] localization levels of more than 80 per cent to reach demanding price points and to defend profits against exchange rate fluctuations. The need to bring down development costs enforces an increasing amount of local R&D. Localization and development of India-adequate vehicles is only reasonable when a significant potential volume can be tapped. Hence, the vehicles of choice are small cars, a voluminous but also extremely competitive segment of the market. Typically, the current volumes in the small car segment that are attainable for new entrants are insufficient by themselves to justify the effort. This is why export opportunities invariably need to be tapped to increase volumes. Exports also provide higher margins compared to local business and contribute to the overall profitability of operations within India. As a consequence, companies such as Hyundai and Renault–Nissan clearly understood that India must be a global hub for small car exports from the start of operations in the country.[84] After a few painful years of adjustment to this reality, other MNCs came to the same conclusion as Hyundai and Renault–Nissan. Clearly, market dynamics position India's small car segment as a global lead market, an enviable position for the Indian automotive industry.[85]

Maruti Suzuki: Moving India[86]

Maruti's beginning goes back to 1981 when Dr V. Krishnamurthy incorporated Maruti Udyog Ltd a company formed for two purposes. The first was to develop an indigenous, small and fuel-efficient car that could adequately provide affordable mobility to India's masses. The second was to modernize and develop India's technological and manufacturing footprint through this venture.

Right from the beginning, Dr Krishnamurthy knew that he could not fulfil this mission by himself but that he needed a foreign partner. While India had three car manufacturers producing vehicles at the time—Hindustan Motors (Ambassador), Premier Automobiles (Padmini, better known as Fiat Padmini) and

Standard Motors in Bangalore—product quality and technology were a far cry from the needs of Indian customers as well as the demands of more developed markets. A relevant supply base did not exist in India as the three dominant players had very high degrees of vertical integration. Krishnamurthy rightfully concluded that these challenges were too daunting to be tackled without competent and committed help.

Suzuki emerged as the partner of choice out of the many potential suitors for a passenger vehicle joint venture, as the focus and mission of the company aligned perfectly with India's needs.[87] Osamu Suzuki was a man of action and was unfazed by the challenges that India had to offer. Taking a minority stake of 26 per cent in a government public sector undertaking (PSU) did not give Suzuki the kind of management control that the company would have liked. Operating under the Licence Raj would imply limitations on the number of vehicles that could be sold and potentially affect break-even calculations. In short, the odds seemed to be fully stacked against a JV between the government of India and Suzuki.

Yet, to the surprise of everyone, Maruti Suzuki not only survived but thrived. Rahul Bharti, vice president, corporate planning, observes,

> From day one we had a very successful blend of Indian and Japanese ways of doing things. We were impressed with the minute detail-orientation of the Japanese. Their way of observing customers in detail, identifying their needs and then aligning the whole value chain to deliver this need at an appropriate value was impressive.

Osamu Suzuki, current chairman and previous CEO of Suzuki Motor Corporation, as well as the Indian and Japanese management teams, played a key role in this. With Suzuki's conviction that cleanliness would drive effectiveness, he and his team drove down 5S principles[88] in the organization. Suzuki would personally inspect the factory as well as offices, open drawers and check corners for signs of inefficiency and waste.

He worried about the width of alleys and the distance between supervisors and their employees, all in the interest of ensuring fast and open information flow. Supervisors were expected to be accessible to their employees, to not intimidate them but to recognize that every employee is equal in the aspiration to make their company excel. Open offices, one uniform and a common canteen for everyone from the sweeper to the managing director— all these ideas helped to reinforce the common responsibility of Maruti Suzuki employees to work for the well-being of their company. All of these concepts were revolutionary in India in the 1980s, even for private companies, let alone PSUs.

Suzuki's conviction—'smaller, lighter, lesser and more beautiful'—became inculcated in Maruti Suzuki's DNA and is relentlessly applied to everything that the company does, whether it is products, machines or headquarter documents. One of the major initiatives launched in this context was the '1 component, 1 gram, 1 Yen' initiative. Osamu challenged the organization to go through all vehicles and to identify cost improvements to the tune of at least 1 Yen as well as weight reduction to the tune of at least 1 gram. The impact of the initiative was enormous. The campaign mobilized an army of about 6000 employees and several thousand vendor employees and generated a meaningful weight reduction per vehicle. More importantly, it also drove the 'smaller, lighter, lesser and more beautiful' philosophy across the extended company. Maruti Suzuki's DNA was aligned to this motto and this alignment is one of the major reasons for the company's continued success in the country.

The quest for truth—the 3G principles—became another part of Maruti's DNA. The 3G principles are *genchi*—go to the spot;

genbutsu—see the actual problem; *genjitsu*—take realistic action based on the facts. Management drives teams to identify problems and to go to the location of the problem to solve them. If there is a problem with a vendor, the teams go and visit the vendor to identify the solution. If there is a challenge with rural marketing, Maruti Suzuki employees visit villages to understand the problem and identify solutions. Realistic actions are being taken based on these observations rather than based on a cascade of management reports.

Efficiency within Maruti Suzuki was driven via 3M. The 3M principles are: *muda*—wastage, *mura*—inconsistency and *muri*—strain. This meant that the management was continuously looking to eliminate wastage, inconsistency and strain.[89] Here Suzuki's global experience in making waste visible in factories, e.g., via videography and other tools, proved invaluable. JIT, Kanban and Kaizen, for instance, became common tools for Maruti Suzuki and the company's vendors long before liberalization started.

Lastly, Maruti Suzuki's Indian employees had to become accustomed to Suzuki's determination to drive *jugaad*, i.e., quick-fix solutions that address acute customer needs, out of their system via the 3Ks. The 3Ks philosophy is the following: *kimeraareta koto ga*—what has been decided; *kihon dori*—exactly as per standards; *kichin to mamoru*—must be followed.

Consequently, driving home adherence to standards and a structured, continuous improvement of standards via Kaizen amounted to a dramatic cultural change programme. A major part in this effort was to not only impart training by Japanese expats in India, but also to send hundreds of employees into Japanese factories to work alongside Japanese workers and to experience 3G, 3K, 3M and 5S in action. This proved to be crucial for Indian employees because they understood the importance of these principles when they saw them applied in Suzuki's factories.

Other efforts, such as having Maruti Suzuki employees take an oath that they would not accept, make or pass on bad quality parts in the course of their work, also drove changed attitudes.

While the company was changing the way India manufactured goods within its walls, the constraints of the phased manufacturing programme, i.e., commitments on localization, made it necessary for Maruti Suzuki to develop a local vendor base as well. Here, the company applied an interesting balance between handholding and leveraging competition. Models of support for suppliers included a one-time sale of technology, technology collaborations, JVs and 100 per cent subsidiaries. Quality of components tended to improve with increased cooperation between OEM and supplier. More than 125 foreign suppliers (Japanese, European and American, in order of relevance) were brought into the country by Suzuki, and Maruti Suzuki supported the suppliers along project management, feasibility studies, sample validation and hand-over. To ensure quality in the supplier JVs, Maruti Suzuki demanded expat quality managers to be present in the JVs for a minimum of two years. In about eighteen suppliers, Maruti Suzuki took equity directly. However, even for these suppliers, second-source suppliers were brought into the fray to prevent complacency, which would ultimately erode value for customers.

In some extreme cases, when suppliers ran into trouble, Maruti Suzuki's own engineers would be stationed in suppliers' factories and run them until the suppliers were able to take over themselves. Management best practices were shared with Tier-1 suppliers, starting with the CEO and covering such things as organizational structures, roles and responsibilities, independence of the quality department, maintenance practices and sound financial practices.

For suppliers, as for dealers, Maruti Suzuki believes in being financially responsible, hence efforts to convince suppliers to show profits on their books rather than to try to evade taxes were pushed. Displaying real profits in books would enable loans at lower rates and higher valuations, and hence create more value than potential tax 'savings'. Many of the suppliers who decided to accept these management practices were able to grow into USD +1 billion companies themselves either in turnover or market cap. Tier-1 suppliers were also strongly encouraged to share these learnings with their own supply base to ensure the development of an automotive quality ecosystem.

Maruti Suzuki encouraged suppliers to build up volume with other OEMs in the market to support their overall business. The company believed that down the line it would benefit from a supplier base that was competitive, even if during the initial years competitors stood to benefit from the investments in vendor management that Maruti had made. Preferable terms with suppliers result from Maruti's dominant volume in the local market, the predictability of production plans[90] that allow suppliers to keep inventories to a minimum, good relations as well as prompt payments and protection against market vagaries resulting from forex or commodity fluctuations.

Efforts and programmes to reduce costs to the company are extended down to suppliers. As shown in Figure A.8 in the Appendix, Maruti Suzuki achieved a net cost reduction in direct material cost[91] despite the fact that it had recently changed the product mix towards higher value vehicles. Activities such as supplier consolidation[92] focus on specific components to improve the performance of Tier-2 and Tier-3 suppliers. Supplier localization and centralization,[93] support with R&D, processes and systems for Tier-2 suppliers, etc., have helped bring down cost and improve performance. Strict supplier management and constant monitoring keeps suppliers motivated to live up to quality and cost targets. Value engineering for existing products, such as the 'one gram, one Yen per component' initiative, focuses on weight and cost reduction. Steel scrap is reused to make child parts,[94] and grades of steel are consolidated to drive volume discounts. Attention to detail is everywhere. For example, Maruti worked together with suppliers to bring down the bumper manufacturing time for the Ertiga from seventy seconds to sixty-six seconds in steps of two seconds per year. In-house automation for new projects saved about INR 26 crore in FY13. Development of local suppliers for equipment and machinery allowed the company to reduce downtime by 50 per cent. Water and electricity consumption was driven down by 58 per cent and 30 per cent, respectively, over a period of twelve years. The list of activities is long. Most of these activities are not revolutionary, but in combination they have afforded Maruti Suzuki with the opportunity to out-price and out-compete all other OEMs in India.

The drive for financially responsible behaviour determines the company's relationship with its dealers as well. Maruti Suzuki does not give credit to dealers but believes that it is their responsibility to plan inventories and market demand. At the same time the company does not push inventory to dealers, a common practice in India, since increased inventory cost would only reduce value for customers. Working with dealers over decades has given Maruti detailed insights into sales cycles, which allow it to fine-tune production and to keep overall inventories low.

Maruti provides detailed training and technical support to dealers that leverages the Japanese management techniques described above. Every activity in the showroom or in the work bays is documented, detailed and imparted to sales and service staff via training. Dealer balanced score cards drive dealer management with both leading and lagging indicators, including standards for training and remuneration of sales and service staff, promptness of salary payments and presence of HR staff in each showroom. Says Rahul,

Initially we needed to work hard to convince dealers that our suggestions would lead to higher volumes and better profits for them . . . Once they realized that high performing dealers were making more money, it became easier to align them to us. The same happened when we suggested investments in driving schools, insurance, used car businesses, etc. Today, our success makes interaction with dealers easy.

Detailed market understanding is driven by own insights, cooperation with dealers and the desire to be intellectually honest, i.e., to do a rigorous analysis of your own and your competitors' performance in the market and to derive the necessary actions. Maruti understands that in the automotive business, it is the right product, the company's commitment to live up to its promises on service and total cost of ownership that make all the difference. Focus on key parameters such as leadership in customer service satisfaction has driven positive word of mouth for the brand and enabled sustained sales success. The product itself has to be a delicate balance of fuel efficiency, engine power and pick-up, space, styling, interiors and price. Says Rahul: 'If you miss any of these points in your equation at a particular price point, your product will not be successful.'

The Japanese influence has been beneficial at Maruti in more ways than just efficiency and productivity. When the Indian organization wanted to focus on cost reduction in its existing line-up as a result of the economic downturn in 1999–2002, Suzuki pushed for the introduction of the first global product, the Swift, into the Indian market. Global observations indicated that customers would want to upgrade to more modern cars with larger wheels and more muscular arches a few years after the crisis was over. When the Swift was launched in 2005, it created a new segment and fulfilled the aspirations of many customers, just as Suzuki had foreseen.

Frugal engineering is a major strength of the company. Various suppliers to several OEMs in India point out that Maruti Suzuki's designs satisfy all regulatory and customer requirements but are still 10–15 per cent cheaper than the competitors'. Frugal engineering is supported by two research centres in the country. The R&D centre in Gurgaon has about 1,250 local engineers and thirty-five expats who support connection with and knowledge transfer from R&D in Japan. Recent centre achievements include the introduction of CNG, LPG and diesel variants for several models, such as the SX4, Eeco, etc. The centre also has full-model-change capability, as demonstrated for the first time in the Alto 800. In addition, a new R&D centre at Rohtak has a test track, crash test facilities, a wind tunnel, a performance and endurance chassis dyno and electromagnetic compatibility labs. This centre greatly enhances the engineering work that can be done in India and is intended to design, develop and test vehicles for the local as well as export markets in Africa, the Middle East and Southern Asia.

All of the activities undertaken by Maruti Suzuki, including efforts to create value for customers and to provide affordable mobility to India's masses, are driven by volume, as shown in Figure 2.4. The product portfolio is designed to hit at least 50,000 units per model launched. Production is stable so that operational efficiencies can be optimized and inventories minimized for the OEM as well as the suppliers. Higher volumes and stable production drive better conditions with suppliers; this translates into lower prices and drives volumes. Higher volumes and better supplier profitability enable suppliers to invest in productivity enhancements and quality improvements which again drive down cost and increase volumes. They also create positive business cases for dealers and allow larger network coverage that in turn increases volumes. Higher volumes enable profitable downstream services such as True Value (used cars), insurance, financing and accessories that increase CSI[95] and hence drive positive word of mouth and volumes as well as dealer profits. Dealer profits can be reinvested in service, again leading to improved margins and improved volumes. With a large distribution footprint and a low cost position of high-volume platforms, niche models become feasible, again driving volumes. Volumes also lead to surplus cash, which can be invested and drive significant below-the-line cash flows. These cash flows provide long-term financial stability or can be re-invested in R&D, the distribution network, etc.

2 FIGURE 4

A Schematic View of Maruti Suzuki's Virtuous Cycle

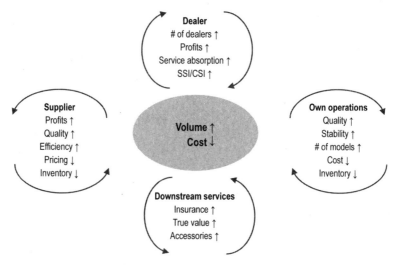

Source: Maruti Suzuki; Roland Berger analysis

Maruti Suzuki's success is unique. Maruti's stock surged 65 per cent in 2014, raising its market capitalization to USD 19.7 billion and overtaking its Japanese parent company Suzuki, which is valued as USD 19 billion. Maruti sold 1.29 million units in FY15, contributing 44 per cent of Suzuki's global sales of 2.9 million units. It accounted for 33 per cent of Suzuki's auto revenue and

55 per cent of EBIT in FY15. Clearly, for Suzuki, India is not a lead market, it is *the* market in which winning is crucial even for the survival of the parent brand. Maruti Suzuki's determination to remain the leader in the Indian PV market based on profitable growth is underlined by its detail orientation and alignment in every little step of the value chain. Opportunities for export markets, such as Africa, the Middle East and Southeast Asia, for which the Indian organization has the global export lead, are waiting to be fully tapped.

Maruti's way forward remains challenging. The company will have to work hard to not fall victim to its own success. Since most of the present older generation has driven a Maruti at some stage in their lives, new products will have to help the company shed the 'daddy's car' image. Also, as India becomes more affluent, Maruti needs to graduate from the small car segments into the medium and potentially large car segments. Maruti's moves have been continuous and evolutionary rather than radical, e.g., exemplified by its journey from the Swift to the Dzire and SX4, and finally to the Ciaz and S Cross. With its premium showroom concept NEXA that the company has launched across India, Maruti is trying to blend into the lifestyle of an Indian customer who is about to upgrade in many aspects of his or her life. The transition from a value-to a lifestyle-oriented brand has been difficult for Suzuki globally. India may just be the market in which it finally cracks the code.

Adani Ports: Opening the Door to India

Not unlike some of their global peers, Indian businesspeople are renowned for their financial prudence. Investments are made after careful deliberation in a step-by-step fashion, often after exhausting existing capacities to the fullest. Adani Ports and

Special Economic Zone Ltd (APSEZL) is the antithesis to this behaviour. As we will see below, massive investments were made early on in anticipation of substantial demand as well as with the determination to become one of the leading port operators globally in terms of efficiency.

India's Maritime Trade: A Quick Overview

Growth in India's exports has outpaced most other nations. At a CAGR of 15.4 per cent from 2002 to 2015, India grew faster than developing Asia (10.1 per cent), the Middle East and North Africa (MENA, 4.2 per cent), the Euro area (3.9 per cent) and Latin America (3.6 per cent). Goods exports are dominated by petroleum products, engineering goods, chemicals and related products, gems and jewellery, and agriculture and related products. Imports have grown even faster at a CAGR of about 17 per cent. The main imports are petroleum crude and products, capital goods, gold and silver, electronic goods, pearls and precious stones, chemicals, and coal, coke and briquettes.

India's increasing engagement with the world has enabled a diversification of trade partners. While the top five export nations for India in FY98 were the US, the UK, Hong Kong, Germany and Japan, the ranking in FY15 is US, UAE, Hong Kong, China and Saudi Arabia. After Singapore, the UK and Germany are ranked seventh and eighth respectively. Overall, Asia and the Middle East have become major export regions. Today, Asia and MENA are India's main trading partners (see Figure 2.5) followed by Europe, Africa, the US and South America.

With India being 'boxed in' by the Himalayas to the north and isolated from the rest of Asia via this impressive mountain range, maritime transportation is the primary mode of foreign trade. Over 90 per cent of the country's trade by volume and

70 per cent by value moves in and out of India via ships. However, total traffic handled in Indian ports only grew at a CAGR of 4.2 per cent in the period from 2005 to 2015, from 384 million metric tons to 581 million metric tons (projected).

2 FIGURE 5

Asia Is Now India's Largest Trading Partner Both in Terms of Exports and Imports Followed by MENA and Europe

Regional trade flow between India and rest of the world[1] [USD bn, FY16]

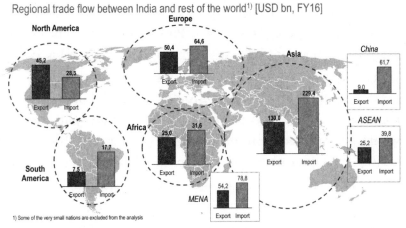

1) Some of the very small nations are excluded from the analysis

Source: Ministry of Commerce & Industry, Import Export Data Bank version 7.1, http://www.commerce.nic.in/eidb/Default.asp, Roland Berger analysis

Performance differences between India's thirteen major ports (of which twelve are government trusts) and about 200 notified non-major ports (of which sixty-nine engage in import and export) are partly to blame for the slow growth in port traffic. As shown in Figure A.9 in the Appendix, capacity utilization (the extent to which installed capacity is used) at major ports has been very high even over the last two to three years, during which both the global economy and India's GDP growth were subdued. High capacity utilization, dilapidated infrastructure due to insufficient investments, a lack of space in which to grow, bureaucracy, corruption, legacy labour practices and the need to tender new projects all drive major ports to perform relatively low on key indicators. While improvements have been observed over the last decades, key indicators, such as the time it takes for a ship to dock at a berth or the turnaround time for a ship in a port, trail international benchmarks significantly.[96] Average turnaround time at India's major ports is 3.84 days compared to Singapore, which reports an average turnaround time of 1.16 days. Hong Kong reports 0.72 days, South Korea 0.68 days, China 0.96 days and the US 1.02 days.[97] Performance across ports is very uneven. Some of the major ports report turnaround times of around five days while Jawaharlal Nehru Port Trust, Navi Mumbai, for example, achieves an average turnaround of 1.08 days despite very high capacity utilization.

According to Business Monitor International, current container traffic in India is approximately one-twelfth of what would be expected from an economy of its size.[98] The current revival of GDP growth, a number of important policy initiatives by the NDA government, easing financial constraints[99] and the Sagar Mala project—which will drive port-centric development, focus on inland water transportation and coastal shipping as well as efforts to reduce red tape—will all drive traffic to India's ports. This untapped potential and double-digit growth in import and export going forward clearly call for solutions beyond the major ports.

As can be seen from Figure A.10 in the Appendix, non-major ports are very effectively leveraging the opportunity that India's growth brings and have been growing at a CAGR of 9.6 per cent, or roughly three times faster than major ports.[100] Many ports have private partners and significant funding behind them, making capacity expansions easier. Also, road and rail linkage is typically better than that of the old state-run facilities. Efficient operations and faster evacuation at non-major ports make up for lower tariffs at regulated major ports. Currently, non-major ports handle about 43 per cent of India's export/import trade. They are likely to take care of more than half of India's needs by FY20.

Gujarat corners 74.3 per cent of the total traffic at non-major ports, followed by Andhra Pradesh (14.1 per cent) and Maharashtra (5.9 per cent). Gujarat benefits in particular from the fact that Jawaharlal Nehru Port Trust has chronic capacity shortages and hence spill-over traffic drives opportunities in the state. Similar comments are true for Chennai, where an overcrowded port that is locked in by the city of Chennai is facing tough competition from ports on India's east coast.

Adani Ports: Invest and They Will Come[101]

APSEZL is one of the key businesses of the Adani Group and uniquely positioned to take advantage of the favourable environment for non-major ports in India.[102] APSEZL's footprint is shown in Figure 2.6, together with India's twelve major sea ports. Cargo volume handled at Mundra, Dahej and Hazira is dominated by coal (38 per cent) and petroleum, oil and lubricants (21 per cent). Mundra has the fastest turnaround time for ships among Indian ports—of eighteen to twenty hours. Mundra was also the first Indian port to cross the 100 million metric tons mark in cargo handling in FY14.[103]

APSEZL's financial performance is outstanding. Revenue growth from FY10 to FY15 was at a CAGR of 34 per cent with FY15 revenue of INR 6,152 crore. Close to 90 per cent of the revenue comes from APSEZL. The company's EBIT margin stands close to an exceptional 60 per cent with a return on capital employed margin of 13–15 per cent over the last two years. APSEZL stands out, in terms of both Indian and international comparisons.

2 FIGURE 6

In FY14, Mundra Handled Around 90% of APSEZL's Cargo Volume; Dahej and Hazira Handled the Remaining 10% of Cargo Volume

Ports in India: APSEZL group ports, major ports, current and proposed capacity

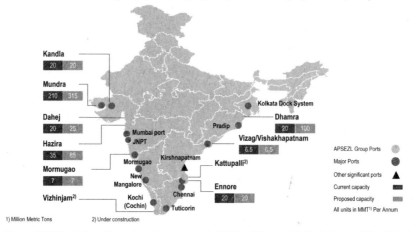

1) Million Metric Tons   2) Under construction

Source: APSEZL website and annual reports, press reports, Ministry of Transport, Indian Ports Association; Roland Berger analysis

So what drives the spectacular success of APSEZL versus both national and international competitors? For Captain Unmesh Abhyankar, joint president, Executive Director's office, and former COO and CEO of Mundra Port, it all began in 1978. As a young mariner, he made his first port call in Bombay. Upon nearing the port itself, he noticed his captain calling a friend in the port authority. His question as to why such a call was necessary was answered with a short reply: 'Without pulling favours we may have to wait for a berth for months. I don't think either of us wants that.' At that point, Unmesh decided that should he ever run a port, he would ensure that berths would wait for ships and not the other way round.

Unmesh got an opportunity to realize his ambition when Gautam Adani decided to build a world-class port in Gujarat. Adani had been a trader who had suffered from his ships being stuck in various ports. He knew first-hand that ports were inefficient and overloaded. Cargo would surely move to alternatives should anyone decide to build them. He also realized that nobody in India had invested in the port sector with the bold ambition of building a global-scale business that integrated both the marine as well as the evacuation side of cargo. He believed this to be a great opportunity.

Adani also realized that a capital-intensive business such as that of ports required volume to break even within a reasonable time frame. Volume required mechanization to ensure fast and efficient handling of containers, coal, fertilizers and other cargo. Mechanization in turn required the right planning and master plan of the port as well as the perfect location for the same.

The cornerstone of the virtuous circle that Mundra leverages is demand. Mundra's hinterland is North India, a land-locked area that corresponds to about 40 per cent of India's GDP. With superior service levels and the shortest distance to these demand pockets, cargo from North India would de facto be assured. As a consequence, investments could be made with the reasonable assumption that cargo and volume would follow.

The right location was found in the port of Mundra. Protected by the Saurashtra landmass, the port did not require heavy investment in the building of breakwaters. Its location allowed it to be a deep draft port[104] with 365 days of operation.

Once the location was identified, Adani and his team went about building a port that would compete with the best and biggest ports globally. Rather than waiting for cargo and then building the subsequent infrastructure, Adani decided to turn the approach on its head. He and his team, led by Malay Mahadevia, Director, APSEZL, developed a twenty-five-year master plan for Mundra that included significant investments in rail and road connectivity, water, electricity and gas. Adani decided to develop this infrastructure himself rather than waiting for government support as speed and scale were essential for his project to succeed. Guided by the principle that berths should wait for ships, the port was constructed with a targeted berth productivity of 65 per cent maximum. In addition, an inverted funnel at a factor of ten between maritime and evacuation capacity was built, i.e., the capacity to discharge any cargo from ships to the hinterland was ten times larger than the berth capacity.

Relatively quickly, Mundra graduated from a multipurpose to a specialized port. Says Unmesh: 'Once we started building dedicated infrastructure, such as a dedicated container terminal, serious enquiries started coming in.' Mechanization allowed highly efficient port operations, which in turn translated into best total cost for customers. This drove cargo traffic. For example, when building the world's largest coal import terminal capable of handling the largest coal ships globally, Adani invested in the latest technology for gravel loaders, unloaders and cranes. It worked with the best consultants to ensure optimal berth layout. Says Sudipta Bhattacharya, ex-CEO of APSEZL, and CTO of Adani Group:

> We have never taken a nickel-and-dime approach to innovation. Investing in the latest technology has allowed us to achieve world-class performance, e.g., in terms of EBITDA ratios. Working with the best consultants enabled us to build our ports much faster than the competition. Minor cost savings in these areas are always more than overcompensated by the gain in contribution margin when you can start operating terminals a few months earlier than planned.

Full automation of the fertilizer terminal created a first in the Indian port industry. Fertilizer is moved fully automatically from ships to the Fertilizer Cargo Complex within Mundra. Bagging of fertilizer is also fully automated, as is loading in railway rakes.[105] As a consequence, Mundra is able to cater to ten to twelves rakes per day versus one to three rakes per day at competing Indian ports. Besides increased speed, the quality of fertilizer handling increases. In addition, the Indian railways are happy to work with Mundra as business volume and predictability is higher than with other ports.

Innovation is a major driver of productivity enhancements at Mundra port. For example, historically, grain was loaded into ships after being sieved through a fishing net in order to remove foreign materials (such as plastic bags). Unmesh challenged his teams to come up with a metallic net instead. Despite initial difficulties in designing the same, the final solution improved grain loading productivity by a factor of three and was quickly copied by ports throughout India. Similar innovations for the loading of steel or the moving of cranes also improved productivity by a factor of three to a factor of five. 'We don't hang people; we hang ideas,' says Unmesh. 'Fast experimentation and quick corrections of errors are necessary since we continuously want to challenge the status quo in port operations.'

People are an important part of value creation at Mundra. Rather than hiring overqualified people for jobs in what is after all a rather remote location in India, APSEZL decided to hire people with the right aptitude and to train them for the job at hand. Unmesh encouraged his tea boys to take the crane operator course, for example. The basic idea behind this is to ensure that people are grateful for the jobs that they have and proud of their accomplishments. As Unmesh puts it, 'If your employee feels that this is the best job that could ever have happened to him, he will be proud and he will work hard. This leads to lower attrition and higher efficiency.' Hand in hand with this idea is the approach to make operations in Mundra goof-proof. A strong focus on processes and certifications aims to reduce the human element as much as possible.[106]

Global benchmarking is key for Mundra. Says Malay:

> It would be easy to benchmark ourselves against Indian ports, but
> that is not our competition. We want to be among the best globally
> and hence we compare our performance in coal, steel, containers,
> etc. against the leading ports globally, whether they are from
> China or Europe or wherever. We also continuously work with
> consultants to ensure that we are abreast of the latest thinking and
> innovation. We can't stop innovating in this game as we would fall
> immediately behind.

With the clear ambition to continue to drive the port sector in India, Mundra's future development is bright. As Mundra has built up an industrial ecosystem with power, cooling and processed water, natural gas, electricity, social infrastructure and holistic logistics services, it can offer foreign companies a service rather than a capex business model for operating in the country. Further developing the industrial ecosystem around the Mundra SEZ will lead to additional revenue streams and also ensure captive traffic for the port.

APSEZL has scaled up its business massively over the last four years. The company went from one port in 1998 to ten ports currently that cover the whole coastline of India[107] and account for 17 per cent of India's port business. This string of pearls increases options for shipping lines who want to call on APSEZL, and opens up opportunities in transhipment and coastal traffic. While global expansion will happen down the line, the team at APSEZL focuses on the India opportunity at present. 'We know India well and the opportunities in the country are highly attractive,' says Malay. 'It makes sense to stabilize the business and to scale it up before we venture out to foreign locations.'

In terms of mechanization and automation, the journey doesn't stop either. As Sudipta points out,

> Our current focus is, among others, on using the Internet of Things to take efficiencies to the next level. Assume, for example, that Pump 101 has a failure. We are working on ways that Pump 101 informs Spare Pump 102 that it has to spring into action, informs the maintenance technician that he has to have a look, checks with the SAP system if the spare parts needed are available and orders new spare parts if inventory levels falls below the threshold level.

Cost, productivity and safety will be greatly enhanced by these applications along with increased visibility in the logistics value chain. 'We believe any business can be fundamentally disrupted by the use of technology and we are working day and night to make that happen,' says Sudipta.

Globally, ports are successful when seven key factors are fulfilled:

1. Different modes of access to hinterland
2. Strong support from government/port authorities (tax regimes, incentives, minimal bureaucracy, etc.)
3. Participation of strategic partners
4. Superior service levels in comparison to peers
5. Locational and geographical advantage (deep draft, location along major trade routes, etc.)
6. Supportive logistics and maritime ecosystem (e.g., 3PL, 4PL, etc.)
7. Presence of vibrant industrial clusters

In the case of Mundra, management worked hard to enable these factors. With an ongoing focus on enabling benchmark maritime transportation for India, APSEZL is likely to continue to challenge the status quo in India and abroad.

EFD: Beating the Germans at Their Own Game

EFD Induction, a machine tool company,[108] was founded in 1996 by the merger of Germany's Fritz Düsseldorf Induktionswärmung and Norway's ELVA Induksjon. Over the last twenty years, the company has grown to be Europe's number one and the global number two induction heating company. The basic process of EFD's technology is simple. Magnetic fields in an induction coil generate currents in metals and heat the same in the process. This process can then be used for hardening of metals, welding, etc. in a very precise and fast way. Turning this principle into industrial applications, however, requires precision engineering and specialized knowhow.

EFD entered India in 1992 under the Fritz Düsseldorf name. Its current managing director, Hubert Reillard, joined the company shortly thereafter in 1995.[109] The company currently has a turnover of about INR 90 crore, healthy double-digit pre-tax profit margins and 220 permanent as well as about 100 contract employees. About a quarter of the turnover is due to exports to sister companies in Europe.

The start in Bangalore was difficult. Hubert remembers:

> We did a market study and remarkably, all the target customers that we identified at the time did not materialize. We managed to enter these accounts, but twenty years later. As a consequence, our financial situation was extremely stressed, so much so that at times we bought basic tools with our own money. The good thing is that we went through this as a team and the team learned the hard way how important it is to be lean and cost-conscious.

At the time, the initial idea was to enter India on a total cost-of-ownership[110] platform. De-contented machines[111] were to be sold with a price discount of 10–15 per cent to quality-conscious MNCs and high-end Indian companies. Relatively quickly, Hubert and his team realized that they were getting nowhere. If the indicative price of a machine in Europe was EUR 750,000 in today's money, their target price for India was around EUR 250,000! India clearly did not fit the preconceived notions that headquarter strategists and consultants may have had at the time. In a true 'hidden champion' manner, the team started localizing and adapting their machines to the Indian context. Local components such as generators, machine housing and switch gears were developed together with suppliers. Other MNCs that had started operations in India, such as Grundfos for cooling systems, Lapp for cables and Festo for high-precision components, were roped in to provide low-cost, high-quality solutions.

Insourcing of components that were outsourced in the parent company provided dual benefits of cost savings and quality improvements. Recycling of scrap material such as copper led to double-digit savings. Today, about 80 per cent of value is localized; the remaining 20 per cent are highly sophisticated control logic modules from Siemens, sensors and clamping devices that cannot be localized in an economically viable way.

Investments in R&D as well as application engineering capability provided the opportunity to react to customer requests quickly. For example, EFD can manufacture parts for customer change requests overnight during customer visits so that customers can take delivery the next day. As a consequence, customer satisfaction increases and inventory within the factory is minimized. Development also plays a key role in front-loading, i.e., special care is taken to choose the right parts for a customer request and to ensure that material costs remain manageable.[112] Cross-functional teams from engineering, production and sales ensure close alignment and optimized customer understanding.

Beyond localization, the EFD team aggressively adapted products to reflect Indian market realities. EFD realized that Indian customers did not need the same amount of automation compared to global customers due to a significant difference in labour cost. Material specifications could be modified and adapted to the Indian environment. For example, volumes in Indian factories tended to be lower than in global factories, allowing for lower machine speeds and different material requirements. As a consequence, changed material specifications allowed import substitution with Indian sources for material. Wall thickness could be reduced since the requirements for NVH (noise, vibration and harshness) in India were not as stringent as in many developed economies. By extrapolating information, the number of sensors could be reduced to three rather than using independent measurements from five sensors. Overall, hardware needed to be reduced and to be replaced by more intelligent software and computer numerical control programming.

EFD also spent significant time and resources to understand the specifics of operations in India and to translate them into machine functionality. For example, while customers drive preventive maintenance via TPM[113] and other initiatives, realities on the shop floor are sometimes not aligned with management intentions. Hence, EFD focused on designing machines that need as little maintenance as possible, e.g., by designing sensors so that they could not get dirty during the production process and therefore never have to be cleaned.

Flexibility is another key success factor for the company. Depreciated assets are used to provide job work for major truck and bus manufacturers in the country. Hubert explains,

While this is not part of the product and services portfolio globally, this type of work has several benefits . . . For one, it generates additional revenue and profits. It also lets us get closer to our customers and embed ourselves in their organizations on a continuous basis. Last but not least, we gather valuable application knowledge and experience both the strengths and weaknesses of our machines first-hand, which allows us to further improve our performance.

With local success came the desire to leverage the labour cost advantage (roughly a factor of ten, i.e., labour cost in India is about one-tenth of the cost globally) for the benefit of EFD Global. Overcoming initial resistance, EFD India managed to supply transformers, copper parts and modules to its European headquarters. While maintaining a fair margin in India, these products can be sold by the parent company at prices that are three to five times that of the Indian transfer price, hence creating significant value for global operations. Specific products that were not economically sensible for European production were transferred to India (e.g., a multipurpose generator, hardening machines for special gears). Leveraging labour cost advantages and the capability of the Indian team to focus on small batch production resulted in economic success. Quality levels of EFD India are on par with or better than European suppliers that compete with EFD India for the parent company's business. Clearly, this export activity is a very beneficial natural hedge against the 20 per cent import of components mentioned earlier.

Training, both on the job and via apprenticeships, was and remains a key concern for the company. Because the product is highly complex and customer requirements and challenges vary, massive on-the-job and theoretical training based on the German dual education model is key. While Hubert is not yet satisfied with the quality of the dual training, it has come a long way since its start twenty years ago. Salespeople also need to be highly trained. Again, an apprenticeship scheme is followed. Sales engineers start out assisting in estimations and deliveries, then graduate to handling smaller projects by themselves before they may take on large projects. This process typically takes about four years.

The layout of the current facility in Bangalore is a simple Bauhaus style.[114] The managing director and the leadership team sit at desks in open offices and are always accessible to the rest of the team. Blue- and white-collar workers are seamlessly integrated, and growth opportunities within the company depend on performance rather than school certificates and degrees. 'Team EFD' is aligned behind the goal of making this company as good as the best competitor in the world, a goal that, according to Hubert, is another three to five years away. Team members are encouraged to think about how to achieve this goal and what their contribution could be.

A reflection of the high employee commitment is the fact that EFD does not have a labour union and attrition rates are exceedingly low. Averaging 1–2 per cent yearly for the last twenty years, attrition in the company is an order of magnitude below industry average. Investment in training key people pays off. Variable pay for employees is significant; up to 40 per cent for top management. Pay-out of variable pay is linked to company performance multiplied with personal performance. In economically challenging times, EFD India manages to avoid variable pay and leave cash-in payments without employee agitation.

The initial investment of about INR 11 lakh is long depreciated; clearly, it pays to be early. A new factory is planned a short distance away from Bengaluru's new airport. The plot was bought four years ago, land prices have appreciated by a factor of three since then. Open communication and Bauhaus style construction will be the hallmarks of the new factory. An optimized layout and new machinery will allow EFD to increase efficiency by 30–40 per cent, further strengthening the company's competitive position.

Improvements will not stop there. Material cost reductions, improvement in customer handling processes, virtual manufacturing of machines, etc., are areas that are tackled in the quest to become as good as the best global manufacturers in the next three to five years. Leveraging India for global operations could be further improved, e.g., by implementing around-the-clock engineering, by developing control concepts within the Indian operation and by carrying out trials for the global company in Bangalore.

A focused strategy rather than a broad market approach is key for EFD India. The melting and forging market is ten times bigger than the hardening market. With lower margins and larger volumes, this is, however, a totally different game than the one EFD focuses on and excels in. The team is keen on finding new applications for their existing areas of strength to fill the new factory quickly and to drive further expansion. However, Hubert and his colleagues realize that melting and forging would not fit with their operational processes and culture and hence will not pursue this opportunity. Leadership clearly also means knowing what not to do, management wisdom that is at the core of many 'hidden champions'.[115]

IN SUMMARY

Value-conscious customers leave companies operating in India no choice but to relentlessly focus on operational efficiency regardless of the customer segment that these companies target. An initial wave of operational excellence improvements in Indian companies was mainly triggered by import duty reductions and FDI norm relaxations during India's liberalization, starting in 1991. However, the cost of operating in India is still high compared to other locations, driven by aspects such as inefficiencies in infrastructure, ease of doing business, and institutional voids. That is why Indian 'heroes', i.e., companies that master the complexities of the Indian market, constantly focus on relentlessly driving operational excellence.

The approaches used vary. Maruti Suzuki aligns every activity around a 'volume up, cost down' approach. Constant focus on everything including the most minute details drives cost reduction (e.g., the '1 Yen, 1 gram' initiative), which is passed on as value to customers. This in turn drives volumes, the cornerstone of Maruti's virtuous cycle in the country. APSEZL combines investment in the latest technologies with a strong focus on employee training and empowerment to achieve global benchmark efficiencies. EFD, the European 'hidden champion', redesigned its product portfolio and business model to suit Indian needs. A strong focus on dual training allows for the creation of sustainable competitive advantage in the clearly defined field of operations of induction hardening.

Succeeding in India may not be easy, but as the case studies above show, it is very much feasible for determined and flexible players, whether they are large or small, Indian or MNC.

3

MADE IN INDIA

THE LONG ROAD TOWARDS BUILDING INDUSTRY-WIDE EXCELLENCE

As the case studies discussed earlier and those in subsequent chapters show, India today can boast of world-class companies across industries. Why then is 'Made in India' not regarded the same way as 'Made in Germany' or 'Made in Japan'? Why do many Indian B2B (Business to Business) suppliers struggle to prove that they are as high-quality, reliable and innovative as the best? Why is India's share in global manufacturing exports or as a percentage of GDP so low in global or Asian comparisons as shown in Figure 3.1? The answer is simple. The current negative country-of-origin bias that many Indian companies experience can only be turned into a positive one by concerted, industry-wide change. While 'hero companies' like the ones we described above are gaining global recognition, quality and performance must be driven down across Tier-1, Tier-2 and Tier-3 suppliers. Solid management techniques must be applied in all industries, even in those that so far could opportunistically leverage factor cost advantages to drive sales.

Clearly, government and society have a role to play in building the 'Made in India' brand. Initiatives such as 'Make in India' (see below) must generate a measurable impact on improving the ease-of-doing-business rankings quickly. 'Swacch Bharat'[116] and similar initiatives are key to improve India's image abroad and to—more importantly— instil basic values that are necessary for operating companies efficiently. Without pride in and concern for the environment that we live in, it is difficult to instil pride in and dedication to the work that we do.

3 FIGURE 1

India's Performance on Key Manufacturing Performance Indicators Is Low Compared to Global and Asian Competition

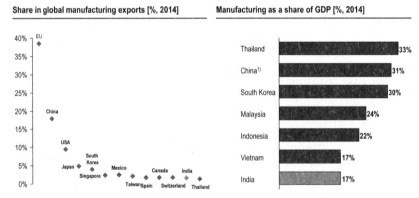

Share in global manufacturing exports [%, 2014]   Manufacturing as a share of GDP [%, 2014]

Source: WTO, International trade and market access data, Manufacturers Merchandise trade https://www.wto.org/english/res_e/statis_e/statis_bis_e. htm? solution=WTO&path=/Dashboards/MAPS&file=Map.wcdf& bookmarkState={%22impl%22:%22client%22,%22params%22: {%22langParam %22:%22en%22}}; Roland Berger analysis 1) For China the data is for year 2013, last available data by World Bank

Source: World Development Indicators, Manufacturing, value added (% of GDP), http://data.worldbank.org/indicator/NV.IND.MANF.ZS; Roland Berger analysis

While government and society need to support it, industry has its work cut out for itself. As shown by Bloom et al.,[117] and reproduced in Figure 3.2, the distribution of the degree of application of management techniques in India is rather wide and its average management practice score rather low in comparison with developed countries. The difference in the management practice score of about 20 per cent versus the US is large, and indicates significant potential for improved productivity and quality in India through the widespread adoption of modern management techniques. While it is comforting that India fares well in comparison to China and Brazil, aiming for a replication of the Chinese low-cost, low-quality production model is clearly not desirable. What worked in the 1980s should not be blindly copied in 2016. The challenge facing India's corporations and government alike is not only to create lots of jobs but also to drive 'Made in India' as a globally recognized brand that stands for quality and innovation.

India's dispersion of the management practice score is qualitatively different from the ones seen in the US, China or Brazil. Rather than presenting a continuous distribution of management practices versus firm density, India sports a double hump, as shown in Figure 3.2. As mentioned earlier, and as discussed in the case studies in this book, India has world-class companies that are able to compete internationally. However, rather than pulling the rest of the companies along and driving them to better performance, the large majority of Indian companies are de facto decoupled from these high-performers. Their average management practice score trails China and Brazil. Clearly, a lot more work is necessary to drive consistent firm performance in various industries.

Performance gaps between industries need to be closed. As can be seen from Figure 3.2, the management score in the Indian textile industry is even lower than India's overall average. Bloom et al. covered about 232 textile firms in their sample and found, in general, shortcomings regarding factory operations, quality control, inventory, human resource management as well as sales and order management. There was a detailed consulting intervention for seventeen plants, all part of family-owned businesses that have been in operation for at least twenty years, across thirty-eight management practices. This led to sizeable increases in profits per plant (estimated to be in the range of 20–50 per cent) as well as productivity (11 per cent through improved quality and efficiency as well as reduced inventory). In addition, establishing better information flow in the factory enabled an increase in decentralized decision-making. Although productivity and quality improvements require work and investments, they are possible and clearly pay off.

Operational excellence in textiles is of paramount importance to India as the industry is of key importance to the country's economy.[118] It accounts for 14 per cent of industrial production, 13 per cent of export earnings, about 4 per cent of GDP and, together with agriculture, is the largest employer, with about 45 million directly employed in the sector. Including allied sectors, employment is estimated to be at more than 100 million people. With exports of about USD 40 billion, India narrowly beats Italy and Germany in textile exports, but trails behind China, who is at the top, by roughly a factor of seven.[119] Increasing India's competitiveness in textiles is hence a sure-shot opportunity to drive manufacturing employment in the country.

India's strength is rooted in its strong production base for both natural fibres (cotton, jute, silk, wool) and synthetic fibres (polyester, viscose, nylon, acrylic). However, both in yarn as well as in readymade garments, competition is stiff from countries such as China, Bangladesh and Vietnam as well as developed nations such as Germany. Yield and quality, e.g., for cotton and wool, are areas of concern, as is the prevalence of outdated machinery. Government supports the sector via a series of initiatives such as export promotion, 100 per cent FDI under the automatic route,[120] provision of e-commerce platforms for the sale of products from the unorganized sector, funds for upgrading technology and cluster development, etc. However, Bloom et al.'s findings clearly indicate significant opportunities for performance improvement that are under the control of management. Rather than waiting for further government support, many companies are well advised to leverage these opportunities quickly. As per our experience across hundreds of consulting assignments across India, similar opportunities exist in other industries as well and are waiting to be leveraged.

3 FIGURE 2

India Trails the Average Management Practice Score versus Developed Nations, Significant Opportunities Still to Be Leveraged

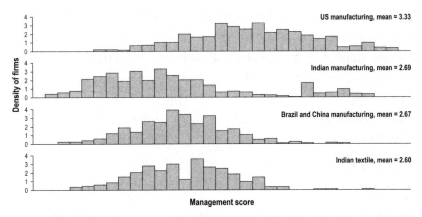

Source: Nicholas Bloom, Benn Eifert, Aprajit Mahajan, David McKenzie and John Roberts, 'Does Management Matter? Evidence from India' (National Bureau of Economic Research, NBER Working Paper 16658, January 2011), http://www.nber.org/papers/w16658.

The Case of the Machine Tool Industry: Recent Success but Still a Long Way to Go

Another example of ongoing opportunities for improvement is the Indian machine tool industry.[121] As shown in Figure 3.3, the Indian machine tool industry has suffered from the overall slowdown in the economy during FY13 and FY14, in terms of both value and volume. The positive for Indian suppliers is the fact that across all categories, indigenous machine tools have outgrown imported machine tools by a wide margin. During FY09–14, imports actually contracted by 6 per cent while the domestic industry managed to grow by about 20 per cent. As a consequence, imports accounted for 59 per cent in value and

50 per cent in volume in FY14 versus 82 per cent and 72 per cent, respectively, in FY09. At the same time, average prices for machine tools have increased by about 50 per cent in FY13 and FY14 versus previous years, showing a remarkable shift towards higher-quality machines. Automotive accounts for 47.2 per cent of machine tool end-use, non-electric machinery for 21.2 per cent, electronics/electrical machinery for 14.9 per cent, and aerospace and defence for 14.5 per cent (FY13 numbers). Clearly, an increasing number of Indian companies are able to fulfil the requirements of very demanding end-user industries.

3 FIGURE 3

India's Machine Tool Industry Achieved Its Highest Sales in FY12; Imports Account for ~65% of MT[1] Requirements by Value

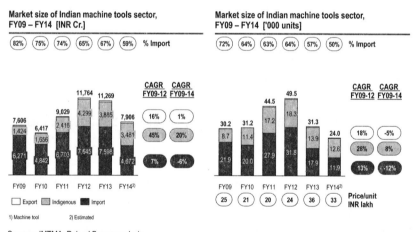

Market size of Indian machine tools sector, FY09 – FY14 [INR Cr.]

Market size of Indian machine tools sector, FY09 – FY14 ['000 units]

Sources: IMTMA, Roland Berger analysis

Going forward, the future of the industry is positive. With a resurgent Indian economy, industry growth of about CAGR 14 per cent till FY20 seems possible. This would lead to an overall market size of about INR 17,000 crore or USD 2.9 billion in FY20. Penetration of indigenous players is likely to increase to about 60 per cent of the overall value.

However, an extensive Roland Berger study for ACMA and IMTMA[122] that took into account the views of sixty automotive suppliers and twenty-two Indian machine tool manufacturers clearly shows that there is more to be done and further opportunities to be tapped. Take the automotive industry as an example. As India matures as a market, customer expectations regarding fit and finish approach global norms. Government regulations also are likely to follow global guidelines regarding emission norms, safety, etc. This translates into higher requirements from automotive OEMs in relation to their suppliers in terms of component specifications, tolerances, finish and process requirements.

Component specifications will be aligned with global trends, especially for small car platforms that are produced in India for global exports. Tolerances have become tighter (<10 μm[123]), surface finish and aesthetics are more challenging[124] and process requirements are more stringent.[125] This in turn translates into modified requirements from auto-component manufacturers when they decide to purchase machine tools. Demands for accuracy, quality, technology and process capability increase. Total cost of ownership driven by machine cost, life and production rate as well as reliability are key decision criteria.

A comparison of imported and domestic machine tools (see Figure A.11 in the Appendix) reveals significant performance differences for some machines. In particular, automotive component manufacturers believe that Indian machine tool players lag behind imported machines in the following areas:

- Technology
  o The machine tool sector is technology-intensive; however, high-accuracy requirements are not met by domestic machines.

- o Imported machine tools come with the latest technology (drives, computer numerical control, etc.), which is missing in domestic machine tools.
- o Domestic machine tool makers fall behind on engineering, design and R&D.
- o Domestic machine suppliers have limited multi-system capabilities, limited adaptive control technology for achieving optimum cutting speeds, limited usage of sophisticated interlocks, longer change-over times, etc.
- Solution and application engineering, machine design
  - o Application engineering is weak, and ownership of complete systems is missing. .
  - o Design decisions in domestic machine tools are not validated, resulting in poor spindle and bearing designs.
  - o Domestic machine makers want to 'sell what they have' versus design solutions for customer needs.
  - o Solution partnering needs to be enhanced.
- Reliability, breakdowns, sub-systems, peripherals and other issues
  - o Breakdown experience with imported machine tools is far superior; downtime is zero for some Japanese machines.
  - o Domestic machines are weak in filtration, electrical systems and chip conveyer solutions, resulting in leakages and frequent breakdowns.
  - o After some time, accuracy and repeatability start to deteriorate.
  - o Peripheral integration is the weakest link and not given adequate focus in domestic machine tools.
  - o Machines are difficult to access for maintenance.
  - o Poor ergonomics reduce ease in machine operations.
  - o Supplier quality needs to be improved via professional supplier management.

- Build quality, aesthetics, size and footprint
  - o Poor workmanship (especially electrical systems, machined parts).
  - o Limited consideration towards making compact machines despite high cost of space in India.
  - o Imported machine tools are compact with small footprint and good aesthetics versus local machine tools.
- Delivery and project management
  - o Project management skills are poor at domestic machine tool manufacturers, with frequent delays and lack of good communication with customers in comparison to Japanese and European suppliers.
  - o Domestic machines are always delayed.
- Commissioning, first time plug-and-play,[126] documentation, training
  - o Domestic machines are not plug-and-play; cycle time and capability achievement take time.
  - o Documentation supplied is inferior compared to imported machines.
  - o Level of training provided is poor.
- Incorporation of customer feedback, lack of sharing of proactive improvements
  - o Customer feedback not incorporated in future design; repeat machines have the same issues.
  - o Lack of sharing proactive improvements.

Despite significant improvements in the past, the list of opportunities for driving performance is long. It is important to realize that this list in modified form is not limited to the tool manufacturing industry alone. We have seen similar problems across a wide range of B2B industries. As a matter of fact, these problems are a reflection of the dispersion of management practices discussed earlier in the context of the textile industry (see Figure 3.2). As in the textile industry example, solutions in the form of standardized approaches to supplier management, R&D roadmaps and governance, HR management, marketing and sales approaches, etc. already exist. Implementing these solutions, e.g., via consultants, has repeatedly shown significant improvements in business performance.

The challenge many companies are faced with is not finding the right way forward, but making the decision to do it. Take R&D as an example. On average, global R&D expenses are 2.5 per cent. Domestic players average 0.5 per cent. Without focused investments, it will be impossible to climb the value chain in a highly competitive, global environment.

In terms of the inherent advantages of Indian machine tool players versus their imported competition, cost, flexibility and spare parts or service were seen as strong points, whereas customer relationship management (CRM) feedback was mixed:

- Cost
  o Indian machines are cost-effective when it comes to initial purchase price; for standard applications, the cost is almost 20–30 per cent cheaper.
- Spare parts or service
  o Availability of spares is an issue with imported machines despite the fact that some manufacturers provide on-site spare parts storage.
  o Domestic machine tool manufacturers have built up an extensive service network as a competitive advantage.
- Flexibility and CRM
  o Flexibility of Indian machine tool manufacturers is a key advantage.
  o CRM feedback is mixed—some customers say it is excellent, some rank imported suppliers better.

As in the case of the weaknesses discussed above, the strengths of Indian machine tool players also apply to many players in other B2B industries.

Opportunities for machine tool manufacturers are significant. Automotive component manufacturers need solutions for low-cost automation, testing, inspection and validation equipment, assembly line automation, tooling and jigs and fixtures. In particular, low-cost automation and high energy-efficiency machines are of interest and seen as a potential opportunity for the frugal engineering approaches often practised by Indian players. Manpower cost as a percentage of sales has increased from 9.4 per cent in FY09 to 10.4 per cent in FY13, and power and fuel cost went up from 3.9 per cent to 4.1 per cent. Both are significant areas that should be optimized given the cost pressures of the automotive industry.

3 FIGURE 4

Global Competition from Japan, Germany and China Forces Indian Players to Become World Class in Their Mindset and Internal Capabilities

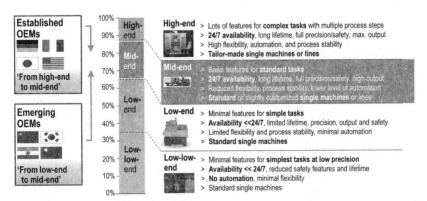

1) 100% = innovative highest performance available on today's market, 1% = manual lowest-cost lowest-performance

Sources: Roland Berger expert panel; company information.

However, it is important to note that global competition is strong and getting stronger. Established global players in automotive and industrial goods are moving consistently from high-end to mid-end technologies (we will talk about this more in the next chapter). Emerging market players, especially the Chinese, are moving aggressively from low- to mid-end technologies. Hence, the real battlefield tomorrow will be the set of machines at the mid-end (see Figure 3.4). To succeed in this environment, Indian players will need to become world-class in their mindset and internal capabilities. Lessons learned can potentially be drawn from the German 'hidden champions',[127] little known B2B players that have come to be dominant or among the top three players in their respective areas of competence globally. These hidden champions focus on leadership in clearly defined areas, marry operational excellence and cost awareness with technology leadership and high employee engagement and leverage scale via global expansion. A champion's cockpit for successful European machinery companies is summarized in Figure 3.5.

3 FIGURE 5

Patterns of Success for European Machinery Champions Centre on the Business Model, Financial Prudence and the Value Chain

Patterns of success: The champions' cockpit

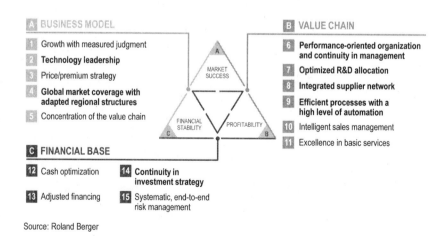

A BUSINESS MODEL

1 Growth with measured judgment
2 Technology leadership
3 Price/premium strategy
4 Global market coverage with adapted regional structures
5 Concentration of the value chain

MARKET SUCCESS

FINANCIAL STABILITY

PROFITABILITY

B VALUE CHAIN

6 Performance-oriented organization and continuity in management
7 Optimized R&D allocation
8 Integrated supplier network
9 Efficient processes with a high level of automation
10 Intelligent sales management
11 Excellence in basic services

C FINANCIAL BASE

12 Cash optimization
13 Adjusted financing
14 Continuity in investment strategy
15 Systematic, end-to-end risk management

Source: Roland Berger

Branding Nations: The Case of 'Made in Germany'[128]

'Mr Schroop', as he was known to the British, was a nice and entertaining man, well regarded in British business circles.[129] He pretended to be on private business and to have a general interest in steel fabrication. His real intention was simple: understand how Britain produces steel, steal the concepts, apply them in his own factory and compete with his hosts going forward. Mr Schroop, it turns out, was none other than Alfred Krupp, one of the key founding figures of the German steel industry.

Krupp was not alone—not by a long shot. In the first half of the nineteenth century, many German companies sent their trusted confidants to Great Britain for a 'study tour', a nice way to describe what was essentially industrial espionage. While Krupp hailed from the Rhineland, Chemnitz was another industrial hotspot where entrepreneurs such as Richard Hartmann were ready to take on the world with their steam engines.[130] Solingen, a small town in North Rhine Westphalia, had been a centre for the production of knives, scissors and other cutting tools for centuries and wanted to leverage global markets for wealth creation.

Companies that were trying to penetrate markets for machines, metal wares or other mass-fabricated products, however, did not succeed at first. The Germans were hampered by a lack of technical knowledge and capital to buy relevant production machinery. Quality levels that were global standards at the time were out of reach. After all, Germany was a latecomer to the industrial revolution. In the early part of the nineteenth century, Germany's exports to Great Britain consisted of sugar, potatoes, wheat, musical instruments, cuckoo clocks from the Black Forest area and other handmade products.

Nevertheless, German companies copied English products relentlessly and dumped their wares on to the world market at attractively low prices. Extremely low labour cost and unregulated, long working hours were the key reasons for Germany's cost advantage. Copying did not stop at products. Solingen's cutting tool producers, for example, mass-produced cheap, iron-made, unhardened knives, scissors, etc.[131] These were made to look identical to Sheffield-made products. Sheffield, a city in South Yorkshire, the heart of the English steel-making industry, prided itself on products that were high-quality, long-lasting, often made by hand and produced from hardened steel. Sheffield-made products consistently outperformed the competition. To compensate, Solingen solved the problem by ripping off Sheffield and falsely labelling their products as 'Sheffield-made'. The impact on the reputation, revenue and profits of Sheffield companies was massive.

Despite these initial sales successes, there was one problem, however. The quality of German products was shoddy at best. Franz Reuleaux, a German professor of engineering from Berlin and a regular judge at global exhibitions, stated during the world exhibition in Philadelphia in 1876 that 'German products are bad and cheap'. This comment was widely picked up in the global press and the Germans had to deal with a major country-of-origin disadvantage.

To make things worse, industrial lobbying in Great Britain led to political action. In 1883, a Paris conference concluded a treaty regarding the protection of patent and brand rights. In particular, the production of wrongly labelled goods was to attract penalties. German representatives refrained from participating in the conference.

In 1887, Great Britain instituted a new version of the 'Merchandise Marks Act of 1862' under the protest of German merchants. All products imported into Great Britain needed to have a label stating where they were manufactured. The government wanted to warn consumers of cheap products and rip-offs from countries such as Germany and hoped that patriotic feelings would drive sales of local goods. While protecting the indigenous industry via import duties would have been easier, it was counterproductive for Britain at the time. Free trade suited the global export champion from the perspective of both exports and imports. Especially, cheap grain imports enabled British citizens to enjoy bread and other staples at reasonable prices.

However, British intentions backfired. Franz Reuleaux's comment on 'bad and cheap' German products and the media backlash that German industry subsequently faced was taken as a grievous, personal insult in German business circles. His advice in Philadelphia to the German industry was to compete on quality. This advice was taken seriously and, over a period of just ten years, a quality revolution was launched in Germany. German industrialists hired English workers, studied the production methods of their British counterparts, leveraged scientific knowledge to improve products and production processes, invested in better machines and trained and educated their workforce.

By the time the 'Merchandise Marks Act' went into effect, German companies were exporting increasingly high-value industrial products rather than cheap rip-offs. Not only did British families suddenly realize how many wares actually originated in Germany—tools, servant jackets, toys, utensils, pencils, water pipes, etc.—German product performance was adequate, often on a par with British wares, while prices were cheaper.[132] Colonial Minister Joseph Chamberlain, the father of British Prime Minister Arthur Neville Chamberlain, tellingly assessed German wares in 1897: 'German clothes are cheaper and more useful, cement is cheaper and of good quality, chemicals are better due to better know-how, watches are cheaper, more attractive and of superior design, tools are cheaper, better tailored to needs and more innovative . . .'[133] The list goes on and highlights the dramatic change that was witnessed in Germany over a short span of time.

Exports from Germany to Great Britain soared. For example, between 1883 and 1893, exports from Germany to England increased by 30 per cent.[134] Several German companies opened up offices in London to support a booming business. By the end of the nineteenth century, German brands such as Aspirin, 4711, Odol, Faber-Castell, Märklin, Steiff, Ibach (piano), Beck's or Lange (watches) were household names in Great Britain that stood for quality superior to that of British producers.

German products drove a 'bottom-of-the-pyramid' revolution of their own. Mass production of high-quality products at attractive prices, attractive commercial conditions and well-trained sales personnel increased the range of many products beyond the middle class. British pianos, for example, were previously only sold via specialized shops. German products were mass-produced and sold via department stores, and could be paid for in instalments. This made products accessible not only to the middle class but also to better paid workers, allowing manufacturers to increase the geographic coverage of their sales outlets, which in turn increased sales.

In parallel, German manufacturers realized that moving up the value chain increased the need for patent protection. Werner von Siemens, the founding father of Siemens AG, developed the initial idea of a *Reichspatentgesetz*, a law designed to protect the intellectual property (IP) of German companies within Germany and abroad. In 1877, it was accepted in the German parliament, the Reichstag. A version of the law which retains the basic characteristics of the Reichspatentgesetz is still valid today.

Germany's ascendance to a major industrial power was in large part possible due to its history of universal education (going back to Martin Luther in 1524). German education focused on apprenticeships (the origins of which are the *Zünfte* or guilds of the Middle Ages) and dual (combined practical and theoretical) education, as well as application-oriented scientific and technical education.[135] Active support by German embassies to support exports from the Reich played a crucial role as well. Within less than a decade, British and German observers realized that the 'Merchandise Marks Act' had backfired brutally. As early as 1896, British journalist E. E. Williams criticized the 'Made in Germany' tag in his work *Made in Germany*,[136] citing it as a free-of-cost way to recommend German products. Even earlier, Germany's Reichstag realized in 1892 that 'Made in Germany' had nearly overnight become a cost-effective way to recommend German manufactured goods.

Today, 'Made in Germany' and related connotations around concepts such as innovation, quality, precision, punctuality, dedication and focus have morphed into a 'corporate identity of a nation' as mentioned by the British author David Head.[137] In many ways, they symbolize the resurgence of Germany from the total destruction of World War II, and are closely connected with democracy and high living standards for all citizens. The 'Made in Germany' story was driven by the combined aspirations of the people and industrial and political leaders. For example, Germany's consensus-oriented culture has time and again seen a cooperation of government and opposition to work for the greater good of the nation. Times of crisis have often brought about a 'grand coalition' of political parties from the left and the right, a coalition determined to do the right thing for the country.

The story of 'Made in Germany' is by no means unique. It has been replicated in a different cultural context in Japan and Korea, again in an impressively short amount of time. It is in the process of being turned into reality in China and with a potential time delay in India. Other nations are sure to follow.

While each country's background and situation is different, some rules of thumb that have played a critical role in Germany's success may be of general relevance. In our view, these are the following:

1. Be peeved: Trying to show the world that you are better than they think can be a powerful incentive.
2. Build capability aggressively: Leapfrogging technology developments is a must.
3. Leverage factor cost advantages aggressively (e.g., labour cost, hours/week, etc.).
4. Face the facts: Accept critics like Reuleaux and attack the problem, not the messenger.
5. Align across industries: Building a national brand requires all companies to perform across all relevant industries.
6. Align between industry and government: Government has a major role to play to create a level playing field that allows companies to compete.
7. Cooperate within the political system.
8. Build institutional frameworks (patents, training, certifications, etc.).
9. Invest in education, training and science: Your workers are the ones that will make change happen. Take them seriously.
10. Dream big.
11. Persevere: A national brand, like any other brand, requires constant renewal and constant 'deposits in the brand equity account'.

Make in India: Timely but Challenging

The vision of 'Make in India' is to facilitate foreign and domestic investment, foster innovation, enhance skill development, protect

IP and build a best-in-class manufacturing infrastructure in India. Targets for this initiative have been clearly spelled out. Manufacturing sector growth should increase to 12–14 per cent per annum over the medium term. Manufacturing's share in GDP should increase from 16 per cent to 25 per cent by 2022. In the same timeframe, 100 million additional jobs should be created in the sector. These targets are ambitious. Adding 100 million jobs, for example, means tripling current employment in manufacturing.[138]

Enablers have also been identified. Unnecessary processes, laws and regulations will need to be eliminated. Time-bound clearances will be given to projects through a single online portal. Appropriate skill sets will have to be inculcated through quality education. The government will have to be made more transparent, responsive and accountable and we will need to increase domestic value addition and technological depth.

Across the spectrum, India's corporations support the government's 'Make in India' initiative. The idea that manufacturing can have a very substantial impact on job creation and hence needs adequate focus is widely accepted today—after years of a narrow-minded focus on IT and services. Overall factors and the current economic environment are also in India's favour, as discussed in Chapter 1.

All these points are laudable and timely. Is it then just a matter of consistent execution that will allow India to leverage her 'demographic dividend' and become another factory to the world similar to China? Can we capture the space that China seems to be vacating by moving from 'Make in China' to 'Innovate in China'? Are government initiatives timely, appropriate and well-executed?

While it is possible to increase low- and high-end manufacturing in the country in an effort to create jobs for all kinds of talents, the window of opportunity for the same is narrow and hence requires decisive action today. Five major trends impact our opportunity to create the intended 100 million jobs by 2022:

1. Competition from other low-cost countries eager to establish manufacturing footprints of their own.
2. Competition from established countries trying to reindustrialize and bring value addition and jobs back home rather than outsource them to countries such as China or India.
3. Increasing pressure for environmentally friendly production not only in developed countries but also in emerging countries due to the latter's significant influence on global greenhouse gas (GHG) emissions.
4. Need to invest in R&D to avoid perpetuating knowledge gaps with developing and emerging economies such as China.
5. Non-uniform capability of Indian companies to compete at global levels of efficiency and quality due to internal reasons as well as lack of a manufacturing ecosystem.

Here, we will look at the first three points and discuss them in more detail in the subsequent sections. The fifth point has already been discussed above and the fourth point will be revisited in the following chapter.

Globally, manufacturing jobs in major economies have declined as a function of time, as shown in Figure 3.6. The only exceptions are China and India. China has added jobs over the last few years as companies started using low labour cost in China as an alternative to further investments in automation and productivity improvements. With relatively high salaries in China and a new focus on efficiency improvement in the triad,[139] this trend is likely to reverse itself. In the case of India, in terms of overall percentages, employment in manufacturing rose marginally from 11 per cent in 1990 to 12 per cent in

2010. The key question going forward is whether India can accelerate this growth and replace China as the factory to the world.

3 FIGURE 6

Manufacturing Jobs Experience a Significant Decline in Percentage of People Employed in Most Major Economies Except China and India
Manufacturing jobs as a % of labour force in major economies

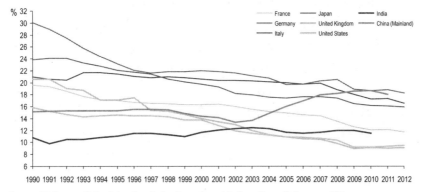

Sources: US Bureau of Labor, International Labor Comparisons, http://www.bls.gov/fls/flscomparelf.htm,
Groningen Growth and Development Center, Groningen 10-sector database, http://www.rug.nl/research/ggdc/data/10-sector-database,
World Development Indicators, 'Labor Force, Total', http://data.worldbank.org/indicator/SL.TLF.TOTL.IN.; Roland Berger analysis

China created a virtuous cycle as the 'world's manufacturing workbench' by, among others,

- leveraging cheap labour,
- creating world-class infrastructure,
- adapting and improving technologies developed overseas,
- achieving cost reductions through deployment at scale and
- achieving incremental process and manufacturing innovation.

While all these points can be copied in principle, they require timely and consistent execution for India to follow in China's footsteps. The new NDA government has launched a number of initiatives to improve the ease of doing business and to drive employment generation in the country.[140] Proactive state governments have supported these efforts by taking adequate steps themselves.

In addition, the government has started a slew of reforms focusing on the maintenance of fiscal discipline, the streamlining of subsidies, investment promotion, domestic manufacturing support, environment/forest clearances, taxation and the financial sector.[141] Some highlights include the implementation of GST,[142] the disinvestment of PSUs, the deregulation of diesel prices, increased limits for FDI in real estate, defence, construction, railways and insurance, the e-auction of coal blocks, a new gas pricing formula, investments in roads, ports and railways, the Mines and Minerals Bill and various amendments to India's labour laws. These initiatives are partially completed, and partially in the process of being rolled out. Consistent execution of these activities will be crucial to drive India's ascent as a manufacturing powerhouse going forward.[143] Consistency will also be required across policies.

We Are Not Alone: Ascent of Low-Cost Competitors

A major consideration of the 'Make in India' campaign is the observation that manufacturing wages in China have risen and are now nearly three times higher than corresponding wages in India (see Figure 1.6). In principle, this opens up opportunities for India to enter into manufacturing activities that are no longer viable in China. However, India is not alone. Manufacturing costs in Vietnam are 53 per cent lower than in China; in Indonesia, that figure is 49 per cent and in the Philippines, it is 66 per cent. In terms of labour availability, India leads the three other countries by a large margin; however, Indonesia and the Philippines trump India in terms of the English-speaking percentage of the population. And while India is the largest market among the four nations that we are considering, the internal market in Indonesia is also large, and that of Vietnam and the Philippines is relevant.

A number of global indicators are cause for concern. In the global competitiveness report 2015–16,[144] India scores a rank of 55 out of 140 countries compared with 37 for Indonesia, 47 for the Philippines and 56 for Vietnam. In terms of the World Bank's ease of doing business 2016 ranking,[145] India is again last, with a rank of 130. Indonesia ranks 109, the Philippines rank 103 and Vietnam ranks 90. In terms of the 2014 International IP index, India ranks behind Indonesia and Vietnam (the Philippines have not been ranked).[146] On the logistics performance index, India ranks 54, behind Indonesia (53) and Vietnam (48), but ahead of the Philippines (57).[147]

Clearly, just because China is forced to vacate parts of the manufacturing space, it does not imply that India is the only or best alternative. As a consequence, the 'Make in India' initiative needs to drive its agenda quickly forward in order to change key global rankings. The latter are important, as global companies do take them into consideration when evaluating their global manufacturing footprint and deciding on fresh investments. Local companies need significant improvements in the same to be able to compete with other global and emerging market competitors on the same footing.

Manufacturing Is Cool: The Reindustrialization of the Triad

In the wake of the global financial crisis, Western nations rediscovered the charm of manufacturing as a driver of innovation, employment and services. The US, UK, France and even Germany, which still has a healthy industrial base, all embarked on various initiatives to ensure manufacturing employment within their own national borders. Rather than going through all the initiatives currently underway, we will focus on 'Industry 4.0', the German avatar of the reindustrialization drive.

The basic premise of Industry 4.0 is that the introduction of intelligent machines, embedded cyber-physical sensors, collaborative technologies and networked processes will once again drive an efficiency revolution in industrial manufacturing. Industry 4.0 was initiated by the German Federal Ministry for Education and Research and officially launched in 2013 with a report called *Securing the Future of the German Manufacturing Industry*.[148] Industry 4.0 aims to build the intelligent factory, which is characterized by adaptability, efficiency and full digital integration. Some components of this factory are smart robots and machines, i.e., multipurpose, 'intelligent' robots that are able to adapt, communicate and interact with each other and with humans. Big data will be leveraged via cloud computing, e.g., for mass customization. Connectivity will reach a new level of quality via constant exchange of information between machines, work pieces, systems and human beings. Optimized production processes will ensure energy efficiency and allow for the decentralization of plants.

European companies in particular are positive regarding the potential of Industry 4.0. Expected cost savings of 14 per cent on average over the next five years would negate a large part of the factor cost advantage that countries like India enjoy today versus developed nations (typically in the range of 15–30 per cent). Efficiency gains are expected to be even higher, at 18 per cent within the next five years. Industry 4.0 is a boardroom-level topic for all European manufacturing companies, with investments in the approach amounting to 3.3 per cent of revenues on average, as shown in Figure A.12 in the Appendix. In comparison, the typical R&D budget of Western automotive OEMs amounts to about 4–5 per cent of revenue.

Established players in the EU are changing their organizations, processes and capabilities in whole or in part due to Industry 4.0. As freedom and flexibility of the production process increases, it will become possible to create products tailored for segment-by-one customer needs, i.e., products personalized for each single customer, at relatively low marginal cost. Also, distribution processes for spare parts or not too complex consumer goods may get easier, e.g., by leveraging 3D printing.

In terms of competition, traditional industry boundaries will become blurred, as are the boundaries between industrial and non-industrial applications. Going forward, the focus will be on industrial working methods, not only of products but also of services.

The value chain will be redefined as well. In a complex and intertwined manufacturing network, the roles of designers, physical product suppliers and the interfaces with customers will change. Supplier hierarchies and pecking orders are likely to be redefined. New companies (such as Amazon, Google and Apple) are increasingly integrating all parts of the value chain to enhance their core service offerings.

In terms of skills, employees will need enhanced social as well as technical skills. Corporate cultures with continuous training and development in the workplace will become a core competency.

Last but not least, the need for offshoring work will reduce as will the overall number of jobs available in manufacturing. Take Baxter, the world's first general-purpose production robot, as an example. Baxter's base version costs only USD 25,000. It can be taught any task due to its learning capability and can work alongside humans due to a range of built-in sensors. Baxter communicates with humans via a visual interface, and can recognize and dynamically adjust to work interruptions, wrong parts, etc.[149] In light of these developments, India's 'demographic dividend' could turn out to be a rather large 'demographic liability'.

The tendency to drive efficiency by leveraging intelligent software is not limited to manufacturing alone. In many service industries, software bots today are able to take over white-collar, professional and creative jobs. Whether it is writing articles for newspapers, diagnosing health problems, writing software or even writing songs, software bots can replace human intervention quite effectively. Overall, experts believe that for a developed economy such as the US, nineteen of the top twenty employment-generating jobs can be easily automated, which accounts for about 37 per cent of the overall jobs in the US.[150] We will have to prepare for a future in which large sections of the population may be unemployable through no fault of their own. This trend has implications for job creation in India's software and services industry as well.

The next industrial revolution is, hence, upon us, and like its predecessors, it will lead to the introduction of new products and new means of producing existing ones. It will disrupt the competitive status quo, on a company, country and/ or regional level, and drive new requirements for workforce and infrastructure alike. Unfortunately, India's automation and digitalization levels are not adequate (see Figure 3.7). Opportunities to leverage the country's pool of well-trained engineers and IT professionals in order to drive an Indian version of Industry 4.0 clearly exist and should be pursued with the necessary effort and investments.

Leading Indian companies are implementing various building blocks of smart manufacturing in an effort to improve quality and efficiency. Supporting such efforts via the creation of targeted industry–academia development platforms (similar, e.g., to Arena2036 in Stuttgart, Germany[151]) should be beneficial.

Creating an industrial commons as part of manufacturing ecosystems would also help to push cross-industry cooperation.

3 FIGURE 7

Indian Manufacturing Industry Has Arrived at an Inflection Point and Is Currently Not Prepared for the Changes Which Industry 4.0 Brings

India currently has only 1/8 the automation rate of China

Current automation rate: industrial robots/10,000 workers

> Industry 4.0 is – besides other challenges – seriously threatening India's position as a low-cost country

> With increasing digitalization of the manufacturing industry in the EU, cost advantage through availability of cheap labor vanishes

> Low automation rate shows that India is not yet ready for Industry 4.0 – urgent changes are needed!

> India needs to reposition itself, and go beyond current efforts to focus on "Make in India"

Sources: World Robotics 2013, Roland Berger analysis.

Environmental Sustainability: A Must for Local and Global Players

Globally, emissions standards are becoming more stringent, with the EU generally leading the charge. Looking at vehicular CO_2 emissions, European targets for 2020 are, for example, about 20 per cent more aggressive than those of the US.[152] India is the world's third largest GHG emitter, with 6.1 per cent of total global emissions (behind China at 22.5 per cent and the US at 12.2 per cent[153]). India cannot abdicate her responsibility towards a cleaner and sustainable future either from a global or, even more importantly, from a local perspective. The current discussions around air quality in major Indian metropolitan areas clearly indicate that awareness of pollution and its impact on quality of life is increasing in India as well.

3 FIGURE 8

Manufacturing Companies Can Address Sustainability Concerns by Focusing on Incremental Measures Covering the Entire Value Chain

Transformation to green manufacturing: Framework

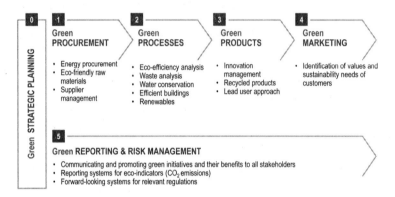

Sources: Roland Berger Product Development, Civil Economics Competence Center.

Manufacturing has a vital role to play in reducing the impact of human activity on the environment. 'Green manufacturing' requires a green manufacturing framework, i.e., a consistent approach to sustainability across the value chain (see Figure 3.8). A green strategy must cover green procurement, green processes, green products and green marketing as well as green reporting and risk management. Procurement, for example, must focus on energy procurement, eco-friendly raw materials and supplier management that drives sustainability down the line to Tier-1, Tier-2 and Tier-3 suppliers.

Processes need to be optimized constantly via eco-efficiency analysis, waste analysis, water and energy conservation, etc. Products need to be designed to minimize ecological impact along the product life cycle. Marketing needs to address and appeal to the values and sustainability needs of customers. Last but not least, reporting and risk management needs to focus on efficient communication of green approaches to all stakeholders and needs to be proactive in terms of anticipating and fulfilling future regulations.

Sustainability will fundamentally change the way citizens look at manufacturing and plants. Take the German company Wittenstein as an example. In 2012, Wittenstein invested in a brand new production facility in the middle of a residential zone near Stuttgart, Germany. In noise- and emissions-sensitive Germany, Wittenstein's factory is low-noise and zero-emission, which allows it to be embedded in an urban environment. Direct benefits from the plant are offered to residents in the vicinity, such as the usage of surplus heat from production for residential heating free of charge. Flexibility of production is enhanced due to the short distances between employees' homes and their workplace. Quality of life of workers is improved at the same time.

Indian companies, especially Indian MNCs, therefore, need to pursue green manufacturing initiatives for a number of reasons, including resource scarcity, climate change, import dependence and government regulations. Customer pull for green products is continuously increasing and—if not taken seriously—may be leveraged by the competition to create product and brand differentiation. Opportunities for profitable and green manufacturing increase due to advances in science and may need to be leveraged to satisfy investors who demand carbon disclosure.

Examples of successful green manufacturing initiatives in India abound. Take Godrej's Fast Card as one example. It is a smokeless paper mosquito repellent that provides a mosquito-free environment for four to five hours at the cost of just INR 1. To reach such an aggressive price point dictated by the needs of the customers (farmers in rural areas who would like to get one night of undisturbed sleep), Godrej had to reinvent the product and its production process. The mosquito repellent formula was changed to reduce water content and to allow for rapid drying, which massively reduced both water and electricity consumption during the production process. Clearly, green manufacturing is not only the right thing to do but also enables companies to provide profitable solutions even for 'bottom of the pyramid' customers.

Godrej's Good & Green Initiative[154] aims to build a more inclusive and greener India via clear targets in key areas. In terms of eco-friendly production, the aims are to reduce energy consumption by 25 per cent and to achieve zero waste, carbon neutrality and a positive water balance. Thirty per cent of energy use is to be achieved via renewable sources. The time frame for all these initiatives is 2020. Taking the Godrej Appliances Shirwal plant as an example, improvements towards a greener business system are being driven via Kaizen and PMO. Results are impressive. Specific energy consumption per appliance was reduced by 56 per cent between FY05 and FY14. In the same time frame, fixed power consumption was reduced from 42 per cent to 31 per cent. Specific water consumption was reduced by 36.4 per cent between FY08 and FY14 and the share of renewable energy consumption went up from 7 per cent in FY11 to 23 per cent in FY14. Hazardous waste disposal to landfill has come down by 55 per cent from FY11 to FY14 and green initiatives have been rolled out to the suppliers via a clear strategic roadmap. Consistent training and awareness creation leads to a rather high number of Kaizen per employee (8.6) and exceedingly high employee participation at 92 per cent.

Leading Indian companies such as Godrej are well-poised to meet the sustainability demands of Indian and global customers. However, as discussed earlier, the success of a 'Made in India' brand will depend on establishing relevant practices across the board. Looking at the state of air, water and soil pollution in India, this aspect of securing jobs as well as the future of young Indians requires a dramatic push going forward.

IN SUMMARY

As we have seen in the previous chapter, the successes of leading Indian companies are impressive especially in light of the challenges of the Indian environment. Building a national 'Made in India' brand, however, requires improvement to management practices across OEMs and Tier-1, Tier-2 and Tier-3 players alike. Such improvements are feasible but require focused action from industry participants, as discussed in the context of the textile and machine tool industries. While government support is needed to allow Indian companies to grow on a level playing field versus international competitors, a lot of progress can be achieved by modernizing management practices in existing value chains. Here, industry players have significant work still ahead of them.

National branding of 'Made in India' as an innovative, high-quality manufacturing destination is important and possible. As the example of 'Made in Germany' demonstrates, success against seemingly overwhelming odds is possible via concerted and sustained action. However, a simple copy-and-paste approach from the Chinese experience is unlikely to succeed. Competition from low-cost countries, the reindustrialization of the triad via Industry 4.0 and similar smart manufacturing initiatives, and a changed environment regarding 'green manufacturing' are some of the factors that render the creation of an additional 100 million manufacturing jobs challenging. Urgent and consistent action by all players is necessary to ensure that India's young population is indeed a demographic dividend rather than a liability.

4

INDIAN INNOVATION

DRIVING DIFFERENTIATION

Successful companies need to create a sustainable advantage and superior value for customers relative to the competition. Generally, this implies creating more value for customers at comparable cost, comparable value at lower cost and hence lower price, or both.[155] In some sense, a focus on operational efficiency and aggressive leverage of factor cost advantages (e.g., lower cost of labour, land, electricity, etc.) seems to be the natural way forward for emerging economies, as the examples of Germany in the mid-nineteenth century and contemporary China have shown.

The case studies discussed in Chapters 2 and 3 and the ones that we will discuss in the remainder of this book reveal a very different approach for India. Besides a strong focus on operational efficiency to earn the right to play, Indian companies simultaneously drive innovation. How innovation in India is played out varies. Business model innovation, application innovation (apply existing products and technologies to innovative uses) and product cost innovation (frugal engineering) are the prominent forms that we have come across in our interactions in this country. Real technological breakthroughs are possible, and are happening in India. Significant impact in this area may require closer cooperation between industry and academia as well as a major quality improvement in tertiary education[156] in the country, as we will argue later in this chapter.

The innovation focus of companies operating in India and their need for a differentiated value proposition stems from the compulsion to compete in higher-margin businesses. As we have seen in the previous chapters, India's government-specific advantages (GSAs)[157] are relatively weaker than those of comparable nations such as China. In terms of country-specific advantages (CSAs),[158] over most of the last two to three decades, India had little advantage in terms of blue-collar labour due to higher cost and stricter labour law regulations. White-collar labour, particularly in IT-related services, provided a much better CSA to Indian companies than pure manufacturing. Firm-specific advantages, i.e., firm-level assets and capabilities that contribute to competitive advantage, are probably India's strong point, as successful Indian companies have had to overcome significant challenges in their environment. With this background, a purely operational excellence, low-cost labour and manufacturing-focused strategy is out of the question since CSAs and GSAs prevent Indian companies from reaching the same cost position as, for example, Chinese companies.

Fundamental research has negligible relevance in an Indian context as well. The weakness of India's tertiary education results in challenges regarding the quality (not the quantity) of qualified labour. Consequences will be discussed in this chapter.[159] We will highlight India's forte, 'frugal innovation', and its growing relevance for Indian companies such as Godrej, Tata, HUL and HPS, as well as global giants (e.g., Siemens). Global MNCs leverage India aggressively as a hub for global R&D, as the case study of Bosch clearly shows. The impressive success of India's start-up and incubator ecosystem will be analysed in the next chapter. There, we will also discuss the case of redBus, a truly innovative Indian start-up with a real impact on the quality of life of India's consumers.

BREAKTHROUGH RESEARCH AND QUALITY OF TALENT: SETTING THE BAR TOO LOW

In global comparisons, India's innovation and R&D efforts still have a way to go. Out of the total global projected R&D spending of USD 1.6 trillion in 2014,[160] India was projected to spend 2.7 per cent as compared to 5.7 per cent for Germany, a remarkable 17.5 per cent for China and 31.1 per cent for the US. With gross expenditures on R&D of about USD 44 billion, on a PPP basis,[161] India equals the UK and leads Brazil and Russia. However, India spends 0.9 per cent of GDP on R&D, and lags behind most major economies in this respect.[162] Thirty-five per cent of R&D expenditure is driven by business, 60 per cent by the government and the remaining 5 per cent by institutes of higher education. Surprisingly, India's split of R&D across basic research, applied research and development is very different from spending patterns seen in the US, China, the EU and South Korea. In India, basic research amounts to more than 25 per cent of the overall money spent, and the rest is nearly equally split between development and applied research. In all other countries, development accounts for more than 60 per cent of total expenditure (more than 80 per cent in the case of China) and the rest is equally distributed between applied and basic research (dominated by applied research in the case of China).[163]

4 FIGURE 1

India's Domestic Filings for Patents Trail Major Economies, Approval Rates Are Equally Low

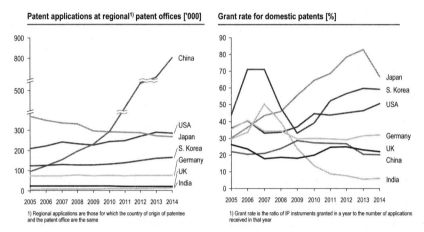

Patent applications at regional[1] patent offices ['000]

1) Regional applications are those for which the country of origin of patentee and the patent office are the same

Grant rate for domestic patents [%]

1) Grant rate is the ratio of IP instruments granted in a year to the number of applications received in that year

Source: World Intellectual Property Office (Online Database), http://www.wipo.int/ipstats/en/statistics/country_profile/; Roland Berger analysis

Research output in India is low, as measured by patent, trademark or industrial design protection applications. As shown in Figures 4.1 and A.13 in the Appendix, India lags behind all major economies in domestic patent applications. In addition, approval rates for domestic patents are extremely low. In terms of international filings, applications are minimal compared to China, the US, South Korea, Japan, Germany and the UK. The only point of light: international approval rates are comparable to the approval rates of other countries. The picture regarding trademarks and industrial design protection applications is similar. Clearly, India does not seem to be getting much bang for its buck as far as research is concerned.

India's challenges are therefore in quantity, in terms of overall R&D investments, as well as quality, in terms of patent output. Plans to achieve a research intensity of 2 per cent of GDP in the next three to five years[164] are laudable. However, this number is likely to be achieved only by significantly increasing private participation in R&D.

While India's investments in R&D are lower than desirable, the output of engineering graduates has mostly been in line with industry needs in terms of quantity. While in FY07, 1511 engineering colleges admitted 659,717 Indian students for undergraduate education, in FY14, 3384 engineering colleges took in more than 1.6 million students.[165] With these numbers, India outpaces both China and the US with 1.3 million and 569,274 engineering entrants per year, respectively.[166] The main employers for these graduates have been the IT industry and manufacturing.

Quality and employability of graduates have been a consistent concern, however. While result-orientation, core domain knowledge and better aptitude are considered primary hiring criteria, a large number of students do not meet the criteria set by companies. A lot of the engineering colleges are understaffed and lack qualified faculty. The course curriculum is mostly theoretical and lacks practical application of the theories. Assignments, projects and evaluation patterns are outdated and routine. Students are encouraged to focus on grades, not learning. Lastly, many engineering institutions are running only for profit and may be influenced by political backers, leading to poor quality of admissions, poor governance and low education standards. To complicate the matter, attractive pay packages in the IT industry are pushing students to opt for IT courses, which leads to an overall neglect of engineering disciplines.

A partial explanation of the relatively low quality of engineering students comes from the educational system itself. Due to lower salaries and lack of career prospects, there is a dearth of faculty at engineering colleges, and hence a very high student-to-faculty ratio, as shown in Figure 4.2. In addition, India has the lowest number of PhDs among the faculty, even among BRIC nations, clearly limiting the quality of education. Consequently, educational mentorship for master's and PhD students is severely constrained.

Tertiary education in India is dreadful, with many universities being driven more by internal politics than by the desire to foster knowledge. The results are visible in simple, indicative output measures. The number of peer-reviewed articles in engineering increased five-fold in China between 2000 and 2010, but only doubled in India during the same period.[167] The same picture emerges when we consider patenting activities as a proxy for the capacity of research institutions to drive applied research. In 2010, India produced less than one patent per 1000 faculty members, trailing her East Asian neighbour by a factor of 160!

4 FIGURE 2

Low Student–Faculty Ratios Due to Dearth of Faculty Has Resulted in Low Research Outputs Compared to India's Peers Globally

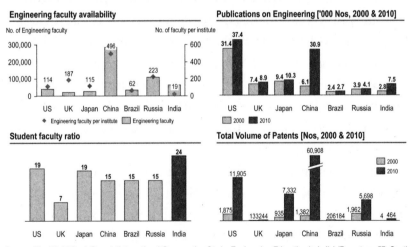

Source: The World Bank Report, 'International Comparative Study: Engineering Education in India' (Report no. 57, South Asia Human Development Sector, April 2013); Roland Berger analysis

India's R&D and educational sector does have bright spots.[168] The Indian Institutes of Technology (IITs) have been able to churn out bright young minds. High levels of academic competition have attracted students to these institutes. With over 50,000 candidates applying for admission, only the top 2 per cent of candidates finally join the IITs. Competition for seats in these institutes has intensified over time, as entrance into an IIT does guarantee a high level of interest from corporate employers and good opportunities for placements. In addition, student-to-faculty ratios are significantly lower and funding levels much higher compared to other engineering colleges. However, there are three commonly voiced concerns with the IIT system. First, an elitist system of specialized training for a few thousand individuals does not address the needs of the country. A trickle-down effect does not exist for education, and a large number of India's youth do not receive education that will enable them to leverage their potential to the fullest. This state of affairs is deplorable. Second, IITs are often not frequented by students interested in engineering, but many have their minds set on high-paying careers in business by combining an IIT degree with another degree from the Indian Institutes of Management (IIMs). While this is understandable from an individual's point of view, it does not support the cause of engineering in India. Lastly, like many other institutions in India, IITs have been accused of being too removed from industrial reality and too focused on 'mugging', learning material by heart to pass exams, rather than focusing on understanding and applying knowledge.

The government has recently announced seven new IITs, bringing the total to nineteen functioning and three planned IITs. Increasing the reach of IITs is a positive move. In addition, a few private universities are successful in driving the Indian innovation agenda. Take Amity University as an example. Amity has adopted a model for commercial innovation through strong patenting office linkages and is a leader in patent submissions. It may be worthwhile to study alternative approaches to education and alternative funding models for IITs and private universities to increase overall impact.

With a limited supply of high-quality talent, the only valid response for corporations is to invest heavily in training themselves. Infosys's training centre in Mysuru (earlier Mysore), built to train about 10,000 software engineers at a time, is a famous example. But even smaller players in India invest aggressively in training. Faurecia, the world's sixth largest auto equipment supplier[169] has two technical centres in India, located in Pune and Bengaluru. The Faurecia TechCenter in Pune was established in 2004 and employs about 600 people. It houses technical centres for interior systems, exteriors and automotive seating and covers areas as diverse as design, development, analysis, knowledge-based engineering, prototyping and testing. The centre evolved from an offshore CAD/CAE-based service facility[170] to a worldwide competence centre in industrial design, e.g., as the global centre of competence for glove boxes. Development of the centre occurred in phases. An initial capability building via 2D drawing, 3D modelling and CAE analysis was followed by a three-year phase to build up understanding in areas such as concept-feasibility, prototyping, production tools and program quality leadership. After that, the centre graduated to testing and validation, manufacturing leadership, complete supply chain management and also expanded its capacity.

Faurecia places special emphasis on workforce training and development in its technical centres. It has built up an Indian engineering academy for developing training as well as trainers, deploying technical training, initiating and supporting knowledge sharing and developing and conducting its flagship programme, the graduate engineer trainee programme. During a six-month period, new recruits go through training modules in software, domain-specific skills and soft skills. The on-the-job training means that trainees are confronted with increasingly complex real-life design problems that were handled before by experienced colleagues at the centre. During the training, engineering performance is monitored against global benchmarks in terms of quality, efficiency, etc. Engineers typically reach about 60–70 per cent of desired performance levels during the training.

Both on the education and innovation front, companies desire better cooperation with academia. As shown in Figure 4.3, corporations identify the lack of effective collaboration between industry and universities and skill shortages as the main barriers to innovation. Top academic institutions have agreements with corporations, e.g., IIT Kanpur with Chevron, Samsung, Eaton, Boeing, Procter and Gamble (P&G), General Electric, Samtel, Autodesk and Hindustan Aeronautics Limited; IIT Delhi with Freescale, Interra, ST, Nvidia, Cisco, Texas Instruments, Mercedes, TCS and NXP; and the Indian Institute of Science with Intel, Microsoft, Honda, Texas Instruments, Cisco, Boeing, Bosch and Pratt & Whitney. However, structured, widespread cooperation between academia and industry, such as it exists in the US, Sweden or Germany, is lacking.

4 FIGURE 3

Stronger Partnerships between Industry and the Academic World Are of Utmost Importance for India to Foster Innovation

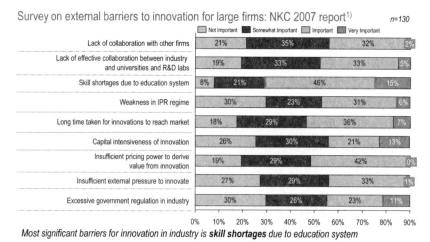

Survey on external barriers to innovation for large firms: NKC 2007 report[1]   n=130

*Most significant barriers for innovation in industry is **skill shortages** due to education system*

1) NKC stands for National Knowledge Commission

Source: National Knowledge Commission Report on 'Innovation in India 2007', Barriers to Innovation, p. 31; Roland Berger analysis

Successful innovation requires the creation of adequate innovation ecosystems or clusters. Beyond universities and industry, all relevant stakeholders need to be part of such an innovation-enabling environment. Initial attempts to build innovation clusters at the state or Central level via so-called innovation councils have been made. Spearheaded by the National Innovation Council and driven via state innovation councils, cluster innovation councils have the following responsibilities:

1. Facilitate collaborations between industry and innovators.
2. Develop technology/business.
3. Act as an incubator for ideas/start-ups.
4. Provide expert advice across domains to all stakeholders.
5. Capture and share knowledge gathered.
6. Actively promote expansion of cluster activities and harness local talent, resources and capabilities to push innovation.
7. Facilitate and help streamline interactions with various government agencies.

The creation of a sustainable partnership model that includes private companies (R&D centres, design and testing centres), innovation platforms (e.g., the National Innovation Council), industry and professional bodies (e.g., CII, FICCI, Assocham[171]), finance (banks, VC, FDI), public research (universities, CSIR, other government centres) and adequate measures regarding infrastructure and policies (physical and social infrastructure, tax policies) is desirable. But to the best of our knowledge, such fully integrated approaches have not been implemented in India as yet.

INDIA'S CLAIM TO FAME: FRUGAL INNOVATION

Technological breakthroughs via structured R&D are not India's current forte. As a consequence, many company executives have come to think of India in terms of jugaad, i.e., quick-fix solutions that address acute customer needs. Examples of jugaad abound—a plastic water bottle used as a gas tank for a modified motorized bicycle, using a motorcycle to drive a pump in the fields, modifying a tractor to turn it into a roadroller, etc. All of these examples can be photographed, and these photos tend to stick in the minds of executives who are less aware of the realities in the country.

While jugaad is a reflection of innovative capability in India, India's real breakthrough innovations have been brought about by 'frugal innovation'. Frugal innovation is a structured innovation process that clearly focuses on delivering customer value at predetermined price points. The basic driver of frugal innovation is the old adage, 'Necessity is the mother of invention'. Resource constraints and the desire to open untapped markets to products and services via adequate price points and acceptable value-for-money propositions are at the heart of the frugal innovation movement.

Frugal markets are driven by the customer and the market rather than by technology. The key questions are: What is the basic functionality that the customer needs? What is the money that he or she may be willing to spend on this functionality? What is the value that convinces the customer to actually buy the product versus continuing with non-consumption? As many of the markets that frugal products target are bottom-of-the-pyramid markets, non-consumption is the main competitor for frugal products. This approach is indeed very different from the technology-focused approach of innovation in developed markets, where 'more complex' and 'more expensive' is often equated with better.

Frugal innovation is not about de-contenting[172] products and reducing quality levels. In some cases, frugal products may have materials and components that cost more than what was commonly used in the original products. This seemingly paradoxical situation is resolved by remembering that frugal products focus on providing exactly the value that is needed. Costly bells and whistles driven by tech-savvy engineers are eliminated in frugal products. This creates cost savings that can be partially reinvested in providing the desired functionality with adequate quality.

Global trends support frugal innovation. As much as 95 per cent of global population growth and 70 per cent of real GDP growth will happen in emerging markets. Asia (excluding Japan) is the main driver, contributing 54 per cent of population growth and 46 per cent of real GDP growth.[173] Developing products and services for the emerging middle class in these countries, slated to constitute around 70 per cent of the global middle class by 2030,[174] is crucial for all players. Frugal products also lead to sustainable development through process optimization and use of environment-friendly methods. Optimized manufacturing processes and reduced product complexity save valuable resources and energy, as already mentioned when we discussed the INR 1 Godrej mosquito repellent. Reusable and recyclable products bring down ownership cost due to residual values and have a positive impact on the environment. Sustainability is inherent in frugal products.

The environment in which much of the new global middle class lives is characterized by a number of constraints:

- low per-capita income in comparison to developed markets,
- weak and highly variable infrastructure,
- non-traditional supply channels,
- weak distribution channels and media infrastructure,
- poor access to electricity and means of transportation,

- low levels of awareness and
- shortage of trained staff to operate modern sophisticated technologies.

Products that can handle such an environment must indeed be frugal, and must therefore fulfil the following criteria:

- Product-related characteristics
  - o **Functional:** Focus on the low-end to middle segment of customer needs, provide value-for-money and quality for customer needs.
  - o **Robust:** Be maintenance-friendly and able to handle challenging infrastructure conditions as described above.
  - o **User-friendly:** Be easy to operate, with little or no training required.
- Market-related characteristics
  - o **Growing:** The business model must be based on high-volume, low-margin innovation rather than the Western approach of low volume, high margin.
  - o **Affordable:** Outcome-focused innovation must provide real value for money to beat non-consumption as the main alternative to frugal products.
  - o Local: Products need to address and solve customer issues in a local context. Exporting products into areas with similar challenges and 'reverse innovation' (see below) are possible, but are not the main driver for frugal products.

The frugal innovation process is as structured as a normal innovation process, with the important difference being that value chain configuration plays an even more important role. Key components of the process are market analysis, product design, value-chain configuration and execution plan, including risk mitigation.

The market analysis starts by identifying customer segments and quantifying potential volumes and growth. A clear definition and understanding of relevant customer segments based on key criteria needs to be established (e.g., related to the type of customer and performance requirements). Market models to assess market volume and growth potential for the segments in focus need to be developed. The total potential needs to be estimated based on scenarios regarding growth, product adoption, price sensitivity, etc. Customer requirements need to be assessed in detail regarding all product dimensions (such as performance, simplicity, robustness). Non-requirements need to be identified equally clearly, as over-specification is not an option in a price-sensitive market. A clear prioritization of customer requirements at this stage also helps decision-making in the development stage. Often, co-creating with customers or quick pilots help identify the needs of customers that are indispensable and really create value.

Subsequently, the revenue model for the product needs to be established. Revenue channels need to be clarified, e.g., for revenue types (for instance, will it be an outright sale or will we offer usage of a product as a service?) or for beneficiary types (e.g., direct beneficiary versus third party). Price points need to be established based on an understanding of the consumption/non-consumption trade-off, available disposable income, estimated price-volume curves, etc.

Product design takes the input of the market analysis and derives potential product options with required features. A high-level bill of materials and target costs are also calculated. The first task is to define realization options and alternatives for the key product features identified in the market analysis phase. Development teams have to ensure that each necessary feature is covered by the various product components and that the number of product components is minimized. The initial bill of materials and product costing can thus be derived from the identified product components.

The value chain configuration phase derives the optimal solution for each step in the value chain, i.e., development, procurement, production footprint and logistics, and marketing and sales. Indicative key questions that are answered include:

- Where and how will we develop the product?
  o What is our engineering footprint?
  o Do we develop components in-house or do we outsource components?
  o What is the product architecture?
  o How can we make it modular and limit the number of components used?
  o How can we optimize the material used? How can we leverage product value management?
- Where do we source from?
  o Which components are potentially available off-the-shelf—preferably in high-volume industries?
  o How can we optimize cost via price optimization, process redesign, technical improvements, supplier integration?
- Where do we produce what?
  o Which production processes optimize cost?
  o Where can we execute them? In-house or via partners?
  o How do we ensure that necessary quality requirements are met?
- What are the material flows?
  o How do we ensure that material flows are optimized?
  o How do we need to configure the supply chain so that cost along the supply chain is minimized yet customers get adequate service?
  o How can we optimize transport costs?

> o How can we optimize planning and forecasting to take out cost?
- Which marketing and sales strategy should we apply?
  > o What kind of marketing channels work with our target group?
  > o How can we reach the target group?
  > o How do we ensure an adequate level of engagement?
  > o How do we ensure after-sales support if necessary?
  > o How do we incorporate customer feedback?

If deviations exist between overall product cost and features and target cost and features, we need to iterate the market, product and value-chain analysis until features and price match customer value-for-money perceptions. Lastly, the results and requirements of the previous three steps will be incorporated into an overall roadmap including business case, risk management, implementation plan and implementation monitoring.

Seen from this angle, frugal innovation shares some commonalities with known innovation and product development processes. The key difference is the focus on payment capability and willingness of customers, and the focus on necessary features that need to be delivered to clients at expected quality levels. This focus drives product and value-chain innovation. This focus is also a cultural break with the common mantra of developed market organizations that concentrate on high-paying customers in the hope that these customers will appreciate the technology that has been developed and will be willing to pay a premium to justify R&D efforts. Cascading across lower-income customers is then seen as an extension of the product life-cycle. Design-to-cost measures and similar approaches exist in companies in the developed world; the new dimension of frugal products is that all these techniques must be brought to bear in an environment of extremely low prices based on a value premise that focuses on high volume and low margins.

Frugal Innovation: Indian Champions Are Leading the Way

Hardly surprisingly, Indian companies have been very adept at understanding customer needs and at fulfilling these needs at affordable price points. This section highlights the efforts of a number of Indian (e.g., Godrej, Tata) as well as fully Indianized global (e.g., HUL) players.

Godrej: Science Rocks![175]

India's fast-moving consumer goods (FMCG) market amounted to USD 47.3 billion in 2015[176] and ranked among the top ten consumer markets globally.[177] A CII study projects a market of USD 103.7 billion by 2020 at a CAGR of 17 per cent.[178] Even if growth only happens at the historic growth rate of 11 per cent, the market size will be USD 79.7 billion in 2020. Either way, it is big. Drivers of the success of FMCG in India are many. Rising incomes are driving purchases, as is an ever-increasing penetration of rural areas. Growth in modern trade and e-commerce supports sales and helps lift up lower penetration and consumption rates to global averages. Favourable demographics and the evolution of consumer lifestyles made more aware by advertisements are driving purchases. Premiumization pushes the demand for higher-priced, better-quality products. Innovative solutions revolutionize the industry by creating new markets at the bottom of the pyramid. In addition, increased scale and spending power in various regions will drive the need towards more fragmented and localized business models. In short, despite a recent tempering in growth rates due to an overall slowdown in economic growth, the Indian FMCG market is complex, exciting and full of opportunities.

The overall FMCG market is split into: food and beverages (19 per cent), healthcare (over-the-counter products and prescription drugs, 33 per cent) and household and personal care (haircare 23 per cent, oral care 14 per cent, home care 6 per cent, skincare 5 per cent, total 48 per cent).[179] Godrej Consumer Products Ltd (GCPL) is mainly present in the household and personal care market with a strong focus on haircare, home care and personal care. GCPL is one of the largest household and personal care companies in India with market leadership in hair colour, household insecticides and liquid detergents, and holds the second position in bath soaps.[180] Direct competitors that cover all three segments similar to Godrej are HUL, P&G and Dabur. GCPL grew at a very healthy CAGR of 22 per cent from FY11 to FY15 to reach a total turnover of INR 8276 crore. Starting from a low base of 34 per cent in FY11, international business amounts to about 47 per cent in FY15. The financial performance of Godrej has been broadly in line with competition, as shown in Figure 4.4.

4 FIGURE 4

The Financial Performance of Godrej Has Been Broadly in Line with Competition

Snapshot of the performance of top players in the Indian FMCG industry

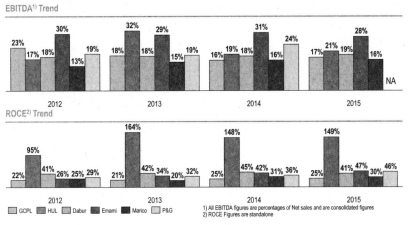

Source: Company annual reports, www.moneycontrol.com; Roland Berger analysis

Godrej's growth has been driven by a stringent execution of the 3x3 strategy, i.e., the desire to build a sizeable business in three geographies (Asia, Africa and Latin America) across three categories (personal care, home care and haircare). The idea is to leverage products in fast-growing, similarly structured markets for the benefit of the overall company.

The execution of this strategy has been a combination of organic growth and acquisitions (rather than JVs). Some of the acquired brands are listed in Figure 4.5. The overall success is impressive.[181] In Indonesia, GCPL leads the market in air fresheners and wet wipes as well as in key modern formats of household insecticides (aerosols, liquid vaporizers and mats). The company leads in ethnic hair colour and hair extensions in Sub-Saharan Africa. In Argentina, Godrej occupies the second position in hair colour. In Chile, it is second in depilatory (hair removal) products and hair colour and third in colour cosmetics. In the UK, it is the leader in stretch mark treatments and second in hand sanitizers. Overall, 37 per cent of Godrej's international sales come from Indonesia, 30 per cent from Africa, 16 per cent from Latin America and 13 per cent from the UK.[182]

4 FIGURE 5

GCPL over the Decade Has Acquired Several Assets in Growing Markets, Eight of Those between 2010 and 2012

GCPL has key international markets in South East Asia, Africa, Latin America and UK

Region	International Net Sales [INR Cr. FY 15]	Segments	Key acquisitions/ brands acquired
> Indonesia	> 1496	> Home Insecticides > Air Care > Baby Care	PT Megasari Makmur, HIT, STELLA, mitu
> Africa	> 1213	> Hair Care > Home Insecticides > Soaps	DARLING/Amigos, Rapidol, Kinky, TURA, FRIKA, e, Valon
> Latin America	> 243	> Hair Care > Color Cosmetics > Skin Care	Argencos, 919ROBY, COSMETICA, U2, Ilicit, PAMELA GRANT, issue, Villeneuve
> UK	> 526	> Personal Care	KEYLINE BRANDS LTD, CUTICURA, Soft& Gentle

Source: Author's calculation using data on international sales from GCPL annual report 2014-15, p. 229, and GCPL company investor presentation, June 2015, p. 14,
http://www.godrejcp.com/Resources/uploads/meet_presentation/GCPLInvestorsPresentationJune2015.pdf; Roland Berger analysis

Key to the successful acquisitions for GCPL is its partnering with the acquired companies. As a general principle, acquired companies and management teams are given significant freedom to continue to drive their markets, as it is expected that they know the local dynamics better than teams from headquarters. Synergies are primarily driven by the backend (such as HR, finance and controlling and IT). Product synergies and cross-selling opportunities are identified via cooperation with teams. A number of examples will be discussed below. Note that while this approach to acquisitions is generally assumed to be pursued by Indian companies, many counter examples exist as well, as we will discuss in Chapter 8.

Today, GCPL sees itself as a global company with a strong focus on fast-growing, emerging markets, since these are best suited to the specific advantages of Godrej. The company is in pursuit of an ambitious vision to grow ten-fold in ten years. This aspiration translates into a CAGR of close to 30 per cent and will be achieved in large part via organic growth and to about a third via inorganic growth. The main drivers for inorganic growth are a significant position of the acquired brands in the local market (usually first or second) and a good cultural fit with Godrej (typically achieved by acquiring family-owned businesses). An overall fit with the 3x3 strategy and an opportunity to create value via backend synergies, innovation or cross-launch of products across geographies are also important.

One of Godrej's strengths lies in its ability to question the status quo and reinvent itself despite a long and illustrious history of 118 years. This is very visible in the R&D division of GCPL. Sunder Mahadeva, head of R&D, points out:

> About nine years ago, we started driving a project to challenge all
> assumptions that we had about our development processes and

products . . . For example, all testing and validation processes were thoroughly analysed to see whether they are still relevant. In some cases, we found that lengthy evaluation processes were inherited from the past, when ingredient quality was not uniform. Today, input material is clearly specified and such processes are no longer relevant. Taking them out greatly reduces our development time versus our competitors and increases our flexibility accordingly. In other cases, we asked if a product that had a particular active ingredient at 3 per cent could also be made with only 2 per cent active ingredient based on a better understanding of customer use cases. Again, such analysis allowed us to drive down cost.

Sunder is convinced that a thorough understanding of the chemistry of product ingredients is necessary to cut down development times and testing cycles. For example, a thorough knowledge of chemistry allows Godrej to use materials with predictable stability criteria for the product in question. Rather than relying too heavily on testing factors such as temperature range or ageing, Sunder drives his team to use materials that fulfil the functional and quality needs of the product from the word go. 'You are not allowed to plug stability testing into your product development timeline,' says Sunder. 'You will understand the raw materials and their interactions and use these such that you will control the properties rather than test for them.'

Continuously driving small innovations pays off. For example, rather than testing hair colour via human hair trials, the team developed multi-fabric strip testing[183] that is easy and fast to use, and allows reproducible testing and formula optimization across a range of colours. The focus is to remove the subjectivity of human testing from testing procedures and to drive R&D towards a number- and data-based approach. According to Sunder, these approaches and continuous improvements allow Indian FMCG players to be faster and more agile than their MNC counterparts. 'Supplier qualification is fast-tracked to one to three months for local players. In comparison, we know that many organizations follow unchallenged protocols that need nearly six to nine months for the same,' he says.

It is important to optimize the way the company rewards and recruits talent as well. GCPL introduced two dual-career tracks in its R&D department three years ago. In addition to the standard management track, a separate technical track was introduced. The importance of the latter was emphasized by giving separate salaries and higher increases to technical contributors. In order to drive thinking out-of-the-box, a number of technical experts outside of the normal talent pool were hired, such as polymer chemists, flavour and fibre experts, etc. In the process, the average age of the research department moved from forty-nine to thirty-six years. Combined with a changed incentive system, where only 30 per cent of the overall bonus was tied to launches and 70 per cent to new initiatives, a significant stimulus towards breakthrough innovation and thinking was created.

Strong cross-functional teams from R&D, marketing, production, and procurement—under the leadership of the CEO Vivek Gambhir and Executive Director Nisaba Godrej— drive cooperation and joint problem-solving. 'In many MNCs and other organizations, marketing and sales is dominant,' says Sunder. 'Here, the various business functions are not subservient to each other, but every brief is thoroughly discussed in the innovation management meeting. It is a multidirectional rather than unidirectional innovation process.'

The process seems to work. The company was able to launch a number of blockbuster successes in the past. For example, the observation that widely used, alcohol-based air fresheners for vehicles often spill under operating conditions in India led to the development of a transparent gel-based solution. This solution has a significantly higher perfume load; this means that not only does it not spill, but it is also less voluminous than the alcohol-based solutions.

Another innovation stemmed from leveraging the Argentinian teams' technology. The Argentinian business sold hair colouring cream in sachets. Godrej assumed that a similar product would be a great opportunity for a 'mastige' (mass prestige) application in India. 'The leading hair colour cream player at that point had a non-sachet based hair care solution for around INR 150; we could have come up with an offer around INR 130,' says Sunder. 'Rather than that, we decided to upgrade our existing hair colour powder customers who would spend INR 15 per colouring to a cream-based product and aimed for a target price of INR 30.' Creating packaging with local suppliers was key in attaining this goal. Machines for filling the cream into the sachets were procured from local vendors at about one-fourth the cost of the imported machines in the Argentinian factory. Productivity in the factory was increased by reducing cycle time in half, from six to three hours. The standard wisdom was that ingredients for the cream had to be mixed hot and cooled down. The team experimented successfully with a 75 per cent hot/25 per cent cold mixture, which brought down cooling times without affecting product stability. Washing times were reduced by adding colour from the bottom of the mixer rather than from the top, reducing splash, a technique borrowed from the toothpaste-making process. Target prices were met via a number of other process innovations, creating a new segment and feeding cost optimization measures back to Argentina to improve business performance over there.

Lastly, the one-rupee Fast Card was created to provide farmers in rural India with a night of mosquito-free sleep by burning a sheet of paper.[184] In this case, a similar product was available since Godrej had acquired an Indonesian brand called Hit. Again, meeting the aggressive cost target was possible via close collaboration with suppliers. For example, the standard process for preparing the paper was a combination of spraying the paper with a water-soluble reagent that increased the burning properties of the paper, drying the paper, then spraying it with oil that contained the active, mosquito-killing agent and drying it again. Rather than working with a cost- and time-intensive spray–dry–spray–dry cycle, the team at Godrej worked with a supplier to eliminate this cycle and integrate with it with the paper pulp drying process. Other challenges—for example, containment of the reagent—were solved by detailed chemical knowhow. Since the active ingredient was known, so were potential chemical barriers, and hence, a plastic sachet was designed, together with the supplier, that contained the active ingredient but did not have to undergo a lengthy trial-and-error process. As in the case of the hair colouring cream, the Fast Card created a new category and was a runaway success with a turnover of INR 120–130 crore after eighteen months. Four months after launch, the company was struggling to meet demand, and shop owners sold ten cards at INR 15, a solid mark-up versus the base price of INR 10 for ten cards. 'The journey is not over,' says Sunder. 'When you go back to basics and avoid doing anything that does not add value, the sky is the limit.'

Sunil Kataria, business head for India and SAARC, believes that the company's persistent focus on its core areas of personal, home and hair care helps it to be successful. While business that is adjacent to these core activities can and sometimes is pursued, the purpose of the company is driven by personal, home and hair care where products, value chains and customers are well known. Overall, he sees Godrej as a very successful mastige player, i.e., a company that upgrades mass consumption segments and thereby creates new markets. He points out:

> Before we entered the hair cream market, the leading cream player had sold hair cream in India at a price point of around INR 150 per unit, which allowed up to three usages. The segment grew steadily at 10–15 per cent annually, but after more than a decade, penetration of hair cream in India only amounted to around 7 per cent. Rather than creating yet another product that marginally increases penetration and fights with the leader for a limited space, we decided to upgrade our mass customers that were using hair powders in the range of INR 15 per usage to a colouring cream. Our whole strategy here is simple. We look at untapped, new, to-be-created market segments to grow volume and to disrupt the market rather than at taking market share from existing players.

A good understanding of customers helps. The cream contains no ammonia, reflecting the widespread perception that ammonia damages the hair during applications. It is easy to use, safe to apply and only takes thirty minutes. With its attractive price point of INR 30 per usage, Godrej's product is a real alternative to henna, the natural hair colour that is otherwise widely used in India. With an upgradation ratio of 25 per cent, i.e., 25 per cent of Godrej hair cream users previously used Godrej hair powder, the conquest rate of 75 per cent speaks for itself.

In hand wash, GCPL also focuses on upgrading mass customers to the mastige segment. Here, design plays a major role to ensure a premium position of Godrej Protect versus competitors such as Dettol. Rather than focusing on clinical efficacy, GCPL positions their products via smell, touch and appealing packaging. Says Sunil:

We have a premium position in the hand wash segment and realize that people would like to have dispensers in their bathrooms that look good. As incomes and aspirations go up, clinical efficiency is not enough to satisfy customers, they need to feel good about your product and happy that it is made out of all natural ingredients.

Overall, GCPL's approach is a combination of disruptive innovations and evolution that demands sharp differentiation. Sunil points out,

You can't expect customers to create the future . . . They will be able to imagine things that differ say by 10 per cent from existing solutions. Real value will be created when you look at differentiation to the tune of at least 30 per cent. For that, you need a collaborative, open culture that realizes that innovation can come from anywhere. Relying only on quantitative and qualitative customer studies with their many in-built filters is just not enough.

To drive an improved, fast and detailed customer understanding, GCPL launched ConQuest (consumer quest), modelled according to data analysis practices prevalent in the telecommunications industry. One component of ConQuest is that managers are trained on how to do qualitative research and go out into the market to test product acceptance. Rather than relying on outsourced research with its complex processes and potentially high transmission losses (write research brief, share with agency, design research, execute in small towns, employ third-party freelancers for the same, etc.), GCPL started to insource qualitative research to challenge outside results and improve their own understanding.

According to Praveen Dalal, executive vice-president, sales,

The cultural change that has happened over the last few years is amazing . . . In the last three years alone, we have had three or four big inventions that have upgraded customers from mass to mastige like the hair colour cream, reinforced our premium, e.g., in hand wash, and taken new solutions to the masses like Fast Card. Solutions have been driven by out-of-the-box thinking. Look at our anti-roach gel as an example. Normal aerosols or chalk that you can use only kills on contact, is rather messy and only effective for a limited time. Our gel is clean, roaches that eat the gel die, and because roaches eat dead roaches, the effect is perpetuated for four or five more months!

With the increased speed of innovation and a slew of new launches for both larger and smaller brands, the rest of the organization had to change to keep up. Processes needed to be strengthened and teams IT-enabled. As an example, all 2000 salespeople work on hand-held devices that are integrated with the management information systems platform. This enables steering of sales processes and outcomes via timely data analysis and predefined workflows. The market approach had to be modified as well. Premium outlets were defined with a wider range and higher-value products. Field representatives need to spend more time with these outlets to go through approximately 300 SKUs.[185] Mass outlets stock only 50–60 SKUs and can be reviewed by field agents that cover a correspondingly larger number of outlets.

Excitement about innovation and the opportunities in emerging markets, a strong social contract between employees and management, as well as a can-do attitude are characteristic of GCPL today. This should enable the company to continue to strengthen its position as a true global giant focused on emerging markets where frugal innovation matters.

ChotuKool: Carrying Cooled Essentials

Conventional refrigerators in India by companies such as Samsung, LG, Panasonic and Godrej cost about INR 8000. Their high cost, big size, high energy consumption and lack of portability are serious issues for rural customers. First and foremost, rural customers need the capacity to keep milk, vegetables and food fresh for one or maybe two days to prevent waste. This functionality needs to be enabled in an environment with erratic power supply.

The potential market in India for refrigerators is huge. As of 2011–12, only 9.4 per cent of rural households and 43.8 per cent of urban households reported possessing a refrigerator, hence the potential market size covers approximately 197 million households.[186] The ChotuKool by Godrej & Boyce[187] was developed as a low-energy cooling solution at a price of INR 3790, i.e., less than half the price of standard refrigerators. In terms of total cost over a five-year period, a conventional refrigerator would cost about INR 13,472 including power cost and maintenance, whereas a ChotuKool is estimated to cost about INR 6919, a 49 per cent difference.[188]

Value chain innovations for the ChotuKool are spread across R&D, distribution and end use. In terms of R&D, the ChotuKool uses a solid-state, chip-based system and no compressors, similar to the cooling system of a computer. It is battery-operated but can also be powered through an inverter. The top-loading cooler keeps cold air in the cooling compartment during opening, versus the front-loading design of standard refrigerators. High-end insulation ensures longer cooling times should electricity fail (cooling time without electricity is more than double that of conventional refrigerators). The ice compartment is eliminated and the overall design is simple with just twenty components versus 200 in standard refrigerators. As a consequence, the refrigerator is service-free, easy to use and easy to clean. The fridge is portable and can be customized in terms of colour and graphics. The product development process heavily leveraged input from villagers and female focus groups to identify essential product needs.

In terms of distribution, Godrej leverages order and delivery through post offices. Home delivery is done through postal vans, postmen are trained to give demos during village visits and special kiosks are set up for display and demos. In addition, B2B sales are happening directly to local shops. Marketing is done mostly through word-of-mouth as this is indeed a very effective way of convincing rural customers that the ChotuKool is a valid alternative to non-consumption.

The performance of the ChotuKool versus conventional refrigerators is summarized in Figure 4.6. Potential niche applications for developed markets are clearly possible, such as for sporting events or fishing trips.

4 FIGURE 6

Low-Cost Refrigerator Developed by Godrej: Portable Cooling at About Half the Price and Operating Cost

IMPACT OF INNOVATION

	Conventional Refrigerators	Godrej's Chotukool
Price	min. INR 8,000	INR 3,790
No of components	200	20
Power consumption	90-100 W	62 W
Cooling time without power	90 min	180 min
Size, weight	80 kg, 4 x 1.9 x 1.2 cu. ft.	7.3 kg, 2.4 x 1.4 x 1.2 cu. ft.
Capacity	min. 150 ltrs	35 ltrs
Cooling range	-5°C - 10°C	5°C - 15°C
Power used	Electricity	Electricity / Battery / Invertor

> An affordable, **low energy solution** for refrigeration for the rural masses
> A potential **market size of around 197 million** households
> No operational and maintenance cost for Chotukool, low acquisition cost

Source: Chotukool website, https://www.chotukool.com/assets/pdf/gck_brochure.pdf; Presentation by Godrej at CII Cost Congress 2011, summarized at 'Godrej chotukool challenges in disruptive innovation', http://jugaadtoinnovation.blogspot. de/2011/12/godrej-chotukool-challenges-in.html; Roland Berger analysis

Low-Cost Water Purifiers: Fighting Diarrhoea and Other Diseases

Existing water purifiers in India from companies such as Kent, Aquaguard, HUL, and others cost around INR 5000 and purify water using ultraviolet rays (UV) or reverse osmosis (RO). The high cost of these water purifiers keeps them out of the reach of a majority of the Indian population. In addition, the poor structure of many of the low-income houses does not permit the installation of these typically wall-mounted devices. Electricity fluctuations and lack of running water in rural areas additionally impact the performance of UV- or RO-based devices. Coupled with the fact that about 8 per cent of India's population does not have access to improved water sources[189] and the widespread lack of awareness about safe drinking water, this creates both a large public health liability and a tremendous market opportunity.

Two companies, Tata with the Tata Swach and HUL with the HUL Pureit, have addressed this market opportunity by developing low-cost purifiers at a price of about INR 1000. These products are suitable for rural use as they do not require running water or electricity. Both solutions are portable and easy to use as well as effective in killing pathogens. They drastically decrease the chances of waterborne diseases, which kill about 1000 children a day in India.[190] Running costs are about 44 per cent lower for Pureit and at least 68 per cent lower for Swach.

In terms of value chain innovation, the Tata Swach replaced the UV/RO process by using paddy husk ash coated with silver nanoparticles in a sedimentation filter so that no electricity is required. Sales are driven via tie-ups with NGOs and micro-finance institutions through village-level entrepreneurs. Also, society and school outreach programmes drove a safe drinking water awareness campaign that reached 20,000 households in three months.

The HUL Pureit uses a four-stage purification method in which a microfibre mesh removes suspended particles, a compact carbon trap removes parasites, a germ kill processor replaces UV/RO to kill bacteria and viruses and a polisher removes chlorine and odour. The device is battery-run and portable, similar to Swach. HUL drives sales via several channels. A direct-to-home demonstration system is in place as well as a doctor partnership programme and a kiosk demonstration programme. In addition, HUL leverages their Shakti network, about 66,000 village-level entrepreneurs who reach most of India's rural areas and sell HUL products.

A technical comparison of the various purifiers is given in Figure 4.7. As we can see, the low-cost water purifiers are as effective as conventional UV and RO systems. In terms of sales, Pureit outperforms Swach by a factor of 1.5 with about 5 million units sold in nine developing countries at the end of 2012.[191] Clearly, effective sales channels are key when bringing frugal products to market. Focusing on the entire value chain rather than just the development effort decides the fate of frugal products.

However, looking at 90–100 million people in India who do not have access to safe drinking water,[192] even the Pureit sales may seem low compared to the obvious benefit that they generate. Here, it is important to remind ourselves that the main competition for frugal products is non-consumption. A case in point is the Prime Minister's Swachh Bharat campaign. A main focus of this campaign is to eradicate open defecation in India.[193] The immediate thought is that building toilets via government and private funds in all villages and in schools would bring down surface-water contamination, reduce diarrhoea and similar disease-related deaths in children, and improve enrolment of girl children in schools due to the privacy that dedicated female toilets provide. In short, it is a no-brainer. However, to the surprise of the Swachh Bharat teams, a sizeable amount of awareness needs to be built up in the villages regarding health benefits, reduced healthcare costs, etc., to drive adoption of toilets. As a matter of fact, rather than donating toilets, it is more beneficial to convince communities to invest or co-invest in toilets themselves. In other words, it is not about spending money, it is about communicating sufficient value to rural consumers so that they want to adopt the products.

As in the case of the ChotuKool, applications of the Swach and Pureit in developed economies exist. Potential opportunities are disaster relief agencies, military applications as well as camping applications. These areas are waiting to be tapped.

4 FIGURE 7

Tata Swach and HUL Pureit: Fighting Disease, Diarrhoea and Loss of Life in an Affordable Manner

IMPACT OF INNOVATION

Features	Boiling	Pureit	Swach	UV	RO
Safety from germs					
• Bacteria kill	✓	✓	✓	✓	✓
• Virus kill	✓	✓	✓	✓	✓
• Parasite removal	✓	✓	✗	✓	✓
• End of life indicator	✓	✓	✓	✗	✗
• Auto-shut of system	✗	✓	✓	✗	✗
No need of electricity	✓	✓	✓	✗	✗
No need of pressurized water tap	✓	✓	✓	✗	✗
Good water taste	✗	✓	✓	✓	✓
No water wastage	✗	✓	✓	✓	✗
Price Range (INR)[1]	Cooking gas used	1,000	800	5,000-11,500	8,500-37,500
Low in-use energy consumption	✗	✓	✓	✗	✗

■ Acquisition cost (INR)
▨ Operating cost per year (INR)[1]

5,000 — 1,025 — 1,000 — 876 — 800 — 438

UV/RO   Pureit   Swach

1)Asuming 10 litre consumption everyday for a family of 4. Cost of electricity ~ INR 3/ unit

SALES UPTO 2012

> Swach ~ 3 million units

> Pureit ~ 5 million units; sold in 9 developing nations

Source: Charles Leadbeater, 'The Frugal Innovator: Creating Change on a Shoestring Budget', p. 107;
C.K. Prahalad, 'The Fortune at the Bottom of the Pyramid, Revised and Updated 5th Anniversary edition', p.. 272

Source: Rangan, V. Kasturi and Mona Sinha, 'Hindustan Unilever's "Pureit" Water Purifier', Harvard Business School Case 511-067, February 2011 (Revised April 2013); Roland Berger analysis

Husk Power Systems: Biomass Power Plants for an Illuminated India

India's lighting and cooking needs are often fulfilled via kerosene lamps and ovens since many areas still don't have electricity. The average household cost for the same amounts to about INR 250 per month per household. In 2011, 44 per cent of rural households lacked access to electricity, and with monthly household income ranging between INR 8,250 and INR 9,500, the potential market size is about 370 million people.[194] In addition, the use of kerosene causes indoor air pollution, which is hazardous.

HPS, an Indian start-up company from Bihar, developed a small biomass power plant that provides a low-cost, safe and reliable source of power. It uses rice husk as a fuel, a waste product of the rice milling process, and brings down the cost of lighting and cooking to about INR 150 per month per household. Rice husk is a renewable and easily available energy resource. India produces enough rice husk to electrify all of India's 1,25,000 villages. Currently, rice husk is disposed of in landfills.

There are a number of value-chain innovations that have been developed by HPS. In terms of R&D, the company developed a new gasification technology that can work with multiple types of feedstock such as rice husk, wheat husk, etc. The engine runs on single-fuel mode; no diesel is required. The design allows easy disposal of biomass char, which otherwise would result in tar formation. Rice husk is purchased from local farmers and fed into the locally manufactured gasifier. Its design is simple and minimalistic, relying on cheap local resources such as bamboo poles instead of cement poles, etc. Each house in the village is connected to the plant via a wire. The business model is a pay-per-use model in which households pay INR 150 per month for six to eight hours of power for two CFL lamps and for cell phone recharging (30 watts) each day. Business subscribers pay INR 225–250 per month (60–75 watts). Cheap prepaid meters have been designed to monitor usage. The operating model is optimized as well. A low-cost, remote plant-monitoring system via the Internet is installed. Local people are trained to operate the plant (four employees per plant), which reduces cost and increases local acceptance of the plant. A cluster of four to five plants is supervised by special personnel to ensure cleaning and maintenance work is done according to specifications.

The HPS business model has been structured along three types to address local conditions. A build–maintain model entails HPS building a plant and selling it to an independent owner who also operates it. A build–own–maintain model implies that HPS owns the plant; however, it is operated by a local who puts in 10 per cent of the cost. Lastly, a build–own–operate–maintain model implies that HPS owns and operates the plant. This model allows flexibility and also scalability, as can be seen in Figure A.14 in the Appendix. In six years, HPS went from one installation to eighty-four installations across the country.

Revenue streams come in from various sources. The immediate revenue stream is linked to electricity sales. In addition, rice husk char, the by-product of the biomass gasification process, can be monetized by making incense sticks, and silica precipitation can be used in cement. Lastly, money is made via certified emission reduction and verified emission reduction credit sales.

HPS's model is economically very attractive. Operational profitability is reached after two to three months with a 20 per cent gross margin at the plant level. Breakeven is possible after two to three years. In terms of equipment life, the gasifier has a lifetime of twelve years, the engine of twenty years and the bamboo poles of one to two years.[195] The installation cost is relatively low, with less than INR 60,000 per kilowatt (less than USD 1300 per kilowatt). The average cost for a gasifier-based biomass power plant installation amounts to INR 2.1 lakh. The operational cost is less than INR 7 per kilowatt hours (less than USD 0.15 per kilowatt hours; see Figure A.14 in the Appendix).[196]

In terms of impact, HPS provides safe, reliable energy (93 per cent availability) to villages and improves their quality of life as well as reduces energy costs by 50 per cent, both for households and for village businesses. Farmers profit from the approach by earning an additional INR 11,500–14,000 a month from selling rice husk to HPS.[197] Plus, employment is generated in the villages via the operation of the plant. Annual savings of 2.7 million litres of kerosene and 18,000 litres of diesel improve India's BoP and at the same time lead to a reduction of GHG emissions by 8100 metric tons of CO_2 per year (see Figure 4.8).

4 FIGURE 8

Husk Power Plants Have Not Only Resulted in Increased Household Savings, but Provided for Additional Incomes for Households As Well

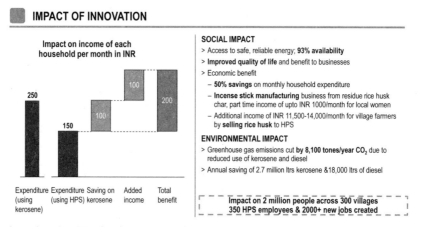

IMPACT OF INNOVATION

Impact on income of each household per month in INR

Expenditure (using kerosene) — 250
Expenditure (using HPS) — 150
Saving on kerosene — 100
Added income — 100
Total benefit — 200

SOCIAL IMPACT
> Access to safe, reliable energy; **93% availability**
> **Improved quality of life** and benefit to businesses
> Economic benefit
  – **50% savings** on monthly household expenditure
  – **Incense stick manufacturing** business from residue rice husk char, part time income of upto INR 1000/month for local women
  – Additional income of INR 11,500-14,000/month for village farmers by **selling rice husk** to HPS

ENVIRONMENTAL IMPACT
> Greenhouse gas emissions cut **by 8,100 tones/year** CO_2 due to reduced use of kerosene and diesel
> Annual saving of 2.7 million ltrs kerosene &18,000 ltrs of diesel

┌───┐
Impact on 2 million people across 300 villages
350 HPS employees & 2000+ new jobs created
└───┘

Source: Sevea Association, 'Case Study: Husk Power Systems', February 2013, http://seveaconsulting.com/page/what-we-do Information from company website, http://www.huskpowersystems.com/innerPage.php?pageT=Community%20Impact&page_id=81; Roland Berger analysis

Frugal Innovation: A Must for Global Players

Frugal innovation is not only for emerging market players—it is also relevant for global MNCs. Leveraging the volume opportunity that emerging markets offer is not possible without a frugal approach. In addition, the fact that frugal engineering minimizes resource utilization is relevant from an overall sustainability perspective. Last but not least, being able to compete with a frugal product and services portfolio does protect global MNCs against emerging market competitors that otherwise could grow unchecked and threaten dominant market positions in emerging and developed markets.

Competitors from the developed world are challenged in emerging markets such as India. Their general assumption is that innovation stems from relatively high-cost research. Their dominant belief is that new technologies will be cascaded from well-to-do to less-well-to-do customers as a function of time in order to optimize financial benefits from the new technology. High-tech is seen as a high-margin, lower-volume game whereas emerging markets play the high-volume, low-margin game and are still able to achieve adequate absolute profits overall. Engineers from the developed world are not tuned to the needs of emerging market customers and hence challenged to develop products that meet their needs. At the same time, headquarter-centric MNCs are not set up for efficient bidirectional communication to and from emerging markets.

The risk of ignoring industry disruption by new MNCs originating out of large, emerging countries such as India and China is real. Take Haier, the Chinese manufacturer of home appliances, as an example. Known for producing low-cost, high-quality appliances with a thorough understanding of customer needs, Haier has limited product lines that are precisely targeted to well-defined market segments. Haier succeeded in market entry into developed markets by first leveraging underserved niche segments. For example, it made its name in the US by providing compact refrigerators to US students and by selling wine coolers. Subsequently, the company established relationships with Walmart, Best Buy and other major distribution partners. It was then quick to expand into other major home appliances such as washing machines, air conditioners and dishwashers. Today, Haier is the world leader in the white goods segment by retail volumes for six years running, with annual sales revenue in 2014 of USD 32.8 billion and a corresponding global market share of 10.2 per cent.[198]

Similarly, Lenovo leveraged its low-cost manufacturing base and dominant market position in China, the world's largest and fastest-growing personal computer (PC) market, to build global scale and dominance. Lenovo's acquisition of IBM's PC business in 2005 put the company in third position in the global PC market. In 2015, with 20 per cent market share worldwide, Lenovo had risen to become the world's number-one PC maker and is a serious threat to global giants such as Dell and Hewlett-Packard.[199]

As a consequence, many global companies have started their own frugal engineering projects. However, a recent Roland Berger survey[200] that covered more than sixty participants across industrials, automotive, consumer goods, pharmaceuticals, services and other industries, highlights that less than half of the surveyed companies are satisfied with the sales success of their frugal products. On the profit front, the news is even more sobering. Only 29 per cent rate the profit success of their frugal products as high or very high. However, in terms of importance, the surveyed companies expect the sales contribution of frugal products to nearly double from 12.3 per cent to 22.3 per cent over a period of five years. A similar growth is expected in terms of profits (growth from 10.4 per cent to 18.4 per cent). Remarkably, these results are homogeneous across industries. In short, developed market companies have woken up to the need of frugal innovation. Many are in the process of adjusting their innovation processes, but few have cracked the frugal innovation code.

Siemens: German Engineering the SMART Way

A few global companies have mastered the frugal engineering game. Siemens, the global engineering giant from Germany, is one such company.[201] Globally, Siemens has a turnover of about EUR 75.6 billion,[202] which is pretty evenly spread over its various lines of business such as power and gas (17 per cent), healthcare (17 per cent), energy management (16 per cent), process industries and drives (13 per cent), digital factory (13 per cent), mobility (10 per cent) and others. The company also offers financial services to its customers, which are not taken into account in the above split. With 3,48,000 employees worldwide, Siemens generates about 20 per cent of its turnover in Asia and Australia (EUR 15.1 billion) where it employs 61,500 people. Siemens' Indian operations generated a turnover of about EUR 1.60 billion[203] with about 16,600 employees in the country. India, hence, amounts to 2.1 /10.5 per cent of Siemens's global/Asian revenues and 4.8/26.9 per cent of its global/ Asian workforce. In India, Siemens generates about 30 per cent of its business through the energy management division, which provides products, systems, solutions and services for transmission and distribution of electrical energy. About 15 per cent of FY15 revenues were earned by the power and gas division,[204] another 15 per cent by the digital factory division,[205] 14 per cent by the process industries and drives division[206] and 14 per cent by the healthcare division.[207]

Despite a long history in the country, it took time for Siemens to realize that German-made and German-engineered products were a tough sell in the extreme value-for-money-conscious Indian environment. Analysing the product value chain from product management, R&D, sourcing, manufacturing and sales, Siemens realized that local sourcing and manufacturing had the potential of reducing cost by 20–40 per cent. Moving to local R&D could drive costs down further with an overall reduction of 40–60 per cent. Clearly, stronger localization provided a significant, untapped opportunity for the company.

Recognizing market opportunities in the mid-market space (see Figure 3.4), as well as increasing competition from emerging market players, Siemens started driving its SMART products initiative. New SMART products were to be developed that were Simple and had basic features, were Maintenance-friendly, Affordable, Reliable and robust, and their Time-to-market had to be minimal. Siemens' traditional segments in India (so-called M1 and M2 in Siemens classification, i.e., high-end machines and solutions) amounted to an overall market opportunity of USD 7.4 billion in FY15. The value and low-cost segments M3 and M4 combined, however, offered a market opportunity of USD 10.3 billion. A potential of 58 per cent of the overall market had so far not been explored by Siemens. This challenge was not limited to India alone. Brazil and China were facing the same issues and launched their SMART initiatives in conjunction with India.

SMART products were launched in FY11 with the clear intention to protect market share in the M1/M2 segments and to enter into the M3/M4 segments. Success was quickly visible. In FY13, SMART products contributed globally to about 9 per cent of the company's turnover (about EUR 1 billion). In India, this number is higher at 13 per cent. Cross-functional teams generated sixty-three SMART product ideas out of which thirty-two have been already realized and launched in the market and another three are in the pipeline. Twenty-two out of the thirty-five ideas are already ready for export. In line with Siemens' business focus in India, most of the ideas are centred around the core areas of business.[208]

While a roughly 50 per cent cost advantage in terms of engineering in India versus Germany was positive for the business case of SMART products, a major benefit also resulted from reduced turnaround times. With 1.8 per cent of Siemens' global turnover,

India is an important part of the Siemens universe, however, there are many other parts of equal or higher importance in terms of revenue and profits. As a consequence, getting time from German engineers proved to be a major challenge, a common experience for many managers in MNCs in India. Giving Indian engineers an opportunity to design market-adequate products gave them a sense of purpose and drive that reduced time to market significantly. With profit margins on SMART products that are only 100–200 basis points (bps) lower than those of standard products, the local teams clearly rose to the occasion.

While SMART has been a success so far, challenges remain. Leveraging SMART products in export markets needs to be aligned with the global sales strategy of Siemens and hence limits volume potential and economies of scale. Intra-company competition in markets where SMART products would substitute conventional solutions is something that most companies would try to avoid. The engineering of SMART products is still tightly integrated with Germany, with German engineers signing off on Indian developments, impacting flexibility and speed to market. So far, SMART has been implemented as a one-off effort. Turning it into a continuous process is necessary and still an open point. However, time is in India's favour. As markets grow in importance, global companies have but one option, that is, to engage deeply with the market across all steps of the value chain.[209]

Frugal engineering is also important in the context of reverse innovation. Bloated healthcare systems in the US and in Europe need cost-effective solutions to provide affordable healthcare to all. Consumers who have suffered from the effects of the global financial crisis are value-conscious and will be open to value-for-money products. Eco-minded consumers would like to consume with the minimum impact on the planet possible. As time progresses, the opportunities of frugal innovation in developed markets are bound to increase. Companies that do not invest in these areas now risk being left behind.[210]

DENYING FACTOR COST ADVANTAGES: THE MNC EMPIRE STRIKES BACK

Infosys, Wipro, TCS and many other Indian software companies have threatened to unseat the traditional dominance of Western players by leveraging Indian labour cost advantages. Promising and delivering quick cost savings by hiring, training and scaling up resources from the unending pool of software engineers provided the Indian players with a convincing value proposition. This value proposition has found favour with US, European and Japanese customers. Some of the incumbents such as Accenture and IBM understood the severity of this challenge and took it seriously. IBM, for example, recognized India as a potential future market as well as a convenient talent pool. The company realized that it needed to work with a global delivery model based mostly on Indian employees to be able to take on the Indian giants, both at home and in IBM's core markets. As a consequence, the company developed a vast pool of human resources in India. This was achieved incrementally via relocation of long-term IBM employees from overseas and by hiring top talent based in India. Within five years, IBM in India employed about 30 per cent of IBM's global workforce (about 4,13,000 people in 2014)[211] and had a dominant market share of 12 per cent (2014), in the Indian software market.[212]

The same desire to leverage factor cost advantages and to pre-empt potential emerging market competition coming out of India explains the rapid increase in R&D centres of multinational companies in the country. During the last fifteen years, the number of MNCs with R&D centres has grown from 191 prior to 2000 to 906 in 2014[213] with major capacity additions happening during 2003–06.[214] Most of the centres are located in cities such as Bengaluru, Delhi, Mumbai, Chennai and Hyderabad. Since 2005, MNCs have also spread out to Tier-2 cities such as Coimbatore in search of lower-cost locations (land, salaries, etc.).

Global trends will require the engineering organizations of tomorrow to have more effective global coverage. The need for frugal engineering and the requirement to be close to frugal customers has been discussed above. In addition, the development of new lead markets due to an overall shift of sales and production to BRIC and other emerging markets has been highlighted in the case study of Maruti Suzuki regarding small cars.

A rise in new technologies (materials, electrification, connectivity, etc.) puts tremendous pressure on engineering organizations in the West to deliver a multitude of technologies at costs that are the same or even lower than today. The shortage of qualified employees, especially in the traditional triad markets, makes it necessary to leverage local talent in emerging markets. Cost and turnaround advantages, e.g., double-shift work for Indian engineers versus single-shift operations in Germany, are equally relevant in today's environment of cut-throat competition.

Last but not least, two major hurdles for offshoring engineering work to India have vanished in the last ten to fifteen years. In the late 1990s and early 2000s, finding engineers with ten to fifteen years' experience, for example, in domains such as automotive, was difficult. Also, global delivery models were still being developed and coordination for communication, quality control, etc., was sometimes cumbersome. Today, these factors no longer apply.

The rise of MNC R&D centres in India is part of a larger trend. Business enterprise R&D investments have diversified over the last decade. The share of various countries in overseas R&D expenditure of US firms between 1994 and 2008 has shifted slightly away from the EU, Canada and Japan (about 80 per cent in 1994,

about 75 per cent in 2008).[215] Countries that benefited from this
trend include China and India, but also Switzerland, Israel and
Korea. Interestingly, reverse BERD investments are happening as
well. While US companies accounted for 82.5 per cent of the BERD
of all non-European companies in the EU in 2007, India ranked
fourth after Japan and Canada with a comparatively small EUR
132 million or 0.8 per cent of total inward BERD.[216] India took the
lead from countries such as South Korea, the Russian Federation
and China. Most of India's investment flowed into the UK (EUR
77 million) followed by Germany (EUR 21 million).

Chinese, Indian and Japanese firms invest disproportionately
more in the high- and medium–high-technology manufacturing
sectors (31 per cent, 35 per cent and 40 per cent, respectively,
versus 22 per cent average for all foreign firms investing in the EU).
They cite domestic collaborations with suppliers and customers
as well as domestic collaboration with academia as major drivers
for investing in the EU. Clearly, these investments are focused on
upgrading the technological skills of the emerging market players,
both for improving their competitiveness at home as well as in
international markets (global expansion of Indian companies will
be covered in more detail in Chapter 8).

As shown in Figure 4.9, several trends have emerged regarding
MNC R&D centres in India.[217] For example, MNCs with global
revenues below USD 1 billion dominate the small R&D centre space
(262 centres with less than 200 employees), as well as the medium
size space (seventy centres with 200–500 employees). MNCs with
revenues between USD 1 billion and USD 10 billion are represented
across the spectrum, including fifty-nine centres with less than 200
employees, forty-five with 200–500 employees, thirty-three centres
with 500–1000 employees and fifteen centres with more than 1000
employees. Global giants with more than USD 10 billion show
markedly different behaviour from the other two groups. They

have a large number of small R&D outlets (fifty-six with less than 200 employees) and a large number of very large R&D centres (forty with more than 1000 employees). Clearly, global giants that have understood how to work a global delivery model effectively and how to leverage cost, talent and turnaround time advantages out of such a model are not afraid to put their money where it matters.

Overall, IT and software have the dominant share in the number of R&D centres (41 per cent), reflecting India's prowess and export success in the sector. In terms of employment, the sector is even more prevalent, covering 57 per cent of the total workforce employed in MNC R&D centres in India. Telecommunications is second, with 17 per cent, followed by semiconductors. Automotive and medical devices/healthcare are comparable, with 6 per cent each, while computing systems (5 per cent) and consumer electronics (4 per cent) round out the picture.

4 FIGURE 9

Many Large Companies Have Over the Years Set Up Larger R&D Centres in India, Primarily in the IT and Software Sector

India spends 0.9% GDP on R&D, becoming the world's eighth largest R&D investor

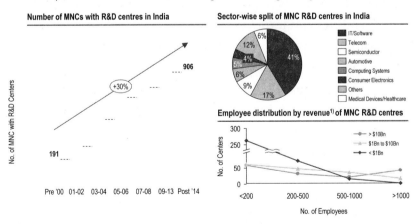

1) Global revenue

Source: Batelle 2014 Global R&D Funding Forecast report, p. 7, Zinnov Consulting Report, 'The Indian Promise', Zinnov Consulting Report, 'Operations Cost Benchmarking Study, 2012', http://www.slideshare.net/zinnov/operational-costs-benchmarking-study-2012; Roland Berger analysis

While small in comparison to IT, the automotive R&D centres in India are numerous and many are large-scale. Both automotive suppliers and OEMs have set up wholly owned (captive) R&D facilities (so-called Global In-house Centres [GIC]) and grown them in the automotive clusters of India.

Several factors need to be addressed to build successful captive centres, as we have seen already in the Faurecia example discussed above:

1. Develop a clear strategy and capability-building roadmap for the centre.
2. Ensure sufficient scale to provide clear career opportunities for employees and attract good talent.
3. Institute solid training processes to ensure quality and efficiency of local talent.
4. Drive lean engineering based on clear processes and key performance indicators (KPIs).
5. Enable continuous and clear communication between geographically dispersed teams.
6. Ensure team exchange across geographies to build up capabilities and informal networks.
7. Ensure acceptance of the global delivery model via top management support.
8. Use continuous improvement to drive process improvements.
9. Leverage global distributed R&D to enhance flexibility, reduce turnaround times and drive down cost.
10. Leverage local centres for 'local for local' engineering and frugal engineering.

In particular, good measurement approaches and KPIs help to reduce room for interpretation and quickly quantify the advantages of globally dispersed R&D. Key quality parameters could be on-time delivery, rework/rejection, customer satisfaction ratings, daily punching ratios, project quality audit results, etc. Operational performance could be measured along dimensions of utilization ratios, efficiency (billable hours as a ratio of project hours), billability (billable hours as a ratio of available hours), benchmark hours versus actual hours, hours per job, number of loops per project, turnaround time per project, hardware/software usage, department-wise workload, etc.

Bosch: The Engineering Giant in Bangalore

An exceedingly successful example of an MNC R&D centre is Robert Bosch Engineering and Business Solutions Ltd (RBEI).[218] The Robert Bosch Group is a EUR 70 billion turnover industrial company (including the recent acquisition of Bosch Siemens Household Appliances). With about 3,75,000 employees spread across 150 countries, Bosch drives innovation in four key fields: mobility solutions,[219] industrial technology,[220] energy and building technology[221] and consumer goods.[222]

Bosch's history in India dates back to 1924 when the company entered the country via imports. The first factory was opened in 1953 and, today, the Bosch Group has nine companies, fifteen manufacturing plants, over 1500 suppliers, more than 4000 sales outlets and about 30,000 employees in the country.

RBEI is part of Bosch India. RBEI is the largest employer of the Bosch Group in the country and most likely the largest engineering services captive in India. RBEI has about 17,000 employees out of which about 12,000 are engineers. RBEI is not only the largest R&D centre for Bosch outside of Germany—about a fourth of Bosch's global engineering workforce is employed in the centre—it is also the only one that serves all business units of Bosch equally rather than being dedicated to any one of them. The largest numbers of employees are based in Bangalore, Karnataka and in Coimbatore, Tamil Nadu. Since RBEI was so successful, the team was also asked to set up engineering centres globally. Today, RBEI engineers also work out of Ho Chi Minh City, Vietnam, and out of Guadalajara, Mexico. A small sales force in Farmington Hills, London, Stuttgart and Tokyo as well as Pune, New Delhi and Bangalore ensures that close contact with customers on-site is maintained and new opportunities for growth are identified.

Competitiveness comes from strong cultural and technical alignment with the global Bosch organizations. Significant investments in German language skills have ensured tight integration with key units in Germany. Consistent management exchange programmes allowed Indian employees to build networks in Germany or other parts of the international Bosch organization. Expats, who served in various positions in India, turned key promoters for RBEI when they returned to their home organizations. Maintaining key IP in-house is another powerful driver for insourcing while offshoring. Similarly, the centre is as qualified as its key external competitors and boasts a number of certifications such as CMMi Level 5 and ASPICE Level 3.[223]

Overall, the centre attracts more technology-affine employees. Challenges in Bosch's key industries and in business-process-focused IT companies are different. Take automotive software as an example. Here, RBEI works with quality targets that are orders of magnitude more stringent than those applicable for business-process-related software.

Moreover, the centre is cost-competitive. Efficiency levels of Indian engineers are at about 85 per cent of those in Germany on average. Selling, general and administration costs, utilization, onsite ratios and attrition are better than the competition. Says Vijay Rathnaparkhe, managing director and president, RBEI:

The value proposition for an employee is very different from Indian IT players. We get to work on technical issues in much more detail than these companies, be closer to and more involved in the key issues that drive Bosch globally. For example, our Powertrain Electronics unit leader is integrated into the global Powertrain leadership team. We also have a good work – life balance.

Cost competitiveness of the centre is demonstrated by external business success. Driven by both the intention to constantly benchmark RBEI versus local best practice and to continue to drive the growth of the centre, third-party business was started about five years ago. Today, third-party business accounts for around 10 per cent of overall revenues. The team at RBEI aims to increase this in the coming years.

RBEI's journey to its current performance has been a long one. R&D activities started in 1990 with five engineers. It took six years, concentrated around proving the concept of India, to build up to a moderate size of 200 engineers. Efficient leverage of cost arbitrage to augment capacity and the decision not to consolidate RBEI headcount in global budgets were key drivers for growth during this period. The subsequent decade drove the build-up of domain capability and process and content quality. Offshoring was maximized as more and more clients realized the business benefits of working with RBEI. The last decade then saw very rapid growth in RBEI's business, driven both by value addition and cost advantage. Integrating the centre into the global Bosch technology roadmaps allowed the team in Bangalore and Coimbatore to scale up and to start to drive innovation in a structured manner.

RBEI describes this journey in terms of its global in-house (GIC) centre maturity model. In the first stage, most centres are operations centres that provide operations support and work under the guidance of engineers in global locations. Their aim and focus is to ensure compliance to the delivery process and to manage customer communication. Typical KPIs are focused around efficient sourcing and onboarding of talent. The second stage is the delivery centre. Here, the centre graduates to being responsible for service delivery and is able to define and manage the global delivery process. Customer orientation increases. Incremental innovation happens and is centred on conceptualizations and process improvements. Typical capabilities that the centre needs to develop are focused on various tools and methods relevant for project delivery, an optimized global delivery model as well as account management. The solution centre is achieved in the third stage. Here, the GIC takes responsibility and ownership of end-to-end solutions as well as provides end-to-end services. Partnering with customers is the name of the game, and in terms of innovation, solution prototyping and structured innovation programmes are pursued. The fourth stage is what the team at Bosch calls the transformation unit. Here the centre leads global functions or business units and drives global technology management regarding design, development and delivery. The GIC partners with customers on strategic initiatives and becomes a technology and innovation hub for the parent organization. As for RBEI itself, stages depend on customers and business units; however, about 5–10 per cent of the overall business today is done at the transformation unit level.

Innovation is a key part of RBEI's journey. As Vijay points out,

> In the first year, we were just looking at various areas and trying to get our feet wet. In the second year, we were trying to understand market requirements, engineer a solution and build a prototype. I call this 'happy engineering' as no real customer connect was there. Finally, in the third year we integrated the market view with

our innovation capabilities. This seems to work. Starting from patents in single digits about five years ago, we have currently 600 patents filed.

Innovation is driven with several separate programmes. Innovations under the new business team are centrally funded projects that need to be unrelated to any existing business unit or core area including adjacent areas. These projects need to address a clear market need and also identify a way to address it. Currently, three to four projects from India are running under this scheme, one of which is a low-cost eye tester for glaucoma and diabetic retinopathy.[224] The second innovation scheme is the India innovation pipeline funded by Bosch India. Here, projects are decided by the CEO of Bosch India, Dr Steffen Berns, and focused on business unit or core-related areas for the Indian market. The third innovation stream is driven by RBEI and the last call on projects lies with Vijay. In the pre-investment initiative, team members are encouraged to move forward ideas that are technology-oriented and require capability that is exclusively available with RBEI. The goal is to address future local and global needs.

RBEI's innovation role for Bosch will continue to become more relevant in the future. Currently, around 100 RBEI engineers are working on the Internet of Things (IoT), with a particular focus on retail, telecommunications and FMCG (manufacturing will follow later). For new IoT technologies, RBEI has a massive location advantage. Besides ready availability of niche talent such as data scientists and visual experts, many of the key players in new technologies such as Intel or EMC are present in Bangalore. Due to this ecosystem, cooperation, partnering and formation of networks become significantly easier than in Stuttgart, Bosch's hometown. RBEI is adept at making these kinds of cooperation work. Also, new technologies are easier to leverage without the disadvantage of legacy. Hence, as Vijay puts it:

> We believe we have a real opportunity to create value for our customers and the global Bosch organization by pursuing orthogonal technologies, i.e., technologies such as open source, HTML5 and others, that complement the capabilities of Bosch globally. These technologies will enable Bosch to successfully transition from the old world to the digital world and will drive the growth and relevance of our centre.

In line with its parent organization, RBEI is propelled by the values and principles of the company's founder, Robert Bosch, who stated, 'I have always acted according to the principle that I would rather lose money than trust. The integrity of my promises, the belief in the value of my products and my word of honour have always had a higher priority to me than transitory profit.' Such principles and a solid track record of performance will continue to drive RBEI's success in scope and scale in India and globally.

IN SUMMARY

'Innovate or die' is a powerful slogan that applies perfectly to the Indian environment. Due to infrastructural deficiencies and institutional voids, a pure cost-leadership competitive model does not work for most companies operating out of India. Indian companies must differentiate their product offerings to ensure long-term survival.

India's fundamental research environment has bright spots. Examples are the cost-effective and successful missions to the moon and to Mars by the Indian Space Research Organisation (ISRO) or the cost-effective patenting activities of select laboratories under the Council for Indian Science and Research. However, spending on fundamental research is low at 0.9 per cent of GDP. An atypically high contribution of 60–65 per cent of research funding from government sources yields disappointing results due to the inefficiencies and failures of India's public research system.

On the talent side, India's educational system manages to deliver a sufficient quantity but an insufficient quality of graduates. Real innovative breakthroughs will require a good, broad-based education of students across colleges rather than a narrow focus on elite institutions such as the IITs. Currently, companies operating in India are forced to compensate for the shortcomings of India's education sector via extensive in-house training programmes.

While companies believe that stronger cooperation between industry and academia can create value, the current situation is not satisfactory. University system reforms and a better implementation of national and local innovation ecosystems are necessary.

India's innovations are, hence, not the result of technology push but of market pull. The country excels in finding new business models and process and product cost innovations that create value at the bottom of the pyramid or that solve challenges that India's environment throws at its citizens and companies alike.

Frugal innovation is a structured innovation process that delivers customer quality and value at precisely determined price points via a radical optimization of the product value chain. Frugal innovation is a forte of Indian players, as the case studies of Godrej, Tata, HUL and others have shown. It is also important for global players such as Siemens both in the context of defending and conquering market share in India as well as serving emerging value-conscious segments in developed markets.

In addition to frugal innovation, MNCs are leveraging Indian talent aggressively for generating IP via captive R&D centres in the country. The Bosch case study clearly highlights the genesis and impact of such centres on the global parent organization.

5

START-UPS AND
INCUBATION IN INDIA

THE START OF AN INNOVATION EXPLOSION

India's start-up ecosystem has been making waves recently with an estimated USD 4.9 billion funds raised in 2015, a jump of roughly 125 per cent from 2014.[225] In terms of the number of investments, the figures are even more remarkable: more than 390 start-ups have received funding in 2015 compared to 179 start-ups in 2014.[226] This trend is spread across industries including IT, automotive, pharmaceutical, biotechnology and FMCG. Bengaluru-based e-commerce start-up Flipkart recently raised USD 700 million in funding to reach an overall USD 15.2 billion valuation.[227] With this, Flipkart has emerged among the top nine Indian unicorns—a term used to describe privately held start-ups who have achieved the rare and exclusive feat of soaring to valuations of USD 1 billion or more within ten years of being founded. Led by Uber, this unicorn list includes eight other Indian start-ups including Snapdeal, Ola Cabs, Mu Sigma, InMobi,

Quikr and recent additions such as restaurant discovery start-up Zomato, digital wallet service Paytm (One97 Communications), and online marketplace ShopClues.com.[228] In comparison, the US has eighty-eight unicorns and Europe has sixteen, according to the *Wall Street Journal.*[229]

The Indian start-up space is sizzling. Venture capitalists and angel investors around the globe have trained their sights on India and are scouting for the next big thing. Large multinational corporations are not sitting back either. In an era where competitive advantage is short-lived and companies need to constantly innovate to stay ahead, engaging with start-ups provides a way to connect with the latest in innovation and thinking.

According to the 2015 NASSCOM report,[230] India has become the third largest base of technology start-ups globally with more than 4,200 start-ups, surpassing 3,900 start-ups in Israel and only trailing 4,500 in the UK (the US leads overall with more than 47,000 start-ups). A large domestic market, improved access to capital and mentors, whitespace opportunities at home and globally as well as increased M&A activity are driving interest in the market. About 83 per cent of 2015's USD 4.9 billion investment in Indian start-ups is B2C-focused, working on areas such as e-commerce (36 per cent), aggregators and online marketplaces (33 per cent), consumer services (8 per cent) and hyperlocal e-commerce (7 per cent). In the B2B space, investment was routed to e-commerce enablers (46 per cent), analytics (17 per cent), robotics (9 per cent), and enterprise software (9 per cent).

Start-ups are not restricting themselves to plain vanilla copies of business models and approaches that have been pioneered in the West. Futuristic technology areas are actively pursued by Indian start-ups. For example, as of 2014,[231] India boasted of more than thirty augmented reality start-ups focusing on marketing and advertising, healthcare and visualization solutions, and at least thirty start-ups were focused on hardware offerings, e.g., in the area of 3D printing, payment solutions and automation. As of 2015, more than seventy-five start-ups operate in the IOT space with applications in wearable tech, home automation and fleet management. Big data and social media analytics is a hot field with more than 400 Indian start-ups covering the same. Other popular topics include health-tech with more than 120 start-ups and payments (with more than seventy start-ups). Cloud computing, security, edu-tech, ad-tech and gaming are other areas in which young (nearly 72 per cent of all founders are younger than thirty-five) Indian entrepreneurs redefine the way India looks at innovation and risk.

The excitement around the start-up explosion (in 2010, India counted only around 500 start-ups versus 4,200 estimated at the end of 2015)[232] is palpable. With above-average compensation, stock options, enhanced growth opportunities and a flexible work culture, start-ups are capable of attracting top talent from industry and consulting companies.[233] In addition, funding has become easier to obtain. The estimated USD 4.9 billion invested in 2015 in the Indian start-up ecosystem has been by 156 VC and private equity (PE) investors, about 292 angels and more than 110 incubators and accelerators.[234] The bulk of these investments stems from VC and PE at over USD 4.7 billion. Investments are concentrated on the expansion stage rather than the earlier seed, early and growth stages and are widespread across the B2C and B2B applications mentioned earlier. About USD 2.3 billion of all VC/PE investments has flown to NCR,[235] nearly double that of Bengaluru (USD 1.2 billion) and Mumbai (USD 1.1 billion). Chennai and Pune follow with around USD 100 million each. Unfortunately, while software-related start-ups have easy access to funding, real-product start-ups are finding it more difficult to be supported.

The main driver for many of India's start-ups is the rapid expansion of Internet usage in the country. With a CAGR of around 30 per cent for more than a decade, India, as of July 2016, has the second largest Internet population globally with 462 million users versus around 721 million for China and 287 million for the US.[236] While it took twenty years from the introduction of the Internet to reach 100 million users, the next 100 million will be reached within three years and the one thereafter in less than a year (see Figure 5.1). Besides rapid growth, there will be a significant shift in the user profile as well. Tomorrow's Internet users will be older, more rural, mostly female, more mobile-led and more vernacular.[237]

In 2013, India's Internet economy already amounted to USD 60 billion or 3.2 per cent of India's GDP. India's Internet economy hence outperformed large sectors such as healthcare (2.5 per cent) and defence (2.5 per cent).[238] By 2018, the Internet economy should contribute about 4.6 per cent of total GDP.[239] Overall, India is among the leading emerging markets in terms of Internet contribution to GDP and trails Internet contribution to GDP in most developed markets by about 200 bps (EU 5 per cent, US 5.2 per cent, Japan 5.5 per cent, South Korea 5.6 per cent, UK 10.2 per cent).[240]

5 FIGURE 1

With Just 34% Population Using Internet, India Lags Behind Other Developing Nations in Terms of Internet Penetration

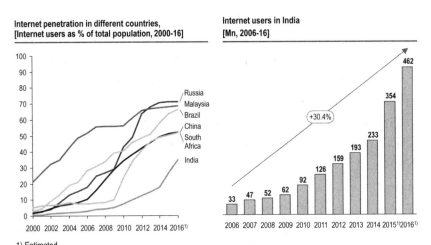

Internet penetration in different countries,
[Internet users as % of total population, 2000-16]

Internet users in India
[Mn, 2006-16]

1) Estimated

Source: Internet Live Stats, www.internetlivestats.com; Roland Berger analysis

Hardly surprisingly, the USD 2.3 billion e-tailing market in India[241] attracts most of the attention of players. The market itself is dominated by large horizontal players[242] such as Amazon, Snapdeal, Flipkart, ShopClues and eBay, who cover about 80 per cent of the action. Vertical players[243] such as Jabong (fashion), Pepperfry (furniture) and lenskart.com (glasses) constitute a smaller share in the market but are growing rapidly. Gross merchandise value (GMV)[244] run rates of major players have exceeded USD 1 billion (Flipkart, Snapdeal, Amazon) and will continue to grow at strong, double-digit rates.

The drivers for India's online shopping revolution are many. Growing mobile Internet penetration and increasingly affordable smartphones have a significant positive impact on overall purchases. In addition, long work hours as well as tedious commutes between work and home limit consumers' spare time. Online purchases therefore provide a convenient way to increase leisure time by eliminating unpleasant drives to overcrowded shopping centres. Increasing purchasing power will continue to drive demand. In rural areas, this is combined with the fact that online shops allow access to products that are not available locally. The fashion store Jabong, for example, generates 50–55 per cent of its revenue in Tier-2 and smaller cities. Last but not least, discounts as high as 30–40 per cent have fuelled the growth of e-tailing. While discounts may be pared down to 15–20 per cent, they are expected to continue to drive the acceptance of e-tailing among Indian shoppers.

Financially, however, e-commerce in India still has a long way to go, with losses for major players outpacing revenues, as shown in Figure 5.2. Efforts to improve overall efficiency and performance are in the works. Last-mile delivery costs for Amazon, for example, are reduced by tying up with hotspots in major universities, kirana stores and petrol pumps, which can carry out deliveries as well as serve as pick-up points. Jabong has institutionalized a similar concept with coffee shops and petrol pumps. High seller count and seller satisfaction is seen as a differentiator, so players are upgrading their seller management capabilities with onboarding, training, operations and financing. Amazon, in conjunction with Narayana Murthy's Catamaran Ventures, (49:51 JV), established Prione Business Services, which has brought around 6,000 sellers from fourteen Indian cities onto Amazon India's portal. Prione's 100 percent subsidiary, Cloudtail, is Amazon's leading seller and merchant, which accounts for approximately 40 per cent of the e-tailer's sales.[245] Flipkart has a dedicated programme, 'Kaarigar Ke Dwar',[246] to guide artisans in using its platform. Based on seller profile and history, Snapdeal facilitates soft loans from various banks to support their partners. Last but not least, all players are in the process of reducing cash-on-delivery due to high direct and indirect costs. While cash-on-delivery stood at 75 per cent in 2012, it has come down to 65 percent in 2014 and is likely to sink further. Despite all these efforts, e-commerce in India is likely to be a GMV-focused game rather than a contributor to bottom line for some time to come.

The future for Indian start-ups seems promising. According to NASSCOM, by 2020, there will be more than 11,500 start-ups in the country employing about 2,50,000 people (up from the currently estimated 60,000–70,000).[247] The development of a start-up culture in India is encouraging and vital to drive India's move up the value chain as well as to create jobs. However, at the time of writing this book, India's start-ups face significant hurdles in the areas of raising capital, taxation, and entry and exit of businesses. These regulatory issues have prompted several Indian start-ups to relocate to more business-friendly countries. According to the software product think tank, iSpirt, in 2014, '54 per cent of the funded young tech ventures resided in Singapore, the US and the UK because of the better regulatory environment in these countries. The figure shot up to 75 per cent this year.'[248]

5 FIGURE 2

With Billion-Dollar Valuations and Strong Fundraising, India's Big E-commerce Players Suffer from Largely Negative Profitability

E-commerce players: Revenue, losses, valuation and funds raised

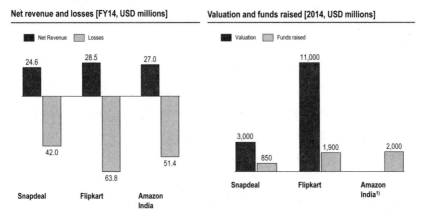

Net revenue and losses [FY14, USD millions]

■ Net Revenue   ▢ Losses

24.6   28.5   27.0

42.0   51.4

63.8

Snapdeal   Flipkart   Amazon
India

Valuation and funds raised [2014, USD millions]

■ Valuation   ▢ Funds raised

11,000

3,000   850   1,900   2,000

Snapdeal   Flipkart   Amazon
India¹⁾

1) Funds raised internally for Amazon. Amazon Global has committed USD 2 bn investment in India

Source: Assocham, 'Future of e-Commerce: Uncovering Innovation', April 2015, p.12; Livemint, 'Amazon Raises Stakes in e-Commerce Battle with Flipkart', 31 July 2014; Roland Berger analysis

Things are slowly improving. In particular, in the area of capital-raising, SEBI has set up an alternate capital-raising platform,[249] known as the institutional trading platform (ITP), approved in June 2015. As the name suggests, this is a trading platform where start-ups can list themselves and raise capital without having to adhere to the extensive requirements of other exchanges, such as the Bombay Stock Exchange (BSE) and NSE. This has been set up in response to the increasing number of Indian start-ups that are choosing to list themselves abroad. The ITP will be made available to 'new-age companies having innovative business model and belonging to knowledge-based sector, where no person holds 25 per cent or more of the pre-issue share capital.'[250]

The number of listing requirements for the ITP has relaxed. The mandatory lock-in period[251] for promoters and other pre-listing investors has been reduced to six months, compared to three years on other Indian exchanges. Further, the erstwhile requirement of at least three years of profit prior to listing has been removed. Now, start-ups need not be profitable prior to listing on the ITP. Within three years of listing, they can list themselves on the SME, and can subsequently graduate to the main boards (BSE and NSE) within two years (even if they continue to be loss-making) provided they have a paid-up capital of INR 100 million (INR 10 crore). Disclosure requirements have also been eased.

While these relaxations are steps in the right direction, they fail to address all the bottlenecks. For instance, only those companies whose promoter shareholding is below 25 per cent after issue can access the ITP. While this makes larger companies such as Flipkart eligible, smaller start-ups with larger promoter shareholding are not. Moreover, the new norms are also ambiguous; for instance, the term 'start-up' has not yet been defined. Finally, ensuring sufficient liquidity will be critical to the success of the ITP. SEBI will need to attract participants to the ITP for this to happen.[252]

Is this initiative enough to completely reverse the trend of Indian start-ups listing overseas? Not yet. Aside from capital-raising regulations, Indian start-ups continue to face regulatory hurdles with regard to taxation, starting up and shutting down, etc. In terms of taxation, no tax exemptions are provided versus countries such as Singapore, which again drives migration of start-ups away from India. In some cases, such as software products, start-ups are burdened with both service tax as well as value-added tax due to ambiguity around the classification of software products as services or products.

A minimum holding period of three years to benefit from capital gains for start-up investments is a major roadblock for potential investors. According to iSpirt, 'Unlisted companies should be brought on par with listed companies by making the minimum holding period of shares (for qualifying for long term capital gains) as one year for all companies.'[253] Further, factors such as the angel tax are challenging, as investments received from individual angel investors continue to be taxed for the amount in excess of fair market value under income from other sources.[254]

Entry and exit of start-ups are burdened by complicated and lengthy procedures, which force start-ups to hire professional consultants to navigate the process, which in turn drives up cost. The liquidation of a company can be a very tedious and time-consuming affair, ranging from six months to several years.[255] Contrast this with the UK, where it takes a week.[256] New compliance requirements for start-ups for capital-raising have increased the cost and time for raising funds by an estimated 25–30 per cent. Mandating the valuation of start-ups by an independent valuation expert for raising capital is troublesome, as the valuation of start-ups in new business segments is subjective and will give rise to conflicting views. High liquidation costs and ambiguity on directives for companies without assets, such as Internet companies, are hassles faced by entrepreneurs in winding down.

Solutions to these problems exist and have been presented to the Indian government. The government in turn is recognizing the impediments to the start-up ecosystem and is beginning to take action. For instance, in June 2015, the Ministry of Corporate Affairs simplified the 2013 Companies Act to help start-ups set up private companies by increasing flexibility in the issue of share capital, reducing compliance burden and easing regulations to raise debt from shareholders.[257]

Moreover, the government of India is taking additional steps to improve the ecosystem for start-ups and entrepreneurship. Prime Minister Modi unveiled the Start-up India initiative on 16 January 2016 with a view to provide a fillip to digital entrepreneurship at the grassroots level and convert the youth into job creators instead of job seekers. In response to the commonly cited challenges to setting up, raising capital, operating and shutting down a new venture, the Prime Minister announced a number of initiatives around three primary areas[258] (see Figure 5.3):

- Simplification and handholding.
- Funding support and incentives.
- Industry–academia partnership and incubation.

5 FIGURE 3

The Start-Up India Action Plan Covers Simplification & Handholding, Funding Support & Incentives, and Industry–Academia Partnership

Key Components of the Government of India's Start-Up India Action Plan, 2016

Simplification and handholding
- > Compliance regime based on self-certification
- > Creation of Start-up India hub
- > Roll-out of mobile app and portal
- > Legal support and fast-tracking patent examination at lower costs
- > Relaxed norms of public procurement for start-ups
- > Faster exit for start-ups

Funding support & incentives
- > Funding support through a fund of funds with a corpus of INR 10,000 crore
- > Credit guarantee fund for start-ups
- > Tax exemption on capital gains
- > Tax exemption to start-ups for 3 years
- > Tax exemption on investments above fair market value

Industry-academia partnership and incubation
- > Organizing start-up fests for showcasing innovation and providing a collaboration platform
- > Launch of Atal Innovation Mission (AIM) with Self-Employment and Talent Utilization (SETU) Program
- > Harnessing private sector expertise for incubator setup
- > Building innovation centres at national institutes
- > Set up of 7 new research parks
- > Promoting start-ups in the biotechnology sector
- > Launching of innovation-focused programmes for students
- > Annual incubator grand challenge

Source: Start-up India, 'Action Plan', 16 January 2016, http://www.pradhanmantriyojana.in/wp-content/uploads/2016/01/Startup-India_ActionPlan_16January2016.pdf; Roland Berger analysis

In addition, initiatives such as Digital India and Skill India were launched in July 2015. Digital India is comprised of three key components, i.e., creation of digital infrastructure, delivering government services digitally and promoting digital literacy.[259] Skill India has four initiatives with a goal of training and skilling 400 million people by 2022.[260]

redBus: All Aboard![261]

An innovative and successful start-up, redBus solves key business challenges of the country. Currently, its business model is being rolled out in other Asian countries such as Singapore and Malaysia.

There are three primary modes of transportation in India: rail, road and air. Rail transport covers most of India and is an economical way to get around the country. Air travel has given a choice to the medium- and upper-class segments of society for travelling long distances in less time (see Chapter 7 for a detailed discussion of India's airline industry). Road transport is probably the most accessible and affordable mode of transportation in India.

High economic growth, increased labour mobility and urbanization have increased the need for inter-city connectivity in India. With state-owned road transport corporations (RTC) focusing on providing basic transport for all classes of society across the country, private bus operators were quick to spot opportunities in the market. For example, private players pioneered the introduction of Volvo luxury buses for long-distance travel (e.g., Mumbai–Bengaluru, 957 km), addressing the need of professionals to travel with more comfort and style from their place of work to their hometowns. Overall, private bus operators have seen positive growth over the years. With a market size of USD 2.5 billion and 220 million tickets sold in 2012 according to redBus, the market is expected to continue to grow with a CAGR of 25 per cent, to a total number of tickets sold of 950 million in FY20.

However, supply-side fragmentation is one of the key challenges in this industry, with large, government-owned RTCs[262] and thousands of private bus operators[263] competing for customer business. About 65 per cent of the market is being served by bus operators with a fleet size of less than twenty buses each. Around 25 per cent of the market is covered by operators with between twenty-five and seventy-five buses. The remaining 10 per cent of the market is covered by large operators with more than seventy-five buses in their fleet. Most bus operators have a local presence in several towns and cities in India; however, bus customers are not familiar with all of these bus operators and rely on travel agents to book seats for inter-city travel via private buses.

Before the advent of redBus, the ticket booking process was cumbersome. Passengers would go to the travel agent's shop. Then, the agent would call up bus operators in the agent's network for ticket availability, and then issue the ticket and the payment receipt subject to availability of a seat. Each travel agent was operating in standalone mode with access to a limited number of bus operators. The agent could not view the status of seats booked by other travel agents. The system provided no flexibility to the traveller in evaluating the service quality of available bus operators, booking return tickets, booking the seat number of choice, etc. This lack of transparency regarding available seat options meant the traveller had to pay the premium fare demanded by the travel agent. The bus operator might suffer from cash flow problems as he was dependent on the travel agent to get his payment and had to bear losses from seats not being booked during travel.

Phanindra Sama, redBus CEO, experienced the inefficiencies of the manual, travel-agent-driven booking process first-hand when he was unable to go home during Diwali in 2005 due to unavailability of tickets. He and two BITS-Pilani alumni, Charan Padmaraju (co-founder CEO) and Sudhakar Pasupunuri, set out to change the way things were done in the bus ticketing business and in 2006 launched redBus in Bengaluru. Phanindra and his colleagues set out to aggregate the inventories of seats in real-time at one end and to provide an online and telephone interface to travellers at the other end. They faced key challenges. First, they needed to convince bus operators to provide seat availability information. Second, they needed to convince customers to book seats via their system. One would not come without the other. They also needed to build a robust software platform, both for bus operators and for travellers. Next, they needed to change the business model of bus operators by convincing largely unorganized players to use their software application for uploading seat inventories in the centralized redBus server. And lastly, should they be successful with all the other challenges, they needed to be able to scale up the business in a short amount of time. These were significant challenges for a business model that in principle is very straightforward. Phanindra explains,

> The business model is very simple. You buy a ticket, you sell a ticket. However, you don't do it with any other company. You do it with 800 operators and 40,000 agents and a million customer gateways and guarantee a comfortable journey by means of transport, which is very emotional and very personal for a customer.

A three-pronged approach to the Indian bus ticketing market was redBus's answer to the above mentioned challenges. The company offers the BOSS application (bus operators software system) to bus operators and RTCs (B2B). It interacts with customers who want to buy tickets via an online Internet website (redBus.in), an offline call centre and franchise contact points (B2C). It also licences the SeatSeller application (B2B) for online travel agents (OTAs). BOSS enables bus operators to upload their inventories to the redBus system and gives redBus real-time visibility on available routes, seats, price ranges, etc. For non-computerized bus operators, the company took the inventory inputs by phone and uploaded the same manually in the redBus system. Customers could search for seats either online or offline. However, redBus was able to provide value-added services such as availability of buses on a particular route, service quality comparisons, fare, seat availability, choice of a seat number, information on pick-up and drop-off points, etc. Offline and online travel agents leveraged SeatSeller, as it provided them with an opportunity to serve their clients better.

All three products and sales channels generate commission earnings for redBus. In addition, money is made by selling BOSS to bus operators. Overall, 80 per cent of redBus's revenue stems from B2C, the rest from B2B channels.

Leveraging data analytics, redBus is able to create significant value for bus operators. Revenues increase because the reflection of real-time inventory to travellers increases transparency and chances for successful sales. Payment for sale of tickets is disbursed in a timely manner, relieving bus operators of cash flow problems. Commission rates are standardized, increasing transparency and predictability of business. Opportunities to gain market share based on outstanding performance are driven by redBus's comparative service quality ratings based on customer feedback. And last but not least, redBus analysis allows bus operators to explore new or underserved profitable routes.

For travellers, redBus creates transparency in the booking process, and less anxiety. It provides a reliable service with real-time access to available tickets on requested routes. Besides transparent pricing, the system gives travellers an opportunity to choose an operator, a bus, seat number, payment mode, ticket delivery, pick-up point, etc. An excellent technology infrastructure with quick navigation and response time, a user-friendly interface and friendly call centre staff as well as wide geographic coverage make bus ticket booking a painless affair for travellers. Lastly, a reliable platform is provided for offline travel agents to improve their service offering for their customers. In addition to standard offerings of trains and planes these agents are now able to provide a complementary travel option via the seamless booking of buses.

Creating a virtuous cycle nevertheless was challenging, and investment in building lasting relationships, especially with operators and distribution partners, was intense. Today, these relationships act as a barrier to entry, i.e., prevent other companies from easily entering redBus's market. As redBus CFO Bharat Singh puts it:

So our customers basically come to us and tell us if there is some unfair trick happening on the ground. It is just because of the relationship that we have developed with them. Our operators tell us how we should run the business, etc. They come to us for counselling as well, what should be done by us on the ground. This kind of relationship is very, very difficult to build and takes a long time to develop.

In addition, building a physical infrastructure keeps competition at bay. In 2012, redBus had built up at least twenty-six regional offices, with 450 employees, a network of 800 bus operators and 40,000 sales and distribution outlets. It managed 19,000 daily transactions with bus services crossing more than twenty states including two RTCs and serviced more than 10 million travellers since inception.

Building an ecosystem of partnerships proved to be vital, not only for the customer-facing front end of the business, but also for the back end. Leveraging the technology capabilities of Amazon by using Amazon web services, redBus built a reliable and scalable cloud-based infrastructure, which could handle all their operational complexities resulting from a huge number of online and offline queries and transactions. The company was also one of the earliest adopters of Google BigQuery, which allowed interactive analysis of the massive datasets that redBus generated. Both of these technologies integrated perfectly to provide a seamless online experience for customers who access the website for evaluating available options and for ticket booking. In addition, the technology platform enabled redBus to closely monitor KPIs for its business, such as server up-time, transaction response time for customer queries, friendliness of user interface, load balancing, real-time inventory upload time, etc.

Besides the revenue streams that we discussed above, redBus profited from a negative cash flow situation. The money that is collected for ticket sales stays within the redBus ecosystem for six to seven days before it is remitted to bus operators. This provides redBus with flexibility and minimizes interest costs. Overall costs are driven by setting up the technology, the regional offices and seven call centres. In addition, operational expenses in terms of salaries, payment gateway costs per transaction (about 18–20 per cent of transaction value), taxes, etc., need to be paid.

Due to rapid growth (more than 200 per cent CAGR since inception) and efficient management the company utilized only INR 120 million against the raised VC of INR 400 million. This enabled redBus to earn its first profit of INR 10 million in 2012. Today, redBus is the largest bus ticketing company in India, whose competitive advantage lies in its scale and reach, the trust and transparency that it built in dealings with suppliers and travellers, its capability to aggregate a large number of bus operators and to manage the operational complexity of real-time inventory management and of processing millions of booking transactions.

A conscious effort to co-opt potential competitors is another aspect of redBus's success. Competition could potentially have come from online travel agencies and travel portals such as Yatra or Expedia. These companies were operating in the business of ticket bookings for air travel, rail travel, package tours and hotels. By providing an application plug-in (SeatSeller) for bus travel bookings, redBus aligned with them as complementary partners. The main entry barrier for these OTAs to compete directly with redBus was the operational complexity of managing a real-time inventory by aggregating the small inventories available with thousands of fragmented bus operators. This was in sharp contrast to the operational simplicity in ticket bookings for air and rail travel.

Competition from individual travel agents who were using manual ticket booking processes was mitigated by again offering SeatSeller as an option to minimize work and increase traveller satisfaction. Real competition could come from other online bus ticket booking companies like Travelyaari and TicketGoose; however, these are regional players whose scale cannot compete with redBus. As shown in Figure 5.4, redBus's integrated value chain aggressively exploits institutional voids in India and provides a very powerful barrier to entry indeed.

 FIGURE 4

The redBus Value Chain

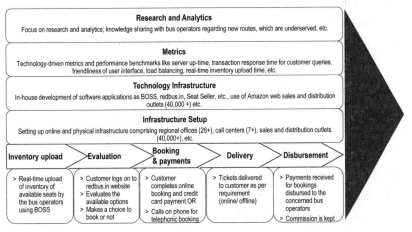

Source: redBus, Porter Prize discussions and documents, 2014; Roland Berger analysis

With the acquisition of redBus by Ibibo Group in 2013, the company has been able to continue to grow aggressively with 80 per cent year on year growth rates. Today, under its new CEO Prakash Sangam, redBus claims a market share of 75 per cent in India with 40 per cent of all bookings coming from mobile applications. In addition, a significant push towards a global platform finally led to redBus's market entry in Malaysia and Singapore, where bus ticketing markets are in similar conditions to India's.[264] Now, redBus seems to be poised to replicate its India success story in relevant global markets.

India Incubates!

Large companies want a slice of the start-up pie. These corporations have resources, scale, market access and the process knowhow needed to run a proven business model efficiently. However, they are plagued by slow and bureaucratic procedural directives that can prove fatal in a dynamic and turbulent environment. Start-ups can only dream of the resources that large corporations have access to. But what a start-up lacks in resources and scale, they more than make up for in innovative ideas, organizational agility and a passionate founding team with aspirations of rapid growth. Business incubators seem to be a viable way to get these two complementary units to work together and to leverage their individual strengths.

Increased activity in the start-up space has catalysed a parallel industry of business incubators and accelerators in India. Business incubators support very early stage start-ups for a period ranging from six months to two years, whereas accelerators provide short and intensive support for early revenue start-ups. Both, in essence, aim to increase the survival rate of start-ups and ensure subsequent commercial success.

Globally, most companies consider incubation as a vehicle for innovation, which is necessary to create and maintain competitive advantage. While several models for corporate incubation exist, companies with a strong track record in incubation have created their own model, which suits their organizational DNA, motives for incubation, capability and resources. Successful stand-alone incubators such as Y Combinator or Rocket Internet have distinguished themselves from the competition due to their emphasis on high-impact mentoring (from domain experts and serial entrepreneurs) and successfully selecting businesses with scalable business models.

Globally, successful corporate incubators have clear motives for incubation that often go beyond profit or return on investment and include factors such as achieving cost competitiveness, enhancing customer satisfaction, etc. The criteria for incubation must be clearly defined, i.e., questions such as which domains, markets, products and technologies will we focus on, will we incubate internally or externally, etc., need to be answered. Internally housed and managed incubators need to follow some basic rules:

1. Be funded separately.
2. Be sponsored and owned by a CXO-level executive of the company.
3. Have a dedicated team with clear roles and responsibilities.
4. Have clear, time-bound goals and milestones.
5. Have systematic performance measurements and incentives along well-defined KPIs.
6. Be given a greater degree of authority and freedom to truly experiment, or else run the risk of becoming another core R&D function.

Business incubation is a nascent topic in India, but is quickly gaining attention, fuelled also by timely government initiatives in this sphere. The venture community has started to look at high-quality incubators as a filtering mechanism. Incubators and accelerators have become prowling grounds for investors looking for innovative and breakthrough technologies that can disrupt entire industries. Large corporations too have thrown their hats into the ring. Corporates across industries are practising incubation as a new-found medium for innovation and as a way to create and sustain competitive advantage.

Roland Berger conducted a rigorous analysis[265] of the Indian incubation landscape through primary interviews with business leaders and managers of more than thirty organizations across the spectrum of industry, academia and incubators, through secondary research, and an analysis of global models. The focus of the study was on for-profit incubation by companies and stand-alone incubators. An overview existing models and incubators/accelerators in India is given in Figure 5.5. Incubation in this context is defined as intensive support provided to for-profit entities to grow at an accelerated pace, typically from infancy to steady-state. Support can be provided in the form of physical facilities, mentoring, market access, funding and administrative services with the overall objective of increasing the incubatee's chance of survival and commercial success.

5 FIGURE 5

Today's Incubation Landscape in India Comprises 3 Key Incubating Groups: Government-Led, Corporate & Standalone Incubators

Non-exhaustive list of incubating organizations in India

1) Corporate Incubators/Corporate Accelerators are specialized corporate units that hatch new businesses by typically providing funding, mentoring and support services

Source: Roland Berger analysis

Corporate Incubation in India

In terms of corporate incubation, the Roland Berger study finds that all companies interviewed, whether Indian or multinational, view incubation as important to their organization and drive it either internally or externally. Companies across a variety of industries are pursuing intra-company incubation, including IT, automotive, pharma, biotech, engineering, telecom, FMCG, chemicals, media and entertainment, retail, etc. However, companies formally incubate external start-ups via incubators/accelerators in only a handful of industries, namely IT/technology, engineering and retail.

Motives for incubation are clear and are typically aligned with a company's strategic objectives. A significant motivator for incubation India is developing innovative technology, products, business models, or services either via licensing from the start-up, by outright purchase of the company or 'aquihiring'[266] teams in question. Additional motivations range from improving competitive advantage to driving an 'intra-preneurial'[267] culture within the company or identifying upcoming technology trends. Exploiting underutilized IP within the organization and spin-off for profit as well as increasing market adoption for existing technologies, platforms or products is witnessed as well. In particular, companies in technology-intensive industries believe that incubation is imperative for strategic reasons and for the long-term survival of the firm. A host of companies have also incubated socially minded businesses internally to engage with bottom-of-the-pyramid groups, e.g., small farmers, self-help groups for women,[268] rural panchayats,[269] etc. While the ideas may have a social agenda, they are typically for profit.

Areas for incubation in terms of domain are normally predefined, usually during the strategic planning process of companies. Incubation is generally focused on core-adjacent or non-core activities as core areas are the domain of traditional R&D departments. Typically, revenue and profitability threshold criteria are determined for these areas. Intra-company incubators[270] support ideas right from inception while external incubator/accelerator programmes by companies focus on start-ups of a certain maturity, i.e., start-ups with a minimum viable product or early-revenue start-ups, which have already received some customer traction and are looking to scale up.

Financial metrics are tracked for internal incubation, however, companies realize that these are experiments and provide longer timelines by which financial metrics have to match corporate hurdle rates. The incubation process itself is monitored according to well-defined quality gates. For external incubation, companies provide funding and seed capital and oversee the budget via a steering committee headed by the managing director or CEO. In some cases, companies have decided not to provide funding but to support new start-ups with mentoring, market access and introduction to potential investors.

In India, many of the rules of corporate incubation that apply globally are also valid locally. The main incubation models for corporate incubation are:[271]

1. **Leveraging:** Increase the top- and bottom-line via commercialization of core or core-adjacent in-house technologies, products and know-how. Often, a separate business division within the company is generated to house the newly developed technologies or products.
2. **Fast profit:** Generate profit or return on investment by commercializing and spinning off non-core areas or technologies. The goal is to exit profitably from these newly created ventures.

3. **Insourcing:** Identify emerging technologies or product start-ups, fund and develop them for potential purchase, spin-in or acquihiring.
4. **Market:** Support development of complementary technology externally to increase demand for parent's product.

Hybrid models also exist, both globally and in India.

India's Stand-Alone Incubators

Stand-alone incubation has found its own ways of operating in the country via four dominant models. Pure facility models provide only a physical space with basic support services while virtual incubators provide funding and mentoring support in exchange for an equity stake. Here, no physical premises are provided. The facility-plus model typically provides the whole gamut of incubation services including market and network access. Similar to the case of external corporate incubation, stand-alone incubators typically have an unstructured incubation process, which they customize to the needs of each start-up. Stand-alone accelerators typically have a structured, time-bound, cohort-based system. In summary:

1. **Facility:** Create an entrepreneurial and collaborative environment for start-ups. Reduce their cost and time spent on non-core activities and make money via monthly rentals.
2. **Facility-plus:** Same as point 1 above but provide mentoring and financing as well. Value is realized by the incubator taking a 5–30 per cent stake in the start-ups.
3. **Virtual:** Generate return on investment by identifying, investing in and providing virtual mentoring to start-ups.

4. **Accelerator:** Generate profit/returns from incubating high-potential start-ups and accelerate their time to market and growth.

For stand-alone incubators, the quality of the founding team is the most important criteria for selecting an external start-up for incubation. Aspects such as domain knowledge, business acumen, flexibility to pivot a product or business model, and congruence between the team are critical. Scalability of ideas is equally important.

India's stand-alone incubator universe is strongly influenced by angel investors, serial entrepreneurs, VC funds and/or high net worth individuals who, beyond a profit motive, often have the expertise and the will to set up a positive ecosystem for start-ups and innovation in the country. Typically, the incubator founders or leaders have expertise in a particular sector and choose to incubate start-ups in their area of expertise. Stand-alone incubators tend to be stage-agnostic, while stand-alone accelerators select incubatees, which have a minimum viable product, or early-revenue start-ups, which have need for scale-up support.

Hybrid models exist in the incubation space. An interesting example is Kyron. Kyron is a sister company of ANSR Consulting, a Bengaluru-based company that sets up offshore captive centres or GICs in India. Customers of ANSR include Wells Fargo, Target, Victoria's Secret, Time, SuperValu and Lowe's. Typically, ANSR establishes a JV with a client company taking about a 20-30 per cent stake in the GIC.[272] Kyron helps these GICs set up their corporate accelerator programme and in addition manages its own start-up accelerator focused on seed funding, product-focused mentoring, provision of access to customers, corporates and investors. Kyron focuses on high-quality start-ups, which provide solutions that are customizable to the needs of large corporations, ideally from ANSR's client portfolio. This way, Kyron acts as a very effective bridge between Indian start-ups and large MNCs. Kyron has incubated about a dozen start-ups since its inception in December 2012.

In June 2015, ANSR Consulting raised USD 9 million in a round led by VC firm Accel Partners, and in July 2015, Infosys invested USD 1.4 million in return for a 5 per cent stake in the firm. This funding will be used to bring in another thirty to forty GICs into India in the next five years. Going forward, Kyron will abandon the traditional accelerator batch system with demo days and instead focus on matching start-ups with an MNC GIC for a six-month period.[273]

IN SUMMARY

Significant excitement centres around today's Indian start-up scene. With more than 4,200 start-ups, India is the third largest ecosystem for start-ups globally and has given birth to some of the world's most impressive unicorns. Companies such as redBus have successfully solved unique Indian challenges but were also able to roll out their technology and business models outside of India.

The government of India is taking steps to improve the entrepreneurial ecosystem. Besides improved regulation, availability of VC and PE funding has greatly supported the development of innovative centres around NCR, Mumbai, Bengaluru, Pune and Chennai. Incubators and accelerators, in their stand-alone, corporate or government avatars, are doing their part to drive entrepreneurial success in the country. While currently most Indian start-ups concentrate on e-commerce, innovative companies in diverse areas such as IOT, analytics, and robotics thrive in India.

In short, as can be seen from the discussion in Chapters 4 and 5, India can and must innovate. While the academic front is disappointing, private enterprises and start-ups will continue to push the limits of Indian innovation. Having sunk its teeth into exciting, profitable innovation opportunities, the Indian tiger is unlikely to let go.

6

CHOICES AND TRADE-OFFS

WHAT YOU DO AND DON'T DO MATTERS

One of the more remarkable stories of the twentieth and twenty-first centuries has been the story of the 'hidden champions', according to author Hermann Simon.[274] Hidden champions are relatively unknown, mostly B2B companies of moderate size (less than USD 4 billion annual turnover) that rank in the global top three in their respective industries. Several common traits emerge across these hidden champions. For one, they have a burning ambition to become or to stay leaders in their respective market segments. This passion is not limited to the management, but runs across the organization, highlighted, for example, by attrition rates that are below industry standards. These companies also define narrow markets for themselves, i.e., they identify clear target customers and serve their needs better than anybody else. This obsessive focus on customer success is what drives management teams and their employees. Their teams have a high level of contact with customers, which drives customer understanding and also increases R&D efficiency. Hidden champions are able to obtain patents at roughly one-fifth the expenditure required by large companies, and still produce five times more patents than them, according to Simon. Rather than pursuing a broad product portfolio, hidden champions typically concentrate on higher-end products and services and drive scale via global penetration.

In terms of Porter's work,[275, 276] these hidden champions understand that they have to be different to succeed and know that their activities need to be fully aligned with their strategy. Hidden champions choose which customers to serve and how to serve them successfully. Company choices can be variety-based, i.e., we choose the product or service that we want to provide versus the customer segment (e.g., oil changes and brake jobs for Jiffy Lube). Choices can be needs-based, i.e., we segment customers based on their needs (e.g., low price, product features, etc.), or access-based, i.e., we segment customers according to where we will serve them. Developing a clear strategic position and a differentiated value proposition for customers is the name of the game. Clear choices about what to do and what not to do, as well as alignment across functions to deliver the desired positioning to customers, are behind the success of hidden champions.

Choices require trade-offs, as a product or service can't be everything to everybody. A premium positioning requires, for example, higher investments in R&D, more qualified employees especially in sales and service, etc. These requirements prevent a simultaneous play based on cost. Kingfisher's attempt to be both a low-cost and a full-service airline ended with the company eventually going bankrupt (see Chapter 7). Trade-offs can be necessary due to an inconsistency in image or reputation (premium versus mass positioning), due to an inconsistency among the activities themselves (product differentiation, e.g., via

R&D versus low cost positioning), or due to the fact that we need to avoid overdesigning or under-designing activities for the task at hand (e.g., overqualified sales people for a given job).

Trade-offs are a company's best friend. Since you can't be everything to everybody, neither can your competition. If your competitive positioning is really creating discernible value for customers, you will deliver this value based on a set of unique activities. This activity system will be hard to imitate for competitors. It is possible to copy training activities for sales people, set up R&D centres that mirror the competence level of your organization, copy HR and incentive systems, adopt the same production practices and philosophy, etc. However, if you get the copies only 90 per cent right, since all these activities are reinforcing in determining the overall business outcome, the overall impact of the benchmark-driven optimization effort diminishes rapidly (indicatively as 0.9^n, with n being the number of activities copied). This is the reason why Toyota is still one of the most revered and successful automotive companies despite the fact that everybody knows about the Toyota Production System and has tried to emulate it.

Straddling, i.e., trying to cover a variety of adjacent market segments by being only 10–15 per cent different from market incumbents is generally not successful and should be avoided. Competitors who are providing a different value proposition based on a set of unique activities won't be able to straddle your space as these activities will often be mutually exclusive as we have discussed above (see also the IndiGo–Kingfisher comparison in the next chapter).

Sustainable competitive advantage is driven and maintained by the company' value chain of a company whose activity systems have been specifically tailored to deliver that value. In the case of EFD discussed earlier, having highly qualified and loyal employees enabled the company to drive ground-breaking frugal engineering in India. But it also implied higher personnel costs when compared to industry, preventing a mass market play in melting and heating. Maruti's value-for-money focus, for example, prevents the company from creating an exclusive experience for its customers similar to that of premium players. Safety features such as high-strength steel cannot be used in the vehicle because target customers are not yet willing to pay for the same.

Not making clear choices and trade-offs leads to a muddled strategic positioning of companies and exposes organizations to medium- and long-term risks. Examples are the Indian textile industry, where a clear positioning as a low-cost, high-quality supplier has not been achieved across the board due to the absence of a consistent set of management techniques. The Indian machine-tool industry likewise has not been able to achieve clear trade-offs by positioning itself as a low-cost, adequate technology player in the mid-market segment, both at home and globally. Shortcomings of this industry due to unclear choices and incomplete execution of strategies have been highlighted in Chapter 3.

In the language of Lafley and Martin,[277] five questions drive good strategies:

1. What is our winning aspiration?
2. Where do we play? (Products, geographies, consumer segments, channels, etc.)
3. How will we win? (Value proposition, competitive advantage)
4. What capabilities must be in place? (Reinforcing capabilities, specific configuration of activities)
5. What management systems are required? (Systems, structures, measures)

The initial three questions all centre around the unique positioning of companies, the last two focus on ensuring that activities are aligned with the overall positioning that we choose. No matter how we look at it, positioning, choices and trade-offs as well as alignment (see next chapter) are crucial for sustainable, profitable growth of companies in today's hyper-competitive environment.

Choices and trade-offs, while important, have not found widespread acceptance in Indian business circles. Driven by a buoyant domestic industry in the run-up to 2010, many Indian business groups were actively looking at diversification and trying to leverage perceived management capabilities and strengths in other areas. Currently, with the NDA government in power and a strong focus on defence and 'Make in India', companies are exploring opportunities for diversification in the defence industry. While diversification is not in and of itself negative, it should not be a distraction from the core business. This is valid in particular when the core business still has room to grow and needs nurturing. As the example of the hidden champions shows, it pays to go deep, i.e., to be the best in something, and then to go broad via global expansion. Only after these growth opportunities seem fully leveraged do most hidden champions look at diversification, mostly by venturing into adjacent opportunities.

In part, the tendency of Indian businessmen to go broad via diversification earlier than many of their international peers may be a direct consequence of operating in an environment characterized by institutional voids.[278] Diversification is often seen as a valid way of de-risking the business. Taking the large Indian business groups mentioned in Chapter 1 as an example, smaller players may be tempted to try to replicate their model. However, the business models that have served India's conglomerates in the past are not necessarily the right role models for smaller companies in today's highly competitive environment. Also, the skill set required to run a company and the skill set required to run a conglomerate of businesses are very different.

As pointed out by Khanna and Palepu,[279] emerging market players successfully fill institutional voids. Conglomerates in emerging markets tend to leverage the parentage advantage in several ways. They may, for example, enter a new line of business by leveraging

- access to capital,
- access to legal and political support,
- an existing talent pipeline,
- brand/reputation,
- distribution footprint and
- R&D capabilities, etc.

They may leverage their position for JVs with MNCs due to their reputation for quality, trust and transparency as well as their track record of previous JVs/alliances. And they may decide to drive innovation as a VC investor by leveraging reach and understanding of the market, their own R&D capabilities and an in-depth understanding of business models and product innovations.

To execute these approaches successfully, groups need to have structured, well-managed capital allocation and portfolio management processes to nurture new areas and to move away from businesses that no longer have sufficient potential. They need to understand clearly where their conglomerate can create value, e.g., in two or three adjacent areas, and how to leverage preferred relationships with governments, suppliers, key customers, unions, etc. Last but not least, a significant amount of attention needs to be paid to building investor confidence to convince investors that the conglomerate creates superior value beyond the 'conglomerate discount' that investors typically associate with large, diversified business groups.

A classic example of a large Indian conglomerate is the Tata group. Operating in more than 100 countries on six continents, Tata generated USD 108.8 billion in FY15. More than 600,000 employees are part of the Tata empire. As shown in Figure 6.1, the group is complex and diverse with over 100 operating companies structured into seven distinct business clusters. In addition, as shown in Figure 6.2, the challenges of managing an array of businesses in different industries, with different sizes, histories and profitability are massive. Typically, a stringent portfolio management approach and good operational practices across the universe of owned companies are necessary to ensure that capital allocation drives desired returns.

6 FIGURE 1

Tata Group Features Complexity and Diversity with Over 100 Operating Companies Structured into Seven Distinct Business Clusters

1) List of companies is not exhaustive
Source: Company website, Roland Berger Analysis

6 FIGURE 2

The Tata Group: Managing a Wide Range of Different Businesses

Return on capital analysis, profitability analysis[1], FY15, of key listed Tata companies[2]

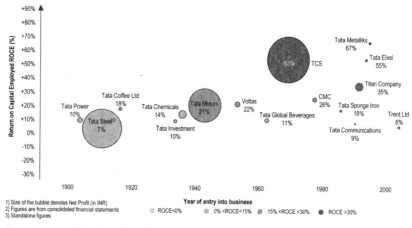

1) Size of the bubble denotes Net Profit (in INR)
2) Figures are from consolidated financial statements
3) Standalone figures

Year of entry into business

ROCE<0%   0% <ROCE<15%   15% <ROCE <30%   ROCE >30%

Source: Company website; Money Control, Roland Berger analysis

Overcoming a conglomerate discount via consistent and effective management of institutional voids is not a valid strategy for many, if not most, players as described above. Companies with insufficient management bandwidth, lack of scalable processes, etc., will not be able to replicate the success stories of the Tatas, Birlas, Adanis, etc. Even for large companies, focus is often the best strategy, as the subsequent cases of Bajaj Auto and IndiGo show. Focus, clear choices and trade-offs often lead to positive business outcomes and do not stress companies to operational breaking points.

BAJAJ AUTO AND THE STORY OF THE INDIAN TWO-WHEELER INDUSTRY

A number of Indian companies have made clear choices regarding where and how they want to play. A prime example is Bajaj Auto, a dominant player in the Indian two- and three-wheeler industry.

The Indian Two-Wheeler Market: A Global Lead Market

India's two-wheeler market is the world's largest, with about 16.5 million units sold in FY16 (see Figure 6.3). Two-wheelers have grown at a CAGR of 9.8 per cent from FY10 to FY16, about 1.6 times as fast as PVs and about 2.3 times faster than the Indian commercial vehicle (CV) market. Two-wheeler sales are primarily driven by utility needs and depend equally on urban and rural customers. Hence both agricultural and industrial output are important to sales, which has made the industry resilient to sudden reductions in demand in one or the other segment. In the domestic market, all three market segments (mopeds, scooters and motorcycles) continue to grow. Scooters are by far the most dynamic segment, with a CAGR of 22.9 per cent over the last seven years compared with 6.5 per cent for motorcycles and 4.2 per cent for mopeds.

6 FIGURE 3

Domestically, the Two-Wheeler Market Is Growing in All Segments; India's Exports Have More Than Doubled in the Past 7 Years

India two-wheeler domestic sales and exports by segment, FY10–FY16

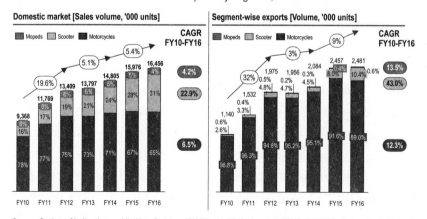

Source: Society of Indian Automobile Manufacturers (SIAM), monthly flash reports FY10–FY16, http://www.siamindia.com/, Roland Berger Analysis

Hero MotoCorp is the clear market leader with a market share of about 39 per cent; Honda comes second with a market share of 26 per cent, but with significantly higher growth rates than all other players (see Figure 6.4). TVS has grown in line with the market and has maintained a number three position in terms of overall volumes. Bajaj has stagnated domestically with a CAGR of 1 per cent and a loss of about 7 per cent of market share.

6 FIGURE 4

Bajaj Dominates the Export Market, Hero Leads the Domestic Market with Honda Being the Fastest Growing Company

India two-wheeler market share development: Domestic & exports, FY10–FY16

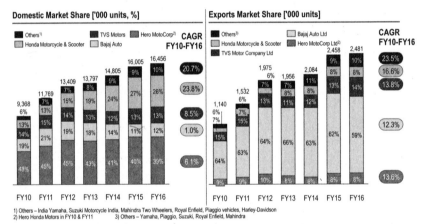

Source: Society of Indian Automobile Manufacturers (SIAM), monthly flash reports FY10-FY16, http://www.siamindia.com/, Roland Berger Analysis

Entry-level bikes (75–125 cc) form the largest base among domestic motorcycle sales, with a volume share of about 80 per cent and a growth of 7.6 per cent CAGR between FY10 and FY16 (see Figure A.15 in the Appendix). Low cost, low maintenance, superior mileage, durability and strong distribution networks are the key requirements for being successful in the segment, especially in the less-than-110cc sub-segment. For bikes between 110cc and 125cc, engine technology, build quality, light weight and other features become important.

The deluxe category of sporty commuter/sports bikes is divided into the 125cc to150cc and 200cc to 250cc sub-segments. Here Bajaj rules the roost due to the success of the Bajaj Pulsar in each sub-category (see Figure A.16 in the Appendix). In particular, Bajaj is able to leverage the partnership with Austrian motorcycle manufacturer Kronreif, Trunkenpolz, Mattighofen (KTM, see below) to drive a premium bike perception in the market. While the overall segment has shrunk over the period of FY10 to FY16 due to the overall weakness of the economy (CAGR −1.2 per cent), strong growth is expected in the future owing to the trend of customers to move to higher-cc categories. In this category, customers upgrade their bikes every 1 to 1.5 years and hence longevity and durability of the products are not that important. Margins on these bikes tend to be higher (EBITDA approximately 20 per cent) than in the entry level 75cc to110cc category (EBITDA approximately 15 per cent).

The biggest winners of the upgradation trend have been premium bikes of more than 250cc. Volumes more than quadrupled over the last four years. Here, Royal Enfield has a strong foothold in the 250cc to 500cc sub-segment and confronts international competition (Harley-Davidson, Triumph, Kawasaki, and others) in the higher segments.

Scooters have made a very strong comeback in India. Growth has been driven by buyers upgrading to higher-cc variants mainly in the 90 cc to 125cc segment. The below-90-cc segment is primarily targeted at young, working women (e.g., TVS Scooty with key USPs such as light weight, convenience and manoeuvrability). Honda rekindled the scooter segment by identifying changing customer preferences towards automatic four-stroke scooters with its undisputed segment leader, Honda Activa. Gearless scooters are easier to handle in urban traffic than bikes which require frequent shifting of gears. Unisex appeal (scooters are driven by both men and women) and ease of use in cities and towns are the key USPs of this segment versus bikes.

Mopeds will remain steady at about 700,000–750,000 units a year. They are still considered a workhorse in rural markets where they provide a low-price, high load-carrying option. Electric two-wheeler sales in India have collapsed from 100,000 units in FY12 to 21,000 units in FY14 due to the withdrawal of government subsidies and the failure to implement the National Electric Mobility Mission Plan. Revival of this segment without dramatic price corrections or substantial incentives is unlikely.

The dynamics of the Indian two-wheeler market remain strong with sales of about 30 million units predicted for FY20.[280] Growth drivers are many. Penetration levels indicate room for improvement. India's population is young (50 per cent is younger than twenty-five), and hence two-wheelers are their preferred mode of transport. The participation of women in the labour force was around 25 per cent in 2010 and leads to good sales for entry-level scooters.[281] Disposable incomes are likely to continue to rise strongly (see Figure 1.3). Urbanization will drive adoption of two-wheelers, since they are often the faster commuting option in highly congested Indian cities. Rising rural incomes bolstered by government schemes such as NREGA and Bharat Nirman as well as by rising minimum support prices for produce will drive rural sales.

Exports from India have also grown rapidly over the same time period, hitting a high of 2.5 million units in FY16. Key export markets for motorcycles and scooters are Latin America, Africa, the Middle East, South and South East Asia.[282] Exports grew only at 3 per cent from FY12 to FY14 since the reductions in incentives under the duty drawback scheme and the withdrawal of DEPB[283] forced players to increase prices, hitting sales in price-sensitive markets. In addition, African markets started seeing fierce competition from aggressively priced products being marketed by Honda and Chinese manufacturers, and Sri Lanka imposed

100 per cent import duties on two-wheelers, with a dramatic impact on volumes. However, export growth has resumed since then (CAGR FY14–FY16 of 9.1 per cent), indicating that players have adjusted to the changed competitive environment.

Growth for Bajaj has come from its exports. Here the company grew at a CAGR of 12.4 per cent (from FY10 to FY16) and maintained a dominant market share of 58.8 per cent (FY16). In FY14, Bajaj had a dominant market share in key export markets:[284] Uganda (88 per cent), Sri Lanka (80 per cent), Bangladesh (54 per cent), Colombia (44 per cent), Nigeria (43 per cent), Congo (37 per cent), Philippines (30 per cent), Central America (28 per cent), Egypt (26 per cent) and Peru (19 per cent). Besides competition from China and Honda, Bajaj will face increased pressure from Hero in Africa[285] and TVS in ASEAN,[286] as well as from Honda and Yamaha, who are using India as an export base for Latin America and Africa.

Bajaj Auto: Money Matters

Bajaj's history with two-wheelers goes back to 1945, when the company was a distributor for two- and three-wheelers in India. A breakthrough in terms of production was reached with the Bajaj Chetak, launched in 1979, based on Vespa's Sprint model. The name Chetak was taken from Maharana Pratap's horse, which was legendary for its bravery and power. In the mid-1980s, Bajaj discontinued the Vespa partnership and started producing scooters without foreign support under the tag line *Hamara Bajaj* (Our Bajaj). The Chetak was extremely successful in India. During the 1990s, monthly sales topped 100,000 units; waiting times for scooters were more than ten years. Bajaj enjoyed a 65–75 per cent market share in the segment and customers were paying extra to get early allocations of their

Chetaks. Low material cost versus industry average ensured good profitability.[287]

However, with increasing competition from Japanese motorcycle manufacturers starting in the mid-1980s, Bajaj's scooter sales declined. The Japanese brought new manufacturing technologies and processes, and suddenly Bajaj saw itself at a disadvantage. Its manufacturing technology had grown historically with heavy and light duty processes mostly done in-house, such as machining of almost all parts, manual fabrication and painting, engine and vehicle lines, etc. The lines were mostly not automated, and batch production limited flexibility. As a consequence, inventories, rejection and rework were high. Productivity was low, as was responsiveness to customers. Fit and finish was not in line with market expectations. Chetak's two-stroke engine did not reflect the needs of a changing market. For example, the fuel efficiency of 45–50 km/l of Bajaj's products trailed Hero Honda's 80 km/l by a wide margin.

To address these issues, Bajaj started cleaning up its manufacturing operations by introducing single-piece flow, 'one man-multiple machine' concepts via multi-skilling, focus on core operations, etc. Step by step, Bajaj eliminated its disadvantages versus Japanese competitors. In later waves of process optimization, TPM[288] and lean manufacturing were introduced. The vendor base was rationalized from 800 down to 200, since a fragmented vendor base did not have the means to invest in new technology, management techniques and capacity expansion. Capacity utilization went up, losses and costs were reduced, lead times were brought down, low-cost automation was introduced and a safe and participatory work environment was created. OEEs[289] and right first time ratios[290] of over 90 per cent were obtained and maintained. Via the Bajaj Automotive Vendor Association (BAVA), these improvements were passed on to suppliers to ensure mutual benefits. A case in point is the capacity extension of the Pulsar that happened in 2013. Rather than requiring vendors to invest in additional machinery, Bajaj worked with the vendors to optimize cell and plant layout to achieve a 30 per cent output increase without investment.

Consistent efforts paid off. The company was recognized with the TPM Excellence Award in 2006 and with the Consistent TPM Excellence Award in 2012. For Bajaj, TPM became 'the prime mover towards excellence'. While factory operations and production costs including vendors were covered in the first phase of TPM, the second phase extended to R&D, engineering, purchasing, service and other areas that could create losses for the manufacturing process. The third phase finally addressed business costs, i.e., applied TPM to sales, HR, finance and controlling, etc.

Bajaj's journey towards lean operations never ends. The latest focus areas are the adoption of new technologies to drive cost effectiveness and to proactively address customer irritants. Improved supply chain management, increased overall line efficiency,[291] logistics optimizations, motion reduction activities, introduction of robotic spot welding, improvements in cathode electrode deposition (CED)[292] and top-coat painting, etc., are among the many initiatives that Bajaj drives to stay competitive. The list of activities is long, and in today's challenging environment is not likely to get shorter any time soon. Cooperation with business partners is key. The larger suppliers of Bajaj, for example, have taken to replicating the Bajaj BAVA approach for their vendors.

The results speak for themselves. Overall line efficiency was brought up by about 20 per cent over the last ten years, standing today at more than 95 per cent while simultaneously increasing output and capacity. Quality improved as well. In-house rejections over the last five years have gone down by more than a factor of three in key areas such as steel, paint and chassis. Warranty costs have reduced dramatically; conversion costs and packaging costs were optimized.

The new plant in Chakan, for example, produces 100,000 vehicles per month[293] with fewer than 1,000 employees. Set up according to Japanese production principles, it has three objectives: first, no stores; second, only most critical and core operations in-house; third, no supervision. 'No stores' implies that all material has to come just in time, which led to the creation of a vendor park around the factory. 'Only critical and core operations in-house' meant a large part of outsourced value addition and hence supplier processes had to be upgraded to bring down inspections and rejections, improve maintenance processes, standardize trainings, etc. 'No supervision' implied a different quality of people that had to be hired in terms of culture and skill. Only diploma engineers are hired on the line, who can handle working versus predetermined time schedules and quality targets. Pradeep Shrivastava, COO, says 'Rather than producing 60,000 scooters with 8,000 employees in Akurdi, Chakan produces 100,000 motorcycles per month with 800 employees and uses 90,000 square metres less space than Akurdi.' Treating employees in Chakan as line engineers rather than blue collar workers and spending additional money on visiting cards, travel arrangements,[294] common facilities of line engineers and management, etc., clearly paid off in terms of improved productivity. Promotions are based on performance rather than being degree-driven, which provides additional motivation to young engineers trying to build a career for themselves.

The extent of the operational excellence challenge cannot be underestimated. A good vendor ecosystem did not exist in the 1990s. Since leveraging Honda's keiretsu[295] would have proved counterproductive, Bajaj worked with alternative vendors to build up their scale and operational and technological capability.

A natural place to look for partners in this journey was Europe. Win–win opportunities with suppliers such as Bosch, who had a large repertoire of technology and wanted to enter the two-wheeler field, were leveraged, and are still creating value today.

While this quality and productivity journey was substantial and required a complete change of company culture, Rajiv Bajaj, who by that time had taken on the role of managing director, knew it was not enough to play the efficiency game. With declining scooter sales in the 1990s, he realized that the company would need a credible presence in the motorcycle space. Initial help was provided by Kawasaki, but soon the team around Rajiv realized that they would have to develop their own technology to be able to withstand the challenges of the market as an independent company. Attempts to hire experts from the Indian industry failed, as competence levels across the board were stuck at engine modifications, not at engine development. A different approach was needed. A small team of bright engineers with no experience in R&D was to become the core of Bajaj's revamped R&D department.[296] The team reported directly to the managing director, and this connection was vital as development efforts proved difficult. To drive success, full responsibility was given to the team, including vendor selection and agreeing on the commercial terms with vendors. De facto, a company within a company was created, full of energy and zeal to build an indigenous four-stroke engine. Today, Bajaj has won several innovation awards, was listed among the top 100 innovative companies globally by Forbes,[297] and has proprietary technologies such as twin spark that deliver tangible benefits to customers (in this case a 10–15 per cent fuel efficiency improvement). As Abraham Joseph, chief technology officer, puts it, 'We have the job of building character into our vehicles, making sure that technology and brand identity become visible and are understood by our customers across the various generations of our vehicles.'

Bajaj's launch of the CT100 followed in May 2004 to take on the entry segment of the motorcycle market. The CT100 was a success and drove market share to 22 per cent from 17 per cent in the entry segment. However, the bike did not result in a real breakthrough. A second attempt to penetrate the entry-level segment was made with the April 2006 launch of the Platina. S. Ravikumar, president of business development and assurance, describes it as 'a good enough commuter bike to take on the Japanese.' But still, the company found itself at a crossroads. While a reputed management consultancy company recommended taking on Hero Honda in the commuter bike segment, as this was the belly of the market, the Platina did not manage to really move the market. Would Bajaj be able to take the competition head-on? Was this the right way forward?

Bajaj chose a different way. Following Rajiv's motto—'Be the number one or be different!'—the company decided to shoot for a de facto non-existing segment of the market, a 150cc sports bike, the Pulsar. Ravikumar says 'In short, we decided to be everything that Honda wasn't. Where they had 100cc bikes that were low-involvement, functional commuting solutions, we had 150cc bikes that were high-involvement for adrenalin-charged riders. Where Honda had a flat seat to accommodate a family, we had a curved seat that would accommodate a rider and his girlfriend. Where Honda was fuel efficiency, we were power!' The Pulsar was a run away success and even today dominates its segment (see Figure A.16 in the Appendix).

At the core of this decision lay the conviction that Indian customers would not shift brand allegiances for a 10–15 per cent difference in product performance. The positioning of Bajaj had to be clearly differentiated, ideally disruptive, to be able to drive sales. As Eric Vas, president for the motorcycle business, puts it:

We believe that there are three types of customers in the motorcycle business. An indifferent or functional buyer for 100cc motorcycles and also scooters, a youthful customer that would fit our Pulsar, and a mature customer more in line with our Avenger. This separation is independent of price; price is a secondary purchase criterion and style is a third, but at every price point you will find these three basic customer types.

The company also believes in understanding these customers in detail, so much so that it has its own market research department rather than relying on external market analysis. Bajaj's interviewing techniques, product exposure approaches, etc., have turned into key competitive advantages for the company.

The basis for Bajaj's success is a strong brand philosophy. Rather than pushing an umbrella brand, the company chose to position strong product brands with clear identities for various segments. The Pulsar is clearly a sports bike, the Avenger a cruiser, the Discover a commuting bike, and the Platina is the ultimate value-for-money bike due to its class-leading mileage, durability and price. Bajaj as a company thus covers mass and mass premium with a clear focus on the mass premium end of the market. Going beyond the Pulsar into premium bikes is not feasible with the Bajaj brand, since it would stretch the brand too far. Customer lifecycle extension is achieved via the partnerships with KTM and Kawasaki, which we will discuss below.

In 2009, Bajaj made another courageous decision: It exited the scooter segment, even though its Chetak had turned Bajaj into a household name. Rather than spread its efforts too thin, the leadership team believed that focusing on the larger global market (where motorcycles dominate instead of scooters) was a more promising and profitable way forward. As a consequence, the team also decided to drive the international business more aggressively, a stance that clearly paid off. Today, Bajaj is at the first or second position in more than 60 per cent of the international markets that it operates in. From an Indian company that also sold some products in international markets, it transformed itself into a major global player with about 50 per cent of its turnover outside of India.

Bajaj's journey would not have been possible without clear leadership, strong processes and solid HR and governance frameworks. Rajiv and his executive team meet three days a month to thoroughly review key management issues. Market performance, product performance, technology road maps, financial performance, vendor/dealer performance and health, HR issues, etc., are discussed in detail according to a predetermined calendar and agenda. Business unit reviews are held in the brand management review committee, while overall issues are discussed in the business review committee. The managing director also heads the BAVA Executive Council, the apex body of all the meeting structures that Bajaj has put in place with its vendors. Strong, bi-directional communication along the value chain ensures consistent alignment between the company and its partners. Clearly defined product development processes are in line with global benchmarks. Product development is overseen by Rajiv and his executive team in regular reviews.

Teamwork and open communication are easy for Bajaj's leaders. Most of them have been with the company for the last twenty-five to thirty years and were instrumental in driving change at Bajaj. The team members know each other: They know the ins and outs of the business and they work together in cross-functional teams in constructive, trust-based relationships based on the premise 'business first'. As Ravikumar states,

> Besides a few courageous calls, this business is about relentless attention to detail along the value chain. Success does not come with grandiose ideas but via consistent and meticulous execution over long periods of time. The teams know this and we challenge each other to live up to the requirements of the company.

HR policies have to be closely aligned with the overall business strategy. 'Our key strategic directions in 2007, the year when I joined, were: first, global penetration, second, sharper brands, and third, efficient back end. I needed to reflect that in the organizational structure as well as policies,' says Amruth Rath, president of human resources. As a consequence, to grow the international business by a factor of six, the position of an international business head was created and put on par with the other management functions in the executive committee. To drive sharp brands, it was obvious that a differentiated customer experience via the ownership of one or two brand attributes was necessary. In the world of motorcycles this meant that style, performance and cost had to speak, i.e., the R&D function needed to be strengthened. The number of R&D employees increased accordingly from less than 400 in 2007 to about 1300 today. Also, brands were sharply positioned by ensuring that international business, KTM India, CV and two-wheeler business are represented from a front-end perspective by separate business unit leaders. At the back end, however, resources are shared ensuring optimal cost position as well as a certain redundancy in the system. Collaboration across functions is ensured via clearly defined processes, roles and responsibilities.

Alignment across the organization is driven via biannual meetings of the top management. In these meetings past performance and future strategy are discussed, challenged and subsequently cascaded across the organization. Systematic job rotation programmes also ensure informal linkages between different departments as well as contribute to developing well-rounded future leaders. Fixed compensation is pegged at the seventy-fifth percentile of the industry; variable components can take this number to the ninetieth percentile. Twenty per cent of the potential variable is tied to quarterly success versus aspirational goals and 20 per cent is tied to overarching goals for the year. The quarterly performance review is stringent, transparent and runs with fixed timelines. It creates a continuous, positive performance tension in the system. In short, the HR system is set up to drive a high-performance culture. To provide meaningful roles to employees, overstaffing of roles and organizational slack are actively avoided. Time is not wasted when employees don't click. Either they are assigned to other roles or asked to go. At the same time, compensation and roles are attractive and enable Bajaj to hire the best available talent from the market.

In the dynamic environment of India's two-wheeler market the strategy of Bajaj Auto stands out due to its consistency and boldness. Bajaj believes in margin before mass, i.e., it has clear requirements as to the profitability of its core business. The company has been the most profitable company among the main players for the past five years in a row (see Figure 6.5). In terms of profitability, Bajaj's EBITDA of around 20 per cent outperformed competitors by a margin of 1.5–3 times over the last years. And while the total revenue is 21 per cent lower than that of Hero, profit after tax is 18 per cent higher, as shown in Figure 6.5. Looking at major cost items in Bajaj's P&L versus competitors, we find[298] that employee costs are very low (4.1 per cent in FY15), indicating a successful HR policy. The same holds true for depreciation costs (1.2 per cent in FY15), which indicates a very efficient use of capital expenditure. Fixed costs overall amount to only 8 per cent while variable cost amounts to 72 per cent of total turnover, thus providing the company with a very large degree of flexibility. Raw material cost as a percentage of turnover stands at 62 per cent, dramatically lower than that of the competition, indicating that both R&D efforts as well as close collaboration with suppliers are paying rich dividends for the company (see A.17 in the Appendix).

6 FIGURE 5

While Bajaj's Revenue Was 21% Lower Than That of Hero in 2015,[1] Its Profit after Tax Was 18% Higher

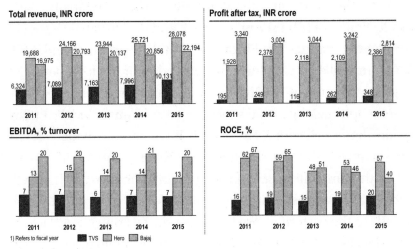

Source: Company annual reports, Roland Berger

Part of the outstanding financial performance results from the focus on higher-margin segments. As discussed above, Bajaj is strong in the premium segment of the Indian motorcycle market as well as in export markets. As far as the premium segment is concerned, Bajaj Auto bets on continued volume growth in the higher-displacement, premium motorcycle segment. To support its premium image, Bajaj has invested early in technology development via cooperation with KTM and Kawasaki.

Take Bajaj's partnership with KTM as an example. Bajaj's engagement with KTM started in 2008 when Bajaj rescued the company from sure bankruptcy in the face of the global financial crisis. Today, KTM has turned around and has more than doubled sales volumes from 70,000 units in 2008 to 181,000 superbikes in 2015, overtaking BMW in the process. Over time, Bajaj has bought an increasing stake in KTM and now owns 48 per cent of the company. Bajaj has full access to KTM's engine technology, which reduces technology risk for the company dramatically. This access also allows Bajaj entry into higher-engine-capacity bikes for both the export and the domestic market. Potentially, Bajaj can leverage KTM's extensive service and dealer network spread throughout markets like Europe. Selling Bajaj products under the KTM umbrella, e.g., in the US, would also circumvent potential negative country-of-origin bias in developed markets and allow margin optimization. Bajaj's sporty, powerful image via the Pulsar brand aligns well with KTM's sports bikes and off-roaders. KTM is in many ways a natural extension of the Bajaj brand.

Both companies use common engine platforms at the back end to achieve cost efficiency while providing very distinctive brands to the customer. Anything that the customer sees, feels or experiences is clearly kept separate. Some technologies, e.g., twin spark from Bajaj, are kept for the respective brands exclusively to ensure brand differentiation. This approach drives operational and R&D efficiencies. It also allows the company to serve very different customer segments. Vice versa, leveraging factor cost advantages and efficient production by Bajaj increases the competitive edge of KTM. Scale effects in procurement and other areas are beneficial to both companies.

Beyond these synergies, Bajaj allows KTM a risk-reduced entry into emerging markets such as China, ASEAN, Latin America and Africa, thereby enabling KTM to become a truly global brand. India can and has been used as a springboard for emerging markets, and Bajaj's home advantage has driven KTM's exceedingly high growth (more than 70 per cent) in the country. In November 2014, KTM became the market leader in its segment, overtaking the Yamaha R15 and Honda CBR.[299] With a dense network of representative 3S[300] facilities across the country and exclusive customer engagement activities, such as an authentic race track experience for core customers, motorsports experiences for amateurs, and overnight touring and camping experiences of 'non-racer' customers, KTM builds a deep customer connect and reinforces its own as well as Bajaj's brand.

The KTM partnership has supported Bajaj's R&D efforts and potentially helped the company to be recognized as one of the world's 100 most innovative companies in 2014 as well as the fifth most valuable brand in the top fifty Indian brands of 2014. As a matter of fact, the Bajaj–KTM cooperation has been so successful that BMW decided to collaborate with TVS to develop and produce 300–400cc bikes in India. These bikes will be double-badged and sold globally via the TVS and BMW sales channels.

Today, Bajaj is a force to reckon with in the global two-wheeler market. Bold decisions, clear positioning and meticulous execution have driven the company into the global limelight. On the back of a large and forgiving domestic market, the company was able to up its game at a time when competitors were trying to find a foothold in the Indian market. As the team suggests, being underrated by competition turned out to be a blessing as well. Large global competitors did not believe that Bajaj would transform into a globally competitive organization. This gave Rajiv and the team the breathing space that they needed to drive performance. With current reports[301] that Bajaj may consider the scooter segment again, especially as the segment is moving to larger, above-90cc scooters, Bajaj may reinvent itself yet again. While the global deck in the two-wheeler space is constantly being re-shuffled, it is clear that Bajaj will remain a trump card for some time to come.

INDIA'S HEALTHCARE SYSTEM: THE GREAT DIVIDE

Healthcare in India is a multi-billion-dollar opportunity with characteristics that vary greatly depending on where healthcare is provided. Vaatsalya Healthcare has turned this uneven performance into a business opportunity via a clear access-based choice.

India's Healthcare Market: A Multi-Billion-Dollar Opportunity

India's USD 74.4 billion[302] healthcare market is split into six segments.[303] As of FY14, hospitals are the largest segment and amount to 51 per cent of the total healthcare expenditure. They are followed by pharmaceuticals at 16 per cent, medical equipment and devices at 7 per cent, medical insurance at 3 per cent, diagnostics at 1 per cent and other allied activities at 21 per cent. In terms of services, the healthcare sector is classified into three service levels: primary care, secondary care and tertiary care, as shown in Figure 6.6. According to Economist Intelligence Unit (EIU),[304] the healthcare market in India is poised to grow at a CAGR of about 14.8 per cent—from about USD 74.4 billion in 2013 to USD 169.9 billion in 2019. This rapid growth, significantly faster than the overall GDP growth of the country is, among others,[305] driven by increasing health awareness. Health insurance has grown at a CAGR of 29 per cent—from USD 463 million in FY06 to USD 3.64 billion in FY14. Additional factors are a dramatic increase in lifestyle-related sicknesses. For example,[306] diabetes cases have increased by about 63 per cent between 2007 and 2014, from 41 million cases to 67 million cases. Overall, India is second only to China in the number of diabetes cases in 2014.[307]

Coronary heart disease[308] increased sharply by 94.4 per cent—from affecting 18 million people in 2005 to 35 million people in 2015. Things do not seem likely to improve in the short run as the rural population is increasingly affected by lifestyle-related diseases.

6 FIGURE 6

Healthcare Delivery Sector Is Classified across Three Service Levels

Classification across levels

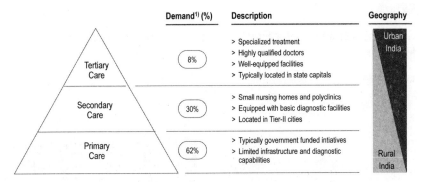

1) Estimates based on Proportion of Ailing Persons (PAP) within Rural and Urban population of India, Key Indicators of Social Consumption: Health (NSS 71st Round, January-June 2014), p. 10
Source: India Hospitals Industry 2015 (Dun & Bradstreet), p. 6, Key Indicators of Social Consumption: Health (NSS 71st Round)), Roland Berger

Overall, India spends about 4 per cent of her GDP in total healthcare expenditure. While this number compares favourably with countries such as Thailand, Bangladesh, Sri Lanka and Indonesia, it trails China (5.6 per cent), Brazil (9.7 per cent), South Africa (8.9 per cent) and Germany (11 per cent).[309] Challenges in the Indian healthcare system are manifold; however, for the purpose of this discussion we will focus on the urban–rural divide, the high level of out-of-pocket expenditure that is required in the Indian healthcare system and the severe shortage of doctors, nurses and hospital beds that the country faces as compared to global averages.

Hospitals in India are split between government hospitals (including healthcare centres, district hospitals and general hospitals) and private hospitals (nursing homes, clinics and other non-government for-profit healthcare delivery entities). As can be seen in Figure 6.7, both rural and urban areas prefer private medical care to government care, and this ratio tilts even further towards the private sector with increasing income. As discussed earlier, India's GSAs are weak, and the private–government split in healthcare is a direct reflection of the same in the health sector.

6 FIGURE 7

65% Households Prefer Private Healthcare in India over Public Healthcare

Sources of healthcare, 2005–06 (*n* = 109,041)

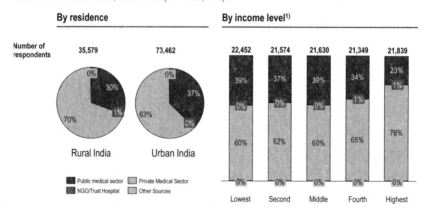

1) Survey respondents classified into quintiles based on annual income
Source: National Family Health Survey 3 (2005–06), Ministry of Health & Family Welfare, pp. 436–40, Roland Berger Analysis

Hospital bed density per 1000 population is estimated at 1.57 (0.95 private, 0.63 government),[310] well below the global median of 2.6 and upper-middle-class-income country average of 3.2.[311] Since 2002, growth has happened mostly in the private sector (CAGR of 8.2 per cent till calendar year 2014) while government investments have been lagging demand dramatically (CAGR of 2.9 per cent in the same time period). About 1.7 million beds are estimated[312] for FY14 (12 lakh in urban centres and 5 lakh in rural areas). Projected growth rates of about CAGR 6.6 per cent till FY19[313] and 7.5 per cent between FY19 and FY25[314] will continue to drag behind projected GDP growth rates.

India's medical workforce is pegged at around 4.7 million practitioners, about 18 per cent of whom are certified allopathic doctors.[315] Registrations of doctors have fallen over the last five years (see Figure 6.8). Overall, one allopathic doctor covers 1218 patients. Corresponding ratios for dentists (10,121), nurses (532) and pharmacists (1987)[316] are modest by global comparisons. On a global average, allopathic doctors serve 709 patients, dental doctors serve 3704 patients and nurses serve 342 patients,[317] almost a two-fold increase in medical workforce availability.

6 FIGURE 8

Registered Allopathic Doctors Constitute Only 18% of the Workforce and Serve a Limited Population Set

Medical workforce (2014)

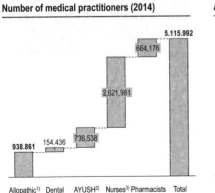

Number of medical practitioners (2014)

5.115.992
664,176
2.621,981
938.861 154.436 736,538

Allopathic[1] Dental AYUSH[2] Nurses[3] Pharmacists Total

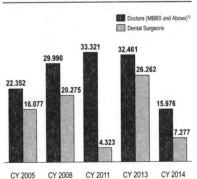

Annual registrations (2014)

Doctors (MBBS and Above)[1]
Dental Surgeons

33.321
29.990   32.461
22.352   26.262
16.077   20.275
                   15.976
              4.323   7.277

CY 2005 CY 2008 CY 2011 CY 2013 CY 2014

1) Only doctors with recognized medical qualifications (under MCI Act): 2) AYUSH = Ayurvedic, Unani, Siddha and Homeopathic doctors; 3) Nurses include auxiliary nurse midwives, registered nurses and registered midwives along with lady health visitors

Source: Human Resources in Health Sector, National Health Profile, 2005, 2008, 2011, 2013 and 2015 (Central Bureau of Health Intelligence), Roland Berger analysis

In terms of out-of-pocket expenditure, India's patients are among the world's most burdened. About 58 per cent of all healthcare expenses are borne directly by India's patients, dramatically higher than China's 34 per cent, Thailand's 11 per cent and Germany's 13 per cent.[318] As Figure 6.9 shows, hospitalization expenses in 2014 were mostly borne from household savings and not covered under insurance.[319] Being sick in India is therefore often life-threatening in more than one way. In addition to illness, it has the potential to wipe out household savings, especially of poorer households. Remarkably, expenditure patterns do not differ much between rural and urban areas, with the notable exception of a 4 per cent insurance penetration in the urban areas versus a 0 per cent penetration in rural areas.

6 FIGURE 9

Hospitalization Expenses Are Mostly Borne from Household Savings and Not Covered under Insurance

Healthcare Expenses, 2014 (n = 333,104)

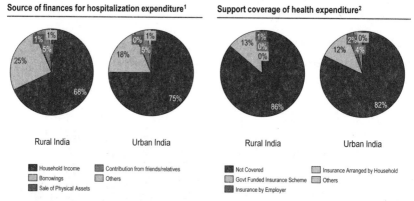

Source of finances for hospitalization expenditure[1]   Support coverage of health expenditure[2]

Rural India   Urban India   Rural India   Urban India

■ Household Income   ■ Contribution from friends/relatives   ■ Not Covered   ■ Insurance Arranged by Household
■ Borrowings   ■ Others   ■ Govt Funded Insurance Scheme   ■ Others
■ Sale of Physical Assets   ■ Insurance by Employer

1) From Key Indicators of Social Consumption: Health (NSS 71st Round), January–June 2014 pp 23; 2) From Key Indicators of Social Consumption: Health (NSS 71st Round), p. 21
Source: Key Indicators of Social Consumption: Health (NSS 71st Round), 2014, http://mospi.nic.in/Mospi_New/upload/nss_71st_ki_health_30june15.pdf, Roland Berger Analysis

Doctors and hospital beds are not only insufficient in India as a whole, in rural settings they are at even more of a premium.

While the population spread in India is roughly 70:30 in terms of rural versus urban, medical facilities are split nearly exactly the opposite way. The public sector, for example, maintains about 433,000 beds in urban areas versus 196,000 in rural areas in 2013.[320] For the private sector, the split is similar. About 654,000 beds are estimated in urban areas versus 296,000 in rural areas (FY11).[321] Even more worrying, the number of private facilities in rural areas has decreased from 440,000 beds in FY01 by about one third. In terms of doctors, about 71,000 government-employed doctors are practising in urban areas vs 35,000 in rural areas (2013).[322] The rural–urban split for the 811,000 private doctors is not available; however, it is unlikely to differ much from the split seen in available hospital beds. Interestingly, while the number of doctors between government and private hospitals is a ratio of 1:7.6, the total health expenditure in the government sector in 2013 amounts to USD 25 billion versus USD 52 billion in the private sector, a ratio of 1:2.1.[323] Higher density of doctors is another reason why private healthcare is clearly preferred over government-run hospitals and care facilities in India.

Healthcare in India's Tier-2 and Tier-3 towns and cities is mostly provided by government healthcare centres, family-owned, husband–wife nursing homes and private clinics. The government healthcare centres lack adequate resources in terms of doctors, nurses and infrastructure as discussed above. Visits to government hospitals are mainly driven by the lack of alternatives as well as very low price points for basic services. Private clinics in small towns typically do not operate around the clock; hence, they do not provide an option in the case of severe, life-threatening diseases. Practical experience on the ground also suggests that these centres are generally reluctant to treat cases in which there is an acute need for support but very little hope of survival. Trust and transparency for patients regarding treatments and charges are an issue with many of these private facilities. This is made more challenging by the fact that hiring and training criteria for nurses and support staff are often inadequate.

Vaatsalya Healthcare: Caring for Underserved Localities

Vaatsalya Healthcare recognized the need for professional, specialized care in India's smaller towns. Dr Ashwin Naik (CEO), a US-trained physician, realized in early 2000 that while his parents had settled down in Hubli, a small town in Karnataka, they had no access to decent medical facilities. He and Dr Veerendra Hiremath (co-founder and CEO) decided to tackle this healthcare challenge in 2004. The mission of Vaatsalya from the beginning was centred on the five As: affordability, accessibility, availability, acceptability and awareness. In other words, the team wanted to provide affordable healthcare in geographically convenient locations centred around four core services (see below) and potential add-on services. It believed in providing quality healthcare on a 24/7 basis and in creating local awareness and acceptance by, for example, training local employees and reaching out to the community via awareness events. Key motivations were to build a hospital infrastructure that would be of the highest standards, i.e., adequate to accommodate the founders' families, would be driven by high ethical values[324] and based on scalability driven by standardization of operating procedures.

To achieve this goal, the company developed an asset-light, no-frills, low-price, hub-based business model. The Vaatsalya approach focuses on offering affordable and high-quality primary and secondary healthcare services in Tier-2 and Tier-3 towns and cities. Within these Tier-2 and Tier-3 towns, Vaatsalya has segmented their customers by income level. Typical customers are individual traders, businessmen, shop-keepers, etc. Patient earnings vary with 50 per cent earning between INR 5,000 and INR 10,000 per month, 30 per cent earning between INR 10,000 and INR 25,000, and the last 20 per cent earning more than INR 25,000 per month. More than 90 per cent of them do not subscribe to newspapers and the majority of customers do not have any form of insurance coverage.

The healthcare services of Vaatsalya are chosen around a core set of specialized services to drive synergies and cost efficiencies. To determine these services, the team under Dr Naik and Dr Hiremath followed a simple logic: One key component of care in Tier-2/3 settings is time. Towns are often at some distance from major care centres and travel does take time due to lacking infrastructure. As a consequence, time-critical services such as neo-natal care and post-birth complications for the baby are a focus for the hospital via specialization in gynaecology and paediatrics. The second component is centred on services that are considered a necessity in today's age. Hence, services like nephrology,[325] intensive care facilities, laparoscopic surgery,[326] etc., are covered by the hospitals, as existing standards for these services in Tier-2/3 cities are weak. Services that require significant movement of people, such as dialysis, provide an opportunity for Vaatsalya versus the hassle in terms of time and cost of getting to major hospitals two to three times a week. Lastly, general surgery and general medicine are part of Vaatsalya's offering as many people prefer a quality, close-to-home solution for these standard services rather than incurring the complexity of travelling to the next major care facility. In addition, recognizing the need in smaller towns, Vaatsalya has also started with preventive care via chronic disease management.

Vaatsalya's marketing and awareness efforts are clearly targeted towards their key clients. In terms of above the line activities, Vaatsalya reaches out to the masses via a weekly healthcare awareness programme on All India Radio called Vaatsalya Aarogya (radio has a much higher penetration rate than newspapers, especially for Vaatsalya's patients). Other activities include campaigns in public places in the localities that it serves. The hospital provides a health helpline in the towns where it operates, which gives patients an opportunity to call in and discuss their problems with a doctor on call.

The company drives a community health project where it goes door-to-door with local health workers to understand the health profiles and needs of the communities in which it operates. This helps in designing and delivering its services accordingly. Patients are given coupons and discount cards for successful referrals of the hospital within their networks. Patient and information exchange clubs for people with diabetes or who need dialysis, for mothers whose babies went into neonatal intensive care, etc., enable improved health awareness and increase customer loyalty to the hospital. Outreach to local NGOs, Rotary clubs, Lions clubs, schools, government hospitals, etc., increases local impact and awareness. Last but not least, tie-ups with a long list of state and Central health insurance programmes have improved customer acquisition and retention. As Dr Naik points out:

> When we started out, about 2 per cent of the revenue came from insurance. Today it is about 16–17 per cent, half of which is from the government. Tying up with various insurance programmes is a key strategy because we realize that when the customer doesn't have to worry about paying you, their compliance is much better.

Focus on customers via stringent feedback mechanisms and increased operational efficiency is another area of differentiation for Vaatsalya. By implementing an interactive voice response booking system, waiting times were reduced by 75 per cent from two to four hours to fifteen to thirty minutes. While the initial worry was that customers would not take appointments, they appreciated the system and are now putting pressure on the rest of the hospital operations as they expect negligible waiting times when interfacing with Vaatsalya. Customer feedback is captured within two to three hours of admission to the hospital and corrective action is taken if necessary. Customer experience is measured via exit feedback and subsequent calls from a third-party provider. Discharge summaries and billing details are generated well in advance, enhancing transparency for the patient. Key performance indicators that are tracked include efficiency of the admission process, quality of service, behaviour of support staff and nurses, efficiency of billing and clearance processes, etc. In addition, Vaatsalya is working on a clinical performance index to track performance for the organization as a whole, at the zonal and unit levels as well as for individual doctors and staff. In addition to creating performance transparency across the value chain, this system has enabled cooperation. Rather than trying to solve key challenges on KPIs alone, doctors and hospitals within the Vaatsalya network reach out to find solutions to problems together and to learn from each other's experiences.

Value for cost-conscious, un-insured Tier-2/3 town patients must come at an attractive price. The hospital's low cost strategy is driven by a dual focus on cost efficiency and optimal utilization of resources. With a network of seventeen hospitals, Vaatsalya can create value by improving price negotiations with vendors, as well as through vendor consolidation and management. It can also work on standardizing operating procedures and hence create efficiencies by leveraging mass production techniques. Local hires help in creating community connections and improving the customer experience. At the same time, lower local salaries have a positive impact on overall overhead costs. Support for local talent is provided through a centralized training school that ensures uniform quality standards across the country.

Vaatsalya's average revenue per occupied bed day (a standard industry metric) is INR 2000, a far cry from the INR 20,000 for high-end Tier-1 city hospitals such as Apollo and Fortis. Clearly, investment levels must be adjusted accordingly. While Tier-1 high-end hospitals have to invest about INR 50 lakh per bed in a full-service model and INR 15 lakh per bed in an asset-light model for Tier-2 cities such as Apollo's Reach, Vaatsalya invests about INR 5 lakh with land on lease. Without land costs (about 30 per cent of the total) the company invests about INR 3 lakh for instruments, etc. Investments are made carefully and tailored to the task at hand.

Cost is optimized in other areas as well. For example, the general ward is larger than in higher-end hospitals, with about twenty in a general ward for a fifty-bed hospital. Even special rooms are not air-conditioned, as customers may not want to pay for this extra. Capital expenses for land are avoided by leasing the land, and because Vaatsalya operates in semi-urban areas such as Hubli, Bijapur and Raichur (all in Karnataka), rentals are low. Overall operating costs per hospital work out to about INR 15 lakh per month while setup costs amount to about INR 1–2 crore.

Revenue is 20–30 per cent higher than in local government hospitals and nursing homes. Customers are willing to pay due to the differentiated service that is provided. The cost–revenue equation allows each hospital, which gets on average 50,000 patients per year, to break even within twelve to eighteen months. 'It took Vaatsalya three years to break even for its first centre in Hubli primarily because it was still in the learning phase,' says Dr Naik. 'Today, a new centre could break even in about eighteen months.'

Getting doctors to move from big to small cities is a big challenge. Initially, Dr Naik and Dr Hiremath solved this problem by enlisting family members. A scalable solution emerged by paying doctors salaries comparable to those paid in Tier-1 cities. The main attraction for doctors in Vaatsalya hospitals then becomes the additional control and independence that they enjoy in a smaller hospital versus some of the large institutions in Tier-1 cities.

A network of hospitals also allows for rotation of doctors and paramedical staff, a key advantage in terms of talent retention.[327] As Dr Naik points out,

> One [advantage] is recruitment, right? Recruitment of doctors, nurses, etc., because we have this network, we can provide much better career options for them, if they decide to move. It's not that they will decide to move every day, but they have the option. Advantages also occur within a town or hospital. Let's say a paediatrician who builds his practice can act as a mentor for three or four surrounding hospitals, be an expert to them.

Vaatsalya's success is based on the key principle of undertaking small field-based experiments. During its launch in 2004, Vaatsalya utilized angel funding and undertook a series of field-based experiments to determine the type of hospitals to be set up, services to be offered, price points, customers, doctors needed, etc. The company kicked off with three hospitals in Hubli, Gadag and Karwar. All three worked on different models. One was an out-patient department services model, the other focused on day care and the third was a nursing home and surgery outfit. In about two-and-a-half years, the company realized that in smaller towns, a nursing home is the only workable model. Vaatsalya shut down the other two models, and since then the company has only built hospitals with fifty to seventy-five beds because anything less than thirty beds was insufficient to differentiate Vaatsalya from small clinics and government centres. In addition, attracting good doctors proved to be difficult for sub-critical units.

Dr Naik points out,

> We didn't start with "This is the market we want to enter." We started with experiments in a town which has about 700,000 people; then we did a pilot in a town which is about 100,000 people, and a pilot in another town which was 200,000 people . . . We ran these pilots for a year or two and understood what is working and what is not working. We found out that four criteria were important. First, there is an opportunity for a third party to come up and set up hospitals in these towns. Patients will come. Second, they will come and obviously pay for it. Third, we will be able to attract doctors who are willing to come and join us, to work with us because of the opportunities. Fourth, we will be able to get enough people to support these doctors, because the pitch that we were making to doctors was that we will provide the nursing team, the support team, the administrative team, so that you can focus on the practice. What happened along the way was that the type of doctors we were attracting were those who wanted to go to small towns but never went because they didn't have the support.

While scalability has been at the forefront of the founders' thinking since inception, in practice, it has its limitations. Clearly, a larger number of hospitals can drive economies of scale, economies of scope (type of services) and economies of learning (experiment-driven learning). However, local context is very important in this business. Scalability has to be driven by an integrated mix of standard operating procedures and customization to local context. As Dr Naik points out,

Another big learning has been how operations in every state have to be different. We started out in Karnataka but could not readily apply those experiences and skills in Andhra Pradesh. Our real estate cost, for instance, has increased in Andhra Pradesh. We will need to factor this in as we expand.

The way forward promises to be exciting. A particular interesting challenge is to provide services for the bottom 30 per cent of the 'base of the pyramid'. In this area, Vaatsalya is working on micro-insurance schemes. It also works on identifying, testing and adopting technologies which can enable healthcare access to the population without the intervention of doctors. This will bridge major challenges in scaling up the business model into new geographies including rural areas.

INSURANCE IN INDIA: VUCA IN ACTION

Turbulent environments test choices that companies make, sometimes forcing them to adjust business models. The Indian insurance industry is a case in point.

Insurance in India: An Overview

The private insurance business in India has a short but very turbulent history of about fifteen years.[328] The industry was opened up to private investments in August 2000 with the hope that consumers and companies would benefit from competition and innovation that private participation was expected to bring. Prior to liberalization, the life insurance sector was dominated by the state-owned Life Insurance Corporation (LIC) which was established in 1956 via the absorption of 245 Indian and foreign insurers into one nationalized entity.[329] Private companies were supposed to increase the security cover for individuals and organizations by providing new, innovative, need-based insurance products to the market. At the same time, this should also stimulate the economy. Insurance is and has always been an instrument to channel household savings into more productive uses by using the capital market to invest its funds.[330] Initial ownership of foreign entities was limited to 26 per cent and the sector was to be regulated by the Insurance Regulatory and Development Authority (IRDA) which was constituted in 1999.

6 FIGURE 10

The Indian Life Insurance Sector Has Gone through Multiple Phases since It Was Opened to the Private Sector in 2000

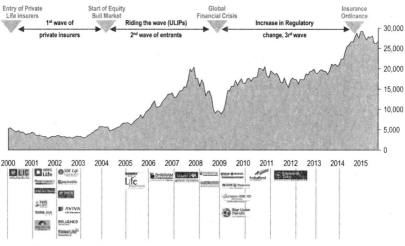

Source: Roland Berger analysis

After liberalization, the insurance industry has seen three distinct waves as far as operating conditions for private life insurers are concerned, as shown in Figure 6.10. The first entry wave of private companies rode the excitement of a large, under-penetrated market such as India opening up for health insurance. Twelve companies entered the fray in an environment that was characterized by low inflation and medium GDP growth of about 5.3 per cent CAGR.[331] Broadly, the entrants were either large Indian financial services companies or conglomerates with the funds to support the relatively long gestation time of the life insurance business. Due to the complex nature of the business, many of these players tied up with external companies possessing the tools to manage the business. Even today, twenty-one out of the twenty-three private health insurance companies have JVs with global majors.[332] Some of these include Bajaj Allianz, ICICI Lombard, etc. In addition, the initial exuberance regarding business opportunities in India motivated some foreign entrants to pay high premiums to partner with domestic players.

Initial market penetration by private players remained rather low, as shown in Figure 6.11. The reasons for this were manifold. By the time liberalization occurred, LIC had gathered enough strength to face the onslaught of private players. The company also had a well-entrenched network of agents across the country that proved unassailable, as it continues to be even today. In addition, consumers were conservative and preferred the traditional, known products of LIC over the newer offerings of hitherto-untried private players. In terms of distribution and products, private players also did not offer much differentiation. The distribution model was agency-led with a clear challenge of building up a national network that could rival LIC. Traditional life insurance policies were offered and only a few segment-led plans for children and pensions were developed. Product development was supported by foreign players and workflow was largely paper-based.

Things started to look up with the start of the equity bull-run from FY04 to FY09. This period was characterized by low inflation of about 5.7 per cent[333] and high GDP growth of 8.4 per cent.[334] The equity market went from 5696 points at the beginning of 2004 to a peak valuation of 20,287 points in December 2007,[335] an ideal time for insurers to build market share by offering unit-linked products or ULIPs.[336] Nine new players, mostly banks, entered the insurance business, and this period was characterized by rapid growth, with the business of private insurance companies shifting to about 85+ per cent in ULIPs. Insurance density measured as the ratio of total premium (in USD) to total population increased by nearly a factor of three from 15.7 in FY04 to 47.7 in FY09 and finally peaked at 55.7 in FY10. Life insurance penetration, which stood at 2.53 per cent of GDP in FY04 peaked at 4.6 per cent in FY09.[337] The insurance industry—and particularly the life insurance industry, which accounts for 90+ per cent of all the assets—was seen as the new sunrise sector in the economy and had an easy time attracting talent.

6 FIGURE 11

Private Sector Insurers Took a Few Years to Gain Traction in the Market. Currently, Their Market Share Is 27%

Overview of Indian life insurance industry, FY01 – FY15

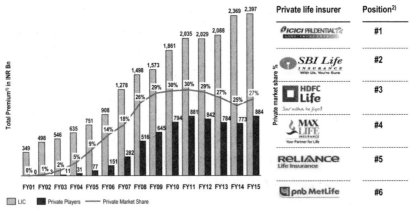

1) Total premium refers to the sum of regular premium, single premium, and renewal premium; 2) Position refers to market position of private life insurers by Retail Weighted Received Premium (RWRP) in 9M FY16

Source: IRDA Annual Reports, ICICI Prudential investor presentation 9M FY16, Roland Berger

However, the boom period brought with it a number of dangerous developments in the market. 'Land grabbing', i.e., building market share aggressively with little concern for profitability, became the name of the game for several competitors. In addition, inefficiencies of private companies versus LIC, the government incumbent, were significant. Private insurers had built up an extensive sales force and agency model, however, with very low levels of activation and based on fixed salaries rather than variable compensation.

Aggressive geographic expansion via branches in Tier-1–3 towns and beyond drove additional, inadequate cost structures. Operational expenditure (OPEX) to total premium ratios[338] of 25–26 per cent were common for key private players[339] versus global benchmarks around 8–9 per cent and a corresponding ratio for LIC of around 6–8 per cent.[340] In addition, insurance companies came to interpret their channel partners as customers and focused less on their end customers, resulting in increasing customer complaints and reduced persistency.

The situation took a turn for the worse when the Indian economy hit a roadblock with the global financial crisis. Combined with the government's policy blunders, India's growth stalled and slowed down to a level not seen since the early 1990s. Financial savings as a percentage of overall savings fell from a high of 12 per cent in FY10 to a low of 7 per cent in FY12 and slightly recovered to 7.2 per cent in FY14.[341] Insurance, typically about 20 per cent of all financial savings, was hard hit. Life insurance accounted for only 17 per cent of all savings in FY14 as against 26.2 per cent in FY10,[342] and life insurance penetration fell from its previous high to a level of 3.1 per cent in FY13, with insurance density going down to USD 41.[343] ULIPs, previously the darling of the insurance companies, found few takers, as customers burned by high surrender charges and low performance opted for traditional products as well as LIC as a primary provider. ULIPs only accounted for 7 per cent of total industry business and 29 per cent of business for private players in FY14.[344] While annual new business volume remained flat, the market share of private health insurers dropped from 29 per cent in FY09 to 25 per cent in FY12, as shown in Figure 6.11. The persistent difficulties of the market forced several international players such as ING and New York Life to exit.

In such a strained environment, investors started focusing increasingly on cost, profits and cash flows. The distribution model of private players shifted even more towards bancassurance[345] as companies reduced the bloated overhead structures of their ineffective agency models. The number of branches of private players contracted sharply from 8785 in FY09 to 6193 in FY14 while at the same time LIC increased its footprint from 3030 offices to 4839.[346] Overall, operational cost ratios (OPEX to total premium ratios, see above) were reduced to about 19 per cent,[347] still significantly higher than global best practices.

In addition, the regulator changed its stance from that of regulation based on good faith to one of micro-management, as excesses in the industry mandated better customer protection. For ULIPs, upfront charges, surrender charges and commission payouts were regulated and hence impacted the basis on which these products were developed. Regulations on minimum sum assured, minimum lock-in periods and minimum guaranteed returns impacted the profitability of the industry as well as companies' opportunity to differentiate themselves via products. Further regulations[348] continued to reign in the flexibility of the industry and turn India into a strongly regulated market versus life insurance markets in China, the US or the UK.

In a relatively short time, India's life insurance industry moved from being a sunrise sector to one that was experiencing all the signs of a VUCA industry. Volatility in regulations, e.g., due to the ULIP charge cap in 2010, turned the industry model on its head and impacted new business margins negatively by 50–75 per cent.[349] The open architecture in bancassurance impacts revenue and will put further pressure on margins along with likely caps on expenses. The overall macro environment of insurance remains complex (low financial savings, unpredictability of inflation, etc.) as does the industry environment (channel economics, product changes, high levels of competition between private players, etc.). Last but not least, greater investments need to be made in technology, channels, and products.

HDFC Life: Thriving in Turbulent Waters[350]

HDFC Life, one among the top three life insurers in India, is a JV between the Housing Development Finance Corporation (HDFC) and Standard Life, a leading UK-based financial services provider. The company has products covering the areas of protection, pension, savings, investments and health. HDFC Life has more than 14,000 employees, enjoys a robust network presence via 414 branches and, together with its partners,[351] covers 980 towns.

HDFC Life overcomes the challenges of the Indian insurance industry by focusing on five key themes:

1. Leader in providing long–term insurance solutions: Set industry standards by driving changes that encourage long-term behaviour by all stakeholders and yield sustainable benefits.
2. Fortify and diversify distribution channel mix (banks, agents, etc.): Retain and grow existing distribution partners and win new relationships to de-risk business in the face of increasing competitive intensity.
3. Own select customer segments and product categories: Select attractive customer segments, develop products based on the

needs of these segments and drive efforts and investments to these segments.

4. Deliver unique customer experience: Improve customer experience and loyalty by offering best-in-class service standards across touch points.

5. Cost leadership across the delivery chain: Run a profitable business by driving cost and productivity efficiencies across the value chain.

These five choices represent a significant shift in the outlook of the company. In the heyday of the insurance industry, HDFC Life was focused on agile reaction to market forces as its main strategy, rather than towards long-term decision-making. It relied heavily on bancassurance via its partnership with HDFC rather than looking at a fortified and diversified distribution mix. Sales were driven in mass-market customer segments rather than focusing on select customer segments. Focus on distributor experience trumped focus on customer experience, and market share leadership took precedence over profitability and cost leadership.

Activities that support the current positioning are many, and an overview of the HDFC activity map is shown in Figure 6.12. Quality of contracts over revenue, for example, is driven by mandating independent verifications of customers before issuance of life insurance contracts. Product sale across distribution channels is limited to products that can be afforded by the cost structure of the respective channel. Multi-distribution platforms are created which drive nimble, low-cost models with channel partners and extend market reach at lower cost. Sales-enabler tools like POS,[352] predictive underwriting, 3-Click[353] and mobility devices enabled with MyMix[354] ensure a smooth, hassle-free issuance and purchase experience for customers while resulting in cost leadership by lowering cost of acquisition. An in-house training programme DNA (develop, nurture, achieve), for experienced sales personnel, and a similar, smart achievers programme, for inexperienced personnel, run together with Manipal Global University to improve the skill base of employees and agents and enhance sales effectiveness. A strong focus on process-led business over person-dependent business has led to writing detailed process documents, executing FMEA analysis,[355] audits and technology-led interventions that improve process adherence and business predictability.

6 | FIGURE 12

HDFC Life's Strategic and Functional Initiatives Are Aligned with Five Central Themes That Drive the Organization

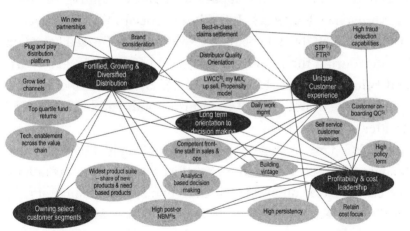

1) STP – Straight-through-processing, 2) FTR – Flexible Term Rider, 3) LWCC – Louisiana Workers' Compensation Corporation, 4) NBM – New Business Margins, 5) QC – Quality Control
Source: HDFC Life Insurance presentation, August 2015

The industry-wide transition from ULIPs (49 per cent of business in FY14 versus 86 per cent in FY11) towards participating[356] plans (36 per cent in FY14 versus 13 per cent in FY11) and non-participating/protection[357] plans (15 per cent in FY14 versus 1 per cent in FY11) was managed successfully. In particular, a number of successful products that are simple to understand and purchase such as maternity protection plans (Click2Protect), cancer care and health plans, as well as low-cost ULIPs (Click2Invest) were launched to support HDFC Life's focus on select key customer groups and low-cost delivery mechanisms.

Technology is a particularly important focus area. HDFC Life has created multiple distribution engines in the online insurance space (its own website, aggregators like PolicyBazaar, partnerships with Flipkart and others, relationships with HDFC Bank and others). Today, the company estimates that it has a rapidly growing online market share of 44 per cent. Clear leadership in the market among all eighteen players in the segment was established via a best-in-class e-commerce setup. This set-up is geared towards mobile applications and expanding its reach via vernacular languages. In addition, social-media presence is strong, with HDFC Life being the second most-buzzed brand on Twitter during the recent Cricket World Cup (after Star Sports and before Emirates, ESPN and Lays). HDFC Life today is the number-one brand in BFSI in terms of both Facebook fans and Twitter followers.

HDFC Life leverages technology not only for marketing, branding and sales but also for product development, operations, and claims and solutions. A focused technology programme aims to create a 360-degree view of the customer. It ensures seamless business processes, improves user experience and drives organizational agility and readiness to respond by leveraging data analytics. As part of this programme, HDFC Life will be able to view and analyse the customer relationship across all touch points via a single-point window. The system will provide alerts for things such as complaints, claims, etc., to ensure timely resolution. End-to-end automation and simplification of processes will improve turnaround times on core processes which can be guaranteed for customers. Mobility-friendly solutions for customers and partners will bring down transactions costs, and integrated lead management systems will drive conversion efficiency. Based on strong processes, new partners and employees will be brought on board faster, and new products and processes will be easier to roll out. Geo-tracking attendance for employees will lead to efficiency improvements and potentially drive agency activation even higher. A complete digitalization of the front office across prospecting, lead creation, lead fulfilment, form filling, online payment, e-signature, document uploading and FR (further requirements) fulfilment will drive a 'sales on the move' rather than a 'brick and mortar' distribution model for HDFC Life and hence improve customer satisfaction and reduce cost.

The positive results of this focused, technology-enabled strategy are clearly visible. Despite all the challenges on the macro-economic, regulatory and customer fronts, total premium for HDFC Life has grown at a CAGR of 16 per cent between FY10 and FY15, driven by renewal premiums (CAGR 21 per cent) and group premiums (CAGR 29 per cent). In the same time frame, assets under management tripled from INR 20,411 crore to INR 67,048 crore. While thirteenth-month persistency[358] remains a challenge at 73 per cent, cancellations and customer complaints have been cut in half to around 2.11 per cent on average in FY15. An operating expenses ratio of 10.2 per cent in FY15 inches closer to the benchmark value of LIC, and overall total premium is within striking distance of the market leader. Says Amitabh Chaudhry, CEO, HDFC Life Insurance Company,

> The changes in the industry during the last ten years have been unprecedented. The challenges that macro-economic changes, increasing customer demands, land-grabbing behaviour by competitors, high-cost structures and regulatory impacts driven mostly in reaction to unethical behaviour of a few companies, etc.,

pose are massive. As a consequence, you have to be constantly self-critical and paranoid. You can't let the competition come close, especially in an environment where the lead time to copy is very small. You have to constantly imagine your next move and prepare for it, which is why we are, among other things, investing heavily in our digital platform.

IN SUMMARY

Choices and trade-offs are core to any business. What we do and what we don't do defines us and our capability to create unique value for our customers. The so-called hidden champions have leveraged this insight very successfully in driving their way to the top three positions in their respective industries. Rather than going broad in terms of products, services and capabilities, they ensure that they go deep first and lead in one narrow, defined market. Scale is generated via global expansion. Only after these opportunities for growth have been exhausted do hidden champions look at other opportunities for diversification.

Indian businessmen and businesswomen historically have had a tendency to go broad via diversification before they have achieved a globally dominating position in their core industry. Often, this is the result of operating in an environment with institutional voids. Being diversified can buffer sudden changes in the operating environment in one of the industries that a diversified company or conglomerate tries to address.

The blueprint for this type of approach to doing business is given by the examples of large Indian conglomerates like the Tatas, Birlas, Adanis, etc. However, running a conglomerate of disparate business entities is not easy and requires discipline regarding capital allocation. While parent age advantage can be leveraged to enter new businesses, the validity of these businesses has to be clearly established. Existing businesses that don't live up to financial or strategic benchmarks need to be rigorously divested. Only then can conglomerates create additional value that overcompensates the common 'conglomerate discount'.

Smaller entities may not be well advised to go for such a conglomerate approach. Management and financial bandwidth, among other factors, need to be substantial to be successful and are not easily available to smaller players. A more focused play, similar to that of hidden champions, promises higher returns as well as a sustainable growth story going forward.

Carefully choosing what to do and what not to do invariably brings trade-offs into play. As the creation of discernible customer value requires consistent activity sets across the value chain, companies can't be jacks of all trades. They need to make sure that their trade-offs, be they variety-, need- or access-based, are well aligned with the overall strategy of the company.

We have seen examples of clear choices in the cases of earlier chapters (e.g., EFD, Godrej, Maruti Suzuki). These insights are reinforced by the story of Bajaj Auto, a company that went for the pursuit of margin over mass by concentrating on premium bikes as well as export markets. Not only did the company clearly choose which customers it wanted to serve, it also decided where it didn't want to play when it exited the scooter segment.

Vaatsalya Healthcare is a prime example of access-based choice. The decision to provide affordable healthcare to patients in Tier-2 and Tier-3 cities addresses an urgent public-health issue in India as well as drives a whole set of decisions and actions down the line. Improvements in operational efficiency in the operating theatre, training of local staff to support doctors, attractive payment packages for doctors comparable to those in Tier-1 locations, an asset-light investment approach, etc., all need to be aligned and implemented to ensure success.

While choices and trade-offs are important, they are not necessarily sacrosanct. Sometimes quickly changing environments can force companies to adjust previous choices. As the example of HDFC Life shows, a very volatile industry and regulatory environment have forced the company to change its focus across the value chain. Starting with the customers that it wants to serve, its products, distribution channels and approaches to operational efficiency, HDFC Life has redesigned its activity system to drive sustainable, profitable growth despite the challenges that the Indian market offers.

As global aspirations of Indian companies grow and competition intensifies within the country, choices and trade-offs are becoming more important. Equally important is the alignment of activities and people across the organization. This will be analysed in the next chapter.

7

ALIGNMENT

DIRECTING AN ORCHESTRA VERSUS PLAYING ONE INSTRUMENT

Otto von Bismarck, the great Prussian chancellor and statesman of the nineteenth century, wrote in one of his letters,

> A Prussian official resembles a player in an orchestra. Whether he plays first violin or the triangle he must play his part without controlling or influencing the whole, just as it is put before him, and without considering whether it is bad or good. I, however, will play good music or none.[359]

In other words, Bismarck considered the only challenge worth pursuing as that of the leader who would align the various parts of the orchestra—in our context, an organization—so that the overall music is beautiful or the organization performs at its best.

Alignment, or 'common purpose', as coined by Joel Kurtzman,[360] is just as important in business as in politics or music. Successful companies are able to create alignment, a common vision of the company's goals, its past and its future, from the chairman to the watchman. Alignment is crucial to enable employees to make independent decisions in an increasingly complex world.[361] While process-focused manuals and documentation are important, it isn't feasible to document everything. Employees need to be relied on to do the right thing for the company in moments of truth, i.e., when they are serving their internal or external customers.

Alignment creates higher outcomes and lowers costs, not only via sets of aligned activities, which we will discuss in the next paragraph, but also through highly motivated employees. Most employees want to create and belong to a winning organization and to contribute to its success. The excitement, long hours and uncertain pay-offs in many modern start-up companies are a clear testimony to the same. Leveraging this innermost desire[362] via the right leadership creates a win-win-win solution for company, employees and customers.

In terms of Michael Porter, alignment or fit is about the combination of activities that create and reinforce a sustainable strategic position. First-order fit is simple consistency between various activities, i.e., the installation of an international business president on par with other executive board members to support international business growth at Bajaj. Second-order fit refers to reinforcing activities, i.e., community outreach of Vaatsalya hospitals to drive awareness and increase business for the hospitals. Third-order fit finally refers to optimizing activities, i.e., installing management information systems at Vaatsalya that encourage collaboration among doctors who face common challenges in meeting quality and cost targets.

As we have seen in the previous chapters, riding the Indian tiger has been a constant VUCA challenge for companies doing business in the country. Companies that have succeeded here have shown a combination of a strong strategy and excellent execution. Those with unclear strategies and/or bad execution have often succumbed to competitive pressure. In other words, alignment of activities down to the last detail is of crucial importance in the Indian context, as the following case studies will show.

The IndiGo case study highlights how strong alignment can enable profitable growth in one of India's—if not one of the world's—most challenging industries. IndiGo's competitor, Kingfisher, demonstrates the dangers of straddling and misaligned activity systems. JSW Steel, similar to the HDFC Life case discussed earlier, is another example of a company whose activity system had to be realigned on a war footing to ensure the survival of the business.

RIDING THE TIGER: THE EMERGENCE OF THE INDIAN AIRLINE INDUSTRY THROUGH TURBULENT TIMES

In late 2013, Phee Teik Yeoh, a senior manager at Singapore Airlines, was given what seemed to be an almost impossible task. After having failed to enter Indian aviation in the 1990s and again in 2001, Yeoh was to drive the third attempt to enter the Indian aviation industry through a JV with the Indian conglomerate Tata Sons. The JV wanted to set up a domestic airline in the subcontinent and make it a success.

From day one, Yeoh experienced myriad difficulties in getting a new airline in India off the ground. Ferocious lobbying by competitors, criticism from politicians and delays at various regulatory levels were just some of the issues he faced. These challenges were testing his patience as well as that of his team. 'He used to come and sit with us with a thick sheaf of application documents and ask politely but firmly to point out the mistake that was holding up a particular approval,' said an aviation ministry official. Yeoh did this repeatedly, whenever the paperwork got stuck, ministry officials recall.[363]

After months of uncertainty, Yeoh's team got through the approval process successfully and finally managed to get the air operator's permit granted in December 2014. Since January 2015, the airline operates under the brand name Vistara as a full-service provider in India, and covers eight domestic destinations from its hub in New Delhi.[364] Vistara is the latest airline to enter the increasingly competitive Indian market.

Looking at the years to come, Yeoh said in a leading Indian newspaper shortly after the inaugural flight: 'We're enthusiastic. There are no doubt challenges, but we believe in the immense potential of the Indian aviation market.'[365] This optimism is based on strong passenger growth in recent years and an overall positive outlook for the industry in the middle- to long-term future. However, the rise and fall of other private players entering India before Vistara is a lesson to not underestimate the unique challenges of the Indian airline market.

Development of the Indian Airline Industry

Historically, the Indian aviation sector has been a laggard relative to its growth potential (for a quick historic overview of the development of the Indian airline industry, refer to Figure A.18 in the Appendix). Excessive regulations and taxations, government ownership of airlines and insufficient infrastructure have hampered the growth of the industry and made it difficult for new players to enter the market. In 1953, the Indian government nationalized all private airlines through the Air Corporations Act and formed Air India (for international travel) and Indian Airlines (for domestic travel) out of the nine existing and mostly regionally operating players.[366] The resulting monopoly on civil aviation in India remained for decades, with both airlines being known for delayed flights, indifferent service, patchy safety records, high fares and constant political interference in matters such as fleet purchase decisions and route selection.[367]

The first signs of deregulation started to show in 1986, when private players were permitted to operate as air taxi operators. However, it took until 1994 to open up the airline sector. At that time, the Air Corporation Act of 1953 was repealed. The monopoly of air corporations on scheduled services was removed and private airlines were allowed to operate scheduled services. Indian Airlines and Air India were converted into limited companies, and private participation in the national carriers[368] was allowed.

Within just a few months of operation, new entrants managed to gain substantial market share, and accounted for approximately 24 per cent of the overall civil aviation market by March 1994.[369] This was mainly due to the latent demand that was previously not served, as well as the different positioning of the new entrants in the market.[370] Damania, for example, one of five airlines that was granted scheduled carrier status during that time, followed a premium approach by offering luxury travel with on-board entertainment such as fashion shows and alcohol with breakfast on domestic early-morning flights.[371] This was a new flight experience for Indian travellers, and helped Damania and other new entrants to quickly grow and expand their leased aircraft fleets. These airlines focused on differentiating factors and gave the government-run carriers stiff competition. Jet Airways became popular for its punctuality and good service; Sahara had excellent connectivity, especially in north India; ModiLuft (supported by Lufthansa) was known for safety and reliability and provided a differentiated flying experience with first, business and economy classes.[372]

Demand for air travel between 1994 and 1997 grew nearly 50 per cent, as shown in Figure 7.1. At the same time, private airlines rapidly gained a substantial share of the previous monopolistic market and accounted for 37 per cent in domestic passenger carriage by 1997.[373] However, these new airlines were struggling to operate profitably. Costs for jet fuel in India were about three times higher than international prices,[374] which was largely triggered by high taxes and limited supply. The government forced airlines to operate on less profitable routes to distant parts of the country. In addition, regulations prevented domestic airlines from serving profitable international routes during the first five years of operation. All these factors, in combination with the underdeveloped airport infrastructure of the late 1990s and intensifying competition due to an increasing number of airlines in the market, resulted in a difficult operating environment.

As a result, the market soon consolidated. Damania Airways was acquired by NEPC group and renamed as Skyline NEPC. Both NEPC and Skyline NEPC were grounded in 1997 for non-payment of dues. Within the first year of operations, ModiLuft fell back on payments to Lufthansa despite profits. Lufthansa alleged that ModiLuft had not paid back dues for leased aircrafts, and ModiLuft discontinued operations in 1996. Only Jet and Sahara continued national operations after 1997. One firm (Jagson) became a regional airline and all other private players shut down.[375]

As a consequence of these failures, the Indian government initiated several policy changes, which included clauses about the minimum size of an airline, in order to ensure economies of scale and the equity base required for operating in India. Further, fuel prices were deregulated in 2001, which resulted in a drop in aviation turbine fuel prices in the years thereafter. As mentioned,

Indian airlines were previously facing aviation turbine fuel costs up to three times as high as international prices.[376]

7 FIGURE 1

Domestic Passenger Traffic Grew Seven-Fold since Liberalization in the Early Nineties, Touching 70 Mn in FY15

Passengers carried [mn]

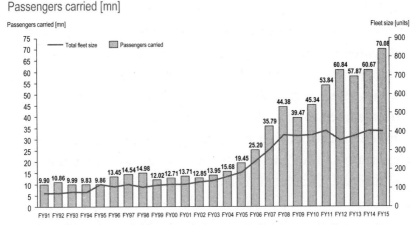

Source: DGCA Statistics website, 'Air Transport Statistics', FY91–FY14, http://dgca.nic.in/reports/Traffic-ind.htm, DGCA, Handbook of Civil Aviation Statistics 2014–15, Fleet size for FY15, www.planespotters.net, Roland Berger analysis

With these changes in place, along with steady growth of the economy and a constant increase in air travellers, a new phase of development kicked off in 2003 with the entry of Air Deccan as the first low-cost carrier (LCC). Air Deccan offered direct flight connections on routes that were previously not served in India.[377] By 2005, Kingfisher, SpiceJet, IndiGo, GoAir and Paramount had started operations—some of them also following the LCC approach, others operating as full-service carriers. The entry of these players led to a significant expansion of fleet size in India. As can be seen in Figure 7.1, fleet size more than doubled between FY05 and FY08, while the number of passengers grew slightly faster. As Figure A.19 in the Appendix shows, the years between FY04 and FY09 also coincide with a dramatic increase in investment by the Airport Authority of India. These investments have brought India within striking distance of China in terms of the number of airports as well as the number of airports per capita (see A.19 in the Appendix). Going forward, the government aims to increase the number of operational airports to 250 by the year 2030, and will spend USD 1.3 billion on non-metro projects between 2013 and 2017, focusing on modernizing and upgrading airports.[378]

Despite good growth and bright prospects, the industry's competitive dynamics became more challenging. With the emergence of e-commerce, the importance of travel agents declined and customers were able to compare offerings easily. Low-cost carriers started to offer discounted prices in a bid to gain market share as well as to be able to compete with long-distance rail travel. As a consequence, only one-fourth of the full-service carrier seats were sold at regular fares by the end of the decade.[379] Fierce competition and limited ability of private and corporate customers to pay for air travel drove available seat kilometre[380] and revenue passenger kilometre[381] rates that were among the lowest globally. While the rates were abnormally low, input prices remained on the higher side, as shown in Figures A.20 and A.21 in the Appendix. Revenue and cost pressures resulted in financial distress and led to another industry consolidation by 2007. Jet acquired Sahara in 2007 and Kingfisher bought Air Deccan in 2011, in order to increase economies of scale. Air India and Indian Airlines merged to continue as the single entity 'Air India' from 2011 onwards, to improve operational effectiveness and leverage synergies in a bid to become profitable.

Consolidation was followed by global expansion, with SpiceJet starting international operations in 2010 followed by IndiGo in 2011. Most recently, Air Asia and Vistara have entered the Indian market. However, to ensure their long-term success in India, these airlines need to find ways to operate in the high-cost environment, to deal with the aggressive fleet expansion plans of other market players and to find the most suitable positioning in a constantly intensifying competitive environment. As we pointed out earlier, and as is shown in Figure 7.2, the competitive dynamics in the Indian airline sector are intense, and only the strongest players survive.

7 FIGURE 2

Competition in Indian Airline Industry Is Fierce. A Number of Players Had to Exit the Market Due to a Lack of Profits

Fleet size of airlines operating in India [number of planes]

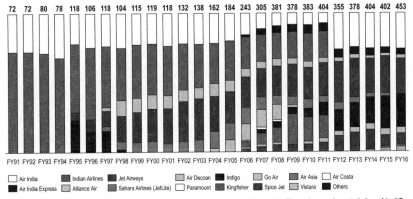

Source: DGCA Transport Statistics, Yearly Statistics, Part II, Table 2.25, Annual traffic and operating statistics of IndiGo, http://dgca.nic.in/reports/stat-ind.htm
DGCA Transport Statistics, Yearly Statistics, Part III, Table 3.12, Annual Total Domestic Traffic and Operating Statistics of Indian Carriers, http://dgca.nic.in/reports/stat-ind.htm
Roland Berger analysis

Despite strong growth and an increase in air travel offerings, air travel penetration in India remains small in global terms. With 0.04 annual trips per capita, against 0.3 in China and more than two in the US,[382] the long-term attractiveness for new players to enter the market despite fierce competition is relatively high. India will be the third largest aviation market by 2020, with 336 million domestic and 85 million international passengers.[383] Indian carriers plan to double their fleet size to over 800 aircraft[384] by then to respond to this emerging business opportunity.

However, setting up a new airline in India requires substantial investment. As a consequence of the bankruptcy of several airlines in the 1990s, the Indian government enforced a minimum capital requirement of INR 30 crore and at least five aircraft, without which airlines are not permitted to take off.[385] Another factor that makes it challenging for new airlines to enter the Indian market is the difficulty in obtaining suitable airport slots for take-off and landing. Established airlines in India already have long-term agreements that secure them prime travel slots at major airports. This leaves the option to use less popular slots at major airports or to fly to non-major airports, which are currently underserved for new entrants.[386]

In addition, the Indian airline industry is still suffering from regulatory restrictions, despite efforts to open up the market. Foreign airlines, for example, have to have a 49:51 JV with a local partner to operate in India and every new airline needs to operate at least twenty aircraft or 20 per cent of its overall fleet on domestic routes before it is allowed to offer overseas flights.

Indian airlines are challenged on the supply front as well. Besides depending on the global duopoly of Airbus and Boeing for plane purchases, there is a shortage of well-trained staff in India—whether it is ground personnel (especially mechanics), flight attendants or pilots[387]—which drives employee costs up. In addition, Indian airlines are heavily dependent on suppliers of fuel and crude oil. These costs account for about a third of the total operating costs, and therefore directly affect the profitability of the airline. Fuel prices have remained relatively stable in 2014, and showed a slight decline in early 2015.[388] However, compared to other international airports, costs for jet fuel have been significantly higher due to substantial tax charges by the government and a limited number of companies supplying aviation fuel in India (see Figure A.21 in the Appendix for a global comparison).

IndiGo—Alignment Drives Market Leadership

The environment in the Indian Airline industry is volatile and extremely competitive. As shown in Figure 7.2, only the fittest survive. Volatile environments due to regulations, lack of or limited infrastructure, extreme price sensitivity of customers, etc. require robust strategies, stringent execution and the ability to constantly adapt to changing environments to ensure success.

IndiGo's approach to air travel in India fits this description very well. The company offers a convenient, on-time, reliable, clean and price-competitive travel experience without unnecessary frills within India (and also to international destinations, starting in 2012). As mentioned by CEO Aditya Ghosh, IndiGo is about a relentless focus on three areas: on-time performance, low cost and a courteous and hassle-free travel experience.[389] As flight distances in India rarely extend beyond three hours, this value proposition is a natural match with price-conscious travellers and businesses alike.[390] International flight destinations for IndiGo are chosen to fit this two- to three-and-a-half-hour model (Dubai, Muscat, Bangkok, Singapore).

While IndiGo is not a full-service airline, it has not blindly copied the Southwest Airlines business model, recognizing important cultural differences between India and the US. While US customers are able to work with a no-frills, do-it-yourself model of air travel, Indian customers are accustomed to a certain minimum level of services that is crucial for customer satisfaction. As a consequence, IndiGo serves, for instance, food for purchase on its flights but the service design is based on pre-packaged items as well as ready-to-eat meals, which require very little special handling and clean-up.

IndiGo not only chooses its value proposition carefully—an India-adequate, value-for-money travel experience—but also consciously selects its customer base. Elite luxury or business travellers will find IndiGo's value proposition not as compelling as other options in the market. The lack of a loyalty programme, no special treatment on check-in, no leniency on excess baggage, an aggressive push for travellers to buy their tickets online, no provision for porters, etc., reduce the comfort level for this class of frequent fliers. At the same time, IndiGo does not chase bargain hunters in an attempt to increase occupancy levels of flights. Aggressive price promotions like Air Deccan's INR 0 tickets are not used to drive sales. Also, in a departure from a standard low-cost model, seats are pre-assigned on all flights, the option to check in online is provided and basic amenities as well as sufficient customer service staffing are maintained at all airports, thus minimizing travel disruptions.

IndiGo's customer base captures the sweet spot of the passenger distribution in the Indian market in terms of volume and purchasing power. Consistent delivery of the promise that low cost does not mean low quality leads to high customer satisfaction within the target group. As Ghosh puts it, 'We truly believe that our customers are our biggest brand ambassadors. While we don't have a frequent-flier programme, our biggest frequent-flyer programme is our reliability, that's what's going to bring people back over and over.' Remarkably, IndiGo translates this conviction into consistent action. For example, the airline does not have a separate marketing department, but just a few junior employees who interact with an external marketing agency.[391]

IndiGo has managed to become the market leader in FY15 with a total market share of 34 per cent, as shown in Figure 7.3.

It is also the only airline in India that managed to generate profit continuously after two years of operation despite massive challenges in the Indian economy (see Figure A.22 in the Appendix).

7 FIGURE 3

IndiGo Is the Largest and Most Successful Airline in India. Starting Its Operations in 2006, It Has Rapidly Become the Market leader

IndiGo has demonstrated consistent growth even during tough market conditions

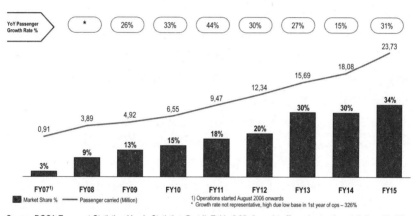

Source: DGCA Transport Statistics, Yearly Statistics, Part II, Table 2.25, Annual traffic and operating statistics of IndiGo, http://dgca.nic.in/reports/stat-ind.htm
DGCA Transport Statistics, Yearly Statistics, Part III, Table 3.12, Annual Total Domestic Traffic and Operating Statistics of Indian Carriers, http://dgca.nic.in/reports/stat-ind.htm
Roland Berger analysis

Driving operational efficiency at IndiGo is a key pillar of the organization, as can be seen in Figure A.23 in the Appendix. The number of employees per plane has reduced by about 18 per cent since launch via a consistent leverage of increased scale and improved operations. The passenger load factor has been about 77 per cent on average since inception, as fleet expansion is in line with increasing demand.

IndiGo drives down operational costs via a focused plane purchasing policy. With a single plane type, a single configuration model—the Airbus A320/Neo configured to all-economy seating—IndiGo minimizes maintenance and spares costs. In addition, one year prior to launch, IndiGo placed a mammoth order of 100 A320s in 2005 and hence secured a significant volume discount from Airbus. In 2006, when the company received its first plane, it sold the plane to a leasing company while leasing it back in a parallel transaction, thus unburdening its balance sheet and freeing up its share capital. Beyond significant cash discounts, IndiGo is able to ensure non-cash discounts from Airbus, e.g., in the form of free training, etc.

In contrast to some competitors, IndiGo started operations with new airplanes rather than leasing used airplanes. This resulted in a hassle-free experience both for customers and for IndiGo staff as maintenance requirements were rather low (see Figure A.24 in the Appendix for a comparison of MRO[392] costs between Indigo and Kingfisher). Each plane is leased for a period of five years and in the sixth year is returned to the lessor. With IndiGo's steady stream of new aircraft being delivered every month, the fleet is always young and low on maintenance, which further reduces costs and turnaround times. Another major advantage is the elimination of the so-called D-Check (the most comprehensive check for a plane) that takes place every five to six years. This check is very expensive and may require almost complete refurbishment. By returning planes before the D-Check is due, IndiGo saves a significant amount.[393]

A 'one plane a month' delivery policy enabled a continuous ramp-up of capacity, i.e., sure and steady growth that gives the organization time to mature in sync with growing business. In addition, cooperation with key stakeholders such as airports became hassle-free since a clear ramp-up plan for IndiGo enabled airports to plan and build their infrastructure accordingly.

Airline purchases were used strategically again when Airbus introduced the Neo, a variant of the A320 with engines that use

10–15 per cent less fuel. With fuel being a major cost driver, IndiGo decided to buy 180 A320 Neos when the plane was launched in December 2010. When IndiGo officially signed the deal at the Paris Air Show six months later, 1000 Neos had been sold already. Hence, if the competition had been late in decision-making regarding the new product, they would have already been 1000 planes behind, which would have ensured a long-term cost advantage for IndiGo. [394]

Another area of operational excellence is the focus on staff training and alignment of staff goals with the overall goals of the airline. To drive on-time performance and fast turnaround times, particular emphasis is placed on recruitment standards and training for all IndiGo personnel. IndiGo employees understand the importance of these factors for the overall success of the airline, live these values and have their compensation tied to turnaround times and fleet utilization. Alignment of value along the service delivery chain is ensured by own check-in, ground and maintenance crews, which are the best in the industry.[395] Streamlined service activities in the airport—e.g., check in a minimum 45 minutes prior to departure, zero tolerance on number of and oversized carry-on baggage, etc. —are explained by friendly yet firm customer-facing personnel. This minimizes boarding disruptions. Constant focus on small, incremental innovations ensures continuous optimization of delivery and cost without impacting customer satisfaction. A good example are boarding ramps, which allow fast boarding of planes even for mobility impaired passengers and also minimize airport charges since the company doesn't have to pay for aero-bridges.

IndiGo's basic principles of offering low fares and being on-time, courteous and hassle-free are embedded in the way the company does business. On-time, hassle-free performance applies not only to planes but also to every aspect of doing business at IndiGo.

Internal trainings have to be on time; if they are not, the trainer will be rewarded with a sad face emoji rather than a smiley face in the daily reports on training activities. The same applies to pilots. Checking of on-time performance is done by the security guard for the trainers and by junior staff members for the pilots, a clear example of an empowered, low-cost feedback system. On-time and hassle-free also means that salaries and vendors are paid on time, reimbursements and promotions happen on time, etc.[396]

The result of all these activities is industry-leading flying time as well as turnaround time at airports. IndiGo's flying time is more than 11.5 hours per day versus eight to ten hours for the competition; its average turnaround time at airports is less than thirty minutes. In addition, IndiGo manages to gain a higher-than-proportionate market share with a lower employee and fleet footprint compared to the competition (see Figure A.25 in the Appendix).

IndiGo's focus is not only directed towards bottom line protection. Top-line opportunities are aggressively leveraged as well. In contrast to a Southwest Airlines model, IndiGo's route selection focuses on high-volume traffic sectors between major cities in India, which drives revenue. The airline's positioning is aggressively driven by on-time performance rather than deals. This is a significant difference from other LCCs who try to buy market share with deals like INR 0 tickets regardless of the bottom-line impact. No frills, pre-packaged meals for sale on board with minimal disposal needs optimize profit potential for the airline while not depriving customers of an opportunity to have a bite during the flight. The same is true for charges on extra baggage, XL seating in the airplane, etc.

Going forward, IndiGo will need to continue to focus on both top and bottom lines. The overall market environment in India remains highly competitive and challenging. Only the fittest will survive, and only as long as they stay fit and ahead of the competition. Or as IndiGo CEO Aditya Ghosh puts it: [397]

> What sets us apart is actually sticking to the smallest of basic boring details that you can get from any book, any case study. Any management-school first-year kid will tell you about these things. But we have to keep our ego aside to say that if this is what works, this is what we will do and this is what we will do over and over again. Not because we are not innovative. We do a lot of things differently but it's all about these small little things. So our classic innovation example is the boarding ramp. Billions of people have walked up a ladder and come down a ladder from an airplane. And we took two inclining planes and put them together to turn them into a boarding ramp. Why? Because it is driven by being hassle-free. But this doesn't mean we are now going to have a fleet of cars bringing people to the aircraft because that will then hit low fares.

IndiGo's aligned activity system, the source of its success in India, is shown in Figure 7.4. As in the case of Bajaj and other companies operating successfully in India, there is no silver bullet. There is no single solution that makes or breaks a company. It is the combination of various, reinforcing activities across the value chain that creates sustainable competitive advantage for the airline. Even after nearly a decade in operation, IndiGo's operating system has not been duplicated in the market. This is despite the fact that protecting ideas, processes and insights from migrating to competition is difficult in India due to highly networked and mobile employees. It is the combination and interplay of activities that cements IndiGo's leadership position. Other companies that try to straddle into IndiGo's space will find it very difficult to replicate their success.

7 FIGURE 4

Strategic Fit Creates Sustainable Competitive Advantage for IndiGo in a Fiercely Competitive Indian Market

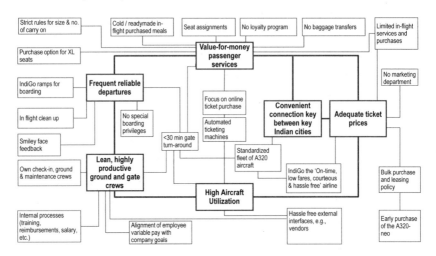

Source: Roland Berger analysis adapted from M.E. Porter, 'What Is Strategy?', *Harvard Business Review*, November–December 1996, https://hbr.org/1996/11/what-is-strategy/; Secondary Research, Roland Berger analysis

Kingfisher: Straddling and Its Consequences

In contrast to IndiGo, many other airlines have found it challenging to define a profitable strategy and business model in India. A case in point is Kingfisher Airlines. The company started out as an all-economy, single-class configuration aircraft with food and entertainment systems. After a year of operations, the airline shifted its focus towards luxury. It changed the configuration of its Airbus A320 aircraft (about 14 of them at that point in time) to 20 business class and 114 economy class seats from 180 all-economy seats.[398] Besides the large cost of reconfiguring the aircraft, additional operational challenges arose, for example, from launching an expensive loyalty programme that promised rapid upgrades and increasing personalized service with each class.

Frequent flyers even had own personalized assistants helping with check-in and, sometimes, security check procedures. Elite guests were pampered by accommodating them with last-minute entry on flights, special boarding privileges, special check-in lines, etc. Additional cost elements such as live television on the entertainment screens, gourmet food and models as flight attendants were added, following the Kingfisher motto of treating customers as if they were guests 'in my own home'. All of these activities increased costs and turnaround times as well as reduced flying time of aircraft.

In a bid to gain market share and to replace the then market leader Jet Airways, the Kingfisher management decided not to charge prices appropriate for that level of service but to compete with the existing airlines at current price levels. Providing more value at the same price was indeed a winning formula for many Indian travellers—however, Kingfisher did not change its strategy even with the entry of LCCs into the Indian airline market. Market share gains continued to trump bottom line considerations and as a consequence operational losses continued to mount and drive up the debt burden of the company (see Figure 7.5).

7 FIGURE 5

Kingfisher Airlines Consistently Posted Losses yet Significantly Added Capacity through Acquisition

High fuel prices in 2012 negated the positive financial direction achieved in FY10 & FY11

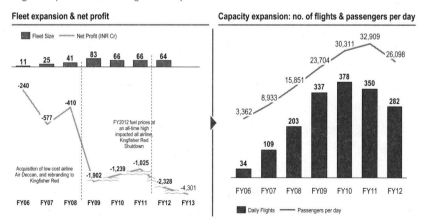

1) High airline fuel price cited as primary reason for compressed results

Source: DGCA, Air Transport Statistics, Part II, FY06, 07, 08 –3.7 FY11 – Table 2.41, FY09 – Table 2.43, FY10 – 2.42, FY11 – 2.41 FY12 - Table 2.7, http://dgca.nic.in/reports/stat-ind.htm; Money Control, http://www.moneycontrol.com/financials/kingfisherairlines/profit-loss/KA02#KA02, Roland Berger analysis

The takeover of the LCC airline Air Deccan, which itself was running at a loss, was intended to give Kingfisher the edge to compete in the LCC space. However, Kingfisher experienced difficulties in making this brand extension work, similar to what some of its international and national competitors had experienced. Kingfisher decided to rename Air Deccan as Kingfisher Red. While the company spent about INR 15 crore on a rebranding campaign, the value proposition and brand promise of the two sub-brands proved to be difficult to delineate clearly. The two brands became even further blurred by management's decision to have the same terminal support staff, check-in staff and ground staff for both airlines and to extend the Kingfisher loyalty programme to Kingfisher Red. This burdened a loss-making LCC airline with further costs. Bridging two strategic objectives— service to elite business class customers and providing no-frills transportation from A to B—proved to be difficult to handle for front-line personnel. As a consequence, the twofold product offering created a mismatch between the expected levels of service for Kingfisher passengers who thought that they had booked a Kingfisher flight but found themselves in a Kingfisher Red flight. This confusion generated a lot of customer dissatisfaction.

In terms of operational efficiency, Kingfisher de facto showed stagnating efficiency during the course of its existence and ended up with substantial operational disadvantages compared to successful competitors such as IndiGo. Fleet complexity and resulting high maintenance costs prevented substantial improvements in operational performance due to large legacy investments.

While the average load factor of 70 per cent was relatively high, transforming high utilization into operating profit proved elusive due to a cost-to-serve per passenger that consistently outpaced the revenue per passenger. Ultimately, this led to the grounding of Kingfisher Red. In September 2011, four years after it was acquired,

Chairman Vijay Mallya announced that they no longer believed in the sustainability of low-cost operations. Kingfisher, the parent airline, having accumulated too many losses, debt and even outstanding taxes, was declared bankrupt and delinquent in 2012–13.

JSW STEEL: WEATHERING THE IRON ORE CRISIS

Judicial or regulatory changes can have a dramatic impact on businesses. A case in point is the German decision to exit nuclear power[399] or the decision of the UK to leave the EU, which forces companies with a significant exposure to the UK to redesign their activity systems. Dramatic and similarly rapid changes have been observed in India as the HDFC Life case study has shown. Another example of a company that was forced to redesign large parts of its activity system to face changes brought on by a Supreme Court ruling is JSW Steel. We will discuss JSW's challenges and fight for survival in this chapter after a short review of the Indian steel industry.

The Indian Steel Industry

Worldwide, India is the third largest producer of steel (calendar year 2015), trailing China and Japan (see Figure 7.6). Since 1980, the industry has grown consistently at a CAGR of 6.6 per cent. Steel currently contributes almost 2 per cent of the country's GDP and employs more than 600,000 people.[400] Domestic demand in sectors such as construction, infrastructure and automotive (see Figure A.26 in the Appendix) drives growth and accounts for more than 65 per cent of the steel consumption in India. However, while continuing to grow, per capita consumption of finished steel in India is still significantly below that of its global counterparts (see Figure A.26 in the Appendix).

FIGURE 6

India is the Third-Largest Crude Steel Producer Globally. Steel Production Has Grown at a CAGR of 6.6% since 1980

Overview of the global steel industry

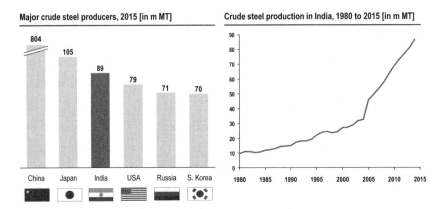

Source: World Steel Association, 'Monthly Crude Steel Production', http://www.worldsteel.org/dms/internetDocumentList/ statistics-archive/production-archive/steel-archive/steelmonthly/Steel-monthly-2015/document/Steel%20monthly%20 2015.pdf, 'Crude steel production 1980–2014', https://www.worldsteel.org/dms/internetDocumentList/statisticsarchive/ production-archive/steel-archive/steel-annually/steel-annually-1980-2014/document/steel%20annually%201980-2014. pdf, Roland Berger analysis

Under its National Steel Policy 2012, the Government of India has set an ambitious target of increasing crude steel production capacity from the current level of around 100 million metric tons to 300 million metric tons by 2025.[401] This is expected to increase employment in the sector by a factor of three. Demand will be driven by current government initiatives (e.g., Make in India), infrastructure projects (e.g., dedicated freight networks), urban transport projects and improving macroeconomic fundamentals.

The Indian steel industry is comprised of large public and private players. PSUs such as the Steel Authority of India Ltd (SAIL) and Rashtriya Ispat Nigam Ltd accounted for 21 per cent of FY14's total crude steel production in the country. SAIL has five integrated steel plants and three special steel plants and is the nation's leading producer of iron ore. In the private sector, players such as Tata Steel, JSW Steel, Jindal Steel and Power Ltd, Essar and Bhushan Steel dominate. All private players collectively account for almost 80 per cent of the country's FY14 steel production (see Figure 7.7). For an overview of the main steel players in the country, please refer to Figure A.27 in the Appendix.

7 FIGURE 7

Private Players Account for ~80% of the Crude Steel Production in India: JSW Steel and Tata Steel Are the Largest Private Producers

Crude steel production, by major producer, FY15 [in m MT]

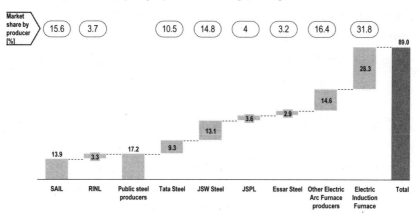

Source: Indian Steel Ministry Annual Report, Annexure IV, p. 120, 2015–16, http://steel.gov.in/Annual%20Report%20(2015-16)/English/Annual%20Report%20(English).pdf, Roland Berger analysis

As a result of the growing domestic demand, both public and private Indian steel suppliers are investing to augment their steel production capacity. However, the government's plans for achieving 300 million metric tons of steel production capacity by 2025 appear daunting. Tata Steel's managing director, T.V.S. Narendran, said, 'We will have to invest more than USD 200 billion to produce an additional 200 million metric tons of steel.'[402]

While the Indian steel sector can leverage strengths such as abundant iron ore reserves, relatively low wages, a consumption-driven economy and rebounding macroeconomic indicators, there are several challenges too. Land acquisition remains a key impediment. Regulatory approvals take a significantly long time, resulting in delayed projects. Access to transportation and logistics infrastructure is a challenge. For instance, it is difficult for the current railway infrastructure to deal with increased volumes, and port capacities and efficiencies need to be enhanced.

The mining scam and the resulting bans (see below) have created a constraint in the domestic supply of iron ore, which declined from a production of 218 million tons per annum in FY10 to 129 million tons per annum in FY15. During this period, India transformed from an iron ore exporter to an iron ore importer.[403] The shortage of domestic iron ore supply is creating challenges for the Indian steel industry. As Ankit Miglani, deputy managing director of Uttam Galva Steel, mentioned,

> Steel plants in India are shutting due to a lack of ore. Though steps have been taken to ease the situation, there is no clarity on when the iron-ore mines will open and supplies will improve. Until the domestic issues are resolved, the government will need to support the sector to tide over this crisis.[404]

The dearth of iron ore and coal in India is exerting upward pressure on the price of key raw materials, thereby making the price of Indian crude steel higher than the global price.[405]

Another addition to the list of challenges is regulatory approval delays and high raw material prices that have had an adverse impact on the financial health of the large Indian steel majors. The financial health of India's large steel companies is a growing concern. Credit Suisse estimates that the collective debt level of major Indian steel producers is about USD 50 billion, which is approximately fifteen times their collective operating profit in FY15.[406] The Financial Stability Report notes, 'Five out of the top 10 private steel producing companies are under severe stress on account of delayed implementation of their projects due to land acquisition and environmental clearances, among other factors.'[407]

Finally, in addition to the domestic challenges, global steel industry dynamics are also exerting some pressure on India. The slowdown in the Chinese economy is resulting in an oversupply of steel, which means that imports from China are cheaper and therefore more competitive than Indian steel. While the US and the EU have taken action against China for dumping its excess steel production in the form of anti-dumping duties,[408] India only increased import duties by 2.5 per cent to 5 per cent on long products and 7.5 per cent on flat products in July and August 2015.[409] Similar concerns exist over steel imports from other countries, such as South Korea, Japan and Russia. [410] For example, due to trade agreements with South Korea and Japan, there is negligible duty on steel imports.[411] In a move to prevent Chinese imports from undercutting domestic mills, the Indian government set a minimum or 'floor price' for imports of steel products on 5 February 2016.[412] The minimum import price is expected to range from USD 341 to USD 752 per tonne on 173 steel products and will be valid for a period of six months.[413]

JSW: Surviving the Iron Ore Crisis

With a 14.3 million tons-per-annum installed capacity at six strategic locations in India, JSW Steel is India's leading steel manufacturer.[414] JSW has integrated steel manufacturing facilities, from raw material processing to value-added product capabilities. It leverages state-of-the-art steel-making technologies such as Corex, DRI and blast furnaces. JSW has an extensive line-up of products such as hot-rolled steel, cold-rolled steel, galvanized, Galvalume®[415] and pre-painted steel, TMT bars, wire rods, special steel bars, etc. The company has a pan-Indian marketing and distribution network[416] and an export presence in about 100 countries across five continents. Production of crude steel has grown at a CAGR of 19.9 per cent from FY03 to FY15, revenues grew even faster at 24.7 per cent to USD 8.13 billion in FY15, and earnings before interest, taxes, depreciation and amortization grew at a CAGR of 21 per cent to USD 1.45 billion in FY15. [417]

JSW's long-term strategy revolves around four key components. The first pillar is linked to raw material security and involves, constant search for new raw material leases for iron-ore, coking coal and fluxes.[418] The second pillar focuses on growth, i.e., on added investments in India, an improved geographical spread and investments in new technologies. The third pillar is centred on operational excellence, with a focused move towards flexible raw material operations, continuous improvement of key operational performance indicators, and operational improvements to generate additional cash flows. All three of these pillars drive the fourth one, i.e., the acquisition and retention of key customers, the move towards higher value-added products and growth via acquisitions and expansions.

JSW's largest plant, with a planned capacity of 12 million tons per annum in FY16, is in Vijayanagar. This plant grew from 0.8 million tons per annum in 1999 to 10 million tons per annum in 2011 to become not only JSW's but also India's largest steel plant. As the land where the plant was built was barren, with poor infrastructure and a significant lack of skilled people to build and operate the facility, a large-scale engagement with the surrounding villages was necessary. JSW's CSR activities include activities designed to minimize the impact of the business on the environment and the ecology (see Figure A.28 in the Appendix), as well as programmes to improve the overall quality of life of villagers living in the surrounding area of the factory (see Figure A.29 in the Appendix).

The significant positive impact that JSW has on the region is reciprocated in kind. All public hearings related to expansion projects of the factory are cleared in one sitting with villagers supporting expansion plans in front of district officials. Land acquisitions for expansions and support infrastructure, areas that can often derail projects in India, are done amicably and village elders take a keen interest in ensuring speedy settlements. During major crises, such as during the iron ore mining ban (see below), village communities represented the company to plead for lifting of the ban to reduce the cost of operations of JSW and safeguard local jobs.

JSW's Vijayanagar plant is located near Bellary, Karnataka. This region is in the iron ore belt, home to large resources of virgin iron ore. The proximity to the main raw material for steel-making provided the company with a competitive advantage as it drastically reduced logistics costs. JSW Steel has been regularly sourcing iron ore fines and lumps from the mines in Karnataka, procuring approximately 11.85 million tons per annum of iron ore in FY11.

The iron ore sector in Karnataka was characterized by large-scale illegal mining, with resulting damage caused to the environment. Based on a piece of public interest litigation, the Supreme Court of India appointed a Central Empowered Committee to investigate and report on the illegality of mining and resultant damage to the environment. The Committee visited the mining areas of Bellary, Chitradurga and Tumkur districts and observed large-scale illegal mining in the area.

In July 2011, the Supreme Court clamped down on mining in Karnataka and banned iron mining in the district of Bellary.

The ban was extended to the other districts (Chitradurga and Tumkur) in August 2011. Mining in Karnataka, with output to the tune of 45–50 million tons per annum (2010–11), was halted immediately. In addition, the Supreme Court closed Goan mines in September 2012. In May 2014, the Odisha government shut twenty-six mines and in September 2014 the Jharkhand government shut twelve mines (see Figure 7.8). Iron ore and coal output was reduced by 40 per cent, with corresponding, long-lasting impacts on the Indian steel industry.[419]

7 FIGURE 8

During the Period FY10 to FY13/14, Iron Ore Production Fell in Most Major States

Iron ore production across key states, FY10–FY14 [in m MT]

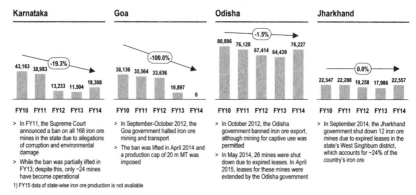

> In FY11, the Supreme Court announced a ban on all 168 iron ore mines in the state due to allegations of corruption and environmental damage
> While the ban was partially lifted in FY13; despite this, only ~24 mines have become operational

> In September–October 2012, the Goa government halted iron ore mining and transport
> The ban was lifted in April 2014 and a production cap of 20 m MT was imposed

> In October 2012, the Odisha government banned iron ore export, although mining for captive use was permitted
> In May 2014, 26 mines were shut down due to expired leases. In April 2015, leases for these mines were extended by the Odisha government

> In September 2014, the Jharkhand government shut down 12 iron ore mines due to expired leases in the state's West Singhbum district, which accounts for ~24% of the country's iron ore

1) FY15 data of state-wise iron ore production is not available

Source: Indian Bureau of Mines, Statistical Profiles of Minerals, FY11–FY14, http://ibm.nic.in/index.php?c=pages&m=index&id=496

Reuters, 'Timeline – India's Moves to Curb Iron Ore Mining, Exports', 6 May 2014, http://in.reuters.com/article/india-ironore-timeline-idINL3N0K30SO20140516

Business Standard, 'Odisha Approves Lease Extension of 26 Mines', 17 April 2015, http://www.business-standard.com/article/economy-policy/odisha-approves-lease-extension-of-26-mines-115041701184_1.html;

Hindustan Times, 'Jharkhand Shuts Down 12 Iron Ore Mines, Steel Plants Hit', 5 September 2014, http://www.hindustan-times.com/india/jharkhand-shuts-12-iron-ore-mines-steel-plants-hit/story-81B858Rt5ucLuOq9sIzvDO.html, Roland Berger analysis

Suddenly, JSW Steel faced a huge shortage of iron ore. The advantage of being in close proximity to vast iron ore resources became almost redundant overnight. A crisis of enormous magnitude loomed large for the company. Moreover, the requirement of approximately 1 million tons per month in 2010–11 increased to approximately 1.2 million tons per month in 2011–12 due to higher demand.

While India had previously been in a surplus iron ore situation and exported up to 102 million tons per annum[420] to other countries in FY10, the situation was reversed overnight and the iron ore market became a sellers' market. JSW's activity systems were highly efficient in a buyers' market situation and needed to be drastically adjusted to ensure survival and to avoid impending catastrophe. As soon as the ban was imposed in Bellary district, the company, as a short-term fix, immediately switched over to sourcing from the neighbouring district of Chitradurga. However, once the ban was extended to Chitradurga and Tumkur, iron ore was sourced on a temporary basis from the state of Odisha.

Ultimately, a more stable and cost-effective solution was needed to ensure the survival of JSW. As a first step, the management team conducted several brainstorming sessions, identified innovative practices and ideas that could improve the situation and ranked those based on their impact and ease of implementation. Internal and external stakeholders were mapped and brought together through various forums to gather feedback and also to communicate the life-threatening challenges that the company faced. The result of these activities was a two-pronged strategy. On the one hand, JSW would actively scout for iron ore from multiple sources. On the other hand, it would redesign the plant operations to cope with multiple input materials of potentially different quality levels.[421] In short, JSW's activity chart, optimized for a stable buyer's market of iron ore, had to be redesigned on the fly for an unstable seller's market, a gargantuan task.

As an initial step, a grade-wise analysis of all ores in the market was conducted together with an analysis of which stocks could realistically be procured. Talks with potential suppliers were initiated both to close short-term gaps as well as to explore long-term cooperation. Lobbying with the Supreme Court to get permissions for starting iron ore transportation in the region as well as starting e-auctions of usable iron ore stock proved successful. The Supreme Court permitted sale, via the e-auction route, of approximately 25 million tons of usable iron ore stock at various mines for the survival of the steel industry. The e-auction turned out to be a significant challenge in its own right. Infrastructure needed to be created at the sellers' place, e.g., weighbridges needed to be installed, computers and printers needed to be provided and linked to the Internet. The latter had to be done via radio frequency connections, as the identified mines were scattered across remote locations in Karnataka. JSW needed to coordinate with the local authorities to ensure the deployment of forest officers in each mine who could in turn issue the necessary forest permits. In a charged atmosphere due to the overall critical situation, confidence-building measures and the establishment of amicable relationships with mine owners and their staff proved to be vital for the e-auction and subsequent evacuation of iron ore. Lastly, the company provided four employees on each weighbridge and mobilized 600 employees for the movement of iron ore in an effort to ensure supply continuity. It also optimized logistics—for example, it released rakes in time to avoid demurrages despite the challenges of massively increased complexity.

Other short-term measures included identification of lower grade (<55 per cent) iron ore combined with an approach to the government of Karnataka to allow the sale of low-grade iron ore. In addition, JSW worked towards reopening of the mines. It filed corresponding affidavits in the Supreme Court and coordinated with various agencies and mine owners for compliance with reclamation (of the natural habitat) and rehabilitation (of the indigenous population) plans, a vital prerequisite for reopening. The company also developed a blending strategy of higher and lower grade iron ores for homogenization of input material.

Despite the announcement of the Supreme Court regarding the sale of iron ore stocks, the demand-supply gap was still too large. Demand from industries in Karnataka was estimated to be approximately 32 million tons, while the available stock of iron ore for sale was only about 25 million tons. Given the situation, it was necessary to adopt alternate strategies to ensure survival and operation of the JSW plant at Vijayanagar. To make things worse, the company had commissioned its largest blast furnace in 2011 at the plant, a significant investment that threatened to lie idle. Clearly, business as usual would not work in such dire circumstances.

The company decided to look for alternative iron sources. A team from the plant found about 25 million tons of waste-grade iron ore at various mines and dumps in Karnataka. The iron (Fe) content of the ore in these dumps was found to be around 45 per cent (+/− 5 per cent), significantly lower than the 62–64 per cent that was normally used in steel production in India. Low-grade iron ore of around 45 per cent had never been used in furnaces operated in India to produce high-quality steel. However, due to the lack of alternative options and given the gravity of the circumstances at the time, JSW engineers at the plant started to work on plans to see if low-grade iron ore could be used for steel production without any impacts on productivity and efficiency.

JSW management lobbied aggressively for the auctioning of these low-grade sources of iron ore. It succeeded in getting Supreme Court permission such that owners could sell waste-grade iron ore through the auction process. However, this was just half the battle. Massive changes in production processes were necessary to enable the Vijayanagar plant to process low-grade iron ore.

Operations needed to be designed for the new iron ore blend. A capacity analysis needed to be done for different areas of operations to identify and clear bottlenecks along the steel value chain of beneficiation, agglomeration, iron making and steel making (for a description of the steel-making process, see Figure A.30 in the Appendix). As input quality variance had increased by a factor of two or three, stringent operations along the process steps were necessary to homogenize the material and ensure high-quality steel as output. Progress in operations was achieved via a combination of benchmarking and ingenuity.

JSW Steel was able to run the furnaces at the Vijayanagar plant by sourcing almost 15 million tons of ore from these dumps during the period of crisis. The productivity of the furnaces, cost per ton of steel production and quality of steel produced at the end of the process, were all kept intact and in accordance with the original plans, despite the poor quality of ore available. At the time of writing, the Supreme Court has lifted the ban on most category A and B mines and mining has resumed, though output has yet not reached previous levels.

JSW is an inspiring example how a company can leverage a life-threatening challenge and transform it into a competitive advantage via a changed and aligned activity system. Today, JSW has superior capability in operations through the use of flexible raw materials. Efforts such as using beneficiation to harmonize input chemistry, evaluation of constraints in the system, coupled with the ability to debottleneck them quickly, a lowered dependence on suppliers and the development of technical solutions through innovative experimentation have strengthened the company's competitive position. Clearly, the ability to run cost-effective operations despite inconsistent and poor raw material quality allowed JSW to redefine rules in the highly competitive steel industry.

IN SUMMARY

Alignment across a company's activity system is crucial to create unique value for customers and to build a sustainable competitive position. IndiGo's obsession with detail around their core value proposition of on-time performance, low cost and a courteous and hassle-free travel experience has driven the company's profitable growth for nearly a decade. JSW Steel's agility and determination to realign its activities in the face of the iron ore crisis ensured the company's survival. It also improved the steel maker's overall competitive position. Whether it is HDFC Life, Bajaj Auto, Maruti Suzuki and or any of the other cases that we discussed in previous chapters, all of these companies excel because of a sound strategy and solid execution through aligned activity systems. As all of these players live in a VUCA environment, one key feature of their approach is a high degree of flexibility, speed and the willingness to learn rapidly from successful and unsuccessful experiments.

The alternative to doing business along the lines of these Indian champions is unattractive. As the case of Kingfisher shows, an unclear strategy, straddling and unaligned activity systems are enough to send even former dominant players into ruin.

8

LEADERSHIP

HAVING THE COURAGE TO
PROVIDE DIRECTION

In India, as in many other emerging markets, opportunity abounds. Change is happening constantly, customer aspirations and behaviour seem to switch overnight, a large number of services and products need to be brought closer to previously under-served customers. In short, twenty-four hours per day, seven days a week seems insufficient time to fully leverage the potential that the rapid development of the country offers.

Yet, not every company succeeds. Many have faltered because of their inability to change organizational processes and cultures to fit new environments. Their hesitation to cut old habits, underperforming employees or inadequate business partners or businesses turned them into losers on the Indian battlefield, outmanoeuvred by more nimble local or global competitors. Others overextended themselves in their desire to grow and to cover as many of the profit-laden opportunities that India seems to present to the unsuspecting businessperson. Burdened with debt and buried under operational complexity, they struggle to keep their heads above water. Some have been drifting along in the flow of opportunistic business opportunities. However, failing to develop a clearly defined value proposition implies a high risk of sinking at the first sign of a storm.

Why do companies make these fatal mistakes? The answer is almost always related to leadership and management. India's opportunities require strong leaders that understand both the market and their own company's abilities. They have to be able to identify where the company and its leadership team can create sustainable, defendable value for customers. This requires clear decisions and trade-offs, a point well understood by Rajiv Bajaj at Bajaj Auto, Nisa Godrej at GCPL, and countless other Indian business stalwarts.

That's why leadership is just as much about saying no as it is about saying yes. Yes to tackling organizational failures ruthlessly, yes to an in-depth understanding of competition and market, no to unguided growth that distracts management's attention away from their core business. Profitable growth that deepens the company's strategic position and increases alignment and fit across the company's activities is the Holy Grail in today's VUCA world. Leadership's main task must have strategy at its core: defining and communicating the company's unique position, creating a fit among core activities and eliminating activities that are not in line with overall positioning.[422]

Successful and some less successful cases in India have been discussed in earlier chapters. As we have seen in Chapter 6, there are also global role models such as the 'hidden champions'— companies that go deep in terms of their products and services but broad in terms of geographical coverage. Generally, globalization is a good conduit for growth that does not impact a company's position negatively. Creation of separate business entities to address customer segments and value propositions that are not in line with the original purpose of the company are also a viable option.

In this chapter, we will look at both globalization and creation of new business units as strategy-compatible growth options for Indian companies. The section on globalization will focus on outward-bound M&A by Indian players while the section on new business units will focus on shared value/bottom-of-the-pyramid businesses[423] that have been launched over the last few years.

THE RISE OF THE INDIAN MNC: CAPTURING GLOBAL OPPORTUNITIES

India's outward foreign direct investment (OFDI) has been the subject of much debate.[424] For the purpose of our discussion, we will focus on four phases of OFDI as shown in Figure 8.1. Phase I covers the investment activities pre-1991. The predominant thinking during this time was that OFDI would be a waste of resources and needed to be carefully balanced against the forex requirements and reserves of the country.[425] OFDI was driven primarily by private enterprises and focused on minority stake JVs to foster cooperative south–south trade[426] with a focus on Africa and Asia. Investments by the Birla group, Tata group and others were mostly market-seeking investments and attempts to try to avoid licensing and anti-trust regulations at home. Most investments (more than 60 per cent) were happening in developing countries. Manufacturing—in particular, chemicals, paper and textiles—dominated Indian OFDI together with raw materials and energy.

Phase II covers the period from 1991 to about 2005. During this time, India's companies were challenged by increasing competition at home and focused on upgrading and restructuring their business, as discussed in earlier chapters. India's economy continued to accelerate and most local players were busy growing and defending their home turf. However, restructuring efforts and high stock market valuations did provide Indian companies with the wherewithal to look at global acquisitions and investments. The economic downturn in 2002/2003 drove Indian businesses to look at foreign markets to potentially hedge demand fluctuations at home. Foreign acquisitions were also made more accessible by the lifting of the OFDI cap in 2003.

Between 2006 and 2010, the amount of OFDI exploded. Indian companies, buoyed by a strong domestic market, were confident and equipped with strong balance sheets. At the same time, the great financial crisis created a unique opportunity in the West as company stocks were beaten down mercilessly. Pent-up demand in OFDI drove OFDI/FDI ratios up to a level of 1:1.9, compared to normal developing country ratios of 1:5. The Indian appetite for global M&A was clearly much larger than what experts would have expected for an economy of India's development profile. Indian investments concentrated on developed economies to acquire brands and leverage them to penetrate both developed and other developing markets. The crisis provided a unique opportunity to gain access to customers, developed markets and technology. The latter could be combined with Indian frugal engineering and scale to drive down cost and to compete more effectively in both international and domestic markets. Indian companies also focused on gaining economies of scope, i.e., leveraging the opportunity to move up the value chain to more complex products and services.

At the height of the M&A frenzy during Phase III, a significant herd mentality could be observed in some business owners and groups that engaged in M&A activities due to personal or national pride. However, similar to M&A activities of companies headquartered in developed nations, many of these M&As did not create value. Insufficient detail orientation in target selection as well as in pre-merger due diligence and post-merger integration often led to failures. In some cases, target companies that were bought either had to be sold off again or even closed down. Managing international firms and marshalling sufficient, internationally experienced personnel became significant challenges for Indian MNCs.

 FIGURE 1

 Roland Berger

India's Outward FDI Performance Has Been Impressive and Grew by 28x since the 1990–99 Period

Overview of India's outward FDI (OFDI) and inward FDI (IFDI)

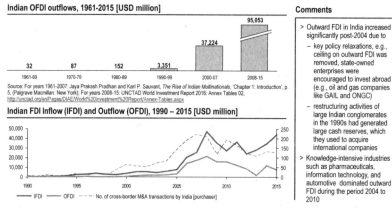

Source: UNCTAD World Investment Report 2016: Annex Tables 01, 02 and 12, http://unctad.org/en/Pages/DIAE/World%20 Investment%20Report/Annex-Tables.aspx, Roland Berger analysis

The mixed results of the Phase III wave of Indian OFDI combined with a dramatic slowing of the Indian economy resulted in a significant reduction of OFDI in Phase IV between 2010 and 2014. The OFDI/FDI ratio collapsed to 1:3.8, close to what would be expected from India based on its GDP per capita.[427] The reasons for the same were mostly driven by two factors. For one, a number of high-level M&A failures increased the level of vigilance across companies as far as acquisition opportunities are concerned. In addition, challenges in the Indian market reduced company profits and required management attention. However, in 2014 and also in 2015 signs of a revival of Indian OFDI were clearly visible.

The composition of Indian OFDI varies significantly from country to country. While Indian OFDI in the US is dominated by IT (around 80 per cent), it is spread much more widely in the EU. There, IT accounts for only 19 per cent of all OFDI, followed by pharmaceuticals (17 per cent), electronics (10 per cent), transportation (9 per cent) and chemicals (7 per cent).[428]

Interestingly, while JVs were the organizational structure of choice during Phase I, from Phase II onwards a clear trend towards wholly owned subsidiaries is observable in developed markets.[429] Indian entities are sufficiently confident to run business in developed markets on their own and prefer the operational flexibility and freedom that this provides. Indian companies have another advantage as well. Privately owned enterprises from democratic countries tend to raise fewer red flags than Chinese enterprises. As far as developing markets are concerned, Indian companies continued to prefer JVs since these seemed to be beneficial in navigating institutional voids in emerging economies.

There is no single, Indian model for M&A. Some authors and industry experts have claimed that Indian companies have a 'non-interfering' way of managing acquisitions, i.e., leaving acquired entities to their own devices and generating synergies over a time frame of several years rather than months. This seems to be the case in some instances, e.g., for Godrej, as discussed in Chapter 4. However, other companies such as Bharat Forge have taken a more front-loaded approach to integration in line with what is generally seen internationally.

The cases that we discuss below reflect a unique capability of some Indian businesspeople to take the lead and to act decisively. Bharat Forge's purchase of the defence assets of the Swiss company RUAG is such an example. Chaand Sehgal, chairman of the Motherson Group, built an empire worth USD 7 billion based on a relentless focus on customer needs that helped him grow his customer base as well as the value share captured from each customer.

The Kalyani Group: Building Indigenous Defence Capabilities

In 1999, during the height of the Kargil War, the Indian army realized that it would quickly run out of ammunition for its 155 mm Bofors Howitzer. The army turned to the Kalyani Group with an emergency order to make 1,00,000 shells. The group rose to the challenge and played its part in winning the war. The experience also whetted the appetite of Baba Kalyani, chairman of the Kalyani Group, to enter the strategically important defence business.

The Indian Defence Sector

The Indian defence sector amounts to about 2.4 per cent of India's nominal GDP[430] and is comparable in size to other key sectors such as education (3.3 per cent)[431] or infrastructure (4.7 per cent). As a budgetary line item, defence spend has never seen contraction but has seen a clear upward trend over the last couple of decades. India has the world's eighth largest annual defence budget (USD 50 billion in 2014)[432] with the sixth highest growth rate (CAGR of 4 per cent from 2004 to 2014) after China, Saudi Arabia, Russia, UAE and Brazil.[433] The FY15 budget of INR 2,29,000 crore accounted for INR 94,588 crore of capital expenditure and INR 1,34,412 crore of revenue expenditure.[434] Capital expenditure is set to grow faster than revenue expenditure and will amount to INR 2,51,000 crore in FY22, an increase of 180 per cent. Overall investment and expenditure is set to shift from army to air force and navy.

Historically, the defence market has been dominated by government entities, i.e., ordnance factories and defence PSUs (DPSUs). However, in addition to questions regarding the capability and efficiency of some of these entities, many DPSUs are heavily overbooked. For example, the order book to turnover ratio for Hindustan Aeronautics Limited is 3.95 years, for Bharat Electronics Limited 3.23 years, and the ratio for Mazagon Dock Limited as well as Bharat Dynamics Limited is at an amazing 36 and 10.11 years, respectively.[435] Together with the government's 'Make in India' campaign and offset opportunities (see below), this situation can potentially give rise to an indigenous military–industrial cluster that India urgently needs.

The Indian offset regime requires local value addition of 30–50 per cent of contract value for any defence procurement from foreign vendors. Offsets arising from the Indian Air Force's Medium Multi-Role Combat Aircraft (MMRCA) programme, air re-fuellers, transport aircraft, attack helicopters, ammunition, upgrades, etc. amount to about USD 18 billion cumulatively over the next ten to twelve years. The Indian army's offset opportunity amounts to about USD 12 billion arising from battle tanks, artillery, air defence, radars, networks, night vision, small arms and munitions. Lastly, the Indian navy contributes about USD 15 billion via frigates, destroyers, submarines, networks, landing platform docks and munitions. Overall, the offset obligation over the next ten to twelve years amounts to about USD 45 billion out of which roughly USD 25 billion still need to be structured. If handled well, this could give a significant boost to an Indian defence industry.

Indian defence programmes are relevant on a global scale and can be leveraged to build local champions. Take the Future Infantry Combat Vehicle (FICV) as an example. This programme is likely to be spread over twelve to fifteen years, will have a total volume of more than 2600 units, and will, together with its variants, amount to a business opportunity of USD 12 billion[436] (at current prices). This amount refers to platform acquisition alone; there will be a further USD 10–12 billion of lifecycle spend, which is over the next twenty-five years. The current market for Infantry Combat Vehicles stands at a yearly volume of USD 5.5 billion,[437] hence the FICV with an average yearly outlay of USD 1 billion will increase the global market by 20–25 per cent.

The defence sector was liberalized in 2001. Prior to 2001, private players were confined to Tier-2 and Tier-3 roles in the defence supply chain. Subsequently, 100 per cent investment by domestic companies and 26 per cent FDI was allowed. In 2014, the foreign investment limit in the defence sector was increased from 26 per cent to 49 per cent. After 2001, a number of private companies entered the field such as Tata Advanced Systems Ltd, Mahindra Defence Systems Ltd, Pipavav Defence and Offshore Engineering Company Ltd, Mahindra Aerospace, Kalyani Strategic Systems Ltd, Maini Aerospace, Dynamatics, and others.

However, even today, India's defence production capability is built largely around the backbone of DPSUs, ordnance factories and DRDO (Defence Research and Development Organization) labs. The government entities are supported by about 24,500 private sector aerospace, defence and homeland security (HLS) channel partners. Almost 80–82 per cent of these vendors are SMEs and 10–14 per cent are medium-sized enterprises. With this MSME backbone only providing 48–52 per cent of the turnover, the vibrancy and scalability of the Indian defence sector is a question mark beyond the large players that provide the rest of the turnover.

The Indian HLS market is set to grow from USD 15 billion in FY14[438] to USD 20 billion in FY18.[439] The overall market is split into internal security, intelligence, perimetric,[440] border and coastal surveillance and control, identification, critical infrastructure and asset protection, disaster management and forensics. Traditionally, HLS has been the preserve of the government; however, more recently, industry and private citizens are increasingly becoming a larger market constituent for some segments, e.g., perimetric access, identification, and limited surveillance.

The way forward in the Indian aerospace and defence and HLS market for private players is still fraught with challenges. Overall, significant technology gaps exist that need to be bridged, for instance, via international cooperation. R&D capability and spend in defence is insufficient, cooperation between entities such as DRDO and private companies must be improved. Bureaucracy, corruption and long project delays create large risks for companies determined to leverage the defence opportunity. Nevertheless, for a large number of small players and an increasing number of large conglomerates, defence seems to be the next growth opportunity.

The Kalyani Group: Pune's Engineering Giant[441]

Bharat Forge is led by Baba Kalyani, an MIT-educated industrialist from Pune. Bharat Forge is the flagship company of the Kalyani Group, a privately held industrial group in India with interests in engineering steel, automotive and non-automotive components, renewable energy and infrastructure, specialty chemicals and defence. Bharat Forge's main business is automotive. The company produces crankshafts, connecting rods, front axles, steering knuckles and transmission parts for PVs as well as for light, medium, and heavy CVs. About 62 per cent of the company's business depends on the auto business,[442] the remaining business is spread across energy (oil and gas, power, nuclear, thermal, wind, hydro), transportation (rail, marine, aerospace), and construction and mining (construction, metals and mining, general engineering). Geographically, the company is equally well diversified. From its FY15 revenues, 32 per cent are generated in India, 41 per cent in Europe, 25 per cent in the US and 2 per cent in Asia-Pacific.[443]

With consolidated revenues of USD 1.3 billion starting from USD 1.3 million in 1971, the year when Baba Kalyani entered the company,[444] ten manufacturing locations across four countries, a global marquee customer base of more than thirty-five OEMs and Tier-1 companies across automotive and industrial applications, Bharat Forge today is one of the leading forging[445] companies globally.

The Kalyani Group has a clear focus on building its empire around its core competencies of metallurgy and metal forming. These core competencies are leveraged across a number of different industries thereby reducing sector risks for the overall company. The defence sector with its extremely high requirements regarding quality, tolerances and metallurgical properties is hence a natural progression for the company based on its experiences and learnings in sectors as diverse as automotive, oil and gas and renewable energy.

However, the Indian defence market is dominated by PSUs and scepticism towards both the technical and financial capabilities of Indian private players runs high. As Rajinder Bhatia, CEO, aerospace and defence, puts it:

> You can't really wait for the defence market to open, you need
> to force it open. For that to happen, you need to have a clear

product strategy, i.e., a clear understanding of which product categories you can master and potentially sell successfully in India and abroad. At the same time, the current focus on defence of the Indian government requires players to be able to deliver solutions with a very quick turnaround time. This can only be done via the combination of organic growth and capability together with an inorganic growth path that aims to acquire technology and know-how via joint ventures or M&A. The latter is like steroids. It provides you an opportunity to run a marathon in record time and enables you to meet relevant deadlines.

Forcing the Indian defence market open has proven to be a difficult challenge for Indian private players. Kalyani's opportunity came when Switzerland's RUAG decided to sell off a gun manufacturing plant. Rajinder remembers,

> Baba Kalyani and our top leadership team were in London when we heard about this opportunity. We flew immediately to Switzerland to convince RUAG to stop the auction process as the plant was to be sold in pieces. Then we flew back to London to delist the items from the auction houses. We bought the whole factory in about 250 lots and concluded the transaction in about ten days.

Fast and bold decision-making are a characteristic of the company and a reflection of flat organizational structures. But even by the group's standards, this decision stood out. As it was an asset sale only, no setup support was provided. The company would have to develop the manufacturing know-how in house. Surely, Bharat Forge had grown to become a technology and cost leader in the automotive forging space, but would this experience suffice to produce gun barrels? While the opportunity to buy a gun manufacturing unit was unique, the group was betting heavily on its trained manpower and their capability to deliver. Would they rise to the challenge?

Baba had realized early on that technology was the key to differentiation and margins. The key to technology is the right workforce. However, while India would produce hundreds of thousands of engineers every year, the best engineers would be hired by investment banks, consulting companies or MNCs. At the same time, a high-technology, low-cost positioning was key to Bharat Forge's global success, so paying the same salaries as MNCs was not a viable option.

To turn this weakness into strength, the company started early on to focus on graduates from Tier-2 and Tier-3 cities. Twelfth-class pass-outs who did not necessarily have sufficient English and presentation skills but excelled in mathematics and physics were chosen. These young recruits would typically be overlooked by MNCs but provided excellent raw talent that could be moulded according to Bharat Forge's needs.

After three to four years of work on the shop floor, the top 10 per cent are given an opportunity to participate in a bachelor's in engineering course that Bharat Forge has tailored for this purpose together with BITS Pilani, one of the top engineering colleges in India. Roughly forty-five to fifty employees are chosen to participate in this three-year course per year. These young engineers then build a core of brilliant employees committed to Bharat Forge. In addition, the company selects about twenty-five engineers yearly to enrol them into a tailor-made, eighteen-month master's course at the IIT in Mumbai. The focus areas for the same are, for example, modelling and simulation. Each year, ten to twelve employees have an opportunity to enrol in a PhD programme in nanomaterials, 3D printing, light-weighting, exotic materials, etc. On the business side, similar programmes exist. For example, employees have an opportunity to do a twenty-two-month master's in management in collaboration with Warwick University, UK.

'Many of our graduates never dreamt of reaching the levels that they reached at Bharat Forge,' points out Rajinder. 'You truly can join on the shop floor and become a vice president in due time. In some sense, this is our version of the American Dream.' Despite wage bills that are significantly lower than those of international competitors, Bharat Forge has access to a highly capable and loyal workforce. Attrition rates are at less than 6 per cent for the company overall and less than 1 per cent for higher-level employees. Says Rajinder:

> In principle, everybody could do this but how many companies are willing to spend 12 per cent of their wage bill on training? At any given point in time, about 10-15 per cent of our manpower is in some kind of training. This is why we maintain EBITDA ratios of around 30 per cent in industries where others are struggling.[446]

The core team of masters and PhDs lent the necessary strength and capability to the gun manufacturing ramp-up. Within less than eight months, the company was able to put up the factory in Pune and produce the first gun barrel. Production of the first breechblock[447] was even faster and happened in less than six months.

As guns today are made not only of metal but also electronics, the group got together with Elbit Systems from Israel. The JV, BF Elbit Advanced Systems, has a clear separation of duties. While the Kalyani group will concentrate on high-tech manufacturing and detailed knowledge of metallurgy and metals, Elbit will focus on fire control systems, electro-optical systems, etc. Together, both companies believe that they have a winning combination for India and beyond. Says Rajinder:

We are convinced that we will become the most competitively priced barrel manufacturer worldwide by a wide margin in the next five to seven years. In emerging markets, we will be able to play a role as a systems supplier while in developed markets we aim to be a components supplier.

The defence market has long lead times which test the patience and financial endurance of market participants. While no major contracts have been won yet, the Kalyani group is in a good position in four out of six gun programmes of the Indian government and recently signed an MoU with Tata Motors for a joint approach towards the FICV platform. Baba and his team are confident that their dedication and persistence will pay off and allow their company to become the cornerstone of an indigenous land systems capability in India.

Motherson and the Story of the Indian Automotive Supplier Industry

The Indian automotive supplier landscape has come a long way since the early days when Maruti Suzuki started developing the first suppliers in the 1980s. While many of Maruti Suzuki's suppliers experienced success, none were as successful as Motherson, which managed to build a USD 7 billion global empire within a span of forty years.

The Indian Automotive Supplier Landscape

India's automotive industry is going strong. As per ACMA,[448] India is the largest tractor manufacturer globally. The country is the world's second largest two-wheeler and bus manufacturer. It is the fifth largest heavy truck manufacturer and the sixth largest car manufacturer. With population and income growth in her favour, India will continue to move up in global rankings.

A strong automotive industry requires strong suppliers. The automotive component industry has grown with a respectable CAGR of 11 per cent between FY10 and FY15 and amounts to about USD 38.5 billion. As shown in Figure 8.2, PVs (45 per cent) dominate automotive components supplies followed by two-wheelers (22 per cent), CVs (18 per cent) and tractors (8 per cent).

8 FIGURE 2

PV Accounts for ~45% of Auto Component Business; Powertrain Parts Account for Over 50%

Percentage breakup of all components manufactured in India by segment

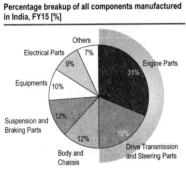

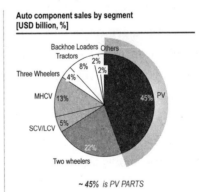

Source: ACMA, http://www.acma.in/docmgr/ACMA_Presentation/ACMA_Presentation.pdf; Roland Berger analysis

Exports have grown even faster than domestic sales, with a CAGR of 29 per cent between FY10 and FY15, to the amount of USD 11.2 billion in FY15. Dominant export destinations are Europe (36.4 per cent), Asia (25.3 per cent) and the US (23.3 per cent). Since exports grew faster than imports (import CAGR of 18 per cent between FY10 and FY15), the negative trade balance in automotive components could be reduced from about USD 3.8 billion in FY10 to USD 2.4 billion in FY15. While Europe is a strong contributor to imports with 32.5 per cent, imports from Asia dominate the show with 58 per cent. This is driven by large Asian players (Suzuki, Hyundai) operating in India as well as by Chinese imports. Imports from the US amount to 7.2 per cent of the total and are less relevant.

Overall, imports account for roughly a third of industry volume. Exchange rate volatility and extreme price pressure drive the indigenization and localization efforts of various OEMs in the country and this percentage should come down going forward.

Capital investment in the automotive component industry reached a high of USD 2.0–2.5 billion in FY11. Since then, low capacity utilization and stagnant or falling demand have resulted in constantly declining investments in the industry. Capital investment stood at USD 0.3–0.5 billion in FY15.

As the tastes of Indian consumers regarding quality and fit and finish converge towards global standards and as exports to global markets—predominantly to OEMs and Tier-1s—have increased, quality has become a central issue for the Indian supply base. The country boasts of fourteen Deming prize-winning companies,[449] the highest number outside of Japan. Many of its companies have various quality certifications (ISO9001, TS16494, ISO14001, OHSAS, etc.). However, concerns about consistency of processes and quality, especially regarding Tier-2 suppliers, are a constant reminder to the industry to up the ante and improve even further.[450]

Motherson: Follow Thy Customer[451]

When Chaand Sehgal, the founder of Motherson, was an eighteen-year-old college boy, his grandfather, who was a jeweller, gave him an opportunity to make some pocket money. Chaand, whose college was close to the Delhi airport, was to take silver from his grandfather's shop to the airport, clear the custom's paperwork and take the paperwork to the banks. For each kilogram of sliver, Chaand would get a commission of INR 1 and earn about INR 1,000 every two to three weeks, a decent sum of money at the time. Chaand remembers:

> Suddenly, for about nine to ten months, everything went haywire. The Hunt brothers were trying to corner the silver market and I found myself selling two to three thousand kilos of silver per day. This turned out to be a lot of money. As taxes were northward of 80 per cent, we, my mother and me, needed to invest the money in a company. We started a wire plant and pretty much made a mess of it. Well, what do you expect from an eighteen-year-old college boy? But the experience of running the plant and going to college was invaluable.

When Maruti Suzuki entered the country in 1983, Chaand was quick to grasp this opportunity. He started supplying wire to Maruti Suzuki and graduated to supplying wiring harnesses.[452] He also realized that Maruti Suzuki's volume predictions were always on the conservative side. As a consequence, rather than waiting for the OEM to ask him for capacity additions, he started going ahead of the OEM by building spare capacity. He did this in an environment where most other suppliers were sweating assets, i.e., they preferred to run plants at more than 100 per cent capacity. Hence, Chaand built a strong relationship with Maruti. In addition, he developed a partnership with the Japanese Sumitomo group whose ability to impart knowledge was 'incredible' according to him. Following both Sumitomo's and Maruti Suzuki's direction in terms of building capability, he was able to cement a strong relationship with both players, creating a solid base for further expansions.

An opportunity for growth presented itself when Daimler attended the Auto Expo in Delhi in the early 1990s. Interacting with Daimler proved to be a long drawn out process. However, in 1995–96, Daimler's plans to enter India ran into a rough patch. The fine print in Daimler's contract with the government to produce cars in India required exports out of the country before an import licence for cars and car parts was to be given. Daimler was unable to fulfil this request and was at risk of losing its India production project. Chaand stepped in to help Daimler out. Within thirty-nine days, he started producing rubber parts in cooperation with Daimler's German supplier, WoCo. On the thirty-ninth day, he was able to export rubber parts worth about 15,000 Deutsche Mark out of India on behalf of Mercedes-Benz and in this way cleared the regulatory logjam. Chaand remembers:

> I didn't have time to pour concrete for the factory, hence I welded ¾-inch steel sheets together, 2200 square metres of it! We put the machines on these steel sheets. I air-freighted about 280 tons of machinery from Germany. WoCo sent three Germans to my factory who lived in the factory 24/7 until we were able to produce and export quality rubber parts. When WoCo's lawyer created trouble, WoCo's CEO told me 'I will support you, we will figure out the details later.' So, instead of starting in a joint venture, I started with a 100 per cent owned entity. All this, just to support Daimler.

Daimler proved to be important for Motherson's international growth in more ways than one. Not only had the company started to export, Chaand and his team had also built strong relationships with the Daimler management. These proved to be vital in the acquisition of Visiocorp about a decade later. Visiocorp was known to Motherson through a successful JV. In terms of revenue, the company itself was larger than Motherson. Nevertheless, key Daimler executives suggested to Chaand that he should acquire the company. 'We started looking at the company in late 2008 just before the Lehman crisis,' says Chaand. 'Our customers assured us that they would stand behind us. So we went through with the transaction despite the fact that by that time Lehman had hit.'

When Motherson's chosen president of Visiocorp communicated that the turnaround would take three to four years, Chaand reacted quickly. As Visiocorp's monthly losses were larger than the profit of Motherson Group, this scenario was simply not an option. He relieved the president of his duties and started working with the original management teams on delivery and quality. Orders proved strong due to customer support. Improvements were quickly visible. After eight months, the OEMs' supplier risk managers took Visiocorp off their risk radar. Rather than turning the company around in three to four years as the OEMs had expected, Motherson achieved a turnaround in less than a year.

The Visiocorp success was an important milestone for Motherson. When the Peguform[453] acquisition opportunity presented itself, both Motherson and the company's OEM customers had the confidence that Motherson would be successful. Peguform's acquisition again nearly doubled Motherson's size, putting the company firmly among globally relevant system suppliers.

The spectacular success of Motherson rests on several pillars. As Chaand puts it:

Our early experience with Daimler and Maruti Suzuki taught us that we have the unique capability to solve problems for our customers. We are extremely fast in our reactions, able to do multiple joint ventures in various configurations, etc. Hence, when you see our mission it is not about being the biggest or the most profitable player. It is centred on being a globally preferred solution provider.

A second management mantra is focused on empowerment. 'Ninety-nine per cent of all the problems in companies are due to lack of empowerment,' says Chaand. 'People want their companies to do well. The various units need to be very efficient in responding to customer needs on a second-by-second basis. Headquarters simply cannot get in the way.' He credits much of the success at Visiocorp to his focus on empowerment and the corresponding corporate culture change. Acquisitions are generally not managed centrally. Also, Motherson does not send Indian talent to run global acquisitions. Chaand's opinion is simple: 'We have equal confidence in talent regardless of their nationality.'

Being clearly focused on serving OEMs rather than branching out into aftermarket sales or other industries is key to Motherson's success. The company sticks with its customers and concentrates on increasing its share of wallet with existing customers as well as increasing its customer footprint. Says Chaand,

No OEM wants a good supplier to go bankrupt. They prefer strategic investors over private equity or hedge funds, as we speak the same language. Also, the first thing we do when we enter an acquired company is to open up the gates for R&D, as products are the lifeline of companies. Private equity and hedge funds tend to choke R&D, IT and other investments. In addition, the global automotive industry continues to grow at a rather steady pace and provides good visibility of customer volumes. With this kind of transparency and a good opportunity to grow in terms of scale and scope, why would I want to invest my money anywhere else?

As M&As and JVs are the lifeline of Motherson, the company has invested in an internal IT company that supports and integrates acquired assets. The CMMI level-three-certified team goes as the first team into acquired assets, understands data structures and data availability and writes patch files to integrate the data from the acquired unit into Motherson's overall reporting dashboard. Software environments are not changed, which increases complexity for the internal software team but minimizes business disruptions for the acquired companies.

Leveraging modern technology at Indian prices drives the data-driven culture at Motherson. Says Chaand,

> You have to go to the units because that is where the money is made. I have 201 units for which all data is either available live when I have an Internet connection or off-line on my laptop or iPad when I am flying. I travel 300 days per year, nobody knows which plant I will be visiting next, but before I get there I have all their data available. This helps us to continue to be on our toes.

Data availability allows Chaand and his leadership team to provide direction and advice regarding improvement potentials. It is also an essential ingredient to Motherson's BYBY approach (by yourself better yourself). Rather than focus on competition, units are encouraged to look at their own data to drive continuous improvement. Data enables the company to be decisive. Says Chaand: 'We don't take time to sit around and imagine what could be. We have data and waste no time taking decisions regarding investments, people, R&D, etc.'

Today, Chaand oversees a network of companies (see Figure 8.3) that generate an overall revenue of USD 7 billion.

The group produces interior and exterior polymer modules. It manufactures polymer components and tools, rear-view mirrors, wiring harnesses and other components. Its customers include Audi, Volkswagen, Seat, Hyundai, BMW, Renault Nissan, Maruti Suzuki, Ford and Daimler. Growth has been breathtaking, with a CAGR of 43 per cent between FY11 and FY15. With facilities across twenty-five countries, Motherson Group is well positioned to reach its 2020 goals of USD 18 billion in revenue, a 40 per cent return on capital employed[454] and its mantra of '3Cx15'— which means that the company works towards a situation in which no country, customer or component amounts to more than 15 per cent of revenue. 'The visibility of the automotive business is incredible,' points out Chaand. 'We have given long-term projections four times in the past and each and every time surpassed our expectations.' Clearly, 2020 is unlikely to be an exception.

8 FIGURE 3   Roland
Berger

MSSL Has Grown as a Result of Organic Growth and Several Key Acquisitions and JVs since 2000

Motherson Sumi Systems Ltd (MSSL): List of subsidiary companies and JVs

1) Has two subsidiaries: Samvardhana Motherson Reflectec (SMR) and Samvardhana Motherson Peguform (SMP)

Source: MSSL FY15 Annual Report

SHARED VALUE: DOING WELL BY DOING GOOD

Following C.K. Prahalad's early work, a lot of attention has been given to identifying business models and developing products that allow companies to generate sustainable profits by serving the world's poor. This focus has been directed towards either emerging markets or the economically less fortunate parts of the developed world. Prahalad's ideas have been rephrased by Porter and Kramer, who talk about 'shared value', i.e., the concept that companies can achieve economic success by building scalable, profitable and sustainable solutions that address large social issues. Leveraging the creative potential of companies for the greater good of mankind is a key task for corporations to re-establish goodwill with a public that is increasingly sceptical as far as the pursuit of profit at the expense of social or environmental values is concerned.

Shared value must not be confused with CSR. CSR tries to address public concerns regarding the social role and commitment of companies, albeit without a profit motive. In India, at the time of writing, 2 per cent of average net profits in the last three years must be spent on CSR initiatives.[455] Investments in social for-profit ventures are explicitly excluded from the list of allowable CSR investments. The CSR regulation unfortunately does not lend itself to providing urgently needed funds for the social venture start-up scene and hence does not support potential significant innovation from such activities. Social causes related to the company's business are also explicitly excluded from CSR spending, increasing the likeliness of activities being unsustainable and not part of the CEO's agenda.

CSR Versus Shared Value: The Case of Hindustan Unilever[456]

For CSR to be part of the CEO's agenda, it has to be tightly linked to core business objectives. A case in point is the 'Shakti Amma' and 'Shakti Maan' campaign by HUL. The initial activities were understood by management as pure CSR. Some poverty-stricken women and, later on, their husbands were given an opportunity to sell HUL products in India's villages, generating income for those individuals with the scale of the total programme being limited by HUL's CSR funds. As this activity was CSR, it was not seen as core to the company, and top-notch talent within HUL avoided taking responsibility for the programme. Things changed when the HUL management realized that Shakti Ammas could provide real competitive advantage by creating massive brand awareness and reach in rural areas. Hence, management decided to treat Shakti Ammas as just one more distribution channel and to steer and measure this channel in the same way it would steer and measure success in organized retail or Kirana stores. Suddenly, the programme was at the core of HUL's activities and management, and the success of this programme turned out to be closely watched by the company's CEO.

Challenges for corporations in reaching rural India, especially villages with less than 2,000 inhabitants, are massive. Small, scattered settlements and poor infrastructure make distribution difficult. A low literacy rate of 59 per cent, especially among females, limits the effectiveness of print media. Overall category penetration and brand awareness is low. Purchasing power is limited For example, SKUs within the price range of INR 0–10 contribute up to 51 per cent of overall Shakti sales in 2013. A total of 84 per cent of all sales fall into the INR 0–50 bracket. With these kinds of purchase volumes, low-cost distribution is the key. HUL's approach was to provide underprivileged women—those who belong to the poorest households in hard-to-reach villages—with capital to invest. These women became micro-entrepreneurs who distributed HUL products. Leveraging its first-mover advantage, HUL was able to build up high customer loyalty and brand equity as well as an extensive distribution network that makes its position in these rural villages nearly impenetrable.

HUL covers the top 17 per cent of all villages, which contribute up to 60 per cent of village wealth, via distributor salesmen. It does not have any representation in the 2,20,000 poorest villages that contribute to 10 per cent of wealth. The company uses the Shakti model to cover all villages between these two extremes. In terms of inbound logistics, the company developed rural distributors who can supply stocks to Shakti Ammas. The Ammas then go door-to-door in the villages, selling HUL products and providing hygiene education to create awareness of the benefits of HUL products to villagers. Shakti Ammas also sell to retail outlets in their own villages as well as to two to three neighbouring villages in a 5–6 km radius. Unsold goods are stored in the homes of the Shakti Ammas, who de facto become brand ambassadors for HUL products in the village.

Since this distribution channel is important, HUL has invested in robust selection and training processes for Shakti Ammas, who distribute goods to over 1 million shops out of the total HUL reach of 3.2 million shops. More than 3000 Shakti promoters report to over 500 rural territory supervisors and are responsible for recruiting, training and retaining Shakti Ammas. More than 45,000 GPRS-enabled mobile phones have been handed out to Shakti Ammas. These run a mini-enterprise resource planning system that helps to book orders and capture sales data that can be mined to further improve understanding of and service for rural customers.

As of 2014, about 66,000 Shakti entrepreneurs covered about 1,65,000 villages and about 4 million households as well as more than 1 million outlets. About 58 per cent of all sales executives were earning more than INR 1000 per month, a significant sum in a rural setting. In poorer states such as Bihar, Jharkhand and UP, Shakti executives earn more than the average per capita income of the state. HUL is constantly innovating to find additional income opportunities by building distribution alliances with non-competing companies (e.g., Tata DoCoMo). Some 69 per cent of all Shakti sales are of detergents, clearly indicating a positive impact of the Shakti model on the livelihoods of rural India.

Today, the Shakti model has become a key distribution channel whose profitability is in line with HUL's standard distribution channels. Its impact on rural India cannot be understated. Its journey from seventeen sales executives in 2001 to a target of 75,000 in 2015 with a CAGR of 82 per cent is impressive. Clearly, none of this would have been possible as a CSR initiative. CSR cannot provide the answers that India and other emerging markets need. These can only be driven by frugal engineering and shared-value businesses.

Rural Housing Construction: A Key Employment Generator

Another powerful example of shared value is the case study of Mahindra Rural Housing Finance, described below. Mahindra's approach successfully leverages group synergies to develop solutions for India's rural poor and to enable them to own their own houses. The approach is tailored to each local community and has a substantial multiplier effect on communities, as housing construction generates a large number of additional skilled and unskilled jobs in a society.

India's Rural Housing Market

According to a recent study by the National Council of Applied Economic Research, residential housing has a major positive impact on the Indian economy. With the overall construction industry divided into residential construction, non-residential construction and other construction sectors, the residential construction or housing sector amounts to 1 per cent of GDP (8.2 per cent for the total construction sector) and 6.9 per cent of the country's employment (11.5 per cent for the construction sector overall).[457]

India's housing finance market grew by 19.7 per cent (annualized) in FY14.[458] Housing loans crossed INR 8.9 trillion[459] in FY15, with 39.1 per cent being financed by housing finance companies[460], 42.2 per cent by public sector banks, and 18.6 per cent by scheduled commercial banks[461] (excluding public sector banks). As shown in Fig. 6.4, the Indian housing market is massively skewed towards loans of INR 25+ lakh, which amount to half of all housing loans. Small loans of up to INR 2 lakh are a marginal 1 per cent of the overall loan pie. In addition, despite the fact that more than two thirds of India's total population lives in rural areas, rural housing loan disbursement is a very meagre 15.5 per cent of all loans. Clearly, the rural market is severely underserved as far as housing loans are concerned. As a consequence, significant employment-generating opportunities in rural areas are lying untapped.

8 FIGURE 4

Roland Berger

Although There Has Been a Significant Growth in the Loans Disbursed, This Has Been Concentrated in Urban Areas and for Larger Loan Amounts
Overview of Indian housing finance industry, 2014

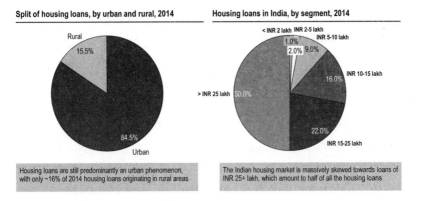

Source: Mahindra Rural Housing Finance Ltd, The Porter Prize Awards 2015 presentation, Roland Berger

With about 15 per cent of all roofs in India made out of grass, thatch, bamboo, wood, mud or similar materials, and about an equal percentage made out of galvanized iron, metal or asbestos sheets, there is a clear opportunity for driving affordable, adequate housing in India in general and in rural India in particular.[462] In fact, the urban housing shortage is estimated at 18.8 million units and the rural housing shortage at 43.7 million units.[463] Growth will be driven by improved affordability of homes, rising disposable incomes, tax incentives, affordable interest rates, favourable growth and government programmes such as 'Housing for All' and 'Smart Cities'.

Transforming rural lives by enabling farmers and agriculture-dependent citizens to own their own homes is not only a noble vision but also a national necessity. However, this need seems to find very few takers among standard private and public sector banks.

Mahindra Rural Housing Finance: Bringing India under a Roof

One company that decided to take on the challenge of enabling home construction in rural India is MRHF, a company promoted by Mahindra and Mahindra Financial Services Ltd (Mahindra Finance) (87.5 per cent) with equity participation by the National Housing Bank (NHB, 12.5 per cent), a 100 per cent subsidiary of the Reserve Bank of India (RBI). The basic idea behind MRHF venturing into the rural housing finance space was simple. The rural market is underserved, so it provides opportunity to play, especially in comparison with the highly competitive, reasonably well-developed urban market. At the same time, MRHF could leverage significant parenting advantages from Mahindra Finance and Mahindra. Mahindra Finance had ready access to funds and a good reputation with RBI. In addition, the company owned a ready-made customer base of more than 3 million across the country, with about 2 million customers in rural and 1 million in semi-urban areas. Mahindra Finance also has a footprint of more than 1100 locations across India. Over about two decades, Mahindra Finance had established a brand name for itself in terms of providing loans to rural customers, e.g., for Mahindra tractors and vehicles or Maruti Suzuki cars, in a responsible manner. The company was able to convince rural customers of its fair dealings and ethics and carried a large amount of trust. Says Anuj Mehra, managing director, Mahindra Rural Finance:

> Rural customers are not swayed by standard advertising and celebrity endorsements by the likes of Amitabh Bachchan or Shahrukh Khan. When they want to buy a tractor, they talk to the village mechanic to understand maintenance cost, performance in the field, fuel efficiency, etc. In case of a house loan, you are asking them to give what is often their only valuable asset, namely their land, as collateral. They will not do that unless they trust you. Hence it is crucial that they can talk to people in the village who have dealt with Mahindra Finance in the past. They need to know that you won't repossess the asset when they get in trouble due to drought or failing crops.

Despite the obvious need for housing finance in rural India, the journey to a scalable offering was tedious. Initially, MRHF thought it could provide housing loans to an average loan size of INR 5 lakh. It was believed that rising rural incomes due to government guaranteed minimum sale prices for basic commodities, government schemes such as NREGA and Bharat Nirman, plus overall GDP growth combined with a young and aspirational customer base should offer significant opportunity for business and growth. Customer demographics clearly supported some of the initial assumptions. For instance, 70 per cent of all clients are between twenty-five and forty-four years of age, i.e., young and driven by aspiration. Some 65 per cent of all clients have at least basic schooling and hence should be able to understand the benefits of a home loan versus the exorbitant rates charged by village money lenders. In terms of occupation, MRHF customers are spread quite uniformly across various professional groups, with farmers (0–2 acres: 7 per cent; 2–5 acres: 10 per cent, 5+ acres: 12 per cent) accounting for close to a third of all disbursed loans, followed by unskilled workers (21 per cent), businesses, shops and traders (19 per cent), skilled workers (12 per cent), salaried (7 per cent), self-employed (7 per cent) and agricultural labour (5 per cent).

However, MRHF misjudged the motivations and attitudes of rural customers with regard to owning a home and the purchase process. According to MRHF, the primary focus for rural Indians is the education of their children. By now, most people understand that education potentially holds the key to a more prosperous life and their focus is to enable the same for their children, even if it is too late for themselves. The second priority is to expand income sources, i.e., to de-risk the income streams from agriculture. The third priority is to provide for the marriage of their children, an expensive affair due to culturally important lavish feasts and dowry payments. Only after these requirements have been fulfilled will rural customers look at building a house. While a house communicates prestige in the village, it is a dead asset in the sense that it does not generate income for the family, hence, its relatively low importance.

With houses being non-income-generating assets and with cash flows from agriculture being unpredictable, rural customers also prefer to pay for houses out of their own savings, obtained, e.g., through bumper crop incomes. Institutional loans occupy the last position of funding opportunities after money lenders and friends and relatives. In fact, by and large, houses are constructed piece-meal (using disposable funds generated by a better-than-average harvest), i.e., walls are constructed but the roof is left as a corrugated sheet and a toilet will be added once the next bumper crop comes around. As so often happens, a bottom-of-the-pyramid product such as finance for rural housing has non-consumption as its greatest competitor!

MRHF quickly realized that the INR 5 lakh average loan size was a pipedream that has little to do with the reality in rural markets. The average investment in housing additions centred around building a toilet, a bathroom, a roof, a kitchen, flooring, or walls. The average ticket size for these transactions was about INR 2.27 lakh, out of which rural customers with average yearly incomes of INR 1.59 lakh would provide INR 1.13 lakh as their own contribution and take INR 0.96 lakh as a loan. Would this be enough to allow MRHF to make money?

MRHF is a profitable company and its financials are in line with industry norms (e.g., PAT/average assets 2.52 per cent, PBT/total income 20.43 per cent). However, building a profitable, scalable business that today is present in nine states and has provided loans to 3,50,000 rural families with an average loan amount of USD 1675 was challenging. It required changing the way business was envisioned at the outset. We will go through the various innovations that MRHF had to drive one by one.

Customer acquisition in an urban setting is typically outsourced to brokers and direct selling agents besides direct tie-ups with builders who provide a constant stream of potential customers. In a rural setting, mass marketing proved ineffective. Convincing customers via concept selling and word-of-mouth is necessary. Hence, the company had to invest in a sales force that had a strong local connection at the village level. It needed to develop brand ambassadors and local champions such as the village elders in much the same way that Mahindra tractors need to convince the village mechanic that the product is solid. Consistency and relationship building pay rich dividends. In FY15, more than 60 per cent of all business came via referrals from existing customers.

Collections in urban settings are standardized and happen via multiple modes. In a rural environment, customers typically don't have a banking habit, so payments have to be collected physically in cash. To avoid pilferage, handheld machines issue payment receipts and upload data to central servers. Schematic approaches such as repossessing land do not work. For one, they would lead to farmer distress with loss of goodwill and (potentially) business losses. In addition, this would destroy all the trust capital that MRHF has built up.

As a consequence, the sales and collection people that MRHF hires cannot be centralized order fulfillers as is the case in urban centres. They have to be trained to understand the products, understand the credit-worthiness and payment capability of the client, and make loan decisions in a decentralized way. All of this needs to be done in an environment in which credit histories and information are not available and where local hires often lack basic education and skills.

Customers in cities also tend to have stable incomes. Again, the situation is different in the countryside. Here, due to the vagaries of nature, cash flows tend to be erratic and bulky. Collections need to happen at the right time and repayment terms must be structured to reflect the customers' cash flows. City dwellers tend to have reasonable savings. This does not apply in a rural setting. Savings are minimal and can easily be wiped out by one or two bad harvests. MRHF's solution to this challenge is a detailed contact programme with customers to constantly keep in touch with what their overall financial situation looks like. The company also offers life insurance coverage with their loans to safeguard their customers against catastrophic loss of life of the primary breadwinners. By handling payment difficulties flexibly, MRHF avoids payment defaults. Says Anuj:

> We do not worry about NPAs—while we are concerned, we do not react quickly, jump for litigation, etc. Farmers and agro-related professions will get into difficulties when crops fail. However, if you have a good relationship you can ensure that the loan is paid back albeit with some delay. While NPAs may fluctuate linked to climatic conditions and cash flows, our credit losses are negligible.

Customers who pay back on time are offered attractive education loans, loans for the marriage of their children, etc. As Anuj points out, 'We want to reward and encourage positive behaviour. At the same time, we understand our customers very well and ensure that we don't overburden them with debt. It is a partnership with customers rather than an attempt to cross-sell products.'

Urban customers are centred in clearly defined locations and can be easily serviced. Rural customers, on the contrary, are widely spread out and expect personalized attention at home. Clearly, such a distribution model costs more than the corresponding model in urban centres. To keep costs from spiralling out of control, MRHF introduced the concept of cluster selling, i.e., sales representatives are in charge of a cluster of eight to ten villages. This brought down overheads as a percentage of average assets in mature markets of the company from about 7.5 per cent to 3.3 per cent.

Credit appraisal is another area where there are major differences between rural and urban customers. In an urban setting, appraisal for loans is heavily documentation-based and this assessment can be easily outsourced. In a rural setting, customers are uncomfortable with the heavy documentation burden that banks require. Often, they don't have the required documents, i.e., the land title may still be in the name of the grandfather rather than in the name of the current owner. MRHF's approach to this challenge is two-fold. The company has developed income models based on type of crop, type of soil or region, size of land holding, etc., that give it a reliable estimate for potential earnings. The so-called 'credit book' documents the insights that local agents have regarding the productive potential of their region. The credit book is constantly upgraded and updated. In addition, after operating for several years in rural markets, MRHF has started to analyse its own data and to develop proprietary software that does risk assessments of rural customers both at the time of awarding a loan as well as during the time when the loan is serviced. Lastly, MRHF employees help customers to create necessary documents for loans and hence enable them to monetize a previously un-bankable asset.

MRHF complements its first mover advantage by aligning with the regulator. Having a 12.5 per cent shareholding of NHB improves its ability to operate in a highly regulated environment.

MRHF is indeed living up to its vision of 'transforming rural lives'. It provides rural customers with a sense of pride by giving them respect and a feeling of self-worth as the company establishes their credit-worthiness. As mentioned above, rural housing has a major impact on employment generation in rural areas as well, so the company plays a role in bettering the lives of India's rural population, both via direct MRHF employment and indirect construction-related employment. With about 273 offices and 3200 employees as of FY15, and a CAGR of 60+ per cent since FY11, it is set to continue to drive prosperity and respect in rural India.

Says Dharmesh Vakharia, chief financial officer, Mahindra Home Finance:

> Our competitive assets such as the relationships that we have built, the field force that we have trained, the pre- and post-loan machine-based learning algorithms that we have deployed for credit scoring and our income estimation methods via credit books give us an edge going forward. Fundamentally, the dynamics in rural markets that drive these competitive advantages won't change over the next ten-plus years.

IN SUMMARY

Opportunity abounds in India. Leveraging this opportunity requires strong leaders that understand both the market as well as their company's abilities in depth. These leaders need the courage to say yes as well as no to growth, depending on the opportunities that present themselves.

While our examples in previous chapters have highlighted companies and leaders that live up to this mantra, the current chapter has focused on two areas where leadership is required: global expansion as well as shared value businesses.

In terms of both organic and inorganic global expansion, Indian companies have come a long way. Overseas FDI is sizeable and several players have used acquisitions to improve their market position at home as well as to build a credible global presence.

The Kalyani group is one such example. Baba Kalyani has identified metallurgy and metal forming as his core competence. He is building the Kalyani group around this competence and expanding from a pure automotive business into diverse areas such as oil and gas and alternative energies. His bold foray into the defence space through the purchase of RUAG's gun manufacturing unit shows the determination, speed and courage characteristic of successful Indian entrepreneurs. His JV with Elbit from Israel ensures that he can offer viable, cost-effective gun solutions to the Indian armed forces as well as down the line to foreign armies.

Chaand Sehgal's sole focus at Motherson Group is Automotive OEMs. He does not waver in capturing a larger share of wallet with these customers, an approach that has led to the creation of a USD 7 billion global automotive component empire. Growth is driven both organically and inorganically. In the latter case, Chaand and his team have developed an impressive, decentralized, data-driven M&A approach that will support Motherson in reaching its revenue target of USD 18 billion by 2020.

Growth can also come by satisfying the needs of the bottom of the pyramid via shared value business models. HUL's Shakti Amma model became scalable by transforming it from a CSR activity to a shared value business model. Today, more than 66,000 Shakti entrepreneurs are a solid competitive advantage for HUL, both in terms of distribution reach as well as in terms of creating brand awareness.

MRHF's approach to rural markets also created formidable competitive advantages, namely a strong distribution footprint, a solid understanding of the needs of rural customers and corresponding data models and analytics. As in the case of HUL's Shakti distribution channel, financial results for MRHF are in line with industry standards. The company lifts rural customers out of poverty, creates substantial employment opportunities both directly and indirectly, and truly does well by doing good.

As our cases have shown, opportunities in India and for Indian companies are aplenty despite of and sometimes due to a VUCA environment. They may not always be suited to the faint of heart. However, visionary and courageous leaders have shown time and again that India is fertile ground for writing your own destiny.

9

TO SUM IT UP

WHAT YOU NEED TO KNOW TO RIDE THE TIGER

Once you take on the helm of a company as the CEO, there is no place to hide, no room for excuses. While you get to ride the positive waves of success, you are held equally accountable for the difficulties that the company faces. Scrutiny from investors, the media, your employees, business partners—including suppliers and dealers—and competition is intense. Everything that you say and do is analysed and sometimes interpreted to fit political agendas within and outside of the company.

On top of this, you have to ride the tiger. You have to steer your business in an emerging economy that is sometimes quite temperamental as it moves through the Indian jungle of changing consumer needs, regulatory requirements, infrastructure challenges and the like. Rules and regulations for your business may change overnight due to the Supreme Court or political decisions. Your product may or may not fulfil the detailed value-for-money equation that Indian consumers expect, despite your having spent a significant amount on customer research. Your competition may exhibit price aggressiveness that you thought inconceivable. Their products may open new market segments that you and your team didn't know existed. Frontline attrition may be so high that you feel you are more of a training institute than a business.

Business under these circumstances is hard, but luckily it is not rocket science. Common sense may not help you to understand interference patterns of gravitational waves or the properties of Higgs bosons. But paired with agility and good execution, common sense can get you quite far in a business environment, even while riding a tiger in a VUCA world.

This book has discussed many approaches to increase your chances of success. We believe that a relentless focus on operational excellence and innovation is key for companies that want to be successful in emerging markets. These organizations need to make choices about what they want to be in regard to their respective customers and they need to implement the corresponding trade-offs. Alignment across the organization is crucial. It is as critical to lead these organizations through growth opportunities that are in sync with choices while staying away from opportunities that are not. Companies have to be agile while responding to market changes, which requires a corresponding culture and organizational structure. And last but not least, serendipity helps. Many large companies and fortunes are built not so much on detailed planning, but as a result of being in the right place at the right time, having the wisdom to recognize the opportunity, and the courage to take advantage of it. To put it in the words of the great French emperor Napoleon Bonaparte, 'I know he is a good general, but is he lucky?'[464]

Hard work and luck often go hand in hand. There is no magic wand or ingenious jugaad that takes away the rigor and focus that is necessary to make a company successful. Life is indeed like the advertising slogan of Apollo Tyres: 'Performance—There are no shortcuts'. This book provides ample evidence of this fact through the detailed analysis of more than sixteen cases across numerous industries in India.

Operational Excellence: The Entry Ticket

Operational excellence is the entry ticket into the Indian game. Maruti Suzuki's minute focus on every detail to drive down costs has enabled the company to increase volumes and to cement its position as India's number one PV manufacturer. With equally determined drive, Bajaj Auto pushes TPM to drive performance and operational excellence across functions. This focus ensured the company's survival when it was threatened by Japanese competition and enabled Bajaj to transform itself into one of the most profitable automotive companies in the world. Vaatsalya Healthcare's asset-light, no-frills service model provides much needed quality healthcare in India's Tier-2 and Tier-3 cities. IndiGo's obsession with on-time performance and low cost operations drives the company's success and has established IndiGo as the market leader in the highly competitive Indian airline industry. Bosch leverages its captive centre model to build capability to scale and to be competitive (relative to external providers) through lower overhead costs, lower attrition rates, higher utilization and offshore ratios, for example.

Life in companies does not have to be about large announcements regarding major strategic shifts or organizational restructurings that lay off thousands of people. While these create publicity, they are normally not desirable from an organizational perspective. As Rajiv Bajaj puts it, 'Yoga is a very useful management concept.' Keeping your body and soul fit via constant exercise works for millions of humans across the globe. In business terms, this translates to constant improvement and proactive management of your business, e.g., Motherson's BYBY approach. Driving performance daily and pushing back boundaries as part of your personal and organizational DNA creates sustainable businesses that fit in and align well.

Customer-Value-Centric Innovation

Innovation is central to creating a value proposition for India's discerning customers. Adani's vision to build a world-class port on India's west coast led to massive investments in mechanization and automation. Today, the company experiments with ways to use cyber-physical systems to increase the efficiency and safety of port operations. The induction heating company EFD invested in R&D capacity to reduce customer turnaround times and to adapt its machines to the local operating environment. With initial assumptions about business in India being flawed, this approach ensured the company's survival. HDFC Life bet its future on best-in-class online delivery systems and integrated, 360-degree views of customers. Not only is HUL's innovative Shakti Amma rural distribution model as profitable as other sales channels, but it also creates unrivalled reach and brand awareness for Unilever's products in India. Siemen's SMART product initiative is designed to secure the long-term prosperity of the company by extending its range of products from the high- to the mid-range. Godrej has modified and streamlined standard development processes through relentless focus on the basic chemistry of its ingredients. This provides the company with an opportunity to react faster to market forces and changes in customer tastes as well as to open up new 'mastige' customer segments.

Choices and Trade-Offs: Focus Is Key

Choices and trade-offs are crucial to ensure that businesses are focused on what they do best and avoid pitfalls such as straddling— the dangerous tendency of some managers to become everything to everybody. Bharat Forge builds its business around its core competence of metallurgy and metal forming. As a consequence, it works across several industries that provide Bharat Forge with a certain hedging effect against market fluctuations. Motherson sees itself as a preferred global solutions provider. It serves only automotive OEMs but aims to increase its share of wallet with each customer as the relationships with the OEMs deepens. Mahindra Rural Finance sees its opportunity in providing housing loans to rural customers. Travel aggregator redBus is the interface between customers, bus operators, travel agents and websites. Each of these companies knows what it stands for and what defines its value proposition in its chosen market. Equally important, these companies are clear about the areas that they do not want to participate in.

Alignment: Moving in the Same Direction

Knowing what you want to do and what you don't want to do must be complemented by alignment, i.e., by activity systems that drive and enable your value proposition. Maruti Suzuki's motto, 'smaller, lighter, lesser and more beautiful', drives employees, suppliers and dealers in their quest to perpetuate the virtuous 'cost down, volume up' cycle. Siemens's SMART product initiative leverages strong engineering capabilities that have been built up in emerging markets in a quest to strengthen its global competitive position in mid-market segments. Alignment between the activities in India, China and Brazil with Siemens's headquarters in Germany is crucial for the success of the SMART initiative. redBus had to align activities between customers, bus operators, travel agents and potential competitors such as travel portals via a range of modern technologies as well as by building trust. JSW Steel's engagement with local communities ensured the support of these communities in times of need. During the iron ore crisis, this support proved vital to the company's survival.

Leadership: Keeping the Eyes on the Horizon

Clear choices and well-aligned activity systems are crucial for companies to survive and thrive in today's hyper-competitive world. However, even companies that have well established choices and activity systems are not immune to straddling, i.e., to diluting their choices in the search for growth. Today's leaders have to ensure that companies stay true to their roots. In cases where the overall environment has changed dramatically, they have to be aggressive in defining new choices and activity systems. Examples for successful leadership include Godrej's focus on growing its position as an emerging market MNC via targeted acquisitions in Latin America, Africa and South East Asia. Bharat Forge's foray into the defence business leverages the core competencies of the company. It found opportunities in the external market, such as the sale of the RUAG gun factory, and formed an alliance with Elbit to open up a new segment for the company. Bajaj's remarkable international expansion and brand extension, via the purchase of a major stake in Austria's KTM, took the company from being a strained Indian player to a global motorcycle powerhouse. Mahindra Rural Finance's approach to improving the lives of rural households via tailored loan products not only had a positive impact on village communities but also provided a profitable business opportunity.

Agility and Courage

India is a subcontinent whose complexity and confusion is a perfect training ground for today's VUCA world. Hardly surprisingly, successful companies in India display a great amount of agility in the face of adversity. Often, it is not the strongest company or the one with the best strategy that survives, but the one that is quick to learn from mistakes and adapt to change. Vaatsalya Healthcare fine-tuned its business model by starting several pilot hospitals across various cities and then adopting the model that worked best. Godrej leverages products from its Argentinian and Indonesian subsidiaries and improves upon them to bring them to market in India. Bharat Forge bought a full-fledged gun factory over a period of ten days. Motherson took about a month to build a factory and start export production for Daimler. Due to regulatory challenges, JSW Steel redesigned its activity system from a buyer's to a seller's market model over a period of a few months. HDFC Life did the same and moved from a market share to a profit-focused model in response to increased regulatory pressures. While the companies in question differ in their businesses and cultures, strong cross-functional cooperation, empowerment of local employees and flat hierarchies seem to be some of the key factors driving their agility and fast response to challenges and opportunities.

Serendipity: Grasping Opportunities

As Napoleon realized, even serendipity helps. Chaand Sehgal's need to invest money that he made from trading silver started a journey that resulted in a multi-billion-dollar business. Baba Kalyani's decision to buy the RUAG gun manufacturing unit opened up defence manufacturing for the group. Yamaha's failure to capture the imagination of India's customers gave the necessary room to Bajaj to grow. The move of Dr Naik's parents to a Tier-2 city initiated his desire to provide decent healthcare in these locations via Vaatsalya. Success comes to those who are able to recognize an opportunity and who have the drive and grit to turn it into lasting success.

Complacency and Its Challenges

The biggest threat for agile, focused and aligned companies like the ones described in this book comes not from technological or competitive disruptions but from within. Complacency, a common trait in many humans, is a constant danger that companies face and often succumb to. Assuming that current success can be extended into the future is an easy misconception that can lead to disastrous restructuring or even company bankruptcies. Keeping the company aligned to its purpose, driving performance day in and day out, pushing back barriers in terms of customer satisfaction, etc., requires constant commitment. It is hard work, and not always rewarding. Yet it is necessary. In some sense, it pays to be paranoid about your company's purpose and performance. In the authors' view, this is the only way to survive in the long term.

As we have discussed in the case of the machine tool or textile industry, there is a significant performance gap between leaders and followers in the Indian industry. Many companies' approach to operational excellence is half-hearted at best. Measures to curb waste are not in place, incentive systems that drive performance are inadequate, and certifications are used for display in company presentations but not as tools to transform the company or drive it to higher performance. Investments in R&D are equally insufficient. In today's world, many companies look to their suppliers as partners that support development and product creation. Companies that focus on build-to-print solutions without R&D investments, processes, and governance are likely to become less relevant in the future and will experience margin pressure. Many players are weak when it comes to choices and trade-offs. Rather than trying to be the best in a chosen field, companies continue to hedge their bets by straddling various product segments and industries. National and international M&A strategies that are not aligned around a clear value proposition lead to increased complexity in business systems and expose companies to medium- and long-term risk. Alignment in such an environment becomes an even bigger challenge than normal. Low employee motivation and misaligned activity sets lead to sub-optimal performance and are the result of poor strategic vision and poor leadership.

The Way Forward

These challenges are not unique to companies operating in India. Similar patterns—and results—can be observed in companies across the globe. When companies are not competitive or not unique in what they do and not important to their customers, they either have to change the way they do business or they will eventually cease to exist. India's economic liberalization was the starting point for many Indian companies to change the way they operated. In today's hypercompetitive world, it is time to accelerate these efforts, not only in a few leading companies but across the board. 'Make in India' will only become 'Made in India'—a sign of reliable quality, performance and innovation similar to Made in Germany—when industrial ecosystems perform at global benchmark levels, rather than just a few companies doing so.

What does all of this mean for you? What does it mean for India and the world? For one, India provides an excellent training ground to sharpen your professional skills and abilities. While just a decade ago, many employees and leaders around the world shook their heads at the confusion that seemed to reign in India, today we can safely say that confusion has become a much broader, even global phenomenon. VUCA is indeed the new normal. For all of us who are operating in India or comparable emerging markets, VUCA is not a new threat but a normal way of life and doing business. This can give you the confidence to take on challenges in this brave, new world of ours.

You also have a set of tools and approaches at your disposal that can greatly increase your chances of success. The concepts described in this book are not theoretical exercises but concepts proven to work by the various companies that we have highlighted in this book (as well as by hundreds of others that we did not have the time and space to include). Diligent and consistent execution of these concepts and adaptation to relevant business situations distinguishes successful players from those who, sooner or later, fall by the wayside.

Indian multinationals are here to stay and will be shaping the future landscapes of their competitive industries. Some players are already sizeable actors in their respective businesses while others are still in the process of building capability, scale and reach. This process will not always be smooth. Not every merger will work and not every market entry in new geographies will be successful. However, the same observations hold true for multinational companies in developed markets. You cannot make bets on products and markets and expect a 100 per cent success rate. We are confident that the inherent strength of many of the leading Indian companies, such as the ones that we have highlighted in this book, will support them in their journey going forward.

India is not only a large market, but also an ideal testing ground for new ideas, products and business models that can be leveraged in other emerging and even developed markets. As a consequence, the country deserves more attention from global businesses and their leaders. For many multinationals, India performs below potential and amounts to only a low single-digit percentage of their profits and revenues. This is sometimes a reflection of different market structures but often also the result of entrenched and encrusted perceptions about the opportunities that emerging markets, such as India, hold. These multinationals need to find a more appropriate approach to doing business in India by empowering local management teams. Successful examples, such as HUL or Maruti Suzuki, do exist. Finding the right approach is critical for all MNCs if they want to become relevant in one of the world's largest consumer markets. Currently, India is the fastest growing economy and it is likely to occupy that spot for several years to come. Now is the time to change perceptions and to take India's opportunities seriously. Now is the time to ride that tiger!

Table 9.1. Key Lessons from Indian Champions (Non-exhaustive)

	Operational Excellence	Innovation	Choices and Trade-Offs	Alignment	Leadership	Agility	Serendipity
Maruti Suzuki (automotive, four-wheeler)	• Minute detail focus via 5S, 3G, 3M, 3K, etc. • Strong integration of employees, dealers, suppliers in cost reduction efforts • Stringent supplier management • Training and technical support on Japanese productivity techniques for suppliers and dealers	• Nexa concept • Rural sales and after-sales penetration • Frugal engineering	• Strong player in volume segment • Nexa as entry into 'mastige' segment	• Align all employees via initiatives, (e.g., 1 gram, 1 Yen) • Financially responsible cooperation with suppliers and dealers • Virtuous 'cost down, volume up' cycle • Employee rotation between Japan and India • Leadership by example • One uniform, one canteen, one purpose • Development of local vendor base	• Motto: 'Smaller, lighter, lesser and more beautiful' as cornerstone of volume strategy		• Good relationships between Dr Krishnamurthy and Indophile Osama Suzuki

	Operational Excellence	Innovation	Choices and Trade-Offs	Alignment	Leadership	Agility	Serendipity
Adani (ports and logistics)	• Drive continuous improvement, (e.g., grain net replacement) • Leverage latent demand and corresponding scale from North India • Drive mechanization and automation, (e.g., fertilizer handling)	• Drive mechanization and automation, (e.g., fertilizer handling) • Leverage state of the art thinking, (e.g., consultants) • Drive IoT for further efficiency gains	• Build world-class port with superior services for shipping lines	• Evacuation capability ten times berth capacity • Dedicated berths rather than multipurpose berths • Invest in integrated master plan (social and business infrastructure) • Invest in training (e.g., don't hire overqualified people) • Develop courses and certifications (e.g., for crane operators) • Strong performance culture	• Motto: Invest and they will come • Build global scale business, (e.g., world's largest coal import terminal) • Benchmarking against other leading ports	• Build up infrastructure (rail, roads, gas, etc.) to speed up the process • Roll out and scale up Mundra processes across multiple ports in India	• Mundra port location

	Operational Excellence	Innovation	Choices and Trade-Offs	Alignment	Leadership	Agility	Serendipity
EFD (machine tools)	• Localization of components (about 80 per cent) • Close collaboration with suppliers • Insourcing	• Build up R&D capability for fast reaction to customer demand • Frugal engineering to avoid unnecessary features and adapt products to Indian operating environment • Virtual manufacturing	• Focus on smaller hardening and welding market • No activity in larger melting and forging market	• Exports to offset currency fluctuations • Training on the job and apprenticeships across the value chain • Bauhaus-style office with direct communication	• Early investments • Strong focus on hardening and welding market	• Change strategy from de-contenting to full localization • Leverage India as production hub for global needs • Leverage depreciated assets for job works	

	Operational Excellence	Innovation	Choices and Trade-Offs	Alignment	Leadership	Agility	Serendipity
Godrej (consumer goods)	• Back-end synergies (HR, FC, IT) with acquired companies • Cross-leverage of products across markets at Indian price points • Close collaboration with suppliers • Separate premium and mass outlets	• Strong focus on understanding basic chemistry • Adapt and streamline innovation and customer research processes • Continuous small and large process innovations	• Targeted acquisitions in emerging markets • Focused development of 'mastige' segments, (e.g., hair cream, Fast Card)	• Strong cross-functional approach • Targeted out-of-the-box recruitment • Empowerment of local teams • Optimized incentive systems	• Emerging market MNC • 3x3 strategy		
Siemens (energy management, power and gas, and others)	• Lean operations in line with global practices	• Localization of input materials • SMART products	• Focus on mid-market segment to complement high-end product segment	• SMART as global initiative across Brazil, China, and India • Strong engineering base in emerging markets with solid talent pipeline	• Leverage SMART products for export to other emerging markets		

	Operational Excellence	Innovation	Choices and Trade-Offs	Alignment	Leadership	Agility	Serendipity
Bosch (engineering services)	• Competition with external providers for benchmark purposes • Low attrition • High offshore ratios • High utilization ratios	• Focused innovation processes at Bosch AG, Bosch India, and RBEI level • Work across all Bosch BUs • Strong focus on Internet technologies • Leverage of Bangalore ecosystem	• Mostly captive centre • IP protection • Gradual ramp-up of capability and scale • Global technology management responsibility in chosen areas • Limited activities in the external market	• Strong focus on capability building (e.g., CMMI, ASPICE certifications) • Strong focus on German language skills • Significant two-way exchange of manpower	• Entry in early 1990s provided opportunity to build strong capability and communication model		

	Operational Excellence	Innovation	Choices and Trade-Offs	Alignment	Leadership	Agility	Serendipity
redBus (B2B, B2C start-up)	• Strong partnerships with technology providers, (e.g., Amazon Web Services, Google, BigQuery) • Stringent monitoring of key operational KPIs • Negative working capital	• Aggregate fragmented supply side on bus tickets via robust software platform • BOSS application for bus operators • SeatSeller application for on/offline travel agents • Provide additional services to end users and channel partners (e.g., via data analytics)	• Aggregator of bus tickets only	• Build strong relationships with bus operators and travel agents • Build consistent online and offline delivery systems • Build up scale and reach • Co-opt potential rivals (e.g., online travel agencies)	• Market entry into Malaysia, Singapore		

	Operational Excellence	Innovation	Choices and Trade-Offs	Alignment	Leadership	Agility	Serendipity
Bajaj Auto (automotive, two-wheeler)	• The prime mover (TPM) towards excellence across the organization • Lean manufacturing/ management • BAVA vendor management • Low-cost automation • White-collar workers at factory level • Clear core/non-core split	• Fully indigenous R&D team, (e.g., twin spark technology) • Recognized among the top 100 innovative companies by Forbes	• Entry into motorcycle business • Exit of scooter business • Focus of motorcycle business on performance bikes (e.g., 'mastige' segment) • Strong international expansion—profit before volume	• Performance-driven culture with clear deliverables and measurements • Consistent communication both internally and externally • Own market research department to understand customer segments in detail • Strong communication along the value chain	• Buy 48 per cent in KTM to extend brand into premium segment • Focused drive towards international expansion	• Draw fast conclusions from product failures and successes	• Yamaha's failure to establish themselves in India

	Operational Excellence	Innovation	Choices and Trade-Offs	Alignment	Leadership	Agility	Serendipity
Vaatsalya Healthcare (healthcare)	• Asset-light, no-frills investment model • Core services drive synergies and cost efficiency (e.g, via standardization) • Stringent customer feedback systems • Clear measurement and continuous improvement of operational KPIs and clinical performance index • Vendor management • Local staff	• Localized marketing activities and community connect • Standardized operating procedures	• Tier-2 and Tier-3 cities • Core service offerings • Key customer groups differentiated by income	• Doctors earn same pay as in Tier-1 cities • Network of hospitals for recruitment, retention, knowledge sharing, etc. • Training of local staff to meet requirements of modern hospitals		• Undertake small, field-based experiments and learn from them	• Dr Naik's parents move to a Tier-2 city

	Operational Excellence	Innovation	Choices and Trade-Offs	Alignment	Leadership	Agility	Serendipity
HDFC Life (insurance)	• In-house training for sales executives enhances effectiveness • Geo-tagged sales force • Process documents and technologies standardize underwriting and eliminate mistakes	• Best in class e-commerce platform (Click-2-buy, 3-Click, My Mix) • Predictive underwriting • Expansion to vernacular languages	• Select profitable customer segments and product categories • Fortify and diversify distribution channel mix to serve these customers • Profitability and cost leadership trump market share	• Independent checks to ensure contract quality • Limit product sales to adequate channels • Use technology to create 360-degree view of customer • Limit personnel discretion via standardization and technology	• Leader in providing long-term insurance solutions • Move away from market share to profit-driven business	• Redesign activity system from agile reaction to market forces to long-term orientation (driven by dramatic regulatory change)	

	Operational Excellence	Innovation	Choices and Trade-Offs	Alignment	Leadership	Agility	Serendipity
IndiGo (airline)	• Limited focus on marketing • Continuous improvement in employee productivity • Focused airplane leasing policy • Early commitment to fuel-efficient A320 NEO • Low maintenance cost • Fast turnaround • High traffic volume due to flights on main routes	• Continuous, small innovations, (e.g., boarding ramp, in-flight cleaning)	• On-time performance, low-cost, courteous and hassle-free travel	• Clear customer selection, no loyalty programmes, boarding privileges, etc. • No competition with low-cost airlines regarding aggressive price promotions • New rather than used aircrafts to ensure hassle-free travel • Recruitment, training and compensation aligned with on-time performance and fast turnaround	• Expansion to international destinations that fit the profile (2.5–4 hour flights)		

	Operational Excellence	Innovation	Choices and Trade-Offs	Alignment	Leadership	Agility	Serendipity
JSW Steel (metals and mining)	• Flexible raw material operations • Continuous improvement of key operational KPIs • Closeness to key input materials	• Redesign plant operations to cope with multiple input materials of potentially different quality levels • E-auction of iron ore	• No captive mines	• Integrate value addition to surrounding villages in overall business plan • Generate strong buy-in and support from villagers • Align stakeholders (forest department, mine owners, Supreme Court, etc.)	• Invest at scale	• Fast response to iron ore crisis via complete redefinition of activity system	
Bharat Forge (defence)	• Leverage best practices from automotive business	• Integrated training system from grade 12 to PhD focused on metallurgy and metal forming • Latest gun production technology	• Build scale across industries around core competence of metallurgy/metal forming • Limit share of profit with automotive customers	• Transfer of know-how and personnel across business units • Strong training systems • Provide dream jobs to employees • Leverage core competence • Fill up competence gaps via partnerships (e.g., Elbit)	• Buy RUAG gun factory over a period of ten days without customer backing/orders • Aim to be emerging market systems supplier and developed market components supplier	• Close RUAG gun factory sales process within ten days	• RUAG's decision to sell gun factory

	Operational Excellence	Innovation	Choices and Trade-Offs	Alignment	Leadership	Agility	Serendipity
Motherson Sumi (automotive supplier)	• By yourself better yourself (BYBY) • Continuous improvement culture • Relentless learning from partners, (e.g., Japanese) • Leverage learnings across company	• Strong commitment to invest in R&D across various products and business lines	• Business is done only with automotive OEMs • Global solutions provider for automotive OEMs	• Strong M&A capability • Data-driven management • Internal IT and data management team integrates data across companies and acquisitions • Guidance of management teams based on internal benchmarks • Empowerment of local teams • Constant on-site interaction of top management with local teams	• Globally preferred solutions provider for automotive OEMs • Courageous acquisitions (e.g., Visiocorp, Peguform) • Go ahead of market and invest in capacity	• Response to Daimler import/ export problem and similar support for other OEMs	• Silver market boom

	Operational Excellence	Innovation	Choices and Trade-Offs	Alignment	Leadership	Agility	Serendipity
HUL (consumer goods)	• Use Shakti Amma distribution to reach villages in a cost-effective manner	• Develop viable BoP distribution model • Tie-up with complementary services to improve profitability • Mobile-phone-based inventory and ordering system	• Complimentary distribution channel combined with normal distributor sales personnel	• Detailed selection and training process • Clear measurement of financial and operational KPIs • Avoidance of working capital requirements for Shakti Ammas	• Unassailable rural distribution footprint and brand recognition	• Turned floundering CSR activity into a scalable sales channel	

	Operational Excellence	Innovation	Choices and Trade-Offs	Alignment	Leadership	Agility	Serendipity
Mahindra Rural Finance (non-banking financial institution)	• Cluster selling concept • Innovative use of technology (e.g., hand-held devices) • Local teams on the ground	• Personalized and localized delivery approaches • Automated cash collection via hand-held devices • Income model for agricultural land, 'credit book' • Default models for agricultural customer segment	• BoP lending as alternative to cash payments/ piecemeal house construction • Focus on underserved rural housing market	• Tie-up with regulator (NHB) • Leverage Mahindra Finance parenting advantage • Fair dealings with customers • Detailed training of local staff • Decentralized decision-making	• Develop trust and affordable value proposition to drive rural housing lending at BoP • Careful expansion into additional segments to not overstretch customers	• Redesign initial business plan centred around INR 5 lakh lending amounts to reality of INR 1 lakh lending amounts	

APPENDIX

A FIGURE 1

Services Has Become the Dominant Industry Sector at the Expense of Agriculture; Industry/Manufacturing/Mining Are Stagnant

India GDP split by sectors[1] [1980, 2000, 2014 - %]

1980	2000	2014
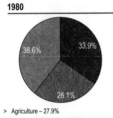		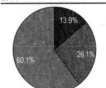
> Agriculture – 27.9%	> Agriculture – 19.6%	> Agriculture – 11.9%
> Mining and Quarrying – 2.5%	> Mining and Quarrying – 3.0%	> Mining and Quarrying – 1.9%
> Manufacturing – 14.9%	> Manufacturing – 15.0%	> Manufacturing – 14.9%

Major sub-segments

> Financing and business services were the fastest growing categories in the services sector, while growth in Industry, mining and manufacturing remained stagnant

Major sub-segments

> Transport, storage and communication services were the main drivers of growth in the services sector, while growth in Industry and manufacturing remained stagnant

Major sub-segments

> Export of software services was the largest contributer to India's services sector, whereas Telecom and software together drive India's global brand image in services

> India's export of financial services too witnessed a high growth of 34.4% in 2013-14

■ Agriculture & Allied services ■ Industry ■ Services

1) Share to total GDP at constant 2004–05 prices

Source: Planning commission data book, http://planningcommission.nic.in/data/datatable/0814/comp_databook.pdf Arpita Mukherjee, 'The Service Sector in India' (ADB Economics working paper no. 352, June 2013); Roland Berger analysis

A TABLE 1

India's Top 50 Companies Grew at an Avg CAGR of 21% in the Past Decade, Taking Advantage of the Opportunities of Liberalization

Consolidated revenue of India's top 50 companies, CAGR 2005–2015 [%][1]

Sr No	Company	Revenue FY05 (INR cr)	Revenue FY15 (INR cr)	CAGR
1	India Oil Corporation Limited	133,407.22	449,508.66	13%
2	Reliance Industries Limited	66,597.00	375,435.00	19%
3	TATA Motors	19,532.84	262,796.33	30%
4	State Bank of India	54,536.32	257,289.51	17%
5	Bharat Petroleum Corporation	63,857.00	238,086.90	14%
6	Hindustan Petroleum Corporation	65,218.33	206,626.19	12%
7	Oil and Natural Gas Corporation	59,747.32	160,894.87	10%
8	Larsen & Toubro	59,747.32	160,894.87	10%
9	TATA Steel	15,998.61	139,503.73	24%
10	Hindalco Industries	10,105.40	104,281.10	26%
11	TATA Consultancy Services	9,748.47	94,648.41	26%
12	ICICI Bank	16,916.83	90,216.24	18%
13	Essar Oil	636.78	83,206.00	63%
14	NTPC	23,516.10	80,622.04	13%
15	Coal India	29,887.12	74,120.07	12%
16	Adani Enterprises	15,005.34	64,581.88	16%
17	Mangalore Refinery and Petrochemicals	20,692.55	57,477.07	11%
18	HDFC Bank	3,730.85	57,466.25	31%
19	GAIL	13,591.38	56,741.98	15%
20	Bharti Airtel	7,903.02	55,496.40	22%
21	Punjab National Bank	10,387.59	54,884.42	18%
22	Infosys	7,129.65	53,319.00	22%
23	Maruti Suzuki	11,033.43	50,801.31	16%
24	Housing Development Finance Corporation	3,688.88	48,315.69	29%
25	Canara Bank	9,115.80	48,300.29	18%
26	Bank of India	7,176.99	47,962.95	21%
27	JSW Steel	7,035.90	46,087.32	21%
28	Bank of Baroda	8,043.95	46,018.04 (2014)	21%
29	SAIL	32,569.53	45,710.78	3%
30	AXIS Bank	2,327.67	43,843.65	34%
31	Chennai Petroleum Corporation	16,295.89	41,865.95	10%
32	Wipro	7,235.50	41,635.00	19%
33	Petronet LNG	1,945.27	39,500.95	35%
34	Mahindra & Mahindra	7,695.59	38,945.42	18%
35	ITC	7,639.45	36,507.40	17%
36	Union Bank of India	5,735.89	35,606.96	20%
37	Motherson Sumi Systems	781.23	35,031.89	46%
38	TATA Power Company	4,954.72	34,366.85	21%
39	Grasim Industries	9,409.99	32,847.34	13%
40	Vedanta	1,409.36	32,502.41	37%
41	HCL Technologies	3,351.20	32,143.66 (2014)	29%
42	Idea Cellular	2,795.25 (2007)	31,279.47	35%
43	Hindustan Unilever	11,060.55 (Dec 2005)	30,805.62	11%
44	Bharat Heavy Electricals	10,686.07	30,182.98	11%
45	IDBI Bank	3,359.05	29,720.25 (2014)	27%
46	Ruchi Soya Industries	3,908.10	28,309.08	22%
47	Central Bank of India	6,143.75	28,303.01	17%
48	Hero Motorcorp	10,086.16 (2006)	27,585.30	12%

| 49 | Aditya Birla Nuvo | 3,189.26 | 26,516.01 | 24% |
| 50 | Indian Overseas Bank | 4,750.61 | 26,076.93 | 19% |

1) If company 2005 revenue not available, CAGR calculated from year of available information

Source: Economic Times, 'ET 500 Companies 2014', http://economictimes.indiatimes.com/marketstats/pid-55,pageno-1,sortby-CurrentYearRank,sortorder-asc,year-2014.cms;

Calculations done using revenue data from www.moneycontrol.com; Roland Berger analysis

A FIGURE 2

Indian GDP/Capita Increased 4x vs 17x for China and Amounts to 29% of Chinese Value in 2014

Indexed GDP per capita growth[1] [1980 – 2014, 1980 = 1]

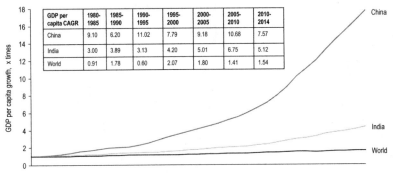

GDP per capita CAGR	1980-1985	1985-1990	1990-1995	1995-2000	2000-2005	2005-2010	2010-2014
China	9.10	6.20	11.02	7.79	9.18	10.68	7.57
India	3.00	3.89	3.13	4.20	5.01	6.75	5.12
World	0.91	1.78	0.60	2.07	1.80	1.41	1.54

1) All GDP numbers used for calculation are in 2010 US dollars.

Source: US Department of Agriculture Economic Research Service, Real per capita GDP (2010 dollars) Historical, http://www.ers.usda.gov/data-products/international-macroeconomic-data-set.aspx; Roland Berger analysis

A FIGURE 3

A Quantitative (3200+) Study of Luxury Customers Identified 6 Consumer Segments with Distinct Characteristics and Value Profiles

Quantitative study of Indian luxury customers [2012-2013]

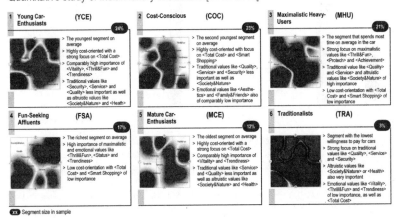

Segment size in sample

Source: Roland Berger

A FIGURE 4

Distribution of the Segments Differs among Regions: Eastern and Central Regions Dominated by One Segment Respectively

Distribution of the customer segments among regions [%]

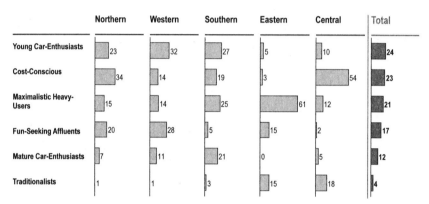

Source: Roland Berger

A FIGURE 5

Proposed Government Investment of INR 55.73 Lakh Crore[1] in Infrastructure under the 12th Five Year Plan Will Fuel the Economy

Investment in infrastructure under the 10th, 11th and 12th Five Year Plans

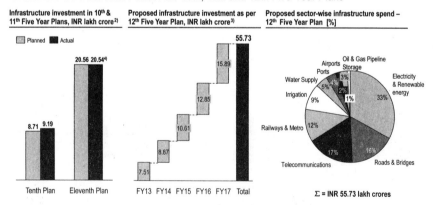

1) About EUR 830 bn at an XR of 1 EUR = 69.5 INR,   2) At 2006-07 prices
3) At current prices   4) Projected value for Eleventh plan actual investment

Source: 'Investment in Infrastructure during the Eleventh Five Year Plan', Secretariat for Infrastructure, Planning Commission, January 2011,
'Twelfth Five Year plan 2012-2017', Vol I, Planning Commission, 2013, http://planningcommission.gov.in/plans/planrel/fiveyr/12th/pdf/12fyp_vol1.pdf; Roland Berger analysis

A FIGURE 6

In 2016, India Ranked 130 among 189 Countries for Ease of Doing Business Mainly Due to Its Complicated Regulatory Environment

Ease of doing business: World Bank rankings 2016

Source: World Bank, Doing Business Report 2016, http://www.doingbusiness.org/rankings

A FIGURE 7

Regional Economics Are Very Different across India and Strategies on Products, Price, Distribution Are to Be Tailored to Each Region

Regional economics

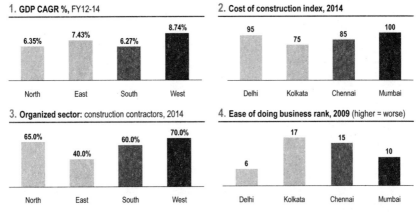

Source: GDP CAGR %: planningcommission.gov.in, 2011–2014; Indian real estate forum, http://www.indiarealestateforum.
com, Roland Berger analysis,
Organized sector, construction contractors: https://www.thebig5constructindia.com, Primary interviews with construction companies
Doing Business in India 2009, The World Bank, 2009 edition, http://www.doingbusiness.org/~/media/GIAWB/Doing%20
Business/Documents/Subnational-Reports/DB09-Sub-India

Key Developments in India from 1991 till Present

Phase	1991–1998	1998–2003	2003–2008	2008–2014	2014 Onwards
CAGR1	6.03	5.81	8.01	7.45	
Politics	• Politically a coalition era. • 4 Prime Ministers in a span of about 7 years. Communal riots followed the Babri Masjid demolition.	• Nuclear tests conducted at Pokhran. • Kargil conflict. • Gujarat riots. • Kargil war and sanctions because of nuclear tests were a setback to the economy.	• Indo-US nuclear deal. Unstable government. • Waning power of BJP at Center. Leadership crisis post Atal Bihari Vajpayee. • RTI bill passed in 2005.	• Scam-ridden government corruption charges in Common Wealth Games, 2G, Coalgate. Significant effort to move towards subsidies. • The Right to Information, Forest Rights, Land Acquisition, Lokpal, Right to Education and National Rural Employment Guarantee Acts add up to an impressive legislative record. • The UID scheme launched to update and modernize the entire infrastructure around providing entitlements and enabling experiments like cash transfers.	• Sweeping majority to BJP in national elections. • Rise of alternative politics, in the form of AAP. • 8 state assembly elections since 2014, of which BJP won or is in coalition in 3 states. • Swachh Bharat Abhiyan (Clean India Mission) – symbolism or serious intent?

Phase	1991–1998	1998–2003	2003–2008	2008–2014	2014 Onwards
CAGR1	6.03	5.81	8.01	7.45	
Economy	• Indian economy opens up. • 51% FDI was approved through automatic route in 35 industries which was then expanded to 111 in 1996. • Strong increase in approved FDI. • SEBI given statutory powers through SEBI Act, 1992. • NSE was established in 1992.	• NHAI kicked off Golden Quadrilateral project. Disinvestment minister appointed for the first time. Institutional reforms in infrastructure. • New law for competition envisaged in this period which got passed in 2005. • More reforms in banking initiated. • FDI opened up in Defense and Insurance sector in 2001.	• Economy witnessed highest ever growth rate. Push towards infrastructure development as well as human development. • According to the Sixth Economic census, new jobs grew at an annual clip of 4.25% between 2005 and 2013.[2] • Spectacular performance of the Sensex under UPA especially up until the 2008 financial crisis.	• Global financial crisis impacts India though less than other global economies. • Indian economy falls prey to faltering growth, rising prices, weakening currency and burgeoning deficit. • Increasing trade deficit since 2011 and rising unemployment.	• GDP growth at 7.2% in FY15.[3] • World Bank rated India very low on ease of doing business in 2014. Modi government has set a goal for India to be at number 50. • 'Make in India' initiative by Modi government aims to boost Indian manufacturing. • RBI focusing on building reserves. • Movement of foreign capital in to stock market.

Phase	1991–1998	1998–2003	2003–2008	2008–2014	2014 Onwards
CAGR1	6.03	5.81	8.01	7.45	
Technology	• IT companies that started in the 80s became internationalized because of policy changes. • US companies started outsourcing work to low cost and skilled talent pool in India.	• Increased investment by Indian companies in R&D. • Increased investment in infrastructure projects. • Start of Indian telecom and internet revolution. • Convergence of data and mobile technologies.	• Indian MNCs came into their own with delivery across the globe. • IT sector particularly active in global M&A activity.	• Technology sector employed more than 12 million people (3 million direct, 9.5 million indirect in FY13)[4]. • Commoditization of Technology— moves from hands of few to many. • In 1991 there were 5.8 million fixed telephone subscribers[5]. In 2011 there were 32.8 million fixed telephone subscribers and nearly 894 million[6] mobile phone subscribers.	• Ecommerce boom in India. • India has leap-frogged in the area of technology with sophisticated technologies coming to India now at the same pace as the rest of the world. • Digital India initiative launched by the government to integrate government departments and people of India.
Consumer	• Fewer choices with consumers. • Spending power not as much. • Consumers more inclined to saving. Automobile, airlines, telecom sectors warming up in India.	• Start of the consumer revolution in India. • Customers getting more choices and sophisticated with exposure to international brands and quality standards.	• Golden age of retail for India. Movement from saving to spending because brands were offering better value propositions to customers. • Spends shifting from necessity to discretionary spending.	• Broad movement with respect to consumer expenditure continues till 2011. • Ecommerce boom starts in India. • Consumer becoming more demanding/ price-sensitive. • Consumer paychecks had gotten bigger but so had expenses.	• Ecommerce momentum continuing in urban areas and also gaining popularity in Tier 2, 3, 4, cities. • Business confidence and investment increased after the slug of 2010–2012, reviving sentiment including consumer spending.

Phase	1991–1998	1998–2003	2003–2008	2008–2014	2014 Onwards
CAGR1	6.03	5.81	8.01	7.45	
Connect between Indian and global economy	• Up until 1991 no significant connect between the Indian and global economy.	• Foreign trade, integration with global economy increased because of acquisition of overseas companies by Indian companies. Rise of multinational Indians.	• Increase in M&A activity.	• MNC R&D centres went up from 191 in pre-2000 to 872 in 2013.[7] • Up until 2008 there's a steady increase in number of students going for higher studies to the US, this number declined for three years post the global financial crisis.	• Effort to bring in foreign investment in the area of manufacturing.

1 United States Department of Agriculture Economic Research Service, 'Real GDP (2010 Dollars) Historical', http://www.ers.usda.gov/data-products/international-macroeconomic-data-set.aspx#26190

2 Central Statistics Office, 'Provisional Results of Sixth Economic Census', 30 July 2014, http://pib.nic.in/newsite/PrintRelease.aspx?relid=107596

3 *Economic Times*, 'RBI Lowers GDP Growth Forecast to 7.6% for FY16', 2 June 2015, http://economictimes.indiatimes.com/news/economy/indicators/rbi-lowers-gdp-growth-forecast-to-7-6-for-fy16/articleshow/47514607.cms

4 Statista, 'Direct and Indirect Employment of the IT Industry in India from 2008-09 to 2012-13', http://www.statista.com/statistics/320729/india-it-industry-direct-indirect-employment/

5 World Bank Indicators, 'Fixed Telephone Subscribers, 1991 and 2011', http://data.worldbank.org/indicator/IT.MLT.MAIN/countries?display=default

6 World Bank Indicators, 'Mobile Cellular Subscriptions, 2011', http://data.worldbank.org/indicator/IT.CEL.SETS

7 *Times of India*, '48% of MNC R&D Talent Is in Bengaluru', 3 February 2016, http://timesofindia.indiatimes.com/city/bengaluru/48-of-MNC-RD-talent-is-in-Bengaluru/articleshow/50828717.cms

FIGURE 8

Net Cost Reduction Was Achieved in FY14 and FY15 in DMC/Vehicle Despite the Launch of Vehicles with Higher Content

Cost cutting at Maruti Suzuki India Limited

Direct material cost (DMC) between FY11 to FY15 [INR'000]

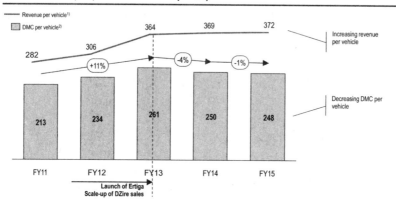

1) Revenue from net sale of products/Total units produced
2) (Cost of material consumed + inventory change) / Total production volume

Sources: Maruti Suzuki annual reports FY11–FY15; SIAM, 'Monthly Flash Reports', http://www.siamindia.com; Roland Berger Analysis

FIGURE 9

Capacity Utilization at India's Major Ports Is High Despite Capacity Additions and Subdued Cargo Growth

India's major ports: Traffic [mn tonnes], capacity [mn tonnes], capacity utilization [%]

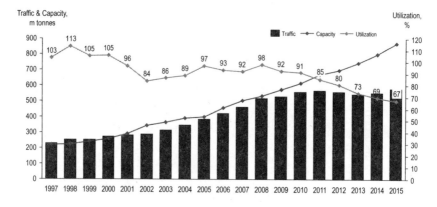

Source: Basic Port Statistics of India 2014–15, Transport Research Wing, Ministry of Road Transport and Highways, http://shipping.gov.in/showfile.php?lid=2272; Roland Berger analysis

FIGURE 9

Capacity Utilization at India's Major Ports Is High Despite Capacity Additions and Subdued Cargo Growth

India's major ports: Traffic [mn tonnes], capacity [mn tonnes], capacity utilization [%]

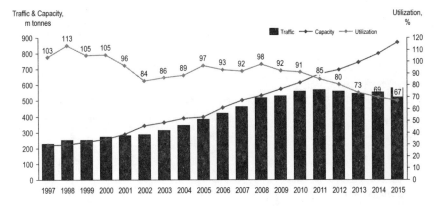

Source: Basic Port Statistics of India 2014-15, Transport Research Wing, Ministry of Road Transport and Highways, http://shipping.gov.in/showfile.php?lid=2272; Roland Berger analysis

FIGURE 10

India's Non-major Ports Have Been Witnessing a Steep Increase in Traffic and Capacity over the Last Few Years

India's non-major ports: Traffic [mm tonnes], Capacity [mm tonnes], Capacity utilization [%]

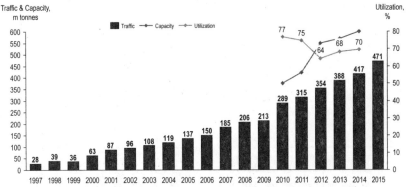

Source: Basic Port Statistics of India 2014-15, Transport Research Wing, Ministry of Road Transport and Highways, http://shipping.gov.in/showfile.php?lid=2272; Basic Port Statistics of India 2013-14, Ministry of Road Transport and Highways; India Infrastructure report, 'Ports in India 2015', February 2015; Roland Berger analysis

A FIGURE 11

Domestic versus Foreign Machine Tools Comparison: Technology, Productivity and Cost

Technology, productivity and cost comparison, based on interview discussions

Illustrative

Metric	Turning centre imported machine (vs domestic)	Internal grinder imported machine (vs domestic)
Component accuracy	30% ⬆	140% ⬆
Repeatability	40% ⬆	50% ⬆
Cutting/milling/grinding speed		80% ⬆
Spindle – rpm, power	30% ⬆	50% ⬆
Tool change over time	30% ⬇	20% ⬇
Cycle time	10% ⬇	30% ⬇
Manpower requirement	50% ⬇	30% ⬇
Cost of machine	100% ⬆	200% ⬆
Power, cutting tool cost	⬌	60% ⬆
Repair and maintenance cost	50% ⬇	60% ⬆

Sources: ACMA–IMTMA interviews & surveys, Roland Berger analysis.

A FIGURE 12

With Smart Manufacturing, Manufacturing Companies in EU Are Expected to Show Significant Efficiency Increases

Average investment of 3.3% of revenue in Industry 4.0-related solutions expected

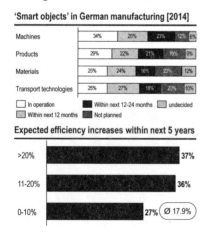

'Smart objects' in German manufacturing [2014]

Machines	34%	25%	23%	12%	6%
Products	29%	22%	21%	19%	9%
Materials	25%	24%	16%	23%	12%
Transport technologies	25%	27%	18%	20%	10%

☐ In operation ■ Within next 12-24 months ▨ undecided
▨ Within next 12 months ■ Not planned

Expected efficiency increases within next 5 years

>20% 37%
11-20% 36%
0-10% 27% Ø 17.9%

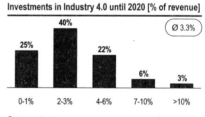

Investments in Industry 4.0 until 2020 [% of revenue]

Ø 3.3%

0-1%	2-3%	4-6%	7-10%	>10%
25%	40%	22%	6%	3%

Comments

> German companies are expected to annually invest about EUR 40 billion in Industry 4.0 related solutions until 2020; manufacturing firms about EUR 8.5 billion per year
> Degree of supply chain digitalization is expected to rise from 19% in 2014 to 85% in 2020 in the German manufacturing sector
> Industry 4.0 and its related solutions are on the CEO agenda of most German manufacturing firms – indicating importance and potential of smart manufacturing

Sources: IDC, PWC, Press releases, Roland Berger analysis.

A FIGURE 13

India's International Filings for Patents Trail Major Economies While Approval Rates Are Comparable

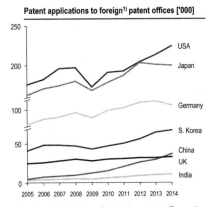

Patent applications to foreign[1] patent offices ['000]

USA
Japan
Germany
S. Korea
China
UK
India

2005 2006 2007 2008 2009 2010 2011 2012 2013 2014

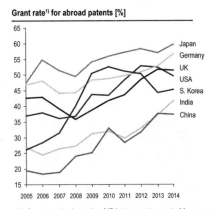

Grant rate[1] for abroad patents [%]

Japan
Germany
UK
USA
S. Korea
India
China

2005 2006 2007 2008 2009 2010 2011 2012 2013 2014

1) Applications which are filed at the patent offices other than the home country patent office of patentee

1) Grant rate is the ratio of IP instruments granted in a year to the number of applications received in that year

Source: World Intellectual Property Office (Online Database) http://www.wipo.int/ipstats/en/statistics/country_profile/; Roland Berger analysis

A FIGURE 14

Biomass Power Plants by Husk Power Systems Innovated to Provide Cheap and Reliable Electricity Access to India's Rural Population

BUSINESS MODEL – THREE TYPES

> **BM:** build, maintain – HPS builds and sells the plant to an independent owner who also operates it
> **BOM:** build, own, maintain – HPS owns the plant but is operated by a local who puts in 10% of the cost
> **BOOM:** build, own, operate, maintain -- by HPS itself

REVENUE STREAMS

> Electricity sales
> Rice husk char, by product of biomass gasification process
> Certified Emission Reduction (CER) & Verified Emission Reduction (VER) credit sales

ECONOMIC SUSTAINABILITY

> **Operational profitability** : reached in 2-3 months; 20% gross margin at plant **Capital expenditures** : breakeven in 2.5-3 years with subsidies
> **Equipment life** : 12 year for gasifier, 20 years for engine and 1-2 years for bamboo poles
> **HPS installation cost** < INR 60,000 per kW (avg. cost for gasifier based biomass power plant installation is INR 175,000)
> **Operational cost** < INR 7/kWh (average cost for gasifier based biomass power plants is INR 23.75)

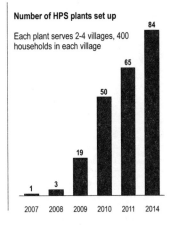

Number of HPS plants set up

Each plant serves 2-4 villages, 400 households in each village

1   3   19   50   65   84
2007 2008 2009 2010 2011 2014

Source: Sevea Association, 'Case Study: Husk Power Systems', February 2013, http://seveaconsulting.com/page/what-we-do; Secondary research sources; Roland Berger analysis

A FIGURE 15

Entry Level Motorcycles (75–125 cc) Contribute to ~80% of Domestic Sales; Significant Growth Seen in Premium Bikes Segment Recently

Category-wise domestic motorcycle sales

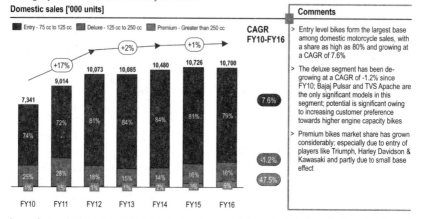

Domestic sales ['000 units]

Legend: Entry - 75 cc to 125 cc · Deluxe - 125 cc to 250 cc · Premium - Greater than 250 cc

CAGR FY10-FY16

Comments

> Entry level bikes form the largest base among domestic motorcycle sales, with a share as high as 80% and growing at a CAGR of 7.6%

> The deluxe segment has been de-growing at a CAGR of -1.2% since FY10; Bajaj Pulsar and TVS Apache are the only significant models in this segment; potential is significant owing to increasing customer preference towards higher engine capacity bikes

> Premium bikes market share has grown considerably; especially due to entry of players like Triumph, Harley Davidson & Kawasaki and partly due to small base effect

Source: Society of Indian Automobile Manufacturers (SIAM), monthly flash reports FY10–FY16, http://www.siamindia.com/, Roland Berger Analysis

A Figure 16

In Deluxe Category, Bajaj Retains Leadership with Variants of Pulsar in Each Sub–Category; Yamaha FZ & TVS Apache Significant Contenders

Bajaj maintains leadership in 125-150 cc and 200-250 cc categories

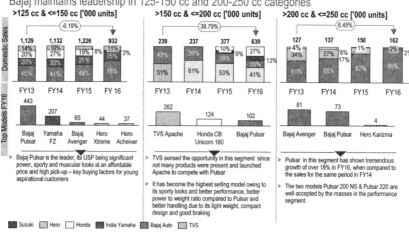

> Bajaj Pulsar is the leader, its USP being significant power, sporty and muscular looks at an affordable price and high pick-up – key buying factors for young aspirational customers

> TVS sensed the opportunity in this segment since not many products were present and launched Apache to compete with Pulsar

> It has become the highest selling model owing to its sporty looks and better performance, better power to weight ratio compared to Pulsar and better handling due to its light weight, compact design and good braking

> Pulsar in this segment has shown tremendous growth of over 18% in FY16, when compared to the sales for the same period in FY14

> The two models Pulsar 200 NS & Pulsar 220 are well accepted by the masses in the performance segment

Legend: Suzuki · Hero · Honda · India Yamaha · Bajaj Auto · TVS

Source: Society of Indian Automobile Manufacturers (SIAM), monthly flash reports FY13–FY16, http://www.siamindia.com/, Roland Berger Analysis

A FIGURE 17

On Major Cost Items, Bajaj Is Significantly More Competitive Than Its Peers

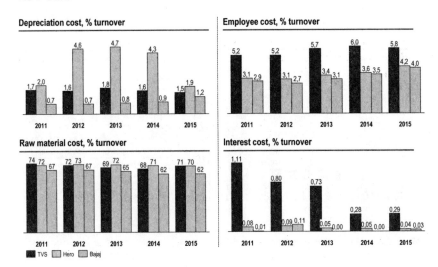

Source: Company annual reports, Roland Berger

FIGURE 18

India: More Than 100 Years of Aviation History

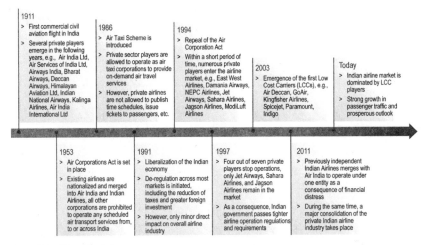

Source: Roland Berger Analysis

A FIGURE 19

Investments by the Government in Airports Have Increased Over the Last Decade; However, Overall Penetration Remains Low

Airport infrastructure

Investments in airport infrastructure in Five Year Plans [INR Cr]

Source: Five year plans, Planning Commission, Volume 1,
available at http://planningcommission.gov.in/plans/planrel/12thplan/pdf/12fyp_vol1.pdf

Centre State Private Projected figures

Number of airports [2015]

US	2.052
Brazil	297
China	188
Russia	140
India	132
Germany	103

Source: The Airport Authority, available at http://airport-authority.com/browse

Airports per capita [per mn people, 2015]

US	6,39
Brazil	1,43
Germany	1,27
Russia	0,97
China	0,14
India	0,10

Source: The Airport Authority, available at http://airport-authority.com/browse
The World Bank, Data, Population total, available at http://data.worldbank.org/indicator/SP.POP.TOTL

Source: Roland Berger analysis

FIGURE 20

Despite Growing at a CAGR of 14% Over the Last Decade, RPK Is Among the Lowest Globally

ASKM[1] and RPK[2] performed on scheduled domestic services by all Indian carriers

ASKM & RPK on services in India [bn]

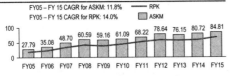

FY05 – FY 15 CAGR for ASKM: 11.8%
FY05 – FY 15 CAGR for RPK: 14.0%

27.79 35.08 48.70 60.59 59.16 61.09 68.22 78.64 76.15 80.72 84.81

FY05 FY06 FY07 FY08 FY09 FY10 FY11 FY12 FY13 FY14 FY15

Source: DGCA, Table 3.19, http://dgca.nic.in/pub/pub13-14/PART-3-%20
DOMESTIC%20ALL/3-19.pdf;
DGCA, Handbook on Civil Aviation Statistics, 2014-15

RPK growth Dec 15 vs Dec 14

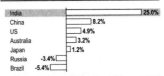

India	25.0%
China	8.2%
US	4.9%
Australia	3.2%
Japan	1.2%
Russia	-3.4%
Brazil	-5.4%

Source: IATA, Press Release No. 4, February 4, 2016,
http://www.iata.org/pressroom/pr/
Pages/2016-02-04-01.aspx

ASKM per week in 2014 [mn]

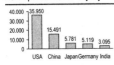

35.950 15.491 5.781 5.119 3.095

USA China Japan Germany India

RPK 2014 [bn]

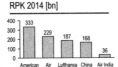

333 229 187 168 36

American Air Lufthansa China Air India
France- - Europe Southern
KLM

ASK growth Dec 15 vs Dec 14

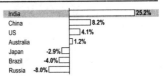

India	25.2%
China	8.2%
US	4.1%
Australia	1.2%
Japan	-2.9%
Brazil	-4.0%
Russia	-8.0%

Source: Statista, Ranking of countries
with highest
ASKM/week, http://www.statista.com/
statistics/270191/ranking-of-the-countries-
with-most-available-airline-seatkilometers/
India: DGCA, Air Transport Statistics, Air
Transport Operating and Traffic Statistics
for 2014-15, All Scheduled Indian Airlines,
Table 1.06, http://dgca.nic.in/reports/
stat-ind.htm

Source: ICAO, Air Transport Monthly
Monitor,
http://www.icao.int/sustainability/Pages/
Air-Traffic-Monitor.aspx;
Air India : DGCA, Air Transport
Operating and Traffic
Statistics for 2014-15, Air India, Table
1.06,
http://dgca.nic.in/reports/stat-ind.htm

Source: IATA, Press Release No. 4,
4 February 2016,
http://www.iata.org/pressroom/pr/
Pages/2016-02-04-01.aspx
Roland Berger analysis

1) ASKM = Available seat kilometre (One seat (empty or filled) flying one kilometre)
2) RPK = Revenue passenger kilometre (A paying passenger flying one kilometre)

A FIGURE 21

Bottom Line Pressure on Airlines Operating in India High Due to Rising Input Costs

Cost drivers

Development of fuel costs[1] [USD/ KL]

Sources: Index Mundi Jet Fuel Monthly Price, http://www.indexmundi.com/commodities/?commodity=jet-fuel&months=120, IATA Fuel Price Monitor, http://www.iata.org/publications/economics/fuelmonitor/Pages/price-analysis.aspx, Indian Oil Corporation, https://www.iocl.com/Products/ATFDomesticPrices.aspx, Roland Berger analysis

Landing charges per single landing[2] in 2014 [USD]

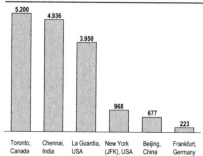

Sources: For other international airports, The Richest, http://www.therichest.com/luxury/most-expensive/10-most-expensive-airportsto-land-your-plane/2/
For Chennai Airport: Airport Authority of India, http://www.aai.aero/misc/Airport-Charges-2014-15.pdf, Roland Berger Analysis
1) Average Aviation turbine fuel for India of four main airports (Delhi, Mumbai, Chennai, Kolkata), 2) Assuming an aircraft weight of 100 MT

A FIGURE 22

IndiGo, Post Its Inception Years, Has Been the Only Consistently Profitable Airline. IndiGo's Capacity Has Continuously Increased

Fleet expansion & net profit

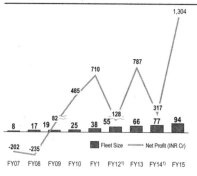

Capacity expansion: No. of flights & passengers per day

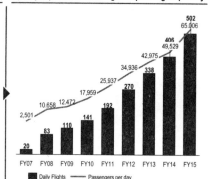

1) High airline fuel price cited as primary reason for compressed results
Source: DGCA, Air Transport Statistics, Air Transport Operating and Traffic Statistics of IndiGo, http://dgca.nic.in/reports/stat-ind.htm, FY07 – Table 3.8; FY15 – Table 1.07; DGCA, Air Transport Statistics, Fleet Personnel & Financial Statistics 2014-15 of IndiGo, Table 1.17 and Table 1.23 http://dgca.nic.in/reports/stat-ind.htm
Roland Berger analysis

A FIGURE 23

IndiGo's Steadfast Focus on Cost Reduction of Controllable Costs Has Helped the Airline Remain Profitable

Utilization is high despite consistent fleet ramp up

Employee strength and employee efficiency[1]

Passenger load factor (Utilization)

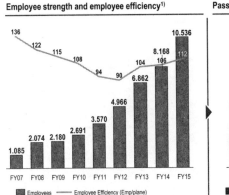
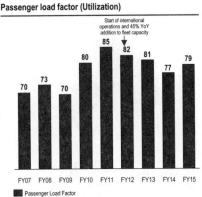

Source: DGCA, Air Transport Statistics, Part II, Operating traffic statistics and other performance indicators of IndiGo, for years FY07 to FY15, http://dgca.nic.in/reports/statind.htm. FY07/08 – Table 3.8, FY09 – Table 2.44, FY10 – Table 2.38, FY11 &12 – Table 2.42, FY13 – Table 2.38, FY14 – Table 2.34; FY15 – Table 1.20 and 1.04, Roland Berger Analysis

A FIGURE 24

With a Single Aircraft Type & Retiring Its Aircrafts after 5 Years, IndiGo Has Managed to Keep MRO Costs Low & Efficiency High

High focus on operations are a key driver of cost competitive advantage for IndiGo

Fleet diversity & flying hours, 2011[1]

IndiGo	Aircrafts	# of aircrafts	Avg Daily Revenue Hrs
	Airbus A320 -200	38	11.8

Kingfisher	Aircrafts	# of aircrafts	Avg Daily Revenue Hrs
	Airbus A 330- 223	5	13.5
	Airbus A 320- 232	23	8.9
	Airbus A321- 232	8	9.0
	Airbus A319- 131	3	8.7
	ATR 72-212A	25	8.9
	ATR 72-212A	2	8.6
	Total (6 Aircraft Types)	66	9.2

MRO cost & personnel (per. aircraft), 2011

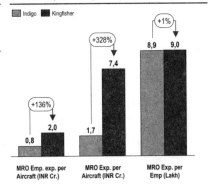

1) We used 2011 as a comparator year it is the most common year of sizable and stable operations that the two airlines share

Source: DGCA, Air Transport Statistics, Part II, Fleet Statistics of Kingfisher Airline during FY11 – Table 2.41 & 2.45

DGCA, Air Transport Statistics, Part II, Fleet Statistics of IndiGo during FY11 – Table 2.42 & 2.46, Roland Berger analysis

A FIGURE 25

IndiGo Has a Higher Than Proportionate Market Share While Maintaining a Smaller Fleet & Employee Footprint versus Competition

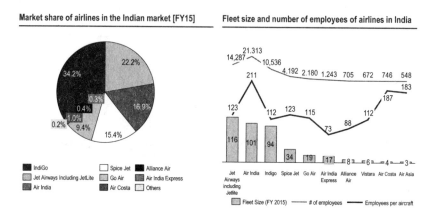

Source: DGCA, Handbook on Civil Aviation Statistics 2014-15; DGCA, Air Transport Statistics, Fleet, Personnel and Financial Statistics 2014-15, Time series data on Fleet Strength and Utilization of Aircraft & Time series data of staff strength, Roland Berger analysis

A FIGURE 26

India Trails Other Countries in Steel Consumption. Construction, Infrastructure & Automotive Drive >65% of Domestic Steel Consumption
Overview of Steel Consumption, India vs Select Countries

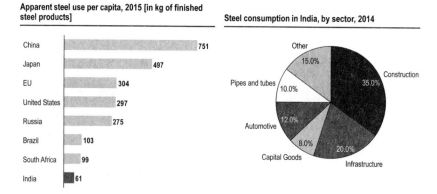

Source: World Steel Association, 'World Steel in Figures 2016', p. 17, https://www.worldsteel.org/dms/internetDocumentList/bookshop/2016/World-Steel-in-Figures-2016/document/World%20Steel%20in%20Figures%202016.pdf;   World   Steel Association, Morgan Stanley Report; Roland Berger analysis

FIGURE 27

The Indian Steel Industry Is Dominated by Large Public and Private Players: SAIL, JSW Steel, and Tata Steel Lead the Industry

Snapshot of Indian steel industry: Competitive environment [standalone]

Company	FY15 Crude Steel Production Capacity [m MT]	FY15 Sales Turnover and Net Profit [INR Cr.]	FY15 Debt & Interest coverage ratio [INR Cr., no.]	Domestic captive iron ore mine, coal mine [Y/N]	
SAIL	12.8	51,129 / 2,093	28,221 2.68	✓ Orissa, Jharkhand, Chhattisgarh	✗ Coal block allotment in Jharkhand
JSW Steel	14.3	50,393 / 2,166	25,761 2.25	✗	✗
TATA STEEL	10.0	46,577 / 6,439	26,210 4.35	✓ Jharkhand, Odisha	✓ Jharkhand
BHUSHAN	3,5	11,735 / -1,254	38,529 0.5	✗	✗ Coal block allotment in Jharkhand
JINDAL STEEL & POWER	3,0	14.652 / -311	26,115 1.08	✓ Odisha	✓ Chhattisgarh
ESSAR STEEL	3,0	17,162 / 648	30,000 N/A	✗	✗

Source: MoneyControl, SAIL: http://www.moneycontrol.com/financials/steelauthorityindia/profit-loss/SAI#SAI
JSW Steel: http://www.moneycontrol.com/financials/jswsteel/profit-loss/JSW01#JSW01, Tata Steel: http://www.moneycontrol.com/financials/tatasteel/profit-loss/TIS#TIS
Bhushan Steel: http://www.moneycontrol.com/financials/bhushansteel/profit-loss/BS14#BS14; JSPL: http://www.moneycontrol.com/financials/jindalsteelpower/profit-loss/JSP#JSP
Essar Steel: http://www.moneycontrol.com/india/stockpricequote/steel-large/essarsteel/ES01; Steel production capacity and captive mine data from corporate website, Roland Berger analysis

 FIGURE 28

JSW's CSR Activities Are Designed to Minimize the Impact of Business on the Environment and Ecology

Utilization solid wastes: Waste to wealth

> Preventing landfills through in-house solid waste utilisation (96%) - Innovative products like mill scale briquettes, micro-pellets, etc.
> Developed innovative solution to replace river sand by slag sand
> Fly ash to cement
> Slime pond tailings use for making bricks

Water conservation

> Zero water discharge campaign to conserve water for community
> Using treated waste water to water trees
> In plant recirculation of water, using blow down for replacing clean water

Sustainability

Improving ecology

> Installed ambient air monitoring facilities at several locations
> Regular monitoring of all water
> Temperatures in the vicinity have gone down by > 5 deg Celsius over the past 10 years
> Rainfall has gone up by 80 mm over the past 20 years

Cleaning & greening all the way

> Planted 20 lakh trees till date in 1300 acres
> Reduction in CO_2 load by 12000t pa
> Committed to carbon credit schemes; building compliant infrastructure

Source: JSW Steel, 'Creating Shared Value – the JSW Way! The Vijaynagar Story', p. 9, 2015; Roland Berger

A FIGURE 29

Programmes Have Been Developed to Improve Quality of Life of the Villagers Living in the Surrounding Areas of the Factory[1]

1 Education

> Mid-day meals in schools (540 schools, 1.35 lakh children)
> Building schools (40 schools, 14000 children), helping with solar lamps, books, computers, teachers

2 Women empowerment

> Training of women for employment (1000 on rural BPO, 750 on textile & apparel, 1100 of entrepreneurship, 2000 on managerial skills, 1500 on self help groups

3 Health

> Antenatal check-ups for women (2000), Institutional deliveries (700)
> Children immunization (600)
> Cataract surgeries (4000)
> Children Vision screening (5600)
> Drinking water

4 Infrastructure development

> >14 kms of village roads constructed
> 6.5 kms of drainages
> 2 new bus stands, 76 bus shelters
> 4000 individual toilets
> >6 tons of garbage collected from villages everyday

5 Sports

> Making School grounds (15),
> Providing sports equipment to schools
> Sponsoring to district level, state level (4) and national level (2) sports events

6 Art, culture & heritage

> 3 nos ancient temples restored and renovated; 16 temples in villages restored
> Restored local arts and culture programs

7 Livestock & agriculture

> Farmers under public-private partnership model (1200) given seeds, fertilizers
> Planted 20 lakh trees in 1334 acres

8 Vocational training

> Vocational training to students (3244)
> Life skills training (350)
> Training for specially abled children (112)
> Sports training (1350)

1) Numbers given are instances

Source: JSW Steel, 'Creating Shared Value – the JSW Way! The Vijaynagar Story', p. 8, 2015; Roland Berger

A FIGURE 30

Blast Furnace, Basic Oxygen Furnace and Electric Arc Furnace Are at the Core of the Iron and Steel Making Process

Iron and steel making process

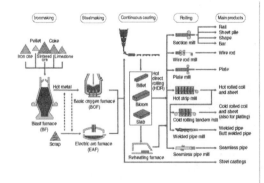

> The integrated manufacturing process for iron and steel using the Blast Furnace (BF) and Basic Oxygen Furnace (BOF) is presently the most commonly used method

> After the BF-BOF process, molten steel is controlled to a target composition and temperature and is then cast by continuous casting machines to produce slabs, blooms, and billets. These castings are rolled to the required dimensions by the rolling mill to produce steel products

> In addition to the BF-BOF process, there is another process which utilizes mainly scrap as an iron source. The direct reduced iron is produced by reducing iron ore with reformed natural gas. The scrap, along with direct reduced iron, is then melted in an Electric Arc Furnace (EAF) to produce molten steel

Sources: JFE 21st Century Foundation, An Introduction to Iron and Steel Processing, 'Chapter 2, Smelting, Refining, and Continuous Casting', http://www.jfe-21st-cf.or.jp/chapter_2/2a_1_img.html; World Steel Association; Roland Berger analysis

NOTES

1. The London interbank offered rate (LIBOR) is 'a benchmark rate that some of the world's leading banks charge each other for short-term loans', http://www.investopedia.com/terms/l/libor.asp.
2. For example, it would currently take about 466 years to clear the caseload before India's Supreme Court. *BBC News*, 'Delhi Justice's 466-Year Backlog', 11 February 2009, http://news.bbc.co.uk/2/hi/south_asia/7883750.stm.
3. Tarun Khanna and Krishna G. Palepu, *Winning in Emerging Markets* (Boston: Harvard Business Press, 2010). Institutional voids are market institutions that are missing in emerging markets, e.g., functioning legal systems, accurate market research capabilities, etc.
4. We use decimal notation and Indian notation interchangeably during the text. In Indian notation, 1 crore equals 10 million; 1 lakh equals 100,000. We also use a mix of currencies in this book. In June 2016, 1 EUR and 1 USD were equivalent to about INR 75 and INR 68, respectively.
5. Centre for Monitoring the Indian Economy, 'Stalling of Projects in March 2014 Quarter Slows Down', 14 April 2014, https://www.cmie.com/.

6. US Department of Agriculture, Economic Research Service, 'Real GDP (2010 Dollars) Historical', Microsoft Excel worksheet, http://www.ers.usda.gov/data-products/international-macroeconomic-data-set.aspx.

7. Figures for the number of people pulled out of poverty in India vary notoriously with different sources. For this book, numbers are calculated from: Pedro Olinto, Kathleen Beegle, Carlos Sobrado and Hiroki Uematsu, 'State of the Poor: Where Are the Poor and Where Are the Poorest?' *Economic Premise*, no. 125, World Bank, October 2013, http://siteresources.worldbank.org/EXTPREMNET/Resources/EP125.pdf. However, another report by the World Bank cites 140 million removed from poverty in India between 2008 and 2011. Still different numbers can be obtained using the poverty estimates published by the Indian government (Tendulkar method).

8. World Bank, *World Development Indicators*, http://data.worldbank.org/indicator/IT.MLT.MAIN and http://data.worldbank.org/indicator/IT.CEL.SETS.

9. German Ministry of Road Transport and Highways, *Annual Report 2013–14*, p. 107, http://www.statistik-portal.de/Statistik-Portal/de_jb16_jahrtab36.asp.

10. Wilfried Aulbur

11. The price of a new Volkswagen Golf 2.0 (or equivalent) has been used for comparison. Deutsche Bank, *The Random Walk: Mapping the World's Prices 2013* (Frankfurt am Main: DB Market Research, 2013), p. 11.

12. RBI, 'Macro-Economic Aggregates (at Current Prices)—Personal Disposable Income', in *Handbook of Statistics on Indian Economy* (Mumbai: RB I, 2015), p. 2, column 14, https://rbidocs.rbi.org.in/rdocs/Publications/PDFs/T00120171321D55840E7A5AE6028D78AB567.PDF.

13. Peter J. Williamson, Ravi Ramamurti, Afonso Fleury and Maria Tereza Leme Fleury, eds, *The Competitive Advantage of Emerging*

Market Multinationals (Cambridge: Cambridge University Press 2013).

14. Unicorns are start-ups, typically across the technology, mobile technology and IT sectors, which have achieved a valuation of USD 1 billion or more.

15. Michael E. Porter, 'What Is Strategy?' *Harvard Business Review* 74, no. 6 (November–December 1996): 61–78.

16. A.G. Lafley and Roger L. Martin, *Playing to Win: How Strategy Really Works* (Boston: Harvard Business Review Press, 2013).

17. Will Durant, *A Case for India* (New York: Simon and Schuster, 1930).

18. See, e.g., Investopedia, 'What Is the "Compound Annual Growth Rate—CAGR"', http://www.investopedia.com/terms/c/cagr.asp for a definition.

19. The time frame has been chosen to cover both the initial years of Chinese reforms which started in 1978 as well as the pre- and post-liberalization period of India. Source: US Department of Agriculture, Economic Research Service, 'Real GDP (2010 Dollars) Historical', Organizational data worksheet, http://www.ers.usda.gov/data-products/international-macroeconomic-data-set.aspx.

20. World Bank, *World Development Indicators*, http://data.worldbank.org/data-catalog/GDP-ranking-table; also see http://data.worldbank.org/data-catalog/GDP-PPP-based-table.

21. In 2015, India's GDP grew faster than China's.

22. If a company's financial information was not available for the entire period considered (2005–15), its CAGR was calculated from the year of available information. For a list of all companies and their performance, see Table A.1 in the Appendix.

23. Between 1990 and 2014, FDI increased by a staggering factor of 146 in US dollar terms. In 1990, gross inflow of FDI to India was USD 236.7 million and this shot up to USD 3.59 billion in 2000; in 2014, it was USD 34.42 billion. United Nations Conference

on Trade and Development (UNCTAD), *FDI Inflows by Region and Economy, 1990–2014*, June 2015, http://unctad.org/en/Pages/ DIAE/World%20Investment%20Report/Annex-Tables.aspx.

24. National Capital Region (NCR) refers to an inter-state planning and development area, which covers the national capital territory of Delhi, Haryana, Uttar Pradesh and Rajasthan.

25. The following enterprises in India are part of the IGCC 15 Index: ZF Steering Gears, Wendt, Siemens, Sanofi, Merck, KSB Pumps, Insilco, Goetze India, FAG Bearings India, Elantas Beck, Clariant Chemicals, BOSCH, Blue Dart Express, Bayer CropScience and BASF India.

26. The IGCC Fact Book 2015 is available at the Indo-German Chamber of Commerce in Mumbai.

27. United Nations, Department of Economic and Social Affairs, Population Division, *World Urbanization Prospects: The 2014 Revision, Highlights* (ST/ESA/SER.A/352) (New York: United Nations, 2014), http://esa.un.org/unpd/wup/highlights/wup2014-highlights.pdf.

28. Interviews by W.G. Aulbur and A. Kapoor with HUL management, Porter Prize, June 2014.

29. UNCTAD, *FDI Inflows by Region and Economy, 1990–2014*, June 2015, http://unctad.org/en/Pages/DIAE/World%20 Investment%20Report/Annex-Tables.aspx.

30. See detailed discussion of Godrej in Chapter 4.

31. In merchandise trade, petroleum crude and products were the major imported commodities (36.7 per cent) in FY14 followed by capital goods (10.9 per cent), gold and silver (7.4 per cent) and electronic goods (6.9 per cent). Regarding exports, petroleum products remained the most exported commodity (20.1 per cent) during the same period, followed by engineering goods (19.7 per cent), chemicals and related products (14 per cent) and gems and jewellery (13.1 per cent). India's major export destinations were the US (12.5

per cent), UAE (9.8 per cent) and China (4.8 per cent), whereas China (11.3 per cent), Saudi Arabia (8.1 per cent) and the UAE (6.5 per cent) constituted the top import sources. India's services trade during FY14 amounted to USD 151.5 billion of exports and USD 78.5 billion of imports. Computer services accounted for 45.8 per cent of India's services exports, followed by business services at 18.8 per cent, transport (11.5 per cent) and travel (11.8 per cent). Regarding imports, business services (34.6 per cent), transport (18.8 per cent) and travel (15 per cent) constituted the major imported services.

32. World Trade Organization, 'Country Profiles: India, 2013', *Trade Profiles 2014*, p. 88, https://www.wto.org/english/res_e/booksp_e/trade_profiles14_e.pdf.

33. U.S. Council on Competitiveness, 'Figure 1: Supplemental Data Analysis: Competitiveness Driven Differently among Most Competitive Nations', *2013 Global Manufacturing Competitiveness Index*, p. 4, https://www2.deloitte.com/content/dam/Deloitte/us/Documents/manufacturing/us-mfg-2013-global-manufacturing-competitiveness-index.pdf.

34. International Labor Organization, *Global Wage Report 2012/13—Wages and Equitable Growth*, (Geneva: ILO, 2013), pp. 24–25, http://www.ilo.org/wcmsp5/groups/public/@dgreports/@dcomm/@publ/documents/publication/wcms_194843.pdf.

35. *BBC News*, 'Delhi Justice's 466-Year Backlog'.

36. Zee News Online, 'Indian Economy: A Journey of Last 66 Years', http://zeenews.india.com/business/slideshow/indian-economy-a-journey-of-last-66-years_68.html/10.

37. RBI, *Report of the Working Group on Savings during the Twelfth Five-Year Plan (2012–13 to 2016–17)*, April 2012, https://www.rbi.org.in/Scripts/PublicationReportDetails.aspx?ID=662#4.

38. A sociologist who studies election trends.

39. *India Today*, 'What Makes NDA's "India Shining" Campaign the "Worst" Poll Strategy in Indian History', 14 May 2013,

http://indiatoday.intoday.in/story/nda-india-shining-worst-poll-strategy/1/270916.html.

40. Also known as MGNREGA, NREGA is an Indian government scheme launched in 2006 that guarantees the right to a minimum of 100 days of paid employment in a financial year to every household volunteering to do unskilled manual work.

41. Bharat Nirman is a time-bound business plan formed by the Indian government to augment growth in rural infrastructure, launched in 2005. Focused sectors are irrigation, roads, housing, water supply, electrification and telecommunication connectivity in rural areas, with a total target investment of INR 1,74,000 crore.

42. The National Food Security Act is an Indian law passed in 2013 that aims at providing cheap food grains to approx. 70 per cent of the country's population through subsidies. It provides food grains at prices lower than market rates through a network of state-run shops.

43. The Right to Information Act of 2005 entitles every citizen to seek information from public authorities and mandates a timely response by the authorities. It aims at increasing transparency and accountability of the government.

44. The Forest Rights Act (enacted in 2006), also called the Scheduled Tribes and Other Traditional Forest Dwellers (Recognition of Forest Rights) Act, grants legal recognition to the rights of forest-dwelling communities over land, resources and occupations in the forests where these communities have been residing for generations.

45. 70 per cent of government spending on food subsidies does not reach beneficiaries on account of leakages and excess economic cost, according to Maitreesh Ghatak, Parikshit Ghosh and Ashok Kotwal, 'Growth in the Time of UPA: Myths and Reality', *Economic and Political Weekly*, vol. 49, issue no. 16, 19 April 2014, http://www.epw.in/journal/2014/16/insight/growth-time-upa.html.

46. Also called the Lokpal and Lokayuktas Act 2013, it is an anti-corruption law in India that seeks to provide for the establishment of an independent body to inquire into allegations of corruption against public functionaries.

47. The Land Acquisition Act, also called the Right to Fair Compensation and Transparency in Land Acquisition, Rehabilitation and Resettlement Act, 2013, regulates the process of land acquisition and governs compensation, rehabilitation and resettlement of the people affected by the acquisition.

48. The Right to Education Act (passed in 2009) aims to ensure that every child in the age group of 6–14 years will get free and compulsory education in a neighbourhood school.

49. *BBC News*, 'Delhi Justice's 466-Year Backlog'.

50. Offsets in defence are 'industrial compensation on arrangements required by foreign governments as a condition of the purchase of defense articles and services from a non-domestic source', according to the Bureau of Industry and Security, U.S. Department of Commerce, 'Impact of Offsets in Defense Trade', https://www.bis.doc.gov/index.php/other-areas/strategic-industries-and-economic-security-sies/offsets-in-defense-trade.

51. Within-plant productivity improvements refer to productivity enhancements within a given plant via Kaizen, Kanban, continuous improvement, etc.

52. Ann E. Harrison, Leslie R. Martin and Shanthi Nataraj, *Learning Versus Stealing: How Important Are Market-Share Reallocations to India's Productivity Growth* (Santa Monica, CA: RAND Corporation, 2011), http://www.rand.org/pubs/working_papers/WR832.

53. Sivadasan Jagadeesh, 'Barriers to Competition and Productivity: Evidence from India', *B.E. Journal of Economic Analysis and Policy* 9, no. 1 (2009): 1–66.

54. Pinelopi Goldberg, Amit Khandelwal, Nina Pavcnik and Petia Topalova, 'Trade Liberalization and New Imported Goods', *American Economic Review: Papers and Proceedings* 99, no. 2 (2009): 494–500.

55. Further productivity improvements could be gained even today, if India would continue to drive down tariff and non-tariff barriers to trade; see, e.g., Pinak Sarkar and Martin Patrick, 'India's Trade Barriers: An Analysis with Reference to Tariffs and Customs Procedures', *Centre for Public Policy Research*, 28 January 2015, http://www.cppr.in/article/5300/.

56. See Jagadeesh, 'Barriers to Competition and Productivity'. Productivity growth rates have been shown to increase by 22 per cent due to FDI and 58.7 per cent due to tariff reductions. Values for productivity improvements due to FDI and tariff reductions vary according to sources; however, all sources point to a larger influence of tariff reductions than FDI in driving domestic firm performance.

57. Jens Matthias Arnold and Beata S. Javorcik, 'Gifted Kids or Pushy Parents? Foreign Direct Investment and Plant Productivity in Indonesia', *Journal of International Economics* 79, no. 1 (2009): 42–53.

58. Harrison et al., 'Learning Versus Stealing'.

59. Jens M. Arnold, Beata S. Javorcik, Molly Lipscomb and Aaditya Mattoo, 'Services Reform and Manufacturing Performance' (Policy Research Working Paper 5948, World Bank, January 2012).

60. Deriving special liberalization indices for the various sectors, the authors show that a one-standard-deviation change in the banking/transportation index leads to a productivity gain of 6.5/19 per cent for all firms. A corresponding one-standard-deviation change in the telecommunications index corresponds to a productivity gain of 7.2/9.8 per cent for domestic/foreign firms. However, a similar change in the insurance index leads to a productivity gain of 3.3 per cent for foreign firms only.

61. J.A. Garza-Reyes, H.S. Parkar, I. Oraifige, H. Soriano-Meier and D. Harmanto, 'An Empirical–Exploratory Study of the Status of Lean Manufacturing in India', *International Journal of Business Excellence* 5, no. 4 (2012): 395.

Darshak A. Desai and Mulchand B. Patel, 'Impact of Six Sigma in a Developing Economy: Analysis on Benefits Drawn by Indian Industries', *Journal of Industrial Engineering and Management* 2, no. 3 (2009): 517–38.

Kaizen is the practice of continuous improvement that has its origins in Japanese companies such as Toyota. Its basic philosophy is that big impact results from small improvements over time. Value stream mapping is a lean-management method for analysing processes and improving their overall efficiency and performance. Total productive maintenance is a practice that uses proactive and preventive maintenance of equipment to reduce unplanned breakdowns and improve efficiency.

62. ACMA, 'India Automotive Industry: Status', http://www.acma. in/docmgr/ACMA_Presentation/ACMA_Presentation.pdf. Six hundred and fifty-one members have ISO 9001 certifications, 546 companies are TS-16949-certified, 287 are ISO-14001-certified and 162 have OHSAS (Occupational Health and Safety Assessment Series) certifications. Fourteen ACMA members have achieved a Deming award (highest number outside of Japan), five have the Japan quality medal, fifteen received a TPM award and two have a Shingo Silver Medallion.

63. OEMs are car companies such as Maruti Suzuki, Mercedes-Benz, Ford, etc.

64. *Economic Times*, 'US FDA Penal Actions Hit Pharma Exports Growth, May Not Exceed 5%', 17 April 2014, http://economictimes. indiatimes.com/industry/healthcare/biotech/pharmaceuticals/ us-fda-penal-actions-hit-pharma-exports-growth-may-not-exceed-5/articleshow/33836244.cms. Indian companies enjoy the

largest share of USFDA approvals granted for abbreviated new drug applications (ANDAs) over the past three years from 2011 to 2013. The USFDA approved a total of 400 ANDAs in the year 2013, out of which 38.5 per cent were by Indian companies. India is the largest producer of active pharmaceutical ingredients and finished dosage forms outside of the US, followed by China, Italy and Germany, with India having 23.7 per cent of the total facilities listed by the USFDA. See, e.g., *Pharmabiz*, 'Indian Pharma Companies Secure 154 ANDAs Approvals from US FDA during 2013', 22 January 2014, http://www.pharmabiz.com/NewsDetails. aspx?aid=79910&sid=1; *GMP News*, 'FDA Publishes List of GMP Facilities Producing for the US Market', 24 October 2013, http:// www.gmp-compliance.org/enews_03940_FDA-publishes-List-of-GMP-facilities-producing-for-the-US-market--generic-drug-products-and-APIs-.html.

65. World Bank, *Logistics Performance Index, International LPI Global Ranking: 2014*, http://lpi.worldbank.org/international/global/2014.

66. Return on sales is a measure to assess a company's operational efficiency. It is defined as the ratio of the net income of a company, before interest and taxes, divided by sales. See, e.g., www. investopedia.com.

67. 100 basis points (bps) amount to 1 per cent.

68. If duties on raw materials are higher than those for finished goods, it becomes challenging for local manufacturers to compete with imported products.

69. H.A.C. Prasad, R. Sathish and S.S. Singh, 'India's Merchandise Exports: Some Important Issues and Policy Suggestions' (Working Paper 3-2014-DEA, Department of Economic Affairs, Ministry of Finance, Government of India, 2014), pp. 22–24.

70. World Economic Forum, *The Global Enabling Trade Report 2014, Country Profiles (India)* (Cologny: WEF, 2014), p. 160.

71. Nicholas Bloom, Raffaella Sadun and John Van Reenen, 'The Organization of Firms across Countries' (Working Paper 15129, National Bureau of Economic Research, July 2009), http://www. nber.org/papers/w15129.

72. According to the National Bureau of Economic Research (NBER), total factor productivity 'is the portion of output not explained by the amount of inputs used in production. As such, its level is determined by how efficiently and intensely the inputs are utilized in production.' See NBER, 'Total Factor Productivity', August 2006, p. 1, http://www.people.hbs.edu/dcomin/def.pdf.

73. According to the RBI's definition, effective as of 31 March 2004, NPAs are those assets which cease to generate income for the bank. Typically, this occurs when the interest and/or principal instalment of a loan amount remain overdue for a period of more than ninety days. See https://www.rbi.org.in/scripts/BS_ ViewMasCirculardetails.aspx?id=5761#L3.

74. *Times of India*, 'Govt Readies INR 70K-Cr Bank Recap Plan', 1 August 2015, http://timesofindia.indiatimes.com/business/ india-business/Govt-readies-Rs-70k-crore-bank-recap-plan/ articleshow/48302234.cms.

75. Chang-Tai Hsieh and Peter J. Klenow, 'Misallocation and Manufacturing TFP in China and India', *The Quarterly Journal of Economics* 74, no. 4 (2009): 1403–48.

76. Roland Berger projects 4.6 million vehicles based on an assumption of a CAGR of 7.4 per cent for 2015–20 for GDP growth. IHS (www. ihs.com) projects 4.2 million, while LMC (www.lmc-auto.com) has published a target of 9.3 million vehicles in 2020.

77. Rahul Bharti, vice president, corporate planning Maruti-Suzuki, Interview with W.G. Aulbur, August 2015.

78. *Reuters*, 'Maruti Suzuki to Sharpen Rural Focus after Q4 Earnings Top Forecasts', 27 April 2015. See http://in.reuters.com/article/ maruti-suzuki-in-results-idINKBN0NI0O420150427.

79. As per Wikipedia,

> e-Choupal is an initiative of ITC Limited, a conglomerate
> in India, to link directly with rural farmers via the Internet
> for procurement of agricultural and aquaculture products
> like soybeans, wheat, coffee and prawns. e-Choupal tackles
> the challenges posed by Indian agriculture, characterized by
> fragmented farms, weak infrastructure and the involvement
> of intermediaries. The programme installs computers with
> Internet access in rural areas of India to offer farmers up-
> to-date marketing and agricultural information.

See https://en.wikipedia.org/wiki/E-Choupal.

80. The mini segment comprises cars such as Maruti Suzuki Alto, Maruti Suzuki A-Star, Hyundai Santro, Chevy Spark, Hyundai Eon, etc.

81. The compact segment includes cars such as Maruti Suzuki Swift/ Zen Estillo, VW Polo, Honda Brio/Amaze, Tata Indica/Vista, Mahindra Vibe, Toyota Liva/Etios, Hyundai i10/i20, etc.

82. 'Earnings before interest, tax, depreciation and amortization (EBITDA) is a measure of a company's operating performance. Essentially, it's a way to evaluate a company's performance without having to factor in financing decisions, accounting decisions or tax environments.' Definition taken from: http:// www.investinganswers.com/financial-dictionary/financial-statement-analysis/earnings-interest-tax-depreciation-and-amortizatio.

83. Deep localization refers to the complete localization of components in India rather than the import of parts and limited value addition/ assembly by suppliers who then sell 'local' components to OEMs. For example, wheels would be produced fully in India rather than the tyre and the wheel rim being imported and only the assembly being done in India.

84. Hyundai's exports predominantly went to Europe until the EU increased import taxes for vehicles made in India. Since then, exports are concentrated in Africa, Latin America and Southeast Asia, similar to what is observed for Renault–Nissan.

85. Rajnish Tiwari and Cornelius Herstatt, *Aiming Big with Small Cars—Emergence of a Lead Market in India* (New York: Springer Verlag, 2014).

86. Many of the points in this section are taken from an interaction with Rahul Bharti, vice president, Corporate Planning, Maruti Suzuki, by W.G. Aulbur in September 2015.

87. R.C. Bhargava and Seetha, *The Maruti Story: How a Public Sector Company Put India on Wheels* (New York: Harper Collins, 2011).

88. The 5S principles are *seiri* (sorting), *seiton* (systematic arrangement), *seiso* (cleaning), *seiketsu* (standardization) and *shitsuke* (sustaining the discipline).

89. Strain refers to overburden, i.e., a blockage of flow in a production environment.

90. On the fifteenth of the month, the day-by-day production schedule for the first two weeks of the next months is frozen and will not be changed. A total schedule for the next two weeks is also fixed.

91. Direct material cost, the cost of the materials which are easily identifiable and directly used in production, has been calculated here using data from Maruti Suzuki annual reports, FY11–FY15; primary interviews with Maruti representatives.

92. The number of Tier-1 suppliers reduced from 355 in FY04 to 250 in FY12.

93. As of FY14, 78 per cent of all suppliers by value were located within a 100 km radius of the plant, as cited on the Maruti Suzuki website: http://www.marutisuzuki.com/greensupply.htm.

94. The overall list of all parts that make up a vehicle is called the bill of materials. The vehicle may contain sub-assemblies. These items

are called child parts. For example, a motor is a child part for a vehicle, a crank shaft a child part for a motor.

95. Customer satisfaction index (CSI) measures the satisfaction of customers with the sales and after-sales processes of a company.

96. As of FY14, average pre-berthing detention (the time a ship has to wait in port before it can dock at a berth; for a detailed definition, see, e.g., https://data.gov.in/catalog/average-pre-berthing-detention) amounts to 1.48 days, average pre-berthing detention on port account equals 0.27 days, average turnaround times stand at 3.84 days and average output per ship berth-day equals 12,179 metric tons. See: Ministry of Road Transport and Highways, Government of India, Transport Research Wing, *Basic Port Statistics of India 2013–14* (New Delhi: Government of India, 2015).

97. C. Ducruet and O. Merk, 'Examining Container Vessel Turnaround Times across the World', *Port Technology International* 59 (2013): 18–20, http://www.porttechnology.org/technical_papers/examining_container_vessel_turnaround_times_across_the_world.

98. Business Monitor International, *India Shipping Report Q1* (2015), p. 33.

99. E.g., banks can provide long-term loans under the 5/25 scheme to the infrastructure sector. The 5/25 scheme, launched by RBI in July 2014, aims at easing financial pressure on the developers of new infrastructure projects with long gestation periods. The scheme allows banks to extend long-term loans of twenty to twenty-five years to match the cash flows of projects while refinancing them every five or seven years.

100. India Infrastructure Research, *Ports in India 2015* (New Delhi: India Infrastructure Publishing, 2015).

101. Comments in this section have been taken from interviews with Adani management by Wilfried Aulbur in November 2015.

102. APSEZL covers three business units: ports and special economic zones (SEZs), logistics, and others (shipyard, warehousing services, etc.). Besides various terminals in some of the ports in India, the

company owns the ports of Mundra, Dahej, Hazira and Dhamra. In FY14, Mundra handled around 90 per cent of cargo volume, Dahej and Hazira the remaining 10 per cent. The Dhamra port was acquired in FY15.

103. Livemint.com, 'Mundra Races Past 100 Mt Cargo Mark—A First among Indian Ports', 10 April 2014, http://www.livemint.com/Opinion/jIu3EuqmWZu311dYPsWAAO/Mundra-races-past-100-mt-cargo-marka-first-among-Indian-por.html.

104. A deep draft or deep water port has a water depth of 18 m and allows the largest tankers currently available to dock directly at the berth.

105. A rake is a formation of coupled coaches or wagons that makes up a train without the locomotive.

106. In some areas, such as crane operator certifications, no certification courses were available in India. These were developed from scratch by the company in order to ensure quality manpower.

107. An eleventh port is in Australia.

108. For an overview of India's machine tool industry, see Chapter 3.

109. This paragraph draws from a series of discussions between the EFD management and W.G. Aulbur that took place during a site visit to EFD's Bangalore facility in August 2015. See also http://www.efd-induction.com/.

110. Rather than focusing on the initial purchasing price, products were developed to minimize the overall cost for the customer across price, usage and recycling.

111. De-contenting refers to the process of taking a product that was developed for developed markets and trying to reduce its cost by eliminating features that are (presumably) less relevant for emerging markets. It has generally proven to be an ineffective approach to emerging markets like India compared to, e.g., frugal engineering approaches. See also Chapter 4.

112. The goal is to move to a full virtual design of machines and virtual testing with real-life software before machines are actually

built. Hence, potential problems are identified early and can be addressed during the design phase, thereby eliminating waste.

113. Total productive maintenance (TPM) is a practice that uses proactive and preventive maintenance of equipment to reduce unplanned breakdowns and improve efficiency.

114. Bauhaus is a German art style in which crafts and art are combined and special focus is placed on functionality, rationality and radically simplified forms. It originated in the early twentieth century.

115. Hidden champions are relatively unknown (mostly B2B) companies of moderate size (< USD 4 billion turnover) that rank among the global top three in their respective industries. See Chapter 6 for more details.

116. The Swachh Bharat Mission or 'Clean India campaign' was launched by the Indian government in October 2014 with the aim of attaining clean roads, streets and infrastructure in the country by 2019.

117. Nicholas Bloom, Aprajit Mahajan, David McKenzie and John Roberts, 'Does Management Matter? Evidence from India' (Working Paper 16658, *National Bureau of Economic Research*, January 2011), http://www.nber.org/papers/w16658.

118. Indian Federal Ministry of Textiles, *Annual Report 2014–15*, http://texmin.nic.in/sites/default/files/ar_14_15_english.pdf. The value chain of the textile industry covers raw material, ginning, spinning, weaving, knitting, processing and garment/ apparel production. The unorganized sector covers handloom, handicrafts, cotton, wool, jute, etc., while the organized sector covers ginning, spinning, weaving, processing, apparel, garment and fashion segments.

119. Apparel Export Promotion Council, as cited in the *Times of India*, 'India Overtakes Germany and Italy, Is New World No. 2 in Textile Exports', 3 June 2014, http://timesofindia.indiatimes.com/ business/india-business/India-overtakes-Germany-and-Italy-is-new-world-No-2-in-textile-exports/articleshow/35973054.cms.

120. 'FDI is allowed under the automatic route without prior approval either of the Government or the Reserve Bank of India in all activities/sectors as specified in the consolidated FDI Policy, issued by the Government of India from time to time.' See RBI website FAQs: https://www.rbi.org.in/scripts/FAQView.aspx?Id=26.

121. ACMA–IMTMA Joint Study 2015, 'Enabling Indian Auto Component Industry Competitiveness—Role of Indian Machine Tool Industry'. See, for example, http://autotechreview.com/news/item/2041-indian-machine-tools-industry-at-$-3-4-bn-by-2020-%E2%80%93-study.html. A copy of the study can be obtained from Wilfried Aulbur, wilfried.aulbur@rolandberger.com. The machine tool industry produces machines for shaping or machining metal or rigid materials.

122. ACMA—Automotive Component Manufacturers' Association of India, and IMTMA—Indian Machine Tool Manufacturers' Association, are the respective industry associations in India.

123. 1 µm equals 10^{-6} metres.

124. E.g., tighter specifications, dent-free and scratch-free components, high-gloss and uniform finish.

125. E.g., higher cutting speeds, robust processes, progressive transfer lines; safety standards and cleanliness; adoption of newer processes to meet new specifications, e.g., ultrasonic/laser welding or water jet deburring of metallic components.

126. Plug and play refers to starting a machine and being able to operate it right away.

127. Hermann Simon, *Hidden Champions* (Boston: Harvard Business Publishing, 1996); Hermann Simon, *Hidden Champions of the 21st Century* (London: Springer Verlag, 2009).

128. The comments in this section are taken from various references. For an overview see, e.g., Wikipedia, 'Made in Germany', https://de.wikipedia.org/wiki/Made_in_Germany#Geschichte.

129. Johanna Lutteroth, 'Dreist, Dreister, Deutschland', Spiegel Online, 24 August 2012, http://www.spiegel.de/einestages/made-in-germany-vom-stigma-zum-qualitaetssiegel-a-947688.html.

130. Mitteldeutscher Rundfunk, ' "Made in Germany"—Wie Aus Einer Warnung Ein Gütesiegel Wurde', 15 September 2015, http://www.mdr.de/zeitreise/weitere-epochen/neuzeit/made-in-germany-chemnitz102.html.

131. Insa Holst and Peter Bräunlein, '"Made in Germany": Wie Deutsche Produkte Die Welt Eroberten', 27 April 2008, http://www.spiegel.de/wissenschaft/mensch/made-in-germany-wie-deutsche-produkte-die-welt-eroberten-a-549197.html.

132. Bayerischer Rundfunk, 'Made in Germany', 22 August 2016, http://www.br.de/themen/wissen/made-in-germany-100.html.

133. See, for example, Politik-forum.eu, '125 Years "Made in Germany"', 26 August 2012, http://www.politik-forum.eu/viewtopic.php?t=32226.

134. Susanne Hilger, '"Made in Germany" Auf Dem Weg In Das Globale Zeitalter', academics.de, October 2011, https://www.academics.de/wissenschaft/_made_in_germany_auf_dem_weg_in_das_globale_zeitalter_51013.html.

135. Wikipedia, 'Schulpflicht (Deutschland)', https://de.wikipedia.org/wiki/Schulpflicht_%28Deutschland%29.

136. E.E. Williams, *Made in Germany* (Brighton: Harvester Press, 1973). See, for example, https://en.wikipedia.org/wiki/Ernest_Edwin_Williams.

137. David Head, *Made in Germany: The Corporate Identity of a Nation* (London: Hodder Arnold H&S, 1992).

138. As of FY12, organized employment in the manufacturing sector accounted for 13.34 million, while unorganized employment stood at 34.88 million, based on FY11 estimates. Therefore, total employment in manufacturing was estimated at 48 million

in FY12. A further addition of 100 million jobs by 2022 would mean a more-than-three-fold increase in total employment. Anwarul Hoda and Durgesh K. Rai, 'Labour Regulations and Growth of Manufacturing and Employment in India: Balancing Protection and Flexibility' (Working paper, Indian Council for Research on International Economic Relations, December 2015), table 2, p. 15, http://icrier.org/pdf/Working_Paper_298.pdf.

139. The triad countries are the US, Europe and Japan.

140. Various measures to e-enable interactions with government are intended to improve ease of doing business parameters such as starting a business, dealing with construction permits, paying taxes, trading across borders, enforcing contracts and resolving insolvency. See, e.g., Confederation of Indian Industry, 'Doing Business Study, Reforms Introduced by India during 2 June, 2014–1 June 2015, Appendix I', in *Government's Initiatives on Improving Ease of Doing Business in India, CII Sector Update*, 24 July 2015, pp. 1–5, http://www.cii.in/ResourceDetails.aspx?enc= MEG9fTomlTCz/SWkRFzdb4uY eOurfQ9X2GTf/tcJ3G8rQnd5 DVG9EKU5pOfurjtB9ALjJiOmmaZrVWlzvY2w6Q==; FICCI–Intel Project on 'Ease of Doing Business—Dealing with Process Inefficiencies/Bottlenecks', FICCI, February 2015. See http://www.ficciqualityforum.com/Ease-of-Doing-Business.pdf.

141. Confederation of Indian Industry, 'One Year of the Government—Major Reforms & Policy Actions and Agenda Going Forward', May 2015. See http://www.slideshare.net/ ConfederationOfIndianIndustry/major-reforms.

142. The Goods and Services Tax (GST) Bill aims to simplify the tax environment in India by introducing a national value-added tax. Its aim is to support a common national market for goods and services.

143. Indications of a certain impatience on the part of industry versus consistent execution are visible, see, e.g., *Times of India*,

'No Change on Ground on Ease of Doing Business, HDFC's Deepak Parekh Says', 18 February 2015, http://timesofindia. indiatimes.com/business/india-business/No-change-on-ground-on-ease-of-doing-business-HDFCs-Deepak-Parekh-says/ articleshow/46288197.cms; *Times of India*, 'Shine Wearing Off Govt, Black Money Law Vengeful, Rahul Bajaj Says', 7 August 2015, http://timesofindia.indiatimes.com/india/Shine-wearing-off-govt-black-money-law-vengeful-Rahul-Bajaj-says/ articleshow/48395739.cms.

144. World Economic Forum, 'The Global Competitiveness Index 2015–16', http://reports.weforum.org/global-competitiveness-report-2015-2016/competitiveness-rankings/.

145. World Bank, 'Ease of Doing Business, Country Rankings', in *Doing Business 2016 Rank, 13th Edition*, p. 5. See http://www. doingbusiness.org/~/media/GIAWB/Doing%20Business/ Documents/Annual-Reports/English/DB16-Full-Report.pdf.

146. US Chamber of Commerce, 'UP. Unlimited Potential—The GIPC International IP Index, 3rd Edition, 4 February 2015. See http:// www.theglobalipcenter.com/up-unlimited-potential-the-gipc-international-ip-index-3rd-edition/.

147. World Bank, *Logistics Performance Index, International LPI Global Ranking: 2014*, http://lpi.worldbank.org/international/global.

148. Download the full report (in German) at https://www.bmbf.de/ files/Umsetzungsempfehlungen_Industrie4_0.pdf.

149. Rethink Robotics, Rethink Robotics Landing Page, company website, http://www.rethinkrobotics.com/baxter/.

150. Roland Berger analysis based on the data from US Bureau of Labor Statistics, 'National Occupational Employment and Wage Estimates United States', May 2013, http://www.bls.gov/ oes/2013/may/oes_nat.htm and C.G.P. Grey, 'Humans Need Not Apply', documentary, 2014, https://www.youtube.com/ watch?v=7Pq-S557XQU.

151. See, for example, http://www.arena2036.de/de/. Arena 2036 is a dedicated research campus based on a close collaboration between industry, research organizations and government. The goal of the teams working within Arena 2036 is to develop new production methods and light weighting approaches within the framework of Industry 4.0. Partners in this endeavour are, among others, Daimler, Siemens, Kuka, Bosch, Festo, BASF, Fraunhofer and the University of Stuttgart.

152. International Council on Clean Transportation, 'EU CO2 Emission Standards for Passenger Cars and Light-Commercial Vehicles', Policy update, January 2014, p. 9, http://www.theicct.org/sites/default/files/publications/ICCTupdate_EU-95gram_jan2014.pdf.

153. World Resources Institute, 'Total GHG Emissions including Land-Use and Forestry 2012', CAIT Climate Data Explorer data, http://cait.wri.org/historical.

154. The Good and Green Policy, 'Green Makes Business Sense', presentation by Godrej Appliances at GreenCo Summit in Chennai, India, June 2014, http://www.greenbusinesscentre.com/site/ciigbc/viewprest.jsp?eventid=432257&event=432257&event=dd&dated=383457.

155. Lafley and Martin, *Playing to Win*; Michael E. Porter, 'What Is Strategy?'.

156. The third level of education which goes beyond high school (undergrad studies and above).

157. Physical infrastructure, human capital, educational systems, quality of governance reflected in policy-making and execution, etc. See, e.g., Peter J. Williamson, Ravi Ramamurti, Afonso Fleury and Maria Tereza Leme Fleury, *The Competitive Advantage of Emerging Market Multinationals* (New York: Cambridge University Press, 2013), p. 239.

158. Land, natural resources, labour, location, climate, etc.

159. For a detailed analysis of the weaknesses of India's university and publicly funded research systems, see Rishikesha T. Krishnan,

From Jugaad to Systematic Innovation: The Challenge for India (Bangalore: Utpreraka Foundation, 2010).

160. Batelle, '2014 Global R&D Funding Forecast', *R&D Magazine*, December 2013, http://www.battelle.org/docs/tpp/2014_global_ rd_funding_forecast.pdf.

161. PPPs are the rates of currency conversion that equalize the purchasing power of different currencies by eliminating the differences in price levels between countries. In absolute terms on PPP basis, India is the seventh largest R&D investor.

162. India's 0.9 per cent compares to 2.8 per cent in the US, 2.9 per cent in Germany, 3.4 per cent in Japan, 3.6 per cent in South Korea and 2.0 per cent in China.

163. Batelle, '2014 Global R&D Funding Forecast'.

164. As announced in the government of India's twelfth five-year plan. See Planning Commission, Government of India, 'Science and Technology', in *Twelfth Five-Year Plan (2012–2017): Faster, More Inclusive and Sustainable Growth*, Volume 1 (New Delhi: SAGE Publications,), p. 235, http://planningcommission.gov.in/plans/ planrel/12thplan/pdf/12fyp_vol1.pdf.

165. All India Council for Technical Education, 'Growth of Technical Institutes in the Country' (Undergraduate), and 'Growth of Intake of Technical Institutes in the Country (Undergraduate)', http://www.aicte-india.org/downloads/Growth_Technical_ Institutions_310514.pdf.

166. Brian L. Yoder, 'Engineering by the Numbers', research article (American Society for Engineering Education, n.d.), p. 37, https:// www.asee.org/papers-and-publications/publications/college-pr ofiles/15EngineeringbytheNumbersPart1.pdf; National Bureau of Statistics of China, 'Number of Regular Students for Normal Courses in Higher Education Institutes', in *China Statistical Yearbook 2014* (China Statistics Press, 2014), http://www.stats. gov.cn/tjsj/ndsj/2014/indexeh.htm.

167. World Bank, *International Comparative Study: Engineering Education in India*, Report no. 57, South Asia Human Development Sector (Washington, DC: World Bank, 2013), p. 17.

168. For instance, ISRO's Mangalyaan mission (Mars orbiter mission) cost just USD 74 million and was about nine times cheaper than NASA's Maven Mars mission (USD 671 million). As a global first, India was the first nation to be successful on their first Mars mission attempt. Chandrayaan, ISRO's mission to the Moon, was also successful, with one orbiter placed in orbit. Since 1999, ISRO has established prowess in launching commercial satellites, having launched forty satellites for foreign customers from nineteen countries using the Polar Satellite Launch Vehicle; Source: *BBC News*, 'Why India's Mars Mission Is So Cheap and Thrilling', 24 September 2014, http://www.bbc.com/news/science-environment-29341850; *Business Insider*, '3 ISRO Achievements That Made Indians Proud!' 4 August 2015, http://www.businessinsider.in/3-ISRO-achievements-that-made-Indians-proud/articleshow/48347077.cms.

169. Globally, Faurecia has leading positions in its four business divisions: automotive seating, emissions control technologies, interior systems and automotive exteriors.

170. Computer-aided design (CAD) and computer-aided engineering (CAE) involve the use of computer software for the creation, modification, analysis and optimization of an engineering design.

171. CII is the Confederation of Indian Industry, FICCI stands for the Federation of Indian Chambers of Commerce, and Assocham for the Associated Chambers of Commerce of India. All three are the apex industrial organizations in the country.

172. De-contenting is a term used, e.g., in the automotive industry, and refers to removing features from a vehicle in order to save cost. Many OEMs have tried (mostly unsuccessfully) to take features out of their global models in an attempt to reach Indian price points.

173. Roland Berger Strategy Consultants, 'Global Topics, 8 Billion, Rising Population Growth and 20 Fast Growing Emerging Markets', in *Think: Act Study*, March 2012, https://www.rolandberger.com/globaltopics/media/pdf/GT_8bn_Introduction_final.pdf.

174. Homi Kharas, 'The Emerging Middle Class in Developing Countries' (Working Paper no. 285, OECD Development Centre, January 2010), pp. 26–29.

175. Many of the observations in this paragraph are based on discussions by Wilfried Aulbur with the Godrej management team (August 2015).

176. Morgan Stanley, Investor Presentation, Dabur India, June 2015, http://www.dabur.com/in/en-us/investor/investor-information/schedule-analyst-investor-meet/presentations.

177. India ranks as the ninth largest consumer market in terms of consumer expenditure, as per constant prices and fixed 2013 exchange rates. Audre Biciunaite, 'Just How Important Is China in the FMCG Landscape?' *Euromonitor International*, 10 February 2015, http://blog.euromonitor.com/2015/02/just-how-important-is-china-in-the-fmcg-landscape.html.

178. Confederation of Indian Industry, 'FMCG Roadmap to 2020—The Game Changers' , 2010, http://cii.in/PublicationDetail.aspx?enc=f49KwfhIDITDK+ZCQkL3deG+Inav4TyC070ZIr5Nt zgrDkgeoFvR8lwa0h62UhlBUdMPzPYP83nXDP2yrDVI6pPva DvHjva2B7Gvx11ZHqEmNi4YafmqrXsgwtF9dzCrD7GkSE9+P+ qTUi4DMUuZQ/sUhCGaY10+VgSUyQts5hmhcW6WvgAHZW Jxc990qtl9.

179. Morgan Stanley, Investor Presentation.

180. Godrej Group, 'Godrej Consumer Products Annual Report (2014–15)', http://www.godrejcp.com/annual-reports.aspx.

181. Ibid.

182. Ibid.

183. Different fabric strips that have the properties of human hair are combined in a bundle and tested with Godrej products. Variations in human hair testing, which invariably occur, can be eliminated in this way. Turnaround times are also improved.

184. Current performance of the Fast Card allows for four to five hours of mosquito-free sleep.

185. A stock-keeping unit, or SKU, 'is an individually identifiable item stored in a specific location and tracked by an inventory system'. William J. Sawaya, Jr, and William C. Giauque, *Production and Operations Management* (Orlando: Dryden Press, 1986), p. 122.

186. Of the 168 million rural households in 2011, only 9.4 per cent reported possessing a refrigerator, while 43.8 per cent of the 79 million urban houses reported owning a refrigerator, thereby creating a market potential of more than 197 million households for ChotuKool.

National Sample Survey Reports, 'Household Consumption of Various Goods and Services in India 2011–12', *NSS 68th Round*, June 2014, p. 39.

187. *Indian Express*, 'Thanks to Postmen, "ChotuKool" Is a Rage in Rural Households', 21 December 2011.

188. Indicative Roland Berger analysis, assuming cost of electricity at INR 3 per kilowatt per hour. The conventional refrigerator compressor runs for twelve hours for the first three years and fourteen hours in the fourth and fifth year with average power consumption of 95 watts; ChotuKool runs for twelve hours daily with average power consumption of 62 watts.

189. According to UN water statistics, improved water sources include piped water on premises (piped household water connection located inside the user's dwelling, plot or yard), and other improved drinking water sources (public taps or standpipes, tube

wells or boreholes, protected dug wells, protected springs and rainwater collection), which are not necessarily safe for drinking. Hence, the potential market size for water purifiers is much larger than 8 per cent of the population. UN Water, 'Percent of Population with Access to Improved Water Sources', 7 October 2014, http://www.unwater.org/kwip; Ameer Shaheed, Jennifer Orgill, Maggie A. Montgomery, Marc A. Jeuland and Joe Brown, 'Why "Improved" Water Sources Are Not Always Safe', *Bull World Health Organization* 92 (2014): 283–89.

190. Charles Leadbeater, *The Frugal Innovator: Creating Change on a Shoestring Budget* (London: Palgrave Macmillan UK, 2014), p. 107.

191. Rajnish Tiwari and Cornelius Herstatt, 'Open Global Innovation Networks as Enablers of Frugal Innovation: Propositions Based on Evidence from India' (TIM/TUHH Working paper no. 73, 12 December 2012), p. 17; 'Pureit Patent Revocation to Have Minimal Impact', *Business Standard*, 5 July 2012, http://www.business-standard.com/article/companies/pureit-patent-revocation-to-have-minimal-impact-112070500041_1.html.

192. WHO–UNICEF, 'Progress on Drinking Water and Sanitation: 2014 Update', WHO–UNICEF Report, 2014, http://apps.who.int/iris/bitstream/10665/112727/1/9789241507240_eng.pdf.

193. Ibid. About half of India's population still defecates in the open due to lack of sanitary facilities.

194. The total number of rural households as of 2011 was 168 million, of which 44 per cent did not have access to electricity. Therefore, approximately 79 million households did not have access to electricity in 2011. Assuming the average size of a rural household to be five persons, this results in a total market potential of around 370 million people in rural India who had no access to electricity and could be potential customers of HPS. Sevea Association, 'Case study: Husk Power Systems', February 2013, http://seveaconsulting.com/page/what-we-do; number of rural households figure obtained

from Census 2011. See C. Chandramouli, 'Houses, Household Amenities and Assets Data 2001–2011 - Visualizing through Maps', presentation, http://censusindia.gov.in/2011-Common/ NSDI/Houses_Household.pdf.

195. Ibid.

196. Installation cost is the landed cost of installation that includes equipment cost, basic construction and cost of wiring a small village. Sources: Gaurav, n.d., Husk Power Systems presentation, http:// www.huskpowersystems.com/admin/upload/presentationsfile/ Husk%20Power%20Systems%20(Introduction%20Updated). pptx; and http://www.cseindia.org/userfiles/Gaurav%20Kumar_ Design%20to%20Scale.pdf.

197. Sevea Association, 'Case Study'. February 2013, http://www. seveaconsulting.com/wp-content/uploads/2016/02/Case_study_ HPS.pdf.

198. Haier, 'Haier Sustains Top Position in the Euromonitor Global Major Appliances' 2014 Brands Rankings for Sixth Consecutive Year', 1 September 2015, press release, http://www.haier.com/in/ newspress/pressreleases/n2014/201501/t20150109_257797.shtml. For the 2014 revenue information on Haier, see Wikipedia, 'Haier', https://en.wikipedia.org/wiki/Haier.

199. *Wall Street Journal*, 'IBM Strikes Deal with Rival Lenovo', 8 December 2004; *Business Wire*, 'Lenovo Marks Decade of Success since Acquisition of IBM's PC Business', 30 April 2015.

200. Roland Berger, 'Frugal—Simple, Simpler, Best. Frugal Innovation in the Engineered Products and High-Tech Industry', *Think: Act*, December 2014, https://www.rolandberger.com/ publications/publication_pdf/roland_berger_tab_frugal_ products_e_20150107.pdf.

201. Many insights in this chapter have been derived from discussions with Siemens management by Wilfried Aulbur during October 2015.

202. Siemens company presentation, 2016, http://www.siemens.com/
     press/pool/de/homepage/Siemens-company-presentation.pdf;
     Siemens financial year ends on 30 September.

203. Siemens India Profile: http://www.siemens.com/about/pool/
     worldwide/siemens_india_en.pdf.

204. This division provides solutions for the generation of clean
     electricity from fossil fuels and for the reliable generation of power
     for oil and gas applications.

205. This division provides software products and automation
     technologies for industrial applications covering the entire life
     cycle, from product design and production execution to after-sales
     services.

206. This division offers a comprehensive portfolio of automation and
     drives for process industries such as chemical, pharmaceuticals,
     food and beverages, etc.

207. This division provides imaging diagnostics, laboratory diagnostics
     and point-of-care solutions.

208. Some examples include A-compact-plus MV motors, steam
     turbines, isolators, gas-insulated switch gears, circuit breakers,
     contactors, SMART cameras for healthcare applications, portable,
     solar-powered X-ray machines, circular pelletizing technology for
     metals, etc.

209. For a discussion on the relevance of India as a market for global
     MNCs, and the importance of internal culture and mindsets
     regarding leveraging India's opportunity, see Ravi Venkatesan,
     Conquering the Chaos (Boston: Harvard Business Review Press,
     2013).

210. For a good discussion on frugal and reverse innovation, see, for
     example, Navi Radjou and Jaideep Prabhu, *Frugal Innovation—
     How to Do More with Less* (London: Profile Books, 2015); Vijay

Govindarajan and Chris Trimble, *Reverse Innovation: Create Far from Home, Win Everywhere* (Boston: Harvard Business Review Press, 2012).

211. *Live Mint*, 'IBM India Profit Falls, Tax Woes Continue', 6 January 2014, http://www.livemint.com/Industry/vQz7Rmn6ow3nTNIXi4DIRP/ IBMIndiaprofitfallstaxwoescontinue.html?facet=print; IBM, 2014, *IBM Annual Report* (Armonk, NY: IBM, 2014), https://www.ibm. com/annualreport/2014/bin/assets/IBM-Annual-Report-2014.pdf.

212. *Business Standard*, 'Indian Software Market Logs Highest 8.3% Growth among BRICS', 30 May 2015, www.businessstandard. com/article/printerfriendlyversion?article_id=115052201485_1.

213. Zinnov Consulting, 'The Indian Promise', 2014, http://zinnov. com/the-indian-promise/.

214. Zinnov Consulting, 'Compensation and Benefits Study 2012', 2012, http://www.zinnov.com/pdfFiles/1338818671orv_Results. pdf.

215. Bernhard Dachs, Franziska Kampik, Thomas Scherngell, Georg Zahradnik, Doris Hanzl-Weiss, Gabor Hunya, Neil Foster, Sandra Leitner, Robert Stehrer and Waltraut, *Urban Internationalisation of Business Investments in R&D* (Luxembourg: Publications Office of the European Union, 2012, p. 31. See https://ec.europa.eu/ research/innovation-union/pdf/internationalisation_business-rd_final-report.pdf.

216. Ibid., p. 40.

217. Zinnov Consulting, 'Operations Cost Benchmarking Study', 2012, http://www.slideshare.net/zinnov/operational-costs-benchmarking-study-2012.

218. This chapter is primarily based on a discussion with the RBEI management team by Wilfried Aulbur in Bengaluru in August 2015.

219. Bosch is the world's largest supplier of cutting-edge automotive technology.

220. The company is the world's largest manufacturer of large gearboxes, drive and control, packaging and progress technology.

221. Bosch is a leading manufacturer of building security and thermo-technology.

222. Bosch is the world's largest power tool manufacturer and leading in the field of household appliances.

223. CMMi or capability maturity model integration level five refers to the highest level of maturity in Carnegie Mellon University's process improvement training and appraisal program. ASPICE is an automotive-specific assessment to gauge both organizational maturity and process capability. A maturity level of three indicates that the organization has established processes.

224. Diabetic retinopathy causes progressive damage to the retina in people with diabetes. American Optometric Association, 'Diabetic Retinopathy', n.d., http://www.aoa.org/patients-and-public/eye-and-vision-problems/glossary-of-eye-and-vision-conditions/diabetic-retinopathy?sso=y.

225. NASSCOM, 'Startup India—Momentous Rise of the Indian Startup Ecosystem', 2015, http://www.nasscom.in/startup-india-%E2%80%93-momentous-rise-indian-startup-ecosystem.

226. Ibid.

227. *Business Standard*, 'Flipkart Confirms Valuation at $15.2 Billion', 24 September 2015, http://www.business-standard.com/article/companies/flipkart-confirms-valuation-at-15-2-billion-115092301144_1.html.

228. *Wall Street Journal*, 'The Billion Dollar Startup Club', March 2016, http://graphics.wsj.com/billion-dollar-club/.

229. Ibid.

230. NASSCOM, 'Startup India'.

231. Updated number of augmented reality and hardware start-ups not provided in the 2015 NASSCOM report.

232. Ibid.

233. Sreeradha Basu, Vinod Mahanta and Madhav Chanchani, 'McKinsey Loses More Than 40 Consultant to Start-Ups, Including 14 of India's Top Team in the Past 18 Months', *Economic Times*, 29 July 2015, http://tech.economictimes.indiatimes.com/news/startups/mckinsey-consultants-indian-startups/48260987.

234. Angel investors are typically high-net-worth individuals who provide seed capital to nascent companies or start-ups in exchange for equity. Venture capital firms provide funding to early-stage growth companies, post the seed stage, in exchange for equity. Typically, this is the first round of institutional funding for a new company, commonly referred to as series A. Private equity is an umbrella term for capital that is not listed on a public exchange; in this context, it is typically provided to firms post the venture capital stage (although PEs can also invest in earlier stages), for an investment horizon of four to seven years.

235. National capital region, or NCR, refers to an inter-state planning and development area, which covers the national capital territory of Delhi, Haryana, Uttar Pradesh and Rajasthan.

236. Statista, 'Countries with the Highest Number of Internet Users as of January 2016', 2016, http://www.statista.com/statistics/262966/number-of-internet-users-in-selected-countries/.

237. Internet and Mobile Association of India (20TK), 'Bharat@Digital.com: Creating a $200 Billion Internet Economy', September 2015, http://company.mig.me/wp-content/uploads/2015/09/bcg-report-on-Indian-internet.pdf.

238. Ibid., p. 4.

239. Ibid., p. 12.

240. Ibid., p. 14.

241. Market estimates for the e-tailing industry range from USD 2.3 billion to USD 4.5 billion. *Technopak*, 'E-Tailing in India @Inflection Point', July 2014, http://retail.economictimes. indiatimes.com/web/files/retail_files/reports/data_file-E-tailing-in-India-1427960066.pdf.

242. Horizontal e-commerce players are those that act as a one-stop shop for customers and offer products across a wide range of categories. Examples include Amazon, Flipkart, and Snapdeal.

243. Vertical e-commerce players are those that specialize in one or a narrow set of product categories. Examples of these include fashion retailers like Jabong, jewellery e-tailers such as BlueStone, and other specialists such as LensKart and Pepperfry.

244. GMV is akin to gross revenue for an e-commerce player, i.e., the sales price charged to the customer multiplied by the number of items sold.

245. *Mint*, 'Amazon's JV Cloudtail Is Its Biggest Seller in India', 29 October 2015, http://www.livemint.com/Companies/ RjEDJkA3QyBSTsMDdaXbCN/Amazons-JV-Cloudtail-is-its-biggest-seller-in-India.html.

246. Literally translated as 'artisan's door', the programme connects artisans in rural areas to the online platform to enable better sales and price realizations. Flipkart signed, among others, an MoU with the ministry of textiles on 25 August 2014 to provide this service to weavers in villages, http://www. jagranjosh.com/current-affairs/textiles-ministry-signed-mou-with-flipkart-to-provide-marketing-platform-to-handloom-weavers-1409033306-1.

247. NASSCOM, 'Tech Start-Ups in India: A Bright Future', 2014, http://www.nasscom.in/tech-startups-india-bright-future.

248. *The Hindu*, 'Oxygen from Silicon Valley', 3 October 2015, http:// www.thehindu.com/sunday-anchor/oxygen-from-silicon-valley-for-startups-in-india/article7720729.ece.

249. SEBI, n.d., 'Discussion Paper on Alternate Capital Raising Platform and Review of Other Regulatory Requirements', http://www.sebi.gov.in/cms/sebi_data/attachdocs/1427713523817.pdf.

250. Ibid. Pre-issue share capital is paid up share capital prior to an initial public offering (IPO).

251. Minimum holding period for company shares for large shareholders after an IPO.

252. *Business Today,* 'Clearing the Decks', 19 July 2015, http://www.businesstoday.in/magazine/markets/stocks/sebi-eases-norms-for-new-age-start-ups-but-bottlenecks-remain/story/221095.html.

253. *Live Mint*, 'iSpirt Seeks Friendly Tax, Regulatory Regime for Software Product Start-Up', February 2015, http://www.livemint.com/Companies/iUDq0wjJmiXneJ1KYVq0MJ/seeks-friendly-tax-regulatory-regime-for-software-pr.html.

254. *Business Standard*, 'Start-Ups Hope "Angel Tax" Will Go', February 2015, http://www.business-standard.com/article/economy-policy/start-ups-hope-angel-tax-will-go-115022800038_1.html.

255. For companies with large assets, such as patents, land, plant, and machinery, liquidator charges can be significant, as high as INR 400,000. See, e.g., *Economic Times*, 'Why Failed Entrepreneurs Can't Legally Close Start-Ups and Start Afresh', March 2014, http://articles.economictimes.indiatimes.com/2014-03-14/news/48222455_1_new-co.

256. Ibid.

257. *Times of India*, 'Eased Companies Act to Help Start-Ups Take Private Company Route', 24 June 2015, http://timesofindia.indiatimes.com/business/india-business/Eased-Companies-Act-to-help-startups-take-private-company-route/articleshow/47793424.cms.

258. *Startup India*, 'Action Plan', 16 January 2016, http://www.pradhanmantriyojana.in/wp-content/uploads/2016/01/StartupIndia_ActionPlan_16January2016.pdf.

259. *Economic Times*, 'Digital India: 15 Salient Things to Know About PM Narendra Modi's Project', 1 July 2015, http://articles. economictimes.indiatimes.com/2015-07-01/news/64004371_1_ digital-india-programme-swachh-bharat-mission-knowledge-economy.

260. These initiatives are the National Skill Development Mission, the National Policy for Skill Development and Entrepreneurship 2015, the Pradhan Mantri Kaushal Vikas Yojana and the Skill Loan Scheme. See, e.g., *Economic Times*, 'Government to Train 40 Crore People under Skill India Initiative', 15 July 2015, http://articles. economictimes.indiatimes.com/2015-07-15/news/64449992_1_ skill-india-prime-minister-narendra-modi-skill-training.

261. The observations in this chapter are based on Prof. Amit Kapoor, Sandeep Goyal and M.P. Jaiswal, 'redBus: The Next Step for Growth', *Harvard Business Publishing*, 15 May 2013, https:// cb.hbsp.harvard.edu/cbmp/product/W13193-PDF-ENG.

262. RTCs such as the Karnataka State Road Transportation Corporation (KSRTC) are large companies. KSRTC, for example, runs a fleet of 7902 buses covering the whole of Karnataka and states such as Maharashtra, Andhra Pradesh, Telangana, Tamil Nadu, Puducherry, Goa and Kerala. Revenue turnover of KSRTC in FY13 amounted to INR 2592.33 crore, profits are at INR 174.2 lakh, and fares for a 10-km journey in Bangalore are as low as INR 7. KSRTC Annual Administration Report 2012–13.

263. Private bus operators have fleet sizes varying from a few to a few hundred buses, e.g., Sharma in South India runs at least 150 buses and Neeta Travels in Mumbai owns a fleet of more than 250 buses.

264. *Financial Express*, 'redBus Looks East, Starts Services in Singapore, Malaysia', 28 July 2015, http://www.financialexpress. com/industry/companies/redbus-looks-east-starts-services-in-singapore-malaysia/109050/.

265. N. Viswanathan, R. Gangal and W.G. Aulbur, 'India & Corporate Incubation: A Practitioner's Perspective & Recommendations', Indian Institute of Corporate Affairs, May 2015, http://iica.in/images/Whitepaper_Corporate%20Incubation%20in%20India.pdf.

266. Aquihiring refers to the process of buying a company to recruit its employees without potentially being interested in the company's products and services. See Wikipedia, https://en.wikipedia.org/wiki/Acqui-hiring.

267. Intra-preneurial means being allowed and able to act as an entrepreneur despite working in a larger corporate.

268. Self-help groups can centre on several topics, e.g., finance, health, education, business.

269. Panchayats are India's statutory institutions of local self-government, https://en.wikipedia.org/wiki/Sarpanch.

270. These are incubators within a corporate that incubate internal ideas via small teams with the intention of value creation.

271. B. Becker and O. Gassmann, 'Corporate Incubators: Industrial R&D and What Universities Can Learn from Them', *Journal of Technology Transfer* 31, no. 4 (2006): 469–83, http://link.springer.com/article/10.1007%2Fs10961-006-0008-6#/page-1.

272. Based on primary interview with Lalit Ahuja, Founder, ANSR and Kyron, in April 2015, Bangalore.

273. *DealCurry*, 'Accel Partners Leads Investment in ANSR Consulting', June 2015, http://www.dealcurry.com/20150610-Accel-Partners-Leads-Investment-In-ANSR-Consulting.htm; *VC Circle*, 'Infosys to Invest in the Firm behind Start-Up Accelerator Kyron', July 2015, http://techcircle.vccircle.com/2015/07/21/infosys-to-invest-in-the-firm-behind-startup-accelerator-kyron/.

274. Hermann Simon, *Hidden Champions* (Boston: Harvard Business School Press, 1996); Hermann Simon, *Hidden Champions of the 21ˢᵗ Century* (London: Springer Verlag, 2009).

275. Porter, 'What Is Strategy?'.

276. Joan Margretta, *Understanding Michael Porter* (Boston: Harvard Business Review Press, 2012).

277. Lafley and Martin, *Playing to Win*.

278. Tarun Khanna and Krishna G. Palepu, *Winning in Emerging Markets* (Boston: Harvard Business Press, 2010).

279. Ibid.

280. Roland Berger *Two-Wheeler Market in India*, October 2014, available from Wilfried Aulbur, wilfried.aulbur@rolandberger.com.

281. ILO, *Economically Active Population, Estimates and Projections*, (sixth edition), October 2011, http://laborsta.ilo.org/applv8/data/EAPEP/eapep_E.html.

282. Colombia, Nigeria, Philippines, Sri Lanka, Bangladesh, Nepal, Argentina, UAE, Egypt, Mexico, Uganda, Kenya, Angola and Peru are lead export markets for motorcycles. Scooters are mainly exported to Sri Lanka, Egypt, Nepal, Angola, Mexico and Bangladesh.

283. DEPB stands for Duty Entitlement Pass Book, an export incentive scheme by the government of India, in effect from 1997 to 2011.

284. Bajaj investor meeting, December 2014.

285. Hero recently set up a CKD assembly plant in Kenya, CKD factories in Columbia and Bangladesh will go live in 2015 and the company plans to expand its Latin America footprint to Brazil and Argentina. Overall global presence will be expanded to fifty countries.

286. TVS focuses strongly on ASEAN countries via their subsidiary in Indonesia. Sixty-five per cent of the local Indonesian production is leveraged for exports to ASEAN and Latin America. Overall global presence of TVS stands at fifty-seven countries.

287. Company annual reports of TVS, Hero and Bajaj, FY11–FY15, corporate websites.

288. Total Productive Maintenance or TPM is a 'system of maintaining and improving the integrity of production and quality systems through the machines, equipment, processes, and employees that add business value to the organization', as quoted in Shahzad Ahmad and Shahwaz Syed, 'Implementation of Total Productive Maintenance in Thermal Power Station (Barauni Refinery)', *International Journal of Engineering Research* 1, no. 3 (2015): 1.

289. Overall equipment effectiveness or OEE 'provides a holistic view of asset utilization. It drives an organization to examine all aspects of asset performance in order to ensure that they are obtaining the maximum benefit from a piece of equipment that has been procured,' as quoted by the Kaizen Institute, 'OEE (Overall Equipment Effectiveness)', n.d., https://www.kaizen.com/knowledge-center/oee.html.

290. Right first time is a 'quality management concept which asserts that defect prevention is more advantageous and cost effective than defect detection and the resulting re-work', as quoted in BusinessDictionary.com.

291. Overall line efficiency measures the productivity of a product line involving machines in series. See, e.g., N. Anantharaman and R.M. Nachiappan, 'Evaluation of Overall Line Effectiveness (OLE) in a Continuous Product Line Manufacturing System', *Journal of Manufacturing Technology Management* 17 (2006): 987–1008.

292. Cathode electrode deposition or CED coatings are paints that are applied using an electrochemical reaction—this has become the widespread method of painting vehicles by leading manufacturers, since it prevents corrosion, provides coatings of a uniform thickness and is more environmentally friendly than other methods.

293. Capacity will be increased to 150,000 or more a month to meet demand for the RS200; see, e.g., *Hindustan Times,* 'Bajaj Auto Scaling Up Chakan Plant Capacity to Meet RS200 Demand', 6 August 2015, http://www.hindustantimes.com/autos/bajaj-

auto-scaling-up-chakan-plant-capacity-to-meet-rs200-demand/
story-cviihY61lPVSoBkzfZedUJ.html.

294. For example, for domestic and international travel, all line engineers fly rather than use buses.

295. Japanese OEMs and suppliers are often locked into a keiretsu, a set of companies with interlocking shareholdings and business relations.

296. Today, Bajaj's R&D department counts about 1300 engineers with access to world-class facilities.

297. *The Hindu*, '5 Indian Firms among Forbes Most Innovative Companies', 21 August 2014, http://www.thehindu.com/business/ Industry/5-indian-firms-among-forbes-most-innovative-companies/article6337573.ece.

298. Bajaj Auto investor meeting, December 2014.

299. Ibid

300. A 3S facility is an automotive dealer outlet which provides sales, service and spare parts on the same premises.

301. *Economic Times*, 'Is Bajaj Bringing 'Chetak' Back?' March 2015, http://auto.economictimes.indiatimes.com/news/two-wheelers/ scooters-mopeds/is-bajaj-bringing-chetak-back/46431863.

302. *The Economist Intelligence Unit, EIU Healthcare Report India,* Q3 (2015), p. 4, http://www.eiu.com/industry/healthcare/asia/ india.

303. Netscribes, *Netscribes Sector Report: Hospital Market in India (Part I)*, February 2014, p. 8, http://www.marketresearch.com/ Netscribes-India-Pvt-Ltd-v3676/Hospital-India-8085252/

304. *EIU Healthcare Report India*, Q3 (2015), p. 4. http://www.eiu.com/ industry/healthcare/asia/india.

305. Other relevant current trends in the Indian healthcare market are the re-emergence of traditional medical care, estimated to be an INR 116 billion market in FY15 and poised to grow at 22 per cent

CAGR till FY18. See e.g., Ken Research, 'India Alternative Medicine and Herbal Products Market Outlook to 2018', November 2014, p. 29, https://www.kenresearch.com/healthcare/skin-and-personal-care-industry/india-alternative-medicine-herbal-market-research-research-report/592-91.html. The government drives the development of a traditional knowledge digital library to prevent companies from claiming patents on such remedies. The Traditional Knowledge Digital Library is a collaborative project between CSIR (Council for Scientific and Industrial Research) and Department of AYUSH. http://www.tkdl. res.in/tkdl/langdefault/common/Abouttkdl.asp?GL=Eng. Additional trends are the emergence of telemedicine in an effort to spread availability of high-quality care around the country, portability of medical records (e.g., driven by websites such as Practo and Healthkart), insurance profiling based on big data to improve the affordability of healthcare premiums by leveraging user behaviour data from several sources, and the emergence of medical tourism. In the latter case, India reported about 2,64,000 medical tourists in 2013 arriving from Africa (17 per cent), Bangladesh (15 per cent), Iraq (10 per cent), Western Europe (6 per cent), Eastern Europe (5 per cent), Pakistan (4 per cent) and others. See e.g., BMI Research, Asia Pacific Pharma & Healthcare, Insight, September 2015, p. 8, http://store.bmiresearch. com/asia-pacific-pharma-healthcare-insight.html. With a projected volume of USD 6 billion by 2018, growth in this particular sector will continue to be driven by cost differentials as, for example, a heart bypass surgery costs USD 5200 in India versus USD 15,121 in Thailand and USD 11,430 in Indonesia. Compared to the US, the surgery can be performed competently at 3 per cent of the overall cost. Refer to JCI (Joint Commission International), a body that certifies that healthcare providers operate at international standards. Twenty-five organizations in India, including Fortis Escorts Heart Institute and Narayana Hrudayalaya, are accredited. JCI, 'JCI-Accredited

Organizations', http://www.jointcommissioninternational.org/about-jci/jci-accredited-organizations/?c=India.

306. International Diabetes Federation, *Diabetes Atlas 2014, sixth edition*, http://www.idf.org/sites/default/files/6th-Edition-Estimates_ Update_2014.xls.

307. Ibid.

308. Wellness, 'Riding the Growth Wave', Third Annual Wellness Conference, 2011, p. 15, https://www.pwc.in/en_IN/in/assets/ pdfs/publications-2011/wellness-report-15-sept.pdf.

309. World Health Organization, 'Global Health Expenditure Database', 2013, http://apps.who.int/nha/database.

310. Government bed density estimates from Central Bureau of Health Intelligence India, Health Infrastructure, 'National Health Profile 2013', http://www.cbhidghs.nic.in/index1.asp?linkid=267. Private sector bed density estimated assuming 60.8 per cent beds in private sector. Planning Commission of India, *Report of High Level Expert Group on Universal Health Coverage for India,* p. 199, http:// planningcommission.nic.in/reports/genrep/rep_uhc0812.pdf.

311. World Health Organization, *World Health Statistics 2014,* 2014, p. 138, http://apps.who.int/iris/bitstream/10665/11278/1/ 9789240692671_eng.pdf.

312. Government and private hospital beds together.

313. Forecast for 2018–19 based on addition of 6.5 lakh beds, from Dun & Bradstreet, 'India Hospitals Industry Outlook', June 2015, p. 20.

314. Forecast for 2024–25 based on addition of 17.5 lakh beds, from FICCI Knowledge Paper, 'Sectoral Investment Landscape across India: An Overview', January 2014, p. 9, http://www.ficci.com/ spdocument/20362/Knowledge-Paper-Book.pdf.

315. The term allopathic doctors is used by homeopathic practitioners to describe mainstream medicine.

316. Central Bureau of Health Intelligence India, *Human Resources in Health Sector, National Health Profile*, 2013, pp. 171–81. http://www.cbhidghs.nic.in/index1.asp?linkid=267.

317. World Health Organization, *World Health Statistics 2014*, p. 138, http://apps.who.int/iris/bitstream/10665/112738/1/9789240692671_eng.pdf.

318. World Health Organization, *Global Health Expenditure Database*, 2013, http://apps.who.int/nha/database.

319. NSS 71st Round, *Key Indicators of Social Consumption: Health*, January–June 2014, p. 21, http://aiihph.gov.in/archives/1100.

320. Central Bureau of Health Intelligence India, *Health Infrastructure, National Health Profile 2013*, p. 207, http://www.cbhidghs.nic.in/index1.asp?linkid=267.

321. Indranil Mukhopadhyay, Sakthivel Selvaraj, Sandeep Sharma and Pritam Datta, 'Changing Landscape of Private Health Care Providers in India: Implications for National Level Health Policy', International Conference on Public Policy, July 2015, p. 5, http://www.icpublicpolicy.org/conference/file/reponse/1435386832.pdf.

322. Central Bureau of Health Intelligence India, *Human Resources in Health Sector, National Health Profile 2013*, pp. 176–80, http://www.cbhidghs.nic.in/index1.asp?linkid=267. Rural estimates for government doctors include doctors at primary healthcare centres (PHCs) and specialists at Community Health Centres (CHCs). Rural/urban split unavailable for private sector doctors.

323. World Health Organization, *Global Health Expenditure Database*, http://apps.who.int/nha/database.

324. E.g., a zero-tolerance policy versus kickbacks for staff, which are otherwise common in Indian hospitals.

325. 'Nephrology is a branch of internal medicine focused on kidney-related illness and diseases', as defined by the Division of Nephrology, Stanford University.

326. 'Laparoscopic surgeries are a type of minimally-invasive surgery which allows a surgeon to access the inside of the abdomen and pelvis without having to make large incisions in the skin', according to the National Health Service UK website.

327. Expansion of Vaatsalya follows both green-field and brown-field models. In the green-field strategy, Vaatsalya rents a place suitable for a hospital and refurbishes it, recruits the doctors and starts operating. In the brown-field model, it partners with an existing hospital and rebrands the hospital as a Vaatsalya Hospital. Overall, the company has built seventeen hospitals across Karnataka and Andhra Pradesh with a cumulative capacity of 1350 beds since 2004, according to Dr Naik. Outreach in FY12 was 460,000 patients per year with a target of 1 million patients per year by FY14. The company treats 3500 in-patients and 35,000 outpatients per month. Turnover was INR 582 million in FY14.

328. See, for example, Confederation of Indian Industry, 'Indian Insurance Sector: In Pursuit of Value', July 2015, http://www.cii.in/ PublicationDetail.aspx?enc=BA05A6VlHsxGBXQ2V 3aalERNwdiuhO/YV3pZHiQvVmR8o33svKYutGIZIoK3DU AKt/gP/NfKE0l0LjYeSlC9E9flXotmteD0zrQEDwSjQLfj0Jm06zA 6yAlTRphX3/l5gwajfEVEtcRYk7Of1NNE0w3/IyH66/ eLrZ0YZ4ZkyL/MCOZdLv+GtVGPS66OiX5y4cGA9DE6WQL3 FYtiDxrSIUUO2+xQvtVL9vkC4NXzCy4   tYP9BrMPBaHx5C 9Sn3h0oj3vBZy/k1X/dZF7G4onP9Q1xYctvl/kRVVZVxUnUz3 hpvix+1TRfY65nwzc4tGrZn+NwTkSVUZH4tCdUV+ e8WhN6SD7xS73VFTi3Jimfh5o9BM6b8JdJpWkThBAXCYfE vGvK7FOdIOQkSR0reuqk3z7/7HEENIXp03d/BSFqG+ g2QEqnF3pOjdAX6OPYukRy.

329. Reasons for establishing LIC were driven by the desire to support nation-building as well as by the need to control malpractice and unethical conduct by private life-insurers.

330. Total value of 'life fund' managed by life insurers in India is about INR 12.9 trillion as of March 2014 (*IRDA Annual Report, FY14*) compared to India's GDP of INR 57.4 trillion in FY14 (*RBI Handbook of Statistics,* FY14).

331. CAGR of GDP at factor cost, constant 2004–05 prices, between FY00 and FY04.

332. IRDA, *annual report, FY14,* https://www.irdai.gov.in/ADMINCMS/ cms/frmGeneral_NoYearList.aspx?DF=AR&mid=11.1.

333. Planning Commission, 'Annual Consumer Price Index and Wholesale Price Index Inflation Rate during 1999–2013', 8 July 2014, https://data.gov.in/community/annual-consumer-price-index-and-wholesale-price-index-inflation-rate-during-1999-2013/.

334. RBI, 'GDP at Factor Cost (Base Year: 2004–05)', in *RBI Handbook of Statistics,* 15 September 2014, https://www.rbi.org.in/scripts/ PublicationsView.aspx?id=15791.

335. BSE Sensex closing data, http://www.bseindia.com/sensexview/ indexview_new.aspx?index_Code=16&iname=BSE30.

336. A unit-linked insurance plan is a combination of insurance and investment with differences between plans arising from investment objectives, risk appetite, investment horizon, etc.

337. IRDA, *Annual Report FY14,* https://www.irda.gov.in/ADMINCMS/ cms/frmGeneral_NoYearList.aspx?DF=AR&mid=11.1.

338. This is a typical key performance indicator measuring the efficiency of insurance companies. The higher the percentage, the less efficient the company.

339. *IRDA, various annual reports, https://www.irda.gov.in/ADMINCMS/ cms/frmGeneral_NoYearList.aspx?DF=AR&mid=11.1.*

340. IRDA, *Handbook on Indian Insurance Statistics 2011–12,* https:// www.irda.gov.in/ADMINCMS/cms/frmGeneral_NoYearList. aspx?DF=AR&mid=11.1.

341. IRDA, *Annual Report FY14*, https://www.irda.gov.in/ADMINCMS/ cms/frmGeneral_NoYearList.aspx?DF=AR&mid=11.1. RBI, Annual Reports, https://www.rbi.org.in/scripts/ AnnualReportPublications.aspx.

342. IRDA, *Annual Report FY14*, https://www.irda.gov.in/ADMINCMS/ cms/frmGeneral_NoYearList.aspx?DF=AR&mid=11.1.

343. Ibid.

344. ICICI Prudential Investor Presentation, November 2015, http:// www.icicibank.com/managed-assets/docs/investor/quarterly-financial-results/2016/investor-presentation-on-ICICI-Prudential-Life-H1-2016-results.pdf.

345. Bancassurance is an arrangement in which a bank and an insurance company form a partnership so that the insurance company can sell its insurance products to the bank's client base. The bank benefits from the additional revenue stream and the insurance company is able to expand its customer base without needing to expand its sales force or pay additional commission to its insurance brokers or agents. Definition from Investopedia.com.

346. IRDA, *Annual Report FY14*, https://www.irda.gov.in/ADMINCMS/ cms/frmGeneral_NoYearList.aspx?DF=AR&mid=11.1.

347. Ibid.

348. Such as the increase in the guaranteed surrender values for traditional endowments, premium payment term linked commissions and constraints on the nature and amount of reinsurance.

349. The numbers in this paragraph are based on HDFC management discussions from August 2015 with Wilfried Aulbur.

350. Many of the comments in this chapter are taken from discussions with the management team of HDFC in August 2015.

351. See, e.g., HDFC Life company website at http://www.hdfclife.com/ about-us.

352. HDFC Life's point-of-sale (POS) application, named Click2Buy, has been an important tool for the company, because it has allowed

it to automate and integrate its business processes. The application is based on two principles: 'first time right' and 'straight-through processing', which allows for a much faster, more hassle-free, and 24/7 selling platform. See India CIO Review, 'POS Has Provided HDFC Life with a 24/7 Selling Platform', October 2013, http://www.indiacioreview.com/interviews/pos-has-provided-hdfc-life-24x7-selling-platform.

353. 3-click refers to a simpler, quicker, hassle-free process of purchasing life insurance products from HDFC Life with merely three clicks.

354. MyMix is HDFC Life Insurance's internal strategic tool which matches customer risk profiles and needs to its product offerings, according to executive director and chief financial officer of HDFC Life, Vibha Padalkar, 'Our Mantra with Click@Invest Is to Sell Online, Deliver Online, Service Online', *India Infoline*, 14 September 2014, http://www.indiainfoline.com/article/news-top-story/vibha-padalkar-executive-director-and-chief-financial-officer-hdfc-life-114091600158_1.html.

355. A failure modes and effects analysis (FMEA) identifies all possible failures in a product or service in a systematic manner.

356. A participating plan typically refers to specific life insurance policies which also act as savings plans, in which bonuses are 'declared at the discretion of the insurer', according to *Mint*, 'De-Jargoned—Participating and Non-Participating Plan', February 2012, http://www.livemint.com/Money/BLsfJVdfl2YfF8vfgUknrM/DeJargoned--Participating-and-nonparticipating-plan.html.

357. Non-participating plans are also specific life insurance policies-cum-savings-plans; however, 'the bonuses or benefits of the policy are clearly defined', according to *Mint*, 'De-Jargoned—Participating and Non-Participating Plan', February 2012, http://www.livemint.com/Money/BLsfJVdfl2YfF8vfgUknrM/DeJargoned--Participating-and-nonparticipating-plan.html.

358. Thirteenth month persistency is an insurance industry term which indicates the ratio of policies on which premium is paid for the second year. Most insurance policies are eligible for renewal one year after their start—typically, an additional thirty days of grace period is provided by insurers to renew their policy, according to Financial Chronicle (MyDigitalFC), 'Life Insurance Persistency Good in First Year, Not in the Long Term', 9 January 2013, http://www.mydigitalfc.com/news/life-insurance-persistency-good-first-year-not-long-term-665.

359. *Chicago Tribune*, 'Show Bismarck in a New Light', 2 December 1900, http://archives.chicagotribune.com/1900/12/02/page/3/article/show-bismarck-in-a-new-light.

360. Joel Kurtzman, *Common Purpose: How Great Leaders Get Organizations to Achieve the Extraordinary* (San Francisco, CA: Jossey-Bass, 2010).

361. Quite different from what was expected from Prussian officials in the nineteenth century.

362. A good reference regarding human motivation is the book by holocaust survivor Viktor E. Frankl, *Man's Search for Meaning* (Cutchogue, NY: Buccaneer Books, 1992).

363. *Economic Times*, 'Meet Vistara Chief Phee Teik Yeoh, the Man Who Gives Wings to Tata–SIA Joint Venture', 5 January 2015, http://articles.economictimes.indiatimes.com/2015-01-05/news/57705256_1_singapore-airlines-indian-airlines-airline-ceos.

364. *Financial Express*, 'New Airline Vistara Plans to Add International Routes, Expand Fleet Size: CEO Phee Teik Yeoh', 31 March 2015, http://www.financialexpress.com/article/companies/new-airline-vistara-plans-to-expand-into-international-routes/59069/.

365. *Zee News*, 'Vistara Is Our New Year Gift to India: CEO Phee Teik Yeoh', 22 December 2014, http://zeenews.india.com/business/

news/companies/vistara-is-our-new-year-gift-to-india-ceo-phee-teik-yeoh_114781.html.

366. Anjan Ghosh, 'Indian Aviation Industry', *ICRA Limited*, 1 March 2012, p. 2, http://www.icra.in/Files/ticker/Indian%20Aviation%20 Industry%20%28NEW%29.pdf.

367. Rishikesha T. Krishnan, *The Indian Airline Industry in 2008* (Bangalore: Indian Institute of Management, 2008), p. 2, http:// www.iimb.ernet.in/~rishi/Indian%20Airline%20Industry%20 in%202008%20v2.0.pdf.

368. Ibid.

369. *Business India*, 'Fighting the Aliens', 20 June–3 July issue, 1994, p. 82.

370. Rishikesha T. Krishnan, *The Indian Airline Industry in 2008* , p. 3.

371. Ibid.

372. Ibid.

373. Jesu Arasu, *Globalization and Infrastructural Development in India* (New Delhi: Atlantic Publishers and Distributors, 2008), p. 271.

374. *Business India*, 'Flying into the Storm', 19 June–2 July issue, 1995, p. 70.

375. Anjan Ghosh, 'Indian Aviation Industry'.

376. *Business India*, 'Flying into the Storm', p. 2.

377. Rishikesha T. Krishnan, 'The Indian Airline Industry in 2008', p. 5.

378. Make in India website, 'Aviation—Reasons to Invest', http:// makeinindia.com/sector/aviation/.

379. Wolfgang Prock-Schauer, *'Full Service Carriers: Adapting to the Environment'*, CAPA Conference, September 2006, http:// www.jetairways.com/EN/IN/Uploads/InvestorRelations/ CAPApresentation_Sept06_Mumbai.pdf.

380. Available Seat Kilometre = One seat (empty or filled) flying one kilometre.

381. Revenue Passenger Kilometre = A paying passenger flying one kilometre.

382. *Reuters*, 'Small City Routes Hold Big Potential for Indian Airlines', 6 October 2014, http://in.reuters.com/article/india-airlines-regions-idINKCN0HV04120141006.

383. Make in India website, 'Aviation—Reasons to Invest'.

384. Ibid.

385. *Economic Times*, 'Big Airlines Seek Entry Barriers against Low-Cost Rivals', 6 July 2005, http://articles.economictimes.indiatimes.com/2005-07-06/news/27501566_1_entry-barriers-spicejet-250-crore.

386. *Marketline*, 'Five Forces Analysis', via EMIS Intelligence Data Portal, 13 August 2012, p. 4.

387. Ibid., p. 5.

388. *Financial Express*, 'Petrol Prices Cut by 49p/Litre, Diesel by Rs 1.21, but LPG Cylinder Rates Hiked by Rs 11', 1 April 2015, http://www.financialexpress.com/article/economy/petrol-prices-cut-by-49-paise-diesel-by-rs-1-21/59382/.

389. Aditya Ghosh, CEO, IndiGo, Porter Prize Interview with Amit Kapoor, August 2014.

390. Popular long-distance travel includes Delhi to Chennai, which can be covered in 2 hours 35 minutes to 2 hours 45 minutes. Schedules retrieved from IndiGo and Jet Airways websites (April 2015).

391. Aditya Ghosh, CEO, IndiGo, Porter Prize Interview with Amit Kapoor, August 2014.

392. MRO refers to maintenance, repair and overhaul, the costs of the services related to assuring an aircraft's safety and airworthiness. Airlines spend between 10 and 15 per cent of their revenues on these costs, according to the Centre for Aviation, 'MRO - Maintenance, Repair & Overhaul', n.d., http://centreforaviation.com/profiles/hot-issues/mro---maintenance-repair--overhaul.

393. *Economic Times*, 'The Secret of IndiGo's Consistent Profits', 22 December 2013, http://articles.economictimes.indiatimes. com/2013-12-22/news/45475783_1_aditya-ghosh-indi-go-interglobe-aviation.

394. Aditya Ghosh, CEO, IndiGo, Porter Prize Interview with Amit Kapoor, August 2014.

395. TripAdvisor, India Air Travel Survey, 2014, https://www.news-pr. in/results-out-for-tripadvisors-annual-india-air-travel-survey-2014-indigo-outshines-other-carriers-to-emerge-as-indias-favourite-domestic-airline.html.

396. Aditya Ghosh, CEO, IndiGo, Porter Prize Interview with Amit Kapoor, August 2014.

397. Ibid.

398. *Business Standard*, 'A Tale of Two Airlines: Kingfisher Vs. IndiGo', 21 February 2012, http://www.business-standard. com/article/companies/a-tale-of-two-airlines-kingfisher-vs-indigo-112022100014_1.html.

399. As a consequence of the March 2011 Fukushima nuclear disaster in Japan, Germany decided to phase out nuclear power. The country shut eight of its seventeen reactors and intends to shut down the rest by the end of 2022 (https://en.wikipedia.org/wiki/Nuclear_power_phase-out). This decision has dramatic consequences on the energy mix (e.g., increased utilization of green energies), the distribution networks, energy cost, etc. It has impacts on energy-generating companies as well as on companies that depend heavily on energy for their production processes and requires a complete re-alignment of activity systems.

400. Ministry of Steel, Government of India, 'Highlights of the Ministry of Steel, FY15', http://steel.gov.in/One%20year%20highlights%20of%20the%20Ministry%20of%20Steel.pdf.

401. Press Information Bureau, Government of India, 'Minister of Steel & Mines Shri Narendra Singh Tomar Chairs Meeting of the Parliamentary Consultative Committee Attached to the Ministry of Steel and Mines', July 2015, http://pib.nic.in/newsite/PrintRelease.aspx?relid=123034.

402. *Times of India*, 'Steel Industry Facing Challenge from China, Government Should Sort Out Internal Challenges: Tata Steel', August 2015, http://timesofindia.indiatimes.com/business/india-business/Steel-industry-facing-challenge-from-China-govt-should-sort-out-internal-challenges-Tata-Steel/articleshow/48495179.cms.

403. Even after the bans were partly lifted in April 2014, iron ore production has been muted in light of caps on output and procedural delays. In FY15, domestic iron ore production stood at approximately 129 million metric tons and 12 million metric tons of iron ore, an all-time high, was imported to meet the domestic demand (exports of iron ore for the corresponding period stood at 7.3 million metric tons). See, e.g., *Business Standard*, 'India Likely to Remain Net Importer of Iron Ore in FY16', April 2015, http://www.business-standard.com/article/economy-policy/india-likely-to-remain-net-importer-of-iron-ore-in-fy16-115042300566_1.html.

404. *Business Standard*, 'Making in India Is Tough, Say Steel Manufacturers,' April 2015, http://www.business-standard.com/article/companies/making-in-india-is-tough-say-steel-manufacturers-115042400047_1.html.

405. Ibid.

406. *Mint*, 'A Troubled Time for India's Steel Industry', July 2015, http://www.livemint.com/Opinion/J17b2iGXgFGdkT0C0bkwgJ/A-troubled-time-for-Indias-steel-industry.html.

407. Ibid.

408. According to the *Business Standard* article, in November 2014, the US imposed anti-dumping duties of up to 100 per cent on Chinese

steel wires, and in February 2015, the EU imposed a 25.2 per cent duty on sheet, coil and strip from China. See *Business Standard*, 'Making in India Is Tough, Say Steel Manufacturers'.

409. Ibid.

410. During the period April to June 2015, China, South Korea and Japan collectively accounted for nearly 75 per cent of the 2.57 million metric tons finished steel imports into India. See, e.g., *Economic Times*, 'China, Korea, Japan Ship 75 Per Cent of India's Steel Q1 Imports', 3 August 2015, http://articles.economictimes. indiatimes.com/2015-08-03/news/65165421_1_steel-product-finished-steel-minister-narendra-singh-tomar.

411. In response to a report from the Directorate General of Safeguards, on 15 September 2015, the finance ministry announced the levy of 20 per cent safeguard duties on steel imports with immediate effect, which would continue for 200 days. This would extend to steel imports from all countries, including S. Korea and Japan, and make the landed price of hot rolled coils from China INR 2000 more expensive than domestic coils, on a per metric ton basis, thereby providing, 'headroom to domestic steel producers to increase prices and volumes, provided Chinese players do not reduce prices further'. See, e.g., *Economic Times*, 'Centre Announces 20 Per Cent Safeguard Duty on Steel Imports,' 15 September 2015, http://articles.economictimes.indiatimes.com/2015-09-15/ news/66568488_1_steel-imports-specific-steel-products-hot-rolled-steel. Analysis as per India Ratings and Research (Ind-Ra).

412. *Reuters*, 'India Sets Floor Price for Steel Imports to Stem Flow from China', 5 February 2016, http://in.reuters.com/article/india-steel-import-price-idINKCN0VE1VF.

413. *The Hindu*, 'Government Imposes Minimum Import Price on 173 Steel Items', 7 February 2016, http://www.thehindu.com/business/ Industry/government-imposes-minimum-import-price-on-173-steel-items/article8203743.ece.

414. JSW Steel is India's largest private steel company. With 12.63 million tons per annum of crude steel production in FY15, the company commands a market share of 15 per cent, second only to the government-owned SAIL (13.91 million tons per annum, 16 per cent).

415. 55 per cent aluminium–zinc-alloy-coated sheet steel, which is licensed from BIEC International Inc. JSW Steel is the first licensee GALVALUME producer in India. See JSW Steel website http://www.jsw.in/shop/galvalume.

416. It reaches Indian consumers via its branded JSW Shoppe distributor outlets, JSW Explore service centres, and JSW Shoppe Connect retail outlets.

417. FY15 figures obtained from JSW Steel Annual Report, 2014–15, p. 8, http://www.jsw.in/sites/default/files/assets/industry/steel/IR/Financial%20Performance/Annual%20Reports%20_%20STEEL/JSW_Steel_Full_AR_2014-2015.pdf. FY03 figures obtained from JSW Steel Annual Report, 2003–04, p. 5, http://www.jsw.in/sites/default/files/assets/industry/steel/IR/Financial%20Performance/Annual%20Reports%20_%20STEEL/13732875612003-2004.pdf.

418. Fluxes are cleaning agents, typically limestone or dolomite, which purify iron ore by fusing or melting the impurities.

419. During the period between FY10 and FY15, domestic iron ore production fell by 40 per cent (simple growth rate).

420. Import–Export Data Bank, Department of Commerce, http://www.commerce.nic.in/eidb/.

421. The first part of the strategy entailed developing a grade-wise market inventory analysis for the short term as well as getting the Supreme Court's permission for restarting ore purchase from existing stocks. In addition, JSW identified lower-grade sources for the long term and worked towards reopening the mines. The second part of the strategy revolved around a beneficiation system redesign, solid waste utilization measures and optimization of

operations of agglomerates (pellet and sinter iron ore pellets are spheres of typically 6–16 mm, which are used as raw materials for blast furnaces. Sinter is a hard material, typically of iron ore and other materials which are prepared for smelting). Beneficiation is a process which removes gangue particles such as alumina and silica from iron ore to produce a higher grade product and a waste stream. Examples of these processes include froth floatation and gravity separation. Beyond these activities, the company established a new operating regime for iron-making operations and stabilized the new steel-making chemistry required for changed input conditions.

422. Michael E. Porter, 'What Is Strategy?'

423. Michael E. Porter and Mark R. Kramer, 'Creating Shared Value', *Harvard Business Review*, January–February 2011, pp. 3–17; C.K. Prahalad, 'Strategies for the Bottom of the Economic Pyramid: India as a Source of Innovation', *Reflections* 3, no. 4 (2002): 6–17; C.K. Prahalad, 'Bottom of the Pyramid as a Source of Breakthrough Innovations', *Journal of Product Innovation Management* 29, no. 2 (2012): 6–12; Stuart L. Hart and Mark B. Milstein, 'Creating Sustainable Value', *Academy of Management Executive* 17, no. 2 (2003): 56–69; Marc Pfitzer, Valerie Bockstette and Mike Stamp, 'Innovating for Shared Value', *Harvard Business Review*, September–October 2013, pp. 1–16; Lalitha Vaidyanathan and Melissa Scott, 'Creating Shared Value in India: The Future for Inclusive Growth, Corporate Social Responsibility: Practice, Theory and Challenges', *Vikalpa* 37, no. 2 (April–June 2012): 108–113.

424. For recent books on the subject, see, for example, Peter J. Williamson, Ravi Ramamurti, Afonso Fleury and Maria Tereza Leme Fleury, eds, *The Competitive Advantage of Emerging Market Multinationals* (New York: Cambridge University Press, 2013); Karl P. Sauvant, Jaya Prakash Pradhan, Ayesha Chatterjee and Brian Harley, eds, *The Rise of Indian Multinationals—Perspective*

of Indian Outward Foreign Direct Investment (New York: Palgrave MacMillan, 2010); Ravi Ramamurti and Jitendra V. Singh, eds, *Emerging Multinationals in Emerging Markets* (Cambridge, UK: Cambridge University Press, 2009).

425. Sauvant, Pradhan, Chatterjee and Harley, eds, *Indian Multinationals*, pp. 1–23.

426. South–south trade denotes trade between developing nations, mostly located in the southern hemisphere.

427. In the case of China, in as late as 2007, its inward FDI was five times its outward FDI. Ravi Ramamurti, 'Foreword' in Sauvant, Pradhan, Chatterjee and Harley, eds, *Indian Multinationals*, p. xxiv.

428. Joel Ruet, 'When a Great Industry Globalizes: Indian Conglomerates Pioneering New Trends in Industrial Globalization,' in Sauvant, Pradhan, Chatterjee and Harley, eds, *Indian Multinationals*, p. 83.

429. Sauvant, Pradhan, Chatterjee and Harley, eds, *Indian Multinationals*, p. 10.

430. Stockholm International Peace Research Institute (SIPRI), 'Military Expenditure Database', last updated 3 November 2015, http://www.sipri.org/research/armaments/milex/milex_database. (Figures are in USD million, constant prices 2011 and 2011 exchange rates).

431. *India Today*, 'Brief Analysis of 5 Key Sectors That Contributed to India's GDP in FY2013–14', February 2015, http://indiatoday.intoday.in/education/story/economic-survey-2013-14-the-analysis/1/421367.html.

432. SIPRI, 'Military Expenditure Database'.

433. Ibid.

434. Indian Federal Ministry of Finance, 'Union Budget of India, FY14–15', http://www.indiabudget.nic.in/ub2014-15/eb/stat02.pdf.

435. Data obtained from FY15 annual reports of the corresponding organizations and press articles. Data from Bharat Dynamics Limited is with respect to FY14, as FY15 data is not available.

436. 'IHS Aerospace, Defence and Security Database', Jane's Information Group and Roland Berger analysis.

437. Ibid.

438. *IFSEC Global India*, 'India's Homeland Security Market to Double by 2018', June 2011, http://www.ifsecglobal.com/indias-homeland-security-market-to-double-by-2018/. The USD 13 billion estimate was provided by then chairman of the Parliamentary Standing Committee on Home Affairs, Venkaiah Naidu. This does not include an additional expenditure of USD 2 billion on disaster management.

439. *IBN Live*, 'Technology Is Increasingly Driving India's Homeland Security Market', July 2014, http://www.ibnlive.com/blogs/india/saurav-jha/technology-is-increasingly-driving-indias-homeland-security-market-10879-748546.html.

440. Perimetric surveillance refers to the surveillance of pre-defined perimeters, e.g., a military base, the grounds of a factory, etc.

441. Most of the points about Bharat Forge's defence business are taken from a discussion with Rajinder Bhatia, CEO, Aerospace and Defence, Bharat Forge, in December 2015 by Wilfried Aulbur.

442. Bharat Forge, '54th Annual Report, FY15', http://bharatforge.com/investors/company-reports/annual-reports.html.

443. Bharat Forge, 'Bharat Forge Investors Presentation, June 2015', http://bharatforge.com/images/PDFs/BFL%20Investor%20Presentation-June%202015_Final.pdf.

444. Bharat Forge, 'Media Kit', http://bharatforge.com/images/PDFs/BABA%20KALYANI%20BRIEF%20PROFILE%20-%20LATEST%20SEPTEMBER%2020143.pdf.

445. Forging is an industrial process which involves shaping of metal by using localized compressive forces such as heating and hammering.

446. The company has maintained EBITDA margins of 29.8 per cent in FY15 and 31 per cent in H1 FY16. Bharat Forge, 'Bharat Forge

Investor Presentations, November 2015', http://bharatforge.
com/images/PDFs/BFL%20Investor%20Presentation%20
November%202015%20-%20Website.pdf and 'Bharat Forge
Investor Presentations, February 2016', http://bharatforge.com/
images/PDFs/BFL%20Investor%20Presentation%20February%20
2016%20-%20Website.pdf.

447. This refers to the block in breech-loading firearms that protects
the rear of the barrel against the force of the charge and prevents
gases from escaping.

448. ACMA is the apex body of automotive component companies
in India. For more information on the industry association, see
http://www.acma.in/docmgr/ACMA_Presentation/ACMA_
Presentation.pdf.

449. The Deming Prize is a global award for companies that have
successfully implemented total quality management.

450. See, e.g., ACMA International Procurement Office Forum, panel
discussion on 'Role of Tier 1 Suppliers in the Development of
Supplier Capabilities', New Delhi, 3 February 2016.

451. Most of the information in this paragraph stems from a discussion
with Chaand Sehgal, chairman, Motherson group, in December
2015 by Wilfried Aulbur.

452. Wiring harnesses are assemblies of cables in a vehicle that transmit
electromagnetic signals.

453. Peguform was a leading expert in plastic technologies in the
automotive industry that had gotten into difficulties. Products
include cockpits, door panels, bumper modules, etc. Motherson
bought the company from PE firm Cerebus and successfully
turned its operations around.

454. Return on capital employed is a financial ratio that measures the
return or profitability of a company vis-à-vis the capital that is
invested.

455. Ministry of Corporate Affairs, 'Notification on 27th February, 2014'. For a discussion of the law, see http://www.mca.gov.in/Ministry/pdf/CompaniesActNotification2_2014.pdf.

456. The information in this paragraph is taken from discussions with management during the Porter Prize application in September 2014 by Wilfried Aulbur and Amit Kapoor.

457. NHB, 'Report on Trend and Progress of Housing in India, 2014', p. 102, http://www.nhb.org.in/Publications/T&P_English_FINAL.pdf.

458. Ibid., p. 100.

459. Total outstanding loan amount for fiscal year 2015.

460. Housing finance companies are companies with the principal objective of lending for housing finance. They are regulated and supported by the NHB.

461. Scheduled banks are listed in the Second Schedule of the Reserve Bank of India Act and are usually private, foreign and nationalized banks operating in India.

462. Census of India, 'Percentage of Households to Total Households by Amenities and Assets', 2011, http://www.censusindia.gov.in/2011census/hlo/Houselisting-housing-PCA.html.

463. NHB, 'Report 2014', p. 100.

464. Goodreads, Quotable Quote, http://www.goodreads.com/quotes/812087-i-know-he-s-a-good-general-but-is-he-lucky.

INDEX

Abhyankar, Unmesh, 54, 56–57
academic institutions, agreements with corporations, 106
Accel Partners, 175
Accenture, 138
Adani group, 53, 56
Adani Ports and special economic Zone Ltd (APSEZL), 27, 49–50, 53–60, 66
Adani, Gautam, 54–56
Air Asia, 236
Air Corporation Act (1953), 233
Air Deccan, 235–36, 240, 248
Air India, 232–33, 236; and Indian Airlines merging of, 236
air taxi operators, 233
Airbus, 238, 242
airline industry, 17, 231–40, 243–48; frequent-flyer programme, 240
Amazon, 91, 155–56, 165

Amity University, 104
Angel investors, 377
ANSR Consulting, 174–75
Apollo tyres, 301
Aquihiring, 171, 381
Arnold, Jens M., 29
Association of Southeast Asian Nations (ASEAN), 32, 189, 200
automation, 56, 62, 77, 86, 153, 302; Sudipta on, 59
Automotive Component Manufacturers Association (ACMA), 30–31, 73, 276
automotive industry, 10, 39, 73, 77, 276–84

Bajaj Allianz, 217
Bajaj Auto, 184–202, 227, 261, 263, 301
Bajaj Automotive Vendor Association (BAVA), 190, 196

Bajaj, 186–87, 189–92, 194–96,
    198–202, 230, 245, 304, 306;
    Chetak, 189; discontinuing
    partnership with Vespa, 189;
    EBITDA of, 198; exports of,
    189; innovation awards for, 193;
    KTM partnership, 201; Rajiv,
    193, 263, 301; R&D of, 193, 201;
    TPM Excellence Award for, 191
Bancassurance, 221–22, 390
banking system, 14
Baxter, 91
BERD investments, 140
Berger, Roland, 73, 170
Bharat Electronics Limited, 269
Bharat Forge, 3, 267, 271–75,
    303–5
Bharat Nirman, 21, 36, 188, 291,
    352
Bharti, Rahul, 40, 45–46
Bhatia, Rajinder, 272, 275
Bhattacharya, Sudipta, 56
Bhushan Steel, 251
biomass power plants 129–34,
    see also Husk Power systems
Birlas, 184, 226, 264
Bismarck, Otto von, 229
Bloom, Nicholas, 68–70
Boeing, 106, 238
Bosch, 100, 106, 143–48, 150,
    193, 301; RBEI's innovation
    role for, 147
Boss application (bus operators
    software system), 163

bus operators, 162–66, 303–4
bus ticketing market, 163
business incubation, 168–74;
    external, 172; corporate
    incubation in India, 168,
    171–73; internal, 172; intra-
    company incubation, 171;
    stand-alone incubators, 169–70,
    173–75
business models, 66, 110, 130,
    149, 152, 163, 174–75, 181–82,
    215
Business to Business (B2B),
    67; industries, 75, 77–78,
    163–64
Business to consumer (B2C), 8,
    163–64

Capability Maturity Model
    Integration (CMMI), 376
Cathode electrode deposition
    (CED), 191, 383
Chamberlain, Arthur Neville,
    81
Chamberlain, Joseph, 81
China: GDP per capita of, 2,
    6; innovate policy of 11; jobs
    addition in, 86; manufacturing-
    led growth model of, 3
ChotuKool, by Godrej & Boyce,
    125–26, 129
Cloudtail, 156
compound annual growth rate
    (CAGR), 1, 3, 35, 50–53, 72,

114, 117, 185–87, 202, 225, 254

connectivity, 32, 90, 139; inter-city, 161; investments in rail and road, 55

consumers, 8, 18, 26, 38, 278, 300

corporate social responsibility (CSR), 285–86, 288

corruption, 15, 22–23, 33, 51, 271; at border, 32; in legal system, 14

country-specific advantages (CSAs), 99

customer-centric innovations, 24

customer-value-centric innovation, 302

Dalal, Praveen, 123

Damania Airways, as Skyline NEPC, 234

decentralization, 33, 90; disadvantage in, 33

Deep localization, 358

Defence Research and Development Organization (DRDO) 270–71

defence sector, 268–72; liberalization of, 270; GDP and, 268

deregulation, 88, 233

Deve, H.D., 19

Digital India, 160

domestic transportation, 32–33, *see also* road transport corporations (RTCs)

Dynamatics, 270

Earnings before interest, tax, depreciation and amortization (EBITDA,) 187, 358

eBay, 155

e-choupal, 358

eco-friendly: consumers, 137; production, 96

e-commerce: horizontal players, 378; vertical players, 378

economic: policies, 19–20; reforms, 2, 20

educational system, 102, 149

e-enable interactions, 365

EFD India, 27, 60–66, 179, 227, 302

EFD Induction, 60–65

Elbit Systems, 275, 298, 304

ELVA Induksjon, 60

emerging markets, 10, 26, 124, 132–33, 139, 200, 308–9

entrepreneurs, 79, 159

environment/forest clearances, 88

Faurecia, 105, 142

Fiat, 16, 38–39

Flipkart, 151, 155–56, 158, 224

foreign direct investment (FDI),
4–5, 17, 20, 23, 28, 88, 107
Foreign Investment Promotion
Board, 17
foreign investments, 10
Forest Rights Act, 21
Fourteenth Finance Commission,
23
Fritz Düsseldorf
Induktionswärmung, 60; facility
in Bangalore, 64
frugal engineering, 47, 77, 99,
133–35, 137, 139, 142, 180,
265
frugal innovation, 99, 107–14,
132, 134, 137, 149–50
frugal products, 108–10, 113, 128,
133–34

Gambhir, Vivek, 119
gasifier, 130–31
GCPL's approach, 115–17, 119,
122–24, 263
General Motors, 38
German: brands, 82;
investments, 5
Ghosh, Aditya, 239, 245
global delivery model, 138–39,
141–42
global expansion, 2, 58, 78, 140,
181, 226, 236, 297, *see also*
mergers and acquisitions
global financial crisis, 21, 89, 137,
200, 219

global giants, 100, 124, 134, 140–41
global greenhouse gas (GHG)
emissions, 86
global in-house centres (GICS),
142, 145–46, 174–75
global opportunities, 264–68
global quality certifications, 30
GoAir, 235
Godrej, 10, 95–96, 99, 114–25,
149, 227, 267; Good & Green
Initiative, 96
Godrej, Nisaba, 119
goods and services tax (GST), 24,
29, 88
Google BigQuery, 165
government-specific advantages
(GSAs), 99
green manufacturing, 94–97
gross merchandise value (GMV),
155–56
Gujral, Inder Kumar, 19

Haier, 133–34
Hartmann, Richard, 79
HDFC Life Insurance, 221–26,
228, 261, 305; point-of-sale
(POS) application of, 390–91
Head, David, 83
healthcare system, 114, 135, 137,
152, 154, 202–11, 213–15, 227, 230
Hero Honda, 190, 194
Hero MotoCorp, 186, 382
hidden champions, 61, 65–66, 78,
177–78, 181, 226–27, 263

Hindustan Aeronautics Limited, 106, 269

Hindustan Motors (Ambassador), 39

Hindustan Unilever Ltd (HUL), 8, 99, 114–15, 127–28, 149, 285–88, 298, 302, 309; Pureit, 127–28; 'Shakti Ammas' campaign by, 285–98; Shakti Maan' campaign by, 8, 286

Hiremath, Veerendra, 208–9, 213

Homeland Security (HLS), 270–71

hospitals, 202, 204, 207, 209–14, 230; hospitalization expenses, 206

Housing Development Finance Corporation (HDFC), 221

housing finance market, 289

'100 smart city' programme, 23

Hsieh, Chang-Tai, 35

Husk Power Systems (HPS), 100, 130–32

Hybrid models, 173–74

Hyundai, 17, 37–39, 284

Ibibo group, 168

IBM, 138

ICICI Lombard, 217

illegal mining, in Karnataka, 255

incremental innovation, 146, 243

India Shining, 20–21

India: GDP of, 1–4, 11, 55, 154; growth driven by services, 3; manufacturing manpower costs in, 11; productivity in, 12

Indian Airline industry, 231–32, 238; deregulation of, 233

Indian Airlines, 232–33, 235–36, 238–39

Indian Champions, 310–23

Indian Institutes of Management (IIMs), 104

Indian Institutes of Technology (IITs), 103–4, 149, 274

IndiGo, 179, 184, 231, 235–36, 239–46, 248, 261, 301; buying A320 Neos, 243

Indo-German Chamber of Commerce (IGCC), 5

industrial design protection applications, 101

industrial licensing requirements, 29

industrial revolution, 79, 92

Industry 4.0, 90–92, 97

information technology, 10

Infosys, 138, 175

InMobi, 151

innovation, 56–58, 69, 83–84, 89, 98–99, 106–8, 117–20, 123–24, 146–47, 152–53; at Mundra port, 57

Institutional trading platform (ITP), 157–58

Insurance in India, 215–21

Insurance Regulatory and Development Authority (IRDA), 216
Internet, 59, 131, 147, 154, 258
intra-preneurial, 171
Inverted duty structures, 32
investments in infrastructure, 8, 21, 34
investments: in India, 8; in infrastructure under Public Private Partnership, 21
investors, 5, 95, 152–53, 158–59, 169, 172, 174, 182–83, 220
iron ore crisis 249–61
iSpirt, 156, 158

Jabong, 155
Japanese: management techniques, 45; production principles, 192
Jawaharlal Nehru Port Trust, 52–53
Jet Airways, 233–34; acquiring Sahara, 236
Jindal Steel and Power Ltd, 251
joint ventures (JVs), 5, 40, 43, 116, 182, 217, 264, 267, 273, 280
JSW Steel, 231, 249–61, 304–5, 398; and iron ore crisis, 253–61; products of, 253–54
jugaad, 108

Kaizen, 26, 29, 42, 96, 355
Kalyani Group, 268–76, 297; Rajinder on, 273–74
Kalyani Strategic Systems Ltd, 270
Kalyani, Baba, 3, 268, 271–74, 276, 297, 305
Kargil conflict, 19–20, 268
Kataria, Sunil, 121, 123
key performance indicators (KPIs), 142, 146, 166, 169, 211
Khanna, Tarun, 182
Kingfisher Airlines, 246–49; 178, 231, 235, 242, 246, 248, 261; buying Air Deccan, 236; declaring bankrupt, 249; and entry of LCCs, 247; rename Air Deccan as Kingfisher Red, 248
Kirloskar, 38
Klenow, Peter J., 35
Kramer, Mark R., 285
Krishnamurthy, V., 39–40
Kronreif, Trunkenpolz, Mattighofen (KTM), 187, 195, 199–201
Krupp, Alfred, 79
Kurtzman, Joel, 229
Kuwait crisis, 16
Kyron, 174–75

labour law, 32, 88, 99
Lafley, A.G., 180
Land Acquisition Act, 353

leadership, 304
Lenovo, 134
lenskart.com, 155
liberalization, 18–19, 27–31, 42,
    215–16
Licence Raj/Permit Raj, 15–18,
    20, 29, 40
localization, 39, 43, 62, 136
logistics, 24, 31–33, 58–59, 89,
    112, 191, 252, 255, 258, 287
London Interbank Offered Rate
    (LIBOR), 347
low-cost water purifiers, 127–32

machine-tool industry, 27, 71–78,
    97, 180, 306
'Made in Germany', 27, 67,
    79–84, 97
'Made in India', 27, 67–69, 96–97,
    307
Mahadeva, Sunder, 117–21
Mahadevia, Malay, 55
Mahindra Aerospace, 270
Mahindra Defence Systems Ltd, 270
Mahindra Finance, 290–91
Mahindra Rural Finance, 291,
    303–4
Mahindra Rural Housing Finance
    (MRHF), 290–98
Mahindra tractors, 291, 294
Maini Aerospace, 270
'Make in China', 85–86
'Make in India', 3, 11, 13,
    23, 27, 33, 68, 84–89, 181;

low-cost competitors, 88–89;
    reindustrialization, 89–96
Mallya, Vijay, 249
Manipal Global University, 223
maritime trade, 50–53
Martin, Roger L., 83, 180
Maruti Suzuki, 27, 35, 37–49, 66,
    139, 227, 279, 291; approach to
    rural marketing, 37; employees,
    41–43; 5s principles, 41; motto
    of, 303; passenger vehicle
    market of, 35–39; sales of,
    36; 3g principles of, 41–42;
    3m principles of, 42; volume
    predictions of, 279; value-for-
    money focus, 180
Mazagon Dock Limited, 269
mechanization, 31, 55–56, 59, 302
medical workforce, 205, see also
    healthcare system
Merchandise Marks Act (1862),
    80–81, 83
mergers and acquisitions
    (M&As), 152, 264, 266–67, 273,
    283, 298, 307
Miglani, Ankit, 252
mines, Supreme Court ban on,
    255–56, 260
MNCs, 4, 24, 39, 61, 66, 119,
    133, 137–43, 150, 264–68, 274;
    R&D centres, 139–41, 143
Modi, Narendra 23–24, 159
Modiluft, 233–34

Motherson group, 268, 276–84, 298, 302–3, 305; acquisition of Peguform, 281

Mr Schroop, 79

MRO (maintenance, repair and overhaul), 242, 394

Mu Sigma, 151

Mundra Port, 53–59

Murthy, Narayana, 156; Catamaran Ventures of, 156, *see also* Infosys

Naik, Ashwin, 208–10, 212–14, 306

Narasimha Rao, P.V., 17–18

National Democratic Alliance (NDA), 20

National Food Security Act, 21

National Housing Bank (NHB), 290, 296

National Rural Employment Guarantee Act (NREGA), 21, 36, 188, 291

National Steel Policy 2012, 250

new technologies, 133, 139, 147–48, 190–91, 254

non-performing assets (NPAs), 14, 34, 295

nuclear tests, Pokhran, 19–20

Ola cabs, 151

online travel agents (OTAS), 163–64, 167

operational excellence, 301–2

outward direct investments, 9

Outward foreign direct investment (OFDI), 264–67

Overall equipment effectiveness (OEE), 383

Padmaraju, Charan, 162

Palepu, Krishna G., 182

Paramount, 235

passenger vehicle (PV) market, 35–38, 40, 49; and consumers, 36; sales of, 38

Pasupunuri, Sudhakar, 162

Paytm, 152

Pepperfry, 155

pharma, 10, 171

Phee Teik Yeoh, 131–32

Pipavav Defence and Offshore Engineering Company Ltd, 270

policy paralysis and economic growth, 21–22

political system, 15–19, 84

Porter, Michael E., 230, 285

Pradhan Mantri Jan Dhan Yojana, 23

Prahalad, C.K., 285

Premier Automobiles (Padmini as Fiat Padmini), 39

Prione Business Services, 156

private airlines, 232–34, *see also under separate names*

private bus operators, 161, 380, *see also* redBus; Volvo luxury buses private universities, 104, *see also* Amity University; Manipal Global University

private: insurance business, 215; life insurers, 216, 218

process improvements, 142, 146

product: components, 111–12; cost of, 98, 113; design, 110–11; innovations, 182; and price-sensitive markets, 111, 188

productivity, 12, 28–29, 46, 59, 70, 120, 190, 259–60; enhancements, 27, 29, 47, 57; growth in India, 27; improvements, 28–29, 86; total factor productivity in, 357

public–private partnership, 21

public research, 107, see also R&D, investments in

purchasing power parity (PPP), 1

purchasing power, 8, 155, 240, 286

Quikr, 152

R&D, investments in, 101–2, 178, 307

Rashtriya Ispat Nigam Ltd, 250

Rath, Amruth, 197

Ravikumar, S., 194

redBus, 100, 161–68, 175, 304

reforms, 1–2, 17, 19, 23–24, 27, 29, 88; of University system, 149

refrigerator, 125

Reichspatentgesetz, 82

Reillard, Hubert, 60–65

reindustrialization drive, 90

Renault–Nissan, 38–39

renewable energy, 10, 271–72

Research output in India, 101

Retail Weighted Received Premium (RWRP), 218

Reuleaux, Franz, 81

reverse innovation, 110, 137

Right to Information Act of 2005, 352

road transport corporations (RTCs), 161, 163, 165, 380

Robert Bosch Engineering and Business Solutions Ltd (RBEI), 143–48; Vijay on innovation in, 146

Roland Berger study, 73, 134, 171

RUAG, 268, 273, 297, 305; alliance with Elbit, 304

rural housing market, 288–90

Sahara, 233–34, *see also under* Jet Airways

Sama, Phanindra, 162–63

Sangam, Prakash, 168

scandals, *see also* corruption

Securities and Exchange Board of
   India (SEBI), 17, 157–58
Sehgal, Chaand, 268, 278, 298,
   305
shared value, 285; CSR and,
   285–88
shopclues.com, 152, 155
Shrivastava, Pradeep, 192
Siemens, Werner von, 82
Siemens, 61, 100, 135–38, 149,
   302–3
Simon, Hermann, 177
Singh, Bharat, 165
Singh, Chandra Shekhar, 18
Skill India, 160
Skoda, 38
small cars, 38–39, 139; demand
   for, 38
Snapdeal, 151, 155–56
social capital, 33
SpiceJet, 235–36
Standard Motors, 40
start-up ecosystem, 151, 153,
   159
start-up India initiative, 159–60
start-ups, 24, 151–53, 156–59,
   161, 168, 171–76
Steel Authority of India Ltd
   (SAIL), 250
Steel Industry, 249–53, 256
Suzuki, 40–43, 46, 48–49
Suzuki, Osamu, 40
Swachh Bharat, 128
Swift, 46, 49

talent, research and quality, of
   100–7
tariffs, 27–28, 32, 52
Tata Advanced Systems Ltd, 270
Tata Motors, 10, 38, 276
Tata Swach, 127
Tatas, 99, 114, 127, 149, 183–84,
   226, 264
Tax exemption, 158
taxation, 88, 156, 158, 232
TCS, 106, 138, see also
   information technology
textile industry, 69, 76, 180, 306
tier-2 cities, 212, 306; MNCs
   in, 139
total productive maintenance
   (TPM), 30, 62, 190–91, 301,
   355, 362, 383
Toyota, 37–38, 179
trade with USSR, 16
trademarks, 101
trade-offs, 178–81, 184, 226–28,
   263, 300, 303, 307
two-wheeler industry, 185–89
two-wheeler market, 185, 188,
   198, 201; import duties on,
   189

United Progressive Alliance
   (UPA), 20–21
US Food and Drug
   Administration (USFDA), 30,
   356
Uttam Galva Steel, 252

Vaatsalya Aarogya, 210
Vaatsalya Healthcare, 202,
    208–15, 227, 230–31, 305–6,
    388; Angel funding of, 213; in
    semi-urban areas, 212
Vajpayee, Atal Bihari, 18
Vakharia, Dharmesh, 297
Value-conscious customers, 65
value-for-money products,
    137
vehicular CO_2 emission, 93, *see
    also* global greenhouse gas
    (GHG) emissions
Visiocorp, 280–82

Vistara, 232, 236, *see also* Indian
    Airline Industry
Volkswagen, 38, 284
Volvo luxury buses, 161, *see also*
    redBus
VUCA world, 33, 261, 263, 298,
    300, 305, 308

Wipro, 138
Wittenstein, 95

Yamaha, 189, 201, 305

Zomato, 152